Praise for
Intimate Partners

"Scarf is a gifted interviewer, and the reader becomes personally involved in the unfolding of each story. . . . Brilliant . . . a sure hit."
—*Psychology Today*

"So much mumbo jumbo about relationships between men and women finds its way into print these days. . . . Mumbo jumbo this is *not*. . . . The testimony of her examples has a momentum all its own."
—*The Atlantic Monthly*

"One of those rare books to offer more than that sort of quick-fix self therapy is *Intimate Partners*."
—*The Seattle Times*

"Her calm, commonsense look at the things that drive most of us nuts is soothing and informative. . . . One of the most compelling nonfiction books about men and women I've read—I think it should be required reading for everyone."
—SUSAN CHEEVER

"Trains a powerful searchlight on our passionate attachments, illuminating conflicts that sabotage couples. It's hard to read two consecutive sentences in this book without experiencing a shock of recognition, followed by an aftershock of understanding."
—*New Woman*

"Probing . . . [a] literate study on the nature of intimacy . . . The author's clear-headed, constructive advice about marital problems . . . should be of help to couples at all stages."
—*Publishers Weekly*

"Every marriage contains a story, and it begins long before the wedding, Maggie Scarf tells us in her ambitious, thought-provoking . . . ultimately compelling study. . . . Read it and feel consoled."
—*USA Today*

"A storehouse of information for committed partners who want to have 'joyful and mutually rewarding' marriages . . . Short of marital therapy itself, *Intimate Partners* may well be the most helpful boost to come along in years for stumbling marriages."
—*The Providence Journal*

"A manual on how to render the marital dilemma not just tolerable but sensational."
—*Kirkus Reviews*

INTIMATE PARTNERS

Patterns in Love and Marriage

MAGGIE SCARF

BALLANTINE BOOKS

NEW YORK

Published in the United States by Ballantine Books, an imprint of
The Random House Publishing Group, a division of Random House, Inc., New York.

BALLANTINE and colophon are registered trademarks of Random House, Inc.

Originally published in hardcover in the United States by Random House, an imprint of
The Random House Publishing Group, a division of Random House, Inc., in 1987.

Grateful acknowledgement is made to the following for permission to reprint previously
published material:

American Association for Marriage and Family Therapy: Excerpts from "Extramarital
Sexual Crisis: Common Themes and Therapy Implications" by Anthony Thomson.
Reprinted from Vol. 10, No. 4 of *Journal of Marital and Family Therapy*. Copyright © 1984
American Association for Marriage and Family Therapy. Excerpts from "Dysfunctional
Marital Conflict: An Integrative Interpersonal Intrapsychic Model" by Larry Feldman.
Reprinted from Vol. 8, No. 4 of *Journal of Marital and Family Therapy*. Copyright © 1982
American Association for Marriage and Family Therapy. Reprinted by permission.

Family Process, Inc.: Excerpts from "Individuation: From Fusion to Dialogue" by Mark
Karpel in *Family Process*, Vol. 15, 1976. Reprinted with permission.

Thomas F. Fogarty, M.D.: Excerpts from "The Distancer and the Pursuer" by Thomas
Fogarty in *The Family*, Vol. 7, No. 1, 1979.

Gardner Press, Inc.: Excerpts from "The Joining of Families Through Marriage: The New
Couple" by Monica McGoldrick in *The Family Life Cycle: A Framework for Family Therapy*,
Elizabeth A. Carter and Monica McGoldrick, eds., 1980.

Grune & Stratton, Inc.: Excerpts from "On Children, Adults and Families: The Critical
Transition from Couples to Parents" by Kitty La Perriere in *Family Therapy: Combining
Psychodynamic and Family Systems Approaches*, John K. Pearce and Leonard J. Friedman, eds.,
1980. Reprinted with permission of the author of publisher.

Hospital Publications, Inc.: Excerpts from "Commentary on a Paper Delivered by Bernard
Greene, Ronald Lee and Noel Lustig," by Stanley Willis. *Medical Aspects of Human Sexuality*
© Hospital Publications, Inc. Published September 1984. Reproduced with permission of
the publisher.

Pantheon Books: Excerpts from *Secrets in the Family* by Lily Pincus and Christopher Dare.
Copyright © 1977 by Lily Pincus and Christopher Dare. Reprinted by permission of
Pantheon Books, a division of Random House, Inc.

Pergamon Press: Excerpts from "A Model of Marital Interaction" by Ellen Berman, Harold
Lief and Ann Marie Williams in *The Handbook of Marriage and Marital Therapy*. G. Pirooz
Sholevar, ed., 1981. Reprinted with permission of the authors and publisher.

Library of Congress Cataloging-in-Publication Data
Scarf, Maggie.
Intimate partners.
ISBN 978-0-345-41820-3
1. Marriage—United States. 2. Interpersonal relations. 3. Love. I. Title.
HQ734.S37643 1987   306.8'1   86-10111

Printed in the United States of America

www.ballantinebooks.com

For Herb

Foreword
to the 2008 Edition

Looking backward from the early twenty-first century, it seems incredible that in 1950 the actress Ingrid Bergman was denounced on the floor of the United States Senate as a "free-love cultist" and a "powerful influence for evil." She had borne a son to her lover, Italian film director Roberto Rossellini, whom she would later marry. However, she was another man's wife at that time, and the child was born out of wedlock. The film industry was scandalized—Bergman was the virginal star of *Joan of Arc*—and she was denounced from pulpits throughout the entire nation.

Bergman's reputation was shattered, for during this period a sexual relationship outside the bounds of marriage was viewed as immoral and an out-of-wedlock birth was considered unthinkable. During the 1950s, only 4 percent of births took place outside of marriage. However, by 2003, 35 percent—that is, *one-third of all births*—were to unwed mothers. This statistic is just one piece of the story of the vast changes in marriage, sexual behavior, childbearing, cohabitation, and divorce that have swept through our society from the 1950s onward.

Of course the fifties were the heyday of marriage in America. Just about everybody got married: 95 percent of the white population and 88 percent of the black population did so. Moreover, they married at younger ages than did any other generation—before them or after them—during the twentieth century. The brides typically averaged around age twenty, and the grooms were about twenty-three. (Earlier in the century, the typical age of new wives was twenty-two, and of new husbands, twenty-six; and in the decades following 1960, the median age at marriage began ascending once again until it reached the un-precedented high of twenty-five for women and twenty-seven for men.) Young though the couples of the fifties were, each newlywed knew with certainty the role he or she was ordained to fulfill. The husband would be the breadwinner, and the wife would stay home to raise the family and support her husband in his career-building ef-forts. He was responsible in the world outside the family; she was re-sponsible within the home, where as a good, subordinate wife and mother she ran the household.

This stark division of roles began to blur as societal changes swept the nation during the 1960s and onward. The Vietnam War brought with it concerted attacks on many forms of authority, including the writ-in-stone rules of the institutional marital bargain. The introduc-tion of effective contraception and legalized abortion changed the game in regard to sexual relationships; it is known that at the current time, most women have had sexual intercourse at least five years be-fore marriage.

The rules about childbearing outside of marriage were being rewritten as well. To be sure, marriage remained a valued ideal, and many couples were still opting to get married. Nevertheless, between the 1960s and the 1990s they were also choosing to divorce in sharply rising numbers. It was not until the 1980s that the divorce rate ap-peared to stabilize, and to even dip downward from its all-time high of 50 percent of all marriages. To complicate this picture further, an increasing number of partners were cohabiting (a term that had re-placed "living in sin") before marriage—or for a period of some nine to twelve months and then splitting apart.

Cohabitation is now so widespread that it has become a fact of everyday life. Over half of young adults live with a partner before marrying, which practically no one did fifty years ago. When partners are asked their reasons for deciding to cohabit, the answers they give are wide-ranging. In some cases, they cite just plain "cold feet": Having experienced the devastating effects divorce has had upon their parents, they want to avoid having it happen to them. In other instances, responders express an aversion to any kind of long-term emotional commitment. Yet another motive cited is economic: The members of the couple have asked themselves, "When we both can share one apartment, why should we pay for two of them?" Another reason reported is that cohabiting is a form of marriage "insur-ance"—a way of screening out undesirable mates before taking that all-important trip to the altar. Still other answers to the question

"Why cohabit?" are along the lines of strong anti-marriage senti-
ments. One or both partners believe traditional marriage to be repressive, entrapping, and irrelevant; he or she dismisses a marriage
license as nothing other than a meaningless piece of paper.

Meanwhile, just as cohabitation has become commonplace, members of the gay community have started to make themselves heard.
Same-sex couples are now declaring their love for each other ever
more publicly, and insisting that they want to live together not only as
partners, but as married couples as well. Also, a changing economic
market has been exerting enormous effects upon relationships between the sexes. Women, married and unmarried, have been entering the workforce in record numbers. For less-educated women, a
variety of service jobs have become available—positions as clerks,
medical assistants, and the like—while for male blue-collar workers,
the availability of manufacturing jobs has dwindled. This has meant
that many less-educated men can no longer play their designated
role as good family providers. This is but one among the changing
kaleidoscope of economic and cultural reasons why the rigid marital norms seen in the 1950s could never be sustained.

In 1982, when I first published *Intimate Partners: Patterns in Love
and Marriage,* a form of union that social scientists called "companionate marriage" had developed and held sway. Although husbands
and wives in this form of marital partnership still adhered to a gen-
dered division of labor—men were the primary breadwinners, and
women were the homemakers—the members of the couple *did*
expect to be each other's closest companions. They looked forward
to equality and love and friendship in ways not conceived of in the
more rule-bound, "institutional" kind of relationships that had flourished at the dawn of the 1950s.

In time, though, long-term trends in the culture were bringing
about an ever-growing focus on finding emotional gratification in
marriage. The companionate marriage was evolving into the so-called
individualized marriage (a term introduced by sociologist Andrew
Cherlin). This type of union is one in which each partner evaluates
the relationship in terms of his or her own sense of personal growth
and self-development. "Am I achieving a fulfilling, independent self
or am I sacrificing my self to my partner?" "Can I express my feelings
openly, and be heard by my mate?" and "Are our roles within the marriage flexible and negotiable?" are questions being pondered by the
members of the pair. In the individualized marriage, these issues take
precedence over those that once had the higher priority, such as "Am

I being a good spouse and a good parent?" and "Am I building a good family?" The search for emotional satisfaction is of the greatest significance to the members of a pair in this kind of marriage; they choose to wed with the hope and expectation of achieving it.

Curiously enough, although years have passed since the original publication of *Intimate Partners*, achieving intimacy while simultaneously developing a sense of both wholeness and separateness happen to be the major themes the book addresses. While mighty cultural changes have taken place in the intervening decades—particularly the widespread growth of cohabitation before or without marriage—intimacy and separateness remain the mutual satisfactions that every couple strives to attain. Thus, there are important things to be learned in these pages, not only by married partners, but by other types of intimate partners—by cohabiting couples, and by same-sex couples as well. For we all struggle with the same, often elusive issues: issues regarding the high-wire act of remaining close to the beloved Other while retaining a sense of oneself as an authentically whole, separate human being.

Preface
Carol Nadelson, M.D.

What is intimacy, and what happens in intimate relationships? In this compelling book, Maggie Scarf takes us beyond the exterior appearances of marriage to explore its underlying architecture. *Intimate Partners: Patterns in Love and Marriage* offers us a comprehensive and absorbing view of the complex problems encountered by couples today.

Our ideas about the nature of the marital relationship have changed in recent years. We no longer look to marriage primarily for offspring, security or caretaking; we also expect companionship, love, sex and "togetherness." We ask a great deal of each other, and the greater the burdens that we place upon our intimate relationships, the more stressed and fragile they become. It is not surprising, therefore, that the field of marital and family therapy has not only evolved within the last few decades, but that it continues to flourish.

Maggie Scarf has a unique ability to enter the lives of the marital partners she interviews and to weave their life stories into a clear discussion of the important theoretical issues of marriage. She explores the interactions within the couple's relationship, and the ways in which the partners' preexisting psychological and cultural histories are affecting what happens between them in subtle, often unnoticed ways.

Contemporary couples are attempting to cope with vast and widespread changes in societal patterns. Ms. Scarf addresses here, with sensitivity and skill, the intricacies of the problems that can and often do develop in intimate relationships. She discusses the ways in which people bring to a marriage disparate expectations and values—dreams and visions often based more on wishes and romanticized fantasies than on what reality can offer. Most important, she delineates the manner in which couples tend to resurrect, in their current relationships, unresolved dilemmas carried over from their original families.

In this lively, absorbing work, Ms. Scarf also discusses the tendency of distressed couples to deflect their difficulties onto a third party—a parent, an in-law, a child, a friend, lover, or even a colleague or boss. Not only does she explore the problematic patterns that can crystallize in close relationships but she also offers some practical and intriguing suggestions for changing them.

Maggie Scarf has captured the essence of our search for intimacy; she alerts us to unanticipated problems and also suggests unexpected resolutions. In her elegant section on sexuality, for example, she points out what might be considered obvious, but is nevertheless often completely unrecognized—the changes in sexual functioning that accompany ordinary aging. These are, as she explains, experienced by many couples as a defeat, rather than a normal human change accompanied by its own promises and challenges.

Anyone who is married, or contemplating marriage, and certainly anyone working in the field of marital therapy will be richly rewarded by the reading of this remarkable book.

Acknowledgments

In the fall of 1981, as I was crossing the Yale campus, I happened to run into an old acquaintance. She asked me whether I was engaged in a writing project at the present time, and I said that I was gathering material for a book on the subject of marriage.

"Do you know Stuart Johnson?" she asked immediately.

I shook my head. Stuart Johnson was someone, she told me, whom I should definitely get in touch with. He had been, for many years, the Director of Family Therapy at the Yale Psychiatric Institute; now, he ran a flourishing practice and was considered to be one of the best couples' therapists in the New Haven area.

She hesitated, blushed slightly, added that she and her husband were in treatment with Stuart Johnson right now. "There is no one *like* him," she said, enthusiastically. "Go and talk to him; you'll see."

I did call Mr. Johnson, the following morning. We arranged for a brief interview, later on that week—but the conversation we began has still not ended. For Stuart Johnson is so erudite, so knowledgeable, so brimming with ideas and information that we have never exhausted our store of interesting subjects to talk about. We soon commenced taping a series of discussions which took place on a weekly and often biweekly basis; over the subsequent years, the tapes have increased in number, spilling over from one long drawerful, to two, to three, to almost four at the most recent counting. These conversations with Stuart Johnson have had a major impact upon my thinking, and upon my writing of this book.

My grateful thanks are due to him, not only for our fascinating talks, but also for the opportunity to sit in on therapeutic sessions with some of the couples in his clientele. Mr. Johnson also arranged for me to take part in the Master's Degree Program in Marital and Family Therapy at the Smith College School of Social Work, which I attended in the summer of 1983. The program offered there was, for me, a great intellectual feast; I emerged from it feeling that several years of study had been packed into one brief, intense, and extremely valuable time period.

Another person who has been of inestimable importance to me, throughout the course of this work, is my longtime friend and mentor, Dr. Carol Nadelson. Dr. Nadelson, who is Professor and Vice-Chairman of the Department of Psychiatry, Tufts University and New England Medical Center, and Immediate Past President, American Psychiatric Association, found time in her hectic schedule to talk with me, at length, about the various couples I was in the process of interviewing. I invariably came away from these intense discussions dazzled by Carol Nadelson's acuity and by the brilliance of her clinical insights.

It was she, moreover, who first introduced me to a number of the other experts whom I consulted while working on this book—most important, to psychiatrist Derek C. Polansky, who teaches marital and sexual therapy at the Tufts University and New England Medical Center, and is also in private practice in Boston. With Dr. Polansky, I explored many of the specifically *sexual* issues that emerged during the course of my interviews with married partners, and I consistently found him to be knowledgeable, sensitive and thoroughly humane.

Other sexual therapists whom I talked with include Dr. Helen Singer Kaplan, Dr. Avodah K. Offit, and Lorna J. and Dr. Philip M. Sarrel. Dr. Anthony H. Labrum read and commented upon the technical information in the chapters about marital sexuality; afterward, Dr. Herant A. Katchadourian reviewed this material again. For their concern and interest, and for the gift of their valuable time, I want to express my appreciation to all of these active and involved professionals.

Early in the research process, I began attending courses at the Family Institute of Westchester, located in Mount Vernon, New York. The other "students" were all practicing clinicians who had come to the institute to develop skills in dealing with distressed couples and families. At the institute, I took classes designed for both first-year and second-year trainees; I also watched therapeutic interviews (both on videotape and live) and attended lectures and seminars.

Most critical to my own learning process was, though, the substantial amount of time I spent in the presence of the Family Institute's Director, Betty Carter, M.S.W., A.C.S.W. Mrs. Carter's skills were extraordinary, her exuberance contagious; her unerring eye for what lies at the heart of an emotional interaction taught me a great deal about what happens to people in intimate relationships.

To Kate Medina, my editor, a special kind of tribute is due. For Kate, always tactful, always gentle, exerted an important and beneficial influence upon the ultimate shape of this book; working with her is a decidedly educational and deeply gratifying experience. In the course of my years of association with her, I have come to rely upon Kate's remarkable talents and upon her wonderfully supportive and sensitive friendship.

Intimate Partners was completed during a stay at the Center for Advanced Study in the Behavioral Sciences, at Stanford, California. To the center's unflaggingly kind and helpful staff, and to its ebullient director, Dr. Gardner Lindzey, I want to express my huge and heartfelt appreciation.

I also want to thank Felicia Dickinson, my longtime pal and assistant, to whom I am indebted for her boundless competence, understanding and patience.

And finally, to the many married couples whom I interviewed—as well as those couples who permitted me to listen and observe while others interviewed them during therapeutic sessions—I want to express my enormous gratitude. Thank you for being so brave, so forthright, so honest—and above all, thank you for allowing me to enter your intimate worlds. I am mindful of the great privilege you bestowed upon me; and it is what I learned from you, most of all, that appears in these pages.

Truro, Massachusetts
July 1986

Contents

Foreword to the 2008 Edition   v
Preface by Carol Nadelson, M.D.   ix
Acknowledgments   xi
Introduction   3

PART I

BECOMING A COUPLE:
THE POWER OF THE PAST

1. The Attraction   27
2. Where the Past and the Present
   Converge: Genograms   40
3. Autonomy and Intimacy   59
4. Love Itself   72
5. Happily Ever After   87

PART II

LOVERS AND OTHER THIRD PARTIES:
EMOTIONAL TRIANGLES

6. Marriage as Systems   103
7. An Intimate System: The Caretaker
   and the Wounded Bird   111
8. Marital Infidelity   127
9. Emotional Triangles   141

PART III

THE COUPLE IN MIDSTREAM: MARITAL PROBLEMS,
MARITAL SOLUTIONS

10. What Marital Prolems Are Made of:
    Couples in Collusion   173
11. Tasks   189

CONTENTS

12. A Classic System: The Silent Husband
and the Hysterical Wife 205

PART IV
SEXUALITY

13. Sexual Symptoms: Psychology, Biology, or Both? 231
14. What, Precisely, Happens During Sex? 252
15. Sexual Cures 260

PART V
THE CHILD-LAUNCHING YEARS:
TIME OF TRANSFORMATION

16. The Second Separation 283
17. A Game for Two Players 313

PART VI
THE POSPARENTING PHASE:
REINTEGRATION

18. Marital Fighting 343
19. The Five Ways in Which Couples Relate 359
20. "We Have a Good Time" 376

Works Cited 393
Selected Bibliography 401
Index 411

INTIMATE PARTNERS

Introduction

When, I was asked recently, did I begin working on the subject of marriage? The answer to that question is that my intensive interviews with couples began in the summer of 1980. Less officially, though, there is a sense in which my exploration of intimate relationships got under way when the cat disappeared.

That happened much earlier, in the 1960s, when our three daughters were very young and my husband, an economist, was teaching at Stanford University. We lived on the campus and had a tiger-striped kitten with pure white paws which looked like mittens; "Mittens" was the name we had given him.

Our closest friends, during this era of our lives, were the D.'s. They were roughly the same age as we, just moving past the twenties and into their early thirties. I customarily spent a good deal of time with the wife, Anne, and had opened myself up to the relationship completely. She was a part-time social worker, who taught at a school for autistic children. On Wednesday afternoons, I took care of her seven-year-old daughter for her. So, aside from other visits, there was always that predictable time together, either when Anne came to pick up her child or to drop her off.

Our two husbands, who were colleagues on the Stanford faculty, were as close to each other as Anne and I were. The friendship had, in fact, originated with the men. Although the two of them related to each other differently than we—they enjoyed getting into long, heated, abstract discussions—they were also, especially for males, unusually disclosing and personal with one another.

In short, the relationship between our two families seemed to work at every level and in every permutation—between the varying adult twosomes, between the four girls of the junior generation, and between each child and any of the respective parents. We had misunderstandings and tensions from time to time, to be sure, but we functioned as a quasi extended family; problems could and did arise, but our attachment to the D.'s was never in question. Going out, in the evening, meant going out somewhere with Anne and Larry, and we did so as often as we could manage it. We went to small restaurants in San Francisco, to the movies, to occasional nightclubs and to afternoon baseball games. As families, we went on hikes, picnics, excursions to the beach at Santa Cruz, and sometimes camping in the Sierra Nevada mountains.

It was on our return from one such trip, to Yosemite National Park, that we discovered that in our absence Mittens had wandered away.

I had actually begun getting anxious about the cat on our way home— I wasn't sure why. We had, before leaving for five days in the mountains, made the usual arrangements for his care. Our neighbor's daughter, a reliable twelve-year-old, was to come in daily and to feed him; she was also to change his litter box. Mittens was, as always, allowed to stay outside in our large enclosed garden during the daytime; this arrangement had never led to any problems in the past. But as we wended our way homeward, I began worrying about the possibility of his having strayed off and met with some sort of accident.

This was ridiculous, I told myself, for he never wandered far from the back patio—not even when the gate of the stockade fence was left open. I felt, nevertheless, extraordinarily uneasy.

Perhaps it had to do with a crazy feeling I'd had, while up in the mountains, that something was different about the D.'s. On the journey back, too, we'd taken a long detour through the old towns of the California gold rush country; I'd been a passenger in Anne and Larry's jeep for a while. I'd felt somewhat confused, while riding with them, felt that something I couldn't understand was taking place.

Something was wrong—or was I imagining it, this difference in the air? I sensed something strained and unnatural about Anne—her wide blue eyes were glassy and blank—or was it Larry who was behaving strangely? Was a fight going on between them? I had seen them when they were overtly angry at each other; neither one seemed angry at the moment. But the atmosphere was subtly toxic . . . or was it my imagination?

"Something is *wrong*," I said to Herb when the personnel in the different vehicles (there were four families on that trip) had reunited us in our own station wagon again. The D.'s jeep was moving around and past us, at that moment, and I nodded my head in their direction.

"*What's* wrong, Mommy?" a voice piped up from the back seat.

"Nothing," I said, signaling to my husband that we would discuss it later on, when the children's attention had turned elsewhere. But when we were able to talk privately, Herb assured me that he had noticed nothing odd or amiss about the D.'s. He believed that I was imagining problems where no problems necessarily existed.

I let myself accept this explanation, even though there had been something *different* about them—about Anne, in particular, who'd been there in body but utterly absent. It was, though, in the wake of this brief discussion (conducted sotto voce) that I began getting so alarmed about the cat.

As we approached Palo Alto, I remember, my sense of foreboding—about something's having happened to Mittens—was experienced as an almost physical, intensely anxious discomfort. I couldn't wait to get out of the car and into the house to prove to myself that I'd been mistaken! But my fears, on this occasion, had been prophetic: Our pet was not there to greet us, and we could not find him anywhere. He was nowhere in the house or in the garden; his food, uneaten, was drying in his blue and white dish.

Our young neighbor, contrite, told us the cat had vanished from the garden a day earlier and had not returned at feeding time. She'd searched the entire area, but been unable to find him. No one, she reported, had seen him—or at least noticed him—and she had no clue to his present whereabouts. She was clearly very upset, and we had to set about reassuring her.

It was not her fault, we told her; Mittens had merely wandered away and was very likely to wander back to us eventually. In the meanwhile, we ourselves would take over the search. Reasonable words, reasonably spoken; and yet, even as we stood on the front lawn talking to her, I felt a sense of queasiness, a sense of awful grief. I could not understand where that feeling emanated from—a missing pet is, after all, low on the list when one thinks of life's potential tragedies! I was, nevertheless, deeply—seemingly irrationally—upset.

Later on, when the children were in bed, I talked about this with my husband, who was able to offer me an explanation that I'd been unable to offer myself. He reminded me of a story that I'd once told to *him*, in the early days of our relationship, but then had apparently forgotten. It had to do with an incident that had occurred on the day of my own parents' separation, a separation which led to their eventual divorce.

I was twelve years old at the time, and the furniture was being moved out of the house. But for me the most terrible part of what was happening was that our cat had gotten his neck caught in the outdoor coal grate. He had hurt himself so badly that the two men from the animal shelter, called to his rescue, had had to carry him off with them.

"Oh, yes," I said to Herb, recognizing that for me that cat had been the symbol of the intact family. The loss of the cat was connected, in my own mind, with the family life that was being taken away.

At the age of twelve one is in part an adult, but also to some large degree a child—still able to give credence to magical ideas and notions. I suppose, looking back, that I probably maintained the belief that if our pet were to return, so would my world's stability. Or perhaps my preoccupation with the loss of the cat—so intense that the breakup of my parents' relationship seemed almost incidental—was due to my finding it easier to confront and mourn the loss of the family pet than to mourn the *intolerable* loss, which was the ending of my parents' marriage.

In the case of the D.'s, history proceeded to repeat itself. For, a few days after our return from that camping trip on which I'd experienced the D.'s as "different," my husband appeared at home—unexpectedly, in the middle of the afternoon—with the warning that he had some bad news he had to tell me. The children were, at that moment, listening to records on their toy phonograph. He and I went outside, to the far end of the garden, and sat down across from each other at a picnic table under a blooming wisteria vine. Anne had, he said without preamble, told Larry that she wanted a divorce.

She had, it appeared, been having an affair for most of this past year; now she was leaving her husband for her lover. He—the other man— wanted to marry her and had already walked out on his own spouse. I sat there, openmouthed. I was doing my utmost to assimilate this barrage of new information, but found it enormously hard to concentrate.

Other matters commanded my attention, such as the perfumed smell of wisteria blossoms and the sight of a lazily droning bee scouting for a likely source of nectar. Also, there were the distant voices coming from the record player; the children were listening to a fairy tale. The only thought that crossed my mind, which felt emptied of ideas, was of the cat, who was still missing. "Will he ever come back again?" I wondered . . . and then realized, at once, that it was not the cat that really concerned me.

It was at that moment, I believe, that my work on marriage actually began.

INTRODUCTION

Room for an Interpreter

"[In] every house of marriage there's room for an interpreter," writes poet Stanley Kunitz, in his lyrical "Route Six." When I began this exploration of intimate relationships, I wondered why there were so few interpreters of marriage about—and so many interpreters of divorce. I felt as if I were in a small auto tootling down the almost empty side of a superhighway while most of the traffic streamed past me in the opposite direction. There was so much attention being given to the *endings* of attachments, and so much less to the important questions of how they form and how to go about maintaining them.

A common assumption about marriage seems to be that it isn't necessary to *learn* anything about working out a satisfying relationship with an intimate partner; you will be able to make this happen very naturally or unable to make it happen at all. This view is similar to the one that used to prevail about sex: You could "do it" (bliss) or you couldn't—that is, you were inept, a failure (disaster). By now, most people appreciate the ways in which sexual relating can be enhanced by information, instruction, enlightenment. But there is not, it seems to me, the same awareness of what could be *learned* that might facilitate better understanding and satisfaction in other areas of a committed, intimate attachment— even though a vast storehouse of clinical information on the subject of marriage does exist.

Such information, if made available to committed partners, could enhance the quality of their relationships immeasurably. My effort, in this book, will be to make this body of knowledge accessible to those who most need and want it—married people who want their lives together to be as joyful and mutually rewarding as they can possibly be.

Genograms

Every marriage begins with the choice of a mate—and how, one might well ask, is that particular person selected? What are the unconscious signals being passed back and forth when partners fall in love; what, that is, makes each of them feel "right," attractive, "special" to the other one?

In my interviews with Laura and Tom Brett, the first couple in this book, I will examine the powerful influences of the past upon the making of marital choices—and the ways in which problematic aspects of each spouse's earlier relationships, in his or her own original family, tend to reemerge in the intimate world that the new couple creates.

7

In talking to the Bretts (and all the other married pairs we will meet in these pages), I made use of an interviewing method or device called a genogram, with which the reader may be unfamiliar. A genogram is a road map laying out the important emotional attachments of each of the partners—attachments that lead backward in time, to the parents' and grandparents' generations, and forward to the new one, the children (if any) of the present union.

Genograms provide, as shall become evident, a widened context in which the spouses can see themselves. For this chart of their extended family system offers the couple a systematically developed overview of the dilemmas, myths, fantasies, loyalties, and internalized guidelines for being in close relationships which each one of them has brought into the marriage. The process of constructing an intimate pair's "family tree" is an intensely affecting experience for both of them—one replete with sudden recognitions and surprises. For the genogram serves to focus the lens of their attention directly upon those patterns for living which their individual histories have imposed upon the relationship. They can literally *see* the ways in which aspects of their intimate world have been picked up from the past generation and are being reenacted and repeated in the present one.

FAMILY TRIANGLES

Genograms also serve another function: that of clarifying the important emotional triangles in which the partners may be involved and embedded. I will, in the course of the discussion that follows, have a good deal to say about the process of "triangling"—which is the automatic tendency of two people, who are experiencing distress in their relationship, to draw a third party into the fray. An example might be a young newlywed couple who were having difficulty dealing with their individual differences— regarding sexual frequency, or how their money should be handled, or how leisure time should be spent, or what was owed to former friends and to each spouse's family. In order to deal with their diverging points of view—which both perceive as potentially threatening to the relationship—the partners might respond by behaving in ways that were provoking to that natural marital scapegoat, the mother-in-law.

Then, whatever quarrels developed could be either *with* her or *about* her, rather than about the tensions between themselves. So long as this emotional triangle persists, the dilemmas of the twosome cannot be resolved (they're being diverted) but the relationship itself will not feel so dangerously threatened.

What is most striking to note, when surveying genograms, is the way in which *a particular kind of triangle* tends to repeat itself from generation to generation—say, for instance, a daughter who is in a covert alliance with the father to sabotage the authority of the mother. Triangles involving a parent and a child against another parent are a configuration commonly encountered in families—and most couples are genuinely startled when they see patterns that recur, generation after generation, as the genogram takes shape. It is as if the red ink with which they opened their marital ledger has suddenly become apparent. A new daughter-and-father-against-mother coalition is "on the books" to develop in the succeeding generation . . . or may already have done so.

This particular two-against-one pattern (which is just one of the many kinds of fixed triangles that can form) exists throughout the extended family's relational system and feels natural to those unconsciously conforming to it. It is a blueprint-for-being with which everyone in that emotional system is familiar.

The trouble is that it may feel totally *unnatural* to the spouse, who comes from a different emotional system and who truly does not understand the unspoken and unspeakable rules by which the family game is being played.

The Couples

Who are the married people who were willing to open their intimate worlds to me by participating in a series of long interviews about their private lives? Were they young, by and large, or were they middle-aged or older? Did they tend to be fairly affluent or were they drawn from a working-class population as well? Had I found it to be true that most couples were relatively happy together—or utterly miserable? What, in situations in which the partners' unhappiness was very apparent, did the difficulties most frequently seem to be about? Did they quarrel about sex, money, responsibility for routine chores, disciplining kids? What, above all, had motivated them to take part in so demanding a project in the first place?

The answer to this last question is the only one that I don't have; I encountered enormous willingness to help, but can't explain *why* it was there. All that I can say is that there were many volunteers—more than I was able to meet with—and that those couples whom I did interview were both extraordinarily generous with their time and brave at a personal level. Participating in these sessions was by no means an easy thing to do.

The marital pairs whom I talked to came to me via a number of differing routes and accessways. Some were couples whom I interviewed during tours of study and participant-observation—at Dartmouth Medical School (in 1980) and at the Family Institute of Westchester (beginning in 1981 and stretching onward over the next several years). Other couples were private patients, who had given permission for me to sit in on sessions with their therapists. I was, during this time of intensive learning and reading in the area of marital and family treatment, talking with a number of married *clinicians* and their own spouses as well.

Perhaps it was curiosity about what I was doing that prompted their participation, or perhaps it was a wish to be on the opposite side of the couch for a while! In any case, these and other psychotherapists (psychiatrists and psychiatric social workers) did, very kindly, continue mentioning my marriage project to their clients. A steady trickle of interviewees came to me in this way. By and large, however, the married couples with whom I talked derived from no clinical source whatsoever. They were recruited via a process that can best be described as "barter."

What the exchange involved was the trading of a lecture (on the subject of women and depression, which my book *Unfinished Business* was about) for a list of twenty-five or so couples who would be willing to be interviewed about their marriages at length. (This procedure, as I later learned, had been used by Kinsey to locate respondents for his research on human sexuality; I had thought then that I had developed it myself.) It did prove to be a most effective means of recruitment, and my first group came to me via the Junior League of a moderately large Connecticut city.

I had my doubts, it must be admitted, about how frank and open these couples would be, but I soon realized that I need not have had concerns of this sort. These intelligent, articulate partners were, for the most part, almost astonishingly honest and forthcoming from the very outset of our discussions.

Other couple volunteers came from many other kinds of groups, organizations, and audiences at functions of all kinds, ranging from a lecture that I gave in a large Washington, D.C., department store auditorium to a variety of church and temple functions. In some such instances, I talked about the study of marriage I'd embarked upon and urged interested parties to get in touch with me. A surprising number of people actually did this— and I was extremely grateful.

I had, eventually, enlisted a full roster of married partners to interview (more than 200), and they resided in a number of differing geographic locations. The couples who were selected to appear in these chapters are but a small subset of the larger number (32) who were interviewed extensively; that is, for a minimum of six one-and-a-half-hour-long sessions. They are a far *smaller* subset of the uncounted number of married people whom I talked with (or observed) in a variety of circumstances, including clinical settings. It was from these committed partners, more than from any other of the expert sources that I was able to tap, that I really learned what I needed to know about intimate relating.

SOME ANSWERS

Before continuing, let me respond briefly to some of those other questions, posed earlier, to which answers can readily be supplied. The couples whom I interviewed included people of all ages; their marriages were, in some cases, only a few months old and in others they were of thirty or forty—or more—years' duration. The people were bright, able to express themselves, and came from blue-collar as well as middle-class and upper-middle-class backgrounds; the group was predominantly, but certainly not exclusively, white.

Such factors as income, occupation, race, ethnic origins and religion obviously do, in a very marked fashion, influence the ways in which any set of partners interact. There are unseen rules for behavior that can differ very widely from group to group—powerful regulations about how much expression of feeling is permissible, for example, or even such seemingly "individualistic" matters as how physical pain is experienced and dealt with.

As anthropologist Mark Zborowski demonstrated, in his remarkable 1969 study, Irish and white Anglo-Saxon Protestant patients have a tendency to be stoic about painful symptoms, while Italian and Jewish patients are far more emotive and much readier to complain about them. When it comes to describing the experience of the pain itself, Italians are melodramatic—and often uninformed—while Irish patients, equally inaccurate when it comes to understanding the true nature of their symptoms, tend to downplay and minimize the degree of pain they are experiencing. The varying cultural rules about dealing with physical suffering are, in differing groups, very different indeed.

So are the rules about expression of feeling. There is a joke, current among family therapists, that if you ask an Irish family to talk about their emotional reactions to a particular event, a silence will descend upon the group. If, on the other hand, a Jewish family is asked to do so, the therapist will be unable to get another word in edgewise! The implicit regulations of the culture serve, generally speaking, to structure the life experiences of its members; the rules provide guidelines for being and behaving, which may work for well or for ill.

White Anglo-Saxon optimism and cheerfulness, as authors Monica McGoldrick, John K. Pearce and Joseph Giordano have observed, lead to confidence and flexibility in situations which require initiative, flexibility, rationality and belief in the efficacy of the individual's acting on his or her own. But such traits can also lead to difficulty in situations of grief, where the expression of painful feelings—mourning—is required. The importance of a couple's cultural assumptions—especially in situations in which the partners come from differing backgrounds—is undeniable, and such internalized existence regulations are something that I shall have more to say about in the pages that follow.

But my own overriding concern, in the course of this project, has *not* been with the ways in which ethnic factors find expression within the emotional environment of the couple. What intrigues me far more, and what I am attempting to explore here, are those basic psychological truths about intimate attachments which cut across social and economic dimensions—which are as applicable to a neurosurgeon and his executive wife as they are to a printer married to a waitress (the latter are, by the way, the jobs held by Angie and Bob Carrano, the third couple in this book). This book is about the way in which marriages are made: the basic materials that are used in their construction and how these affect the structure of the relationship that develops.

Finally, a word about whether or not most couples—or at least most of the couples that I interviewed—are happy. This is not an easy question to reply to; certainly, few relationships, analyzed at length, are without clouds of any kind. There were, nevertheless, couples who clearly were in far *more* rewarding and gratifying marriages than others, and couples who were in ones that were much *less* so. In the latter instances, where dissatisfaction reigned, a power struggle was very frequently in full sway— a battle for ascendancy and dominance in the emotional system that the pair inhabited.

What issue or issues did such power battles tend to be about? Sex and money were the most volatile and frequently encountered conflictual topics. These tend to be the great arenas in which a fight that two people are having—a struggle for mastery and control of the relationship—becomes transformed into something real and tangible, something that can be put into words and *fought about*. An ongoing war about finances, unlike a war about the partner's utter failure to meet one's needs, is one in which losses can be sustained and tolerated. It is easier to battle about issues that don't threaten the existence of the emotional system itself.

Discipline of children, or of a particular child, was another frequent source of tension—a ground upon which two disaffected partners had elected to stand fast and fight it out. Whatever the nature of the issues being struggled about, however, they did tend to be evident in the overall family picture. "Hot" problems of the prior generation were frequently the same as those being dealt with by embattled partners in the present one.

The true nature of marital control-contests, and the almost reflexive fashion in which third parties (child, in-law, lover) are "triangled" into them, will be one of the important subjects examined in the course of the chapters that follow. I shall also, happily, be able to offer some remarkably effective suggestions for blocking the power struggle's ongoing and remorseless continuation, no matter what the particular issues or problems happen to be.

THE MARITAL CYCLE

The five couples whose marriages are explored at great length in these pages (as distinct from those partners whose relationships are described more briefly, and in passing) have been selected for inclusion because they seemed to embody and exemplify the problems and tasks associated with a phase of life and a particular stage of an ongoing intimate relationship.

These emotionally bonded pairs—the Bretts, the Kearneys, the Carranos, the Gardiners, the Sternbergs*—are dealing, to some considerable extent, with age-related concerns and dilemmas. For not only are each wife and each husband moving through an individual process of adult growth and change, connected to the passage of time and the successively shifting circumstances of adult life, but the marriage itself is undergoing similar periodic challenges and demands for adaptive change. A good way of conceptualizing this is to think in terms of *his* life cycle, *her* life cycle, and the marital cycle as a kind of supraentity—a whole which is more

---

* These names are pseudonyms, used in order to preserve the couples' anonymity and privacy.

than and different from the sum of the two intimate partners involved in it. The *relationship itself* goes through a series of sequential phases, has its own set of internal dynamics and its own ongoing agenda.

Psychiatrists Carol Nadelson, Derek Polonsky, and Mary Alice Mathews have sketched out the stages of the marital cycle as a movement from "idealization" to "disappointment and disenchantment" to "productivity" (that is, parenting, career development) to "redefinition and child launching" and, finally, to the "reintegration and post-parenting period" when the pair are a twosome, living by themselves once again.

The couples discussed in this book are of different ages and in different phases of the relational cycle described above. They do not always slip into these categorical slots perfectly neatly—Tom and Laura Brett were, for instance, recently married but not in the exalted "being in love" state and not overidealizing each other—yet they were working at the marital tasks of this period. These have to do with making the internal shift from the family of origin to a commitment to the new attachment that is forming.

The Bretts were, I should say, atypical of the early idealization phase, because they had consulted a therapist in advance of the wedding to talk over some of the concerns they had about the relationship. (More couples ought to do it, though; most divorces occur within two years after the pair has married!) But usually, in this period of high energy and excitement, Nature takes over in ways that encourage mating to occur. Positive feelings reign, and negative ones are pushed under the rug of the relationship. Wonderful fantasies of perfect happiness in a bliss-filled future ensure that coupling will take place and, eventually, the production of a new generation. It is during the first stage of marriage, when love is blinder than it will ever be again, that the intimate bond between the partners is being so assiduously woven and the unspoken rules of the relationship are being negotiated.

But the descent to disenchantment and disappointment is in the cards, for with the passage of time it becomes apparent that the person of one's dreams is not precisely the same as the partner one is living with in reality. And this feels, somehow, like a betrayal—the expectations that he would complete one's world, meet one's every need, make up for the wrongs of the past, and other irrational notions that many partners cherish are experienced as a kind of treason. The recognition of the mate's essential *differentness* from the idealized image that one had of him is what is hard to bear. The struggle to get him to conform to that desperately cherished fantasy may be initiated at this point—and lead to a battle without ending, for *he* wants to be accepted as the person whom he is.

How long do most marriages remain in the phase of illusionment, and when does disenchantment begin? The answer to that question is that there is enormous variability: the inner acknowledgment of certain disappointments in the relationship may begin on the wedding night itself. This had been true for one pair whom I interviewed, whose sexual life before the marriage had been wonderful. But with the falling of the parental mantle upon their shoulders—as he became "husband" and she became "wife"—their physical desire for each other precipitously ended. Theirs was, however, an unusual case; more often the idealizing, glorifying, romantic phase persists for one, two, three or more years. It may last until the birth of a baby (or until efforts to conceive get under way), which often creates unexpected stresses in the twosome's relationship. For the shift from being somebody's child to being somebody's parent—however joyful and gratifying in certain ways—can also engender feelings of anxiety, fear and competitiveness. The spouse, too, is no longer simply a mate; he or she is the parent, or prospective parent, of one's child. Gordon Kearney, who depended upon his wife to be his own caretaker, had found another woman to love him during the very summer when he and his wife were struggling to get a pregnancy started.

The Kearneys were in their early thirties at the time of our interviews, and their daughter, Susannah, was seven and a half months old by then. They were, undoubtedly, in the phase of disappointment and disenchantment—a stage of the marital cycle which is, for obvious reasons, prime time for straying outside the marital boundaries. For if the partner does not accord with the inner fantasy—the golden dream of perfect union with an all-knowing, all-caring other—there may be someone out there who *is* more like the ideal.

It is tension in the intimate twosome, more than anything else, which leads to the creation of a triangle. Love triangles, like other triangles, come into being as a means of coping with anxieties in the marriage that one or both partners are finding unbearable. The "eternal triangle" is a way not only of finding solace with another partner, but of introducing a third party into a relational dilemma. Affairs are often initiated as a means of diverting off and diluting some of the tensions that an intimate dyad is experiencing.

The Carranos, the third couple in the book, were in the productivity phase of their relationship—they had been married for fourteen and a half years and had a daughter, age ten, and a son who was almost seven. This period of the marital cycle is usually a time when unresolved relational problems are shelved for the meanwhile; it is a time of busyness, involvement in childrearing and career building, when the strains of the disenchantment stage are usually not being felt so keenly and painfully. Many spouses, during this phase of marriage, experience a second wind of commitment to the relationship. It is as if the bond between them, severely strained during the time of disillusionment, has been found equal to the test and durable. They are working teammates, and there is a sense of deepening investment in the life enterprise which the pair have created together.

But for many other couples, this sense of mutuality never develops. Instead of the increase in intimacy which emerges in relatively good relationships during the productivity phase, this period of the marital cycle brings nothing other than increasing frustration, anger and disappointment. It is as if the relationship is stuck and cannot get beyond the phase of disenchantment. This was what it was like for Angie and Bob Carrano who, at the time of our talks (when she was thirty-five and he was thirty-seven years old), were bogged down in a stable but highly unsatisfactory marriage.

The pair of them were in a type of relationship which will be readily recognizable and very familiar: that most commonplace of unions between a woman who cannot get enough warmth and closeness and a man who is undemonstrative, superlogical and emotionally unreachable. They were also, as shall be seen, engaged in a desperate power struggle—a battle for control of the relationship which was, in their case, taking place between the sheets. The Carranos' sexual difficulties were of the kind that led me to wonder: Was sex the basic cause of the problems in the marriage, or had the problems in the marriage led to their sexual dilemmas? Were the sexual symptoms they were struggling with, moreover, fundamentally biological or psychological in their origin and nature? In different situations and circumstances, the latter kind of question is one that can be answered in vastly different ways.

One couple whom I interviewed had, for example, had their sex life sabotaged by a prescription medication which rendered the husband impotent. Another suffered from a long-standing difficulty which had resulted from their lack of information about the ways in which aging affects male and female sexuality. These same partners (the Gordons) were also struggling with competitive issues—relating to the dramatically different directions in which their careers were heading—at the time when their quarrels about sex began erupting and bringing the marriage's existence into serious question.

There is, it seems to me, far too little known about the variety of sexual problems that burden so many marital relationships. Many couples, who assume that they "know the facts," are true innocents when it comes to understanding what happens during a *normal* coital experience, much less what to do when a sexual symptom begins to emerge! Intimate partners who are dealing with a sexual issue—such as inability to reach orgasm, or impotence, or premature ejaculation, or some other complaint—are frequently baffled by questions to which answers *could* readily be obtained.

Not only could their questions be answered, but their sexual lives could be improved *significantly*. For there do exist, at the current time, remarkably effective techniques for dealing with sexual dilemmas of all sorts and varieties. Much information about these techniques, or sexual exercises, has been included in this book—and not only for the benefit of those partners who are feeling perplexed and disconcerted. On the contrary, the erotic "tasks" to be described—basic training in the art of the caress—ought to be made part of *every* couple's kit bag of basic knowledge about human sexuality.

CHANGE

The successive phases of a committed, intimate relationship, as sketched out by Drs. Nadelson, Polonsky and Mathews, correspond closely to those "expectable events" of the family life cycle (getting married, having a child, having the oldest child reach puberty, etc.) which involve successive turns of the wheel into a future that is unknown and unknowable. In a sense, such life cycle transitions are expected and utterly predictable; in another sense, they are fearful to contemplate. It is in any case true, as every clinician knows full well, that it is during times of transitional change—which induce adaptive stress—that crises tend to develop.

Change, change itself, is something which stirs deep anxieties in so many people, although, very frequently, the real thoughts associated with the anxious feelings never succeed in ascending to awareness. The newly budding breasts of a pubescent daughter may, for example, be considered faintly humorous by her intrigued parents, and yet send a shiver of apprehension throughout the entire household. Her emerging sexuality, like the faint sound of a distant horn, signals the approach of womanhood, independence, and a far-off but inevitable leavetaking. So ordinary and predictable a happening as her beginning to develop secondary sexual characteristics stirs subliminal alarms in the family—relating to separations, losses and the demise of their world as it exists in the present.

Demands for change, even expectable, normative changes, can summon up inchoate fears of many sorts, for the rules and regulations by which the members of the emotional system live and relate are suddenly no longer reliable. The rules are being reevaluated, tested, not working in the way that they did earlier. This stirs up memories, hard to tolerate, of other times when life felt out of control—of times when one felt helpless and of the feelings of rage that that sense of helplessness engendered. It arouses worries about being stranded, abandoned, left alone in an uncaring environment. Such fears and feelings, because they are so linked to what is primitive, irrational and frankly infantile, can in turn unleash completely incomprehensible and sometimes downright destructive kinds of feelings and behaviors. This was certainly true in the case of the fourth pair of intimate partners in this book, Kathleen and Philip Gardiner. For, as the departures of his adolescent children began looming into view, Philip—in his mid-forties at the time—became possessed of the notion that he needed to leave home as well.

The couple's three teenaged children were, during this phase of the family's development, engaged in the normal adolescent process of loosening their emotional ties to the caretaking parents. They were, inexorably, moving outward into the world of their peers and—despite the usual periodic regressions into childish dependence—becoming increasingly autonomous, self-sufficient human beings. In the course of this difficult detaching process, however, some of the senior generation's *own* unresolved separation issues had been reactivated. The slumbering dogs of adolescence had shaken themselves and wakened with a vengeance.

The problems that had erupted in the Gardiners' marriage, during the redefinition and child-launching phase of their long (twenty-three-year) relationship, had everything to do with developmental challenges—related to leaving home and developing an authentic, individual self—that had never been confronted in their families of origin or at least adequately dealt with. Philip was, at the time of our conversations, engaged in a restaging of the difficulties of his own adolescence, and Kathleen was colluding to help him do so—for reasons that harked back to earlier relational dilemmas that she, too, thought she had left well behind her.

The Gardiners were engaged in a "second separation" process, a pained effort to address certain issues that had been avoided and bypassed during the normal separation from home base that occurs during the adolescent period. Philip's belief, in this middle era of his life, was that he had to leave the marriage in order to find himself—that "self," hidden deep within, which he experienced as having been imprisoned by the demands of the relationship to Kathleen.

For him, the reappraisal of the self, the intimate other and the relationship itself that tends to occur during this period was proving to be an extraordinarily painful experience. This time of marriage was, for both the Gardiners, the hardest that had ever been encountered.

In the subsequent—reintegration and postparenting—phase of the marital cycle, a shift toward greater empathy, companionship and sharing can often be discerned. It was certainly present, and readily recognizable, in the tender and mutually pleasurable relationship of Nancy and David Sternberg. They had, at the time of our interviews, been married for twenty-seven years; David was about to turn fifty, and Nancy was just one year younger. Their children, who were in their early to mid-twenties, had all departed from the family household into jobs (but no marriages thus far) and lives of their own.

The post-childrearing period of a marriage is one that used to be an extremely *brief* one at the beginning of this century. In the early 1900s one partner (generally the husband) usually died within two years of the marriage of the couple's youngest child. For this reason, as clinician Betty Carter has noted, the marital problems of partners in this life period were frequently resolved by the death of one of them! Now, however, owing to increasing longevity, most couples can expect to spend some fifteen years together after their offspring have departed.

This can be a most rewarding phase of life for the spouses if they have mastered the developmental tasks posed at previous stages of their continually evolving relationship. Many of those tasks have, very clearly, had to do with the flexible handling of intimate relationships. At the time of the marriage itself, the members of the couple had to complete the transformation of the emotional bonds linking them to their original caretakers—to establish more peerlike relationships with their parents—and to weave together a new attachment that would be the primary one for both of them. Then, in the years that followed, they had to make space in their intimate world for the children of their creation and, eventually, to be ready to let their offspring depart the nest to go off and create new worlds of their own making.

To the degree that the partners have been able to meet and deal with these sequential adaptive challenges, they will be ready to cope with the new ones of the postparental, reintegration period. For many new things are happening to both of them. They are reviewing the lives that have been lived thus far, in terms of career dreams that have been met or surrendered—and the ways in which the children's lives reflect the goodness or the failings of the family atmosphere—and the mounting, unavoidable evidence of their own physical aging (to name just a few of the problematic issues of this period). They can, at this juncture, either comfort one another and be true companions, withdraw and distance themselves, emotionally, or rail at each other about the disappointments and resentments of a lifetime.

For the Sternbergs, the prospect of being alone again had been frightening—so much so that they'd behaved in ways that had impeded their children's progress out of the household. The bitter things that had happened in the relationship had certainly left each of them feeling apprehensive about and mistrustful of the other. There had been a period in the marriage, as Nancy acknowledged, when she wished that her husband would just *die*—even though she knew that she loved him.

By the time that my series of conversations with the Sternbergs took place, however, their relationship had changed profoundly. It had shifted, become a different kind of relationship entirely. The marriage had been transformed, as they moved out of the child-launching phase into the postparental one, from a battlefield into a safe haven. It had become an emotional shelter in which each of them was finding it possible to work through certain painful dilemmas that had been posed in their original families—the families in which they had grown to adulthood. They had, for the first time in their lives, begun to recognize the real nature of the issues that were generating so much tension between them—and to integrate their own individual pasts and their present life together. The desperate, hopeless effort to *remake the past* in the context of the current relationship had been abandoned, and the entire structure of the marriage had changed.

BEING CLOSE, BEING DIFFERENT

Certain issues of the marital cycle cannot, clearly, be placed in any particular time frame, in terms of a decade or a period when they will most predictably be confronted. Marital infidelity—as a latent or actual concern—can generate tension between the partners at any phase of an ongoing, committed relationship. This problem can be horribly painful for a couple to deal with and feel unique and shocking to that pair, but it is nevertheless very ordinary among the general population.

Sex outside marriage is something that happens often. An overview of eleven large surveys of extramarital sex indicate that 50 percent of married men engaged in intercourse with outside partners, and the figure for married women is rapidly approaching that level. Another important finding, cited in this same review of recent research, was that the most common motivator cited by unfaithful spouses was marital dissatisfaction.

The lower the evaluation of the relationship, and the lower the frequency and quality of the sex with the spouse, the more likely was it that extramarital sex would occur.

This is why, even though the timing of any extramarital romantic fling or affair cannot be foretold, the phase of disillusionment and disenchantment—when disappointment and restlessness are prominent—is one during which sexual acting out is much likelier to happen. Not only is infidelity more probable during this period, but the betrayal of the bond will feel most justified. For it is at this point in their relationship that the husband who has married the "girl of his dreams" is being forced to come to terms with her fundamental *otherness*. He must, now, recognize the dream for what a dream *is*—a fantasy that has sprung from the dreamer's own head. But he may, instead, blame her for being different from the person he'd thought he'd married, who conformed more to the unique vision that existed within his own imagination.

The capacity to recognize her as a person in her own right—as an independent center of motivation, with needs, wishes, desires, opinions, preferences of her own, which will differ from his at times—is what will be required of *him* during this "period of adjustment." But for some people, the acceptance of the mate as a separate and different human being is an impossible acceptance to make. The spouse's *otherness* feels too much like a betrayal from within—which it is, in a way, because it is the dream that has been wed rather than the real-life individual who is the actual partner.

Her (or, as the case may be, his) essential differentness from the idealized image is experienced as a painful disappointment, and revenge may take the form of an affair. Or a struggle to get the mate to be *more like* the fantasy may commence, and continue (without any outside sexual activity's having taken place) all the way through the productivity-and-parenting phase of the marital cycle. Then, however, during the midlife period—when feelings about what has been given up in order to remain with *this* partner, in *this* relationship intensify—the likelihood of an extramarital affair will rise sharply.

For if the spouse cannot conform to the inner fantasy, there may be someone else out there who is able to do so. Like the disillusionment phase of the marital cycle, the redefinition and child-launching period is another prime time for sexual acting-out. It is the time of the midlife crisis. What is involved, in both these charged and difficult phases of the relationship, is a confrontation with what has been given up in order to be in the relationship—with those lost aspects of the self which are perceived as having been surrendered to the relationship and to the partner who turned out to be so dismayingly different from the golden dream.

This brings me to the problem of separateness, which is to say, the crucially important capacity for recognizing the difference between the real qualities of the marital partner and the fantasies (bad or good) about that person which exist in one's own head. The question of how to be one's own self (autonomous) and yet remain close to the marital partner (intimate) is the major marital dilemma that we all must confront. The tension between being an "I" and part of a "we" is one that is felt in *every* phase of the marital cycle and must be addressed and readdressed continually.

Generally speaking, when couples are experiencing a great deal of distress, confusion and unhappiness, the underlying conflict is about trying to remain in an intimate relationship while being a full, whole, separate human being simultaneously. The wish to pursue one's own interests and goals, and the wish to pursue interests and goals that are shared with the mate, *feel* as if they are totally incompatible. One feels that one can be fully autonomous *or* be intimate with the partner, but being both at once is impossible.

How, in troubled partnerships, is the inner struggle between being close and being separate handled? Usually, one spouse (often the wife) experiences herself as wanting more warmth, intimacy, closeness—and having few needs for autonomy and independence. The other spouse (most commonly the husband) experiences himself as always needing more personal space and emotional distance—and no vulnerabilities or need for closeness in relation to the partner. Neither mate, in such a situation, has any conscious awareness that the seemingly irreconcilable wishes and needs to be "an independent self" and "be in a close relationship" *exist inside their individual heads*. The worst kind of confusion, which is the confusion of the self and the other, is what results.

There are, as shall become evident, myriad forms and differing guises in which married couples play these autonomy/intimacy struggles out. In order, however, to fully understand the ways in which partners come together to construct their intimate relationships, the reader will have to become familiar with the manner in which a certain mental process (its technical name is projective identification) operates. Some familiarity with this process is, in my view, essential. The term itself, which derives from a certain form of psychoanalytic thinking, cannot be explained in a moment. Once it *is* understood, however, something vitally important about the nature of intimate attachments will have been learned.

In the course of the interviews that follow, what is meant by the term will become readily apparent. But here let me just say, by way of a very preliminary explanation, that projective identification has to do with one person—say, me—seeing my own denied and suppressed wishes, needs, emotions, etc., in my intimate partner and not experiencing those wishes and feelings as anything coming from within my own self. If, for instance, I were a "never angry" person, I might see anger as coming *only* from my husband—and actually get him to collude in this by forcing him to lose his temper and *express my anger for me.*

Or if, to take another instance, my mate could not accept his vulnerabilities and distresses, I could do the work of getting upset and distressed *for him* every time he began giving me the cues that this was necessary. But because the process occurs at an unconscious level, he might become extremely critical of my constant complaining—might see in me, and dislike and *fight* in me, the feelings that he cannot perceive within himself.

Intimate partners often perform this function for one another: experience and express what are actually the spouse's unacknowledged and repudiated emotions. When one person is always angry and the other is never angry, it can be presumed that the always angry spouse is carrying the anger for the pair of them. And similarly, when one partner is very competent and the other nonfunctional (depressed, for example), there is usually an unconscious deal in effect, a collusion about who will take ownership of which particular feelings.

Most couples haven't, even when in the midst of ferocious autonomy/intimacy struggles—which usually involve massive projections of inner conflicts onto the intimate partner—any idea of what their basic problems are about. (Nor do they know that there are some very down-to-earth, realistic ways in which such dilemmas can be dealt with, as described in Chapter Eleven, "Tasks.") Author Abigail Trafford, discussing the end of her twelve-year marriage, writes:

> Alone now, I hated the king-size bed and got rid of it. I put away the wedding pictures and took off my ring. The children wanted a puppy. I said I couldn't handle it. The house was always cold. We lived off eggs and granola. At night in bed came the pain in my chest. As I lay there, awake and afraid, my mind racing over the past and back to the future, I tried to bring logic to my despair.
>
> In the end, I was haunted by three disturbing thoughts that wouldn't go away: I didn't really know the person I had been married to for twelve years. I wasn't too sure what kind of person I was, either; I certainly didn't like myself or some of the things I had done. But . . . [most] of all, I realized that the official issues that broke us up were not the real ones. Something else was at work, something deeper that neither one of us was

able to explain. It was tantalizing, this chimera, this hint that understanding was there somewhere. I felt that if I could just understand what it was—this mysterious something between us—I would not only understand what had gone wrong in the marriage; I could get over the marriage and on to a new life.

I also sensed that this mysterious something might be a key to why relationships generally don't work—and why they do.

It is this "chimera," this butterfly of understanding, which shall be pursued in this book.

PART I

BECOMING A COUPLE:
The Power of the Past

1

The Attraction

It is a fact of marital reality, well known to experts in the field, that those qualities cited by intimate partners as having first attracted them to each other are usually *the same ones that are identified as sources of conflict* later on in the relationship. The "attractive" qualities have, in time, been relabeled; they have become the bad, difficult things about the partner, the aspects of his or her personality and behavior that are viewed as problematical and negative.

The man who was, for example, attracted by the warmth, empathy and easy sociability of his spouse may at some future point redefine these same attributes as "loudness," "intrusiveness," and a way of relating to others that is "shallow." The woman who initially valued a man for his reliability, predictability and the sense of security he offered her, may—farther down the line—condemn these same qualities as dull, boring and constricting. Thus it is that the admirable, wonderful traits of the partner become the awful, terrible things that one wishes one had realized in time! Although they are, throughout, *identical* qualities, earlier and later on in the relationship they go under different names.

What is most attractive about the partner is often what is also most charged with feelings of ambivalence. That is why my conversations with couples always started out in the same way that my interview with the Bretts, seated side by side across from me, was beginning now. "Tell me," I asked the young couple, "what first attracted you two to one another?" My glance moved from the primly attentive Laura to the slightly wary face of her husband, Tom. "What was it that made you—and you—special to each other, do you think?"

Mundane though the questions sounded, in my own ears, they evoked the usual surprised, even startled response. Laura inhaled sharply, picked up a hank of her long brown-blond hair, flipped it over her shoulder. Tom looked as if he were about to spring from his seat, but instead of rising, he leaned backward against the plush maroon sofa. They turned to each other, with a smile; Laura blushed, and then they both laughed.

No one spoke. I had already conducted enough of these interviews to be well aware that I could soundlessly choose the partner who would answer. If, at this point, I looked directly at Laura, she would be the person who replied. Similarly, if Tom's and my eyes were to meet, he would be my first responder. In order to avoid giving either one of them such a cue, I fastened my eyes on a bookcase which took up most of the wall to the left of the rocker in which I sat. Even though Laura Brett was a theology student, in training for the ministry, and Tom Brett worked as a reporter and writer for a newsmagazine with a nationwide circulation, the books whose titles caught my eye were, by and large, novels.

There was *Laughter in the Dark*, by Nabokov, frayed and in paperback; *The Cancer Ward*, its dustcover looking impeccable; and two novels by Henry James, in the *Modern Library* edition. One of them, *The American*, was, come to think of it, the story of a courtship—but one which ends in disaster for both of the people involved; the marriage never takes place.

Laura and Tom Brett had come close to being in that same situation, a year and a half earlier; they'd veered very near to calling the entire enterprise off. When they'd consulted a couples' therapist, in the fall months before their marriage (which was scheduled for that forthcoming Christmas), it had been for assistance in making a critical decision: whether to continue work on their wedding plans or to dissolve their engagement and end the relationship completely.

It was the therapist whom they'd seen at that time who had telephoned them, much later —just after their first anniversary—and told them about the marriage study that I was engaged in. Would they, he inquired, be interested in talking with me? The Bretts had liked the idea. The pair of them had, I knew, attended only four clinical sessions, after which their decision to marry had been reaffirmed.

The cause of their premarital distress, I had been told, was a painful quarrel that kept erupting between them—a quarrel about the nature of Tom's relationship to his ex-girlfriend. The battles about this subject had grown so wild and confusing that the pair of them had become frightened. If they were fighting this much *in advance* of the wedding, what was it going to be like afterward? They cared about each other, and didn't want to part, but had felt that this ongoing, crazy argument had to be resolved beforehand. . . . Tom Brett cleared his throat, interrupting my ruminations.

"She Challenged Me"

"For me"—Tom began tentatively, his voice surprisingly fulsome and resonant coming from so tall and gangly a person as he—"it was . . . there were two things. Laura met what you might call my prerequisites in terms of being attractive and smart and funny, but then she also challenged me. I guess it's true that I've known other people who had these various qualities—who were pretty, smart, funny, and so forth, or had various combinations of these qualities—but with *her*, there was more of a challenge. A challenge because of her sincerity, I suppose, and her honesty, too. It's all there," he added, with a small shrug, "in her language."

"Her language?" I gazed at him quizzically. He, however, was exchanging a knowing, fond look with his wife.

"Church language," he explained, running a quick hand through his curly brown hair. "Listening to Laura talk to her friends, you hear certain terms come up again and again. Things like 'letting yourself be vulnerable' and 'investing yourself in a decision.' . . . Ways of talking, and of thinking too, that go along with ideas like that." He paused, as if to formulate another thought, then merely shook his head. "I found it mysterious . . . attractive," he said, then added, "and eventually," he turned back to face me, "a little—uh—disturbing, hard to take." He swallowed; I waited for some elaboration, but Tom said nothing more.

Why, I wondered, had he begun to find qualities like "sincerity" and "honesty" hard to take? Because when one's intimate partner is honest and sincere, it seems to demand that one relate to her or him in a similarly honest and emotionally open fashion? "All right then," I said after a somewhat uncomfortable pause, "we'll get back to the attraction—and what was disturbing, later on."

Turning to Laura, I asked her what qualities, in particular, had first attracted her to Tom.

"He Challenged Me"

The fixed, demure smile that she wore as a customary expression—a smile in the shape of a V which, I thought, resembled that seen on archaic Greek statuary and on certain Madonnas—had not left Laura's face or changed in the slightest. "Oh," she said enthusiastically, "I was just *fascinated* by him! And for me, it was almost the same thing . . . an attraction and then later on . . . things that got hard to take. And for me, too, it was a challenge. He was just—oh, I couldn't figure him out! He was so unlike people who had been my friends and people whom I tended to think of as my *potential* friends! His whole way of thinking about life—his values, I mean—seemed absolutely unlike my own. I guess I was caught up short by somebody who didn't think in the ways I think, at all, but whom I *respected*. It was as if, starting out with really different premises, here was someone who'd come to a lot of the conclusions that I'd come to, but by another route."

It was odd, I mused, how often intimate partners had buzzwords—words like "adventure" or "security" or "glamour" or "challenge," which were of immense significance to both people in the relationship. The lattermost word—"challenge"—was clearly important to the Bretts. And yet I knew that if this interview were being conducted with another couple (myself and my husband, for example), that word might never have come up.

"In other words, you each saw in the other a possibility of 'otherness'?" I said. "A totally other kind of way to be?"

Tom, leaning forward in his seat, shook his head as if to say that Laura's ideas had never been completely alien to his own. "I guess the notion that there could be honesty and sincerity, real openness with one another, and so forth was something that I'd thought about before. But in my line of work, in a pretty pressured environment, people don't operate on this kind of level. I mean, it could get you into all kinds of trouble. . . . And I hadn't operated this way, in my personal life either, I guess." He ended his statement with a short, somewhat cynical-sounding laugh.

I hesitated, in the face of his objection, then decided to pursue the idea of "otherness" a step or two farther anyway. "It may be," I spoke in a tentative tone of voice, for I had nothing in mind other than a hunch, "that having seen this different way of operating, you each saw the other as having a piece of something that was unfamiliar and interesting . . . and maybe a little dangerous, and frightening, and even a little—unpleasant, at times, perhaps?"

Laura sat motionless. Tom, shifting his position, said, "Yes, although I don't think the unpleasant part occurred for me, right away." His wife, tempering her words with that serene Greek smile, assented. "The dangerous and frightening part catches it for me."

There was a charged silence, a feeling that we'd come very far very suddenly. I tried to slow things down by asking Laura whether she had been attracted by Tom's differentness and yet, at the same time, had wanted to get him to be more *like* her. She shook her head energetically, almost as if she'd heard the question as an accusation.

"No, the way he was was almost a *reproach* to me," she explained, "because I had gone through life thinking that people who are not like me are not okay people. I mean," she added hastily, as if forestalling any misunderstanding that might arise between the two of *us* about social or religious values, "they could become like me—and then they would be good people instead of mean, dreadful people—and with Tom, it was a *challenge* for me! That he could see things so differently, and talk about them so differently, and have a different kind of integrity!" She shot a swift glance at her husband, then turned back to me to say, "Could come out with compassionate kinds of political stances and so forth," in a proud voice. She was sitting up, like a cooperative schoolgirl, high and straight on the sofa.

"Is what you're saying," I asked, "that you were surprised to find that Tom could be compassionate without a real religious conviction?"

"Not only without a religious conviction," answered Laura, "but without any sort of basic ideals whatsoever."

The anger, which I had expected to see in response to Tom's initial use of the expression "hard to take," had at last come into full view. A round spot of color stood out on each of her broad-boned cheeks.

Had I, I wondered, stumbled into the middle of a quarrel—or was I, as interviewer, starting one? "What sort of basic ideals does Tom not have?" I asked his wife directly, attempting to sound neutral. Laura became disconcerted. "Well, at least at *that* time, he didn't . . . Things like emotional openness. . . ." She seemed confused. Turning to her husband, however, she asked, "Shall I go into this little story, or not?"

So she was not confused; they both knew what she was talking about.

"HE NEVER OPENED HIMSELF TO ANYONE"

Tom's only response to her question was a shrug—the elaborate gesture of someone who is resigning himself to the hearing of a too-often-told tale. "Shall I?" she urged, her voice sounding uncertain, like a child asking permission. "Go ahead," I intervened, and he nodded at the same time.

"When Tom and I were getting to know each other better—getting into a couple relationship, I mean, because we'd known each other, casually, before—I was telling him about what a really rough time of it I'd had, since the last time we'd run into one another . . . which happened to be in Africa, if you can believe it, about a year and a half earlier. And I was describing to him this painful, traumatic involvement that I'd had with a guy who turned out to be such a jerk—someone who was just *using* me all along! Tom's response to this was to say, 'Well, you must really have opened up to this guy, didn't you?' and I told him that of course I had; we were going out for a whole year, and it was a *serious* relationship! . . . *Obviously.*" Her voice was rising.

"That in itself seemed an awfully peculiar question to ask," she continued, "and then Tom told me that this was something he never really had done. " 'You've *what?*' I asked him, and then Tom told me that he wasn't open with people, generally, and that he'd never really opened up in any relationship, whatsoever." Laura blinked her eyes rapidly, several times in succession, as she parodied her own amazed response to that statement.

She added, as if soliciting my agreement, "To me, it was strange—he'd never shown his feelings to anyone! And I found it—*him*—impossible to understand!"

Tom had been, it seemed, initially attracted by such qualities as "honesty," "openness," "willingness to make a commitment." Laura had, apparently, been "challenged" by the man who'd claimed that he had never been emotionally open with any intimate partner, before—for had this not been the case, she could obviously have gone away. But at what point in the course of their developing relationship had Tom actually made that particular comment?

The Bretts gazed at each other questioningly, both trying to remember. Laura thought it was the second time they'd gone out; but Tom reminded her that it had been the *first* night, recalling the party at which they'd had this conversation—and she then recalled the occasion, and agreed.

So she had known from the outset that she was getting into a relationship with a man who was chary about sharing his feelings, I remarked. Had *that* been part of the initial attraction, did she think?

Laura's brown eyes opened very wide, and she said, quietly and distinctly, "I don't know." Tom, as if coming to her rescue, took his wife's hand in his own.

The Bone of a Memory

Laura and Tom Brett had, as I mentioned, consulted a couples' therapist in the fall just prior to their marriage. It had been a question either of resolving the battle—a battle about whether Tom *had* in fact been emotionally involved with his former girlfriend (whose name was Karen) and was unwilling to admit it—or of abandoning their own relationship, because the difficulties between them could not be resolved.

Their escalating, rage-filled quarrels had been terribly confusing to them both. Laura, insisting that Tom had been lying to her from Day One—and that he *had* had an intimate, deeply committed relationship to Karen—had kept demanding that he tell her (i.e., admit to) the truth. She'd felt, at some gut level, that if he got away with the deception about Karen—or what she felt had been, at the very least, a misrepresentation—then there would be the threat of other deceptions and misrepresentations to come. Real intimacy would be impossible with a partner who withheld his inner truths and real feelings, for who knew what such a person might think, or do, behind one's back? If he won the ongoing "Karen" argument, which in Laura's view meant getting away with being deceptive, she herself had too much to lose.

Tom, in this game without end, could not allow matters to be settled in his partner's favor either. If Laura won and took control of his former life, she would control parts of himself and of his past that really belonged to *him alone*. Losing this argument would be akin to being swallowed up alive; she would possess him, in terms of possessing his sense of separateness and autonomy. Since he, as well as she, had too much to lose, both had a stake in seeing that the quarrel about Tom's ex-girlfriend was never settled satisfactorily. The fights about Karen had, therefore, never ended with clarification of anyone's position; they'd only ended when the pair of them got worn out.

What was the ongoing argument actually all about? Basically, about Laura's fear that Tom was hiding his real feelings about his ex-girlfriend because they were still extremely powerful—that he was protecting his cherished memories of Karen because he still cared about that former relationship more than he would acknowledge. As Tom saw it, though, his past involvement might be open to reinterpretation, as he looked back upon it, but it was still part of his own experience, over which Laura had no real claim. Thus it was that they had been fighting over the meaning of that former attachment like two dogs over a bone.

At another level, though, intimacy (she wanted more) and autonomy (he wanted more) were what the underlying quarrel was about.

SETTLING A FIGHT

The Bretts' obsessive fighting had been dealt with by means of a simple-sounding and yet powerfully effective therapeutic device. What the Bretts' clinician had done was to suggest to the pair that they abide, for a period of time, by the following "contract": Laura was to be permitted to complain about Tom's ex-girlfriend—and her own belief that Tom and Karen really *had* had an intimate and involved relationship—for one full hour on one designated evening each week. Not only was Laura to be *allowed* to do this complaining, but it was given to her as a "task," a therapy homework assignment. She was to nag, whine, rage, scream about Karen for a whole hour—from 7:00 to 8:00 P.M.—every Tuesday, without fail.

Tom's homework assignment was to listen. His task was to give her his full attention and, at the same time, to remain silent. He was to sit there, with his gaze upon her, as she said whatever she liked, and he was *not* to respond verbally, no matter how inflammatory her accusations became.

That was all—aside from one other clause in the agreement: Laura was to limit all discussions of Karen to *that one hour per week*. She was forbidden to bring up the subject of her fiancé's ex-lover aside from the 7:00 to 8:00 P.M. hour of her Tuesday evening therapy assignment. It was then, and only then, that she could vent her anger about things that Tom might have said or done in relation to Karen (or things that Laura feared he might one day say or do). Aside from that one hour per week, when *she had to talk* and *he had to listen*, Tom's ex-girlfriend was a prohibited subject.

A Struggle for Control of the Relationship

Innocuous though these instructions may sound, this therapy homework had served to end a deadly impasse—a struggle over who was going to take control of the relationship. For Laura, by merely introducing the subject of Karen, had been able to define herself, her partner, and the very nature of the attachment that they shared. She became, immediately, the good, wronged person; he became the lying, guilty one; and the way in which they related was as the indignant, morally upright female and the guilty, bad, thoroughly deceptive male.

Tom, in order to prevent this from happening—prevent his wife from taking charge of the relationship and running it in such a way as to meet her own needs and satisfy her own inner agenda—had had to spring into an almost reflexive action each time the subject of Karen came up. He would interrupt Laura, deny he'd said things that he really had said to her before; he would confabulate and confuse his fiancée, talking in ways that made Laura feel that she was going crazy. He'd felt compelled to do this, because he had realized, at a subterranean level, that otherwise she would end up with most of the power—which is to say, the ability to say who *he* was, who *she* was, and what their relationship was fundamentally all about.

Accusations have this effect: They *define* the parties concerned in the interaction and the nature of the interaction itself.

WRITING THE MARITAL SCENARIO

Marriage is, as sociologists Peter Berger and Hansfried Kellner have observed, "a *dramatic* act in which two strangers come together and redefine themselves." For each of the partners, getting married involves a rupture with his or her former reality and the construction of a new, private sphere which is the special turf of the two people involved.

How does the new couple go about creating their own emotional world? Principally, suggest Berger and Kellner, in the course of the marital conversation that moves from bed to breakfast table and involves the effort "to match two individual definitions of reality. By the very logic of the relationship, a common overall definition must be arrived at—otherwise the conversation will become impossible and, *ipso facto*, the relationship itself will be endangered," they write.

Each member of the pair has, however, come into the marriage with a different autobiography; the specific family cultures from which they spring have impressed certain ideas and beliefs into their psyches. Each has an internalized set of images about what being in a close attachment is like, a set of images that psychiatrist H. V. Dicks has called "interaction models" or "role models of relationships"—expectations about what one's own behavior and the behavior of the spouse will be like. These will not fit together in a lock-and-key fashion; each partner will have to give up certain parts of the past in attempting to find a "fit" with the other's deeply cherished views and notions.

Their inner scenarios in regard to intimate connections will have to be revised and rewritten. The major struggle, in the early phase of marriage, is about what the themes of their new, jointly constructed scenario will be. For if they cannot agree upon the nature of their shared reality, the marital conversation will eventually reach its ending. They will be "from different worlds" and have nothing whatsoever to say to each other. The effort to reach a mutual understanding of what the relationship is about is, therefore, a desperately important and serious one.

The partners have—and this is an issue to be explored at greater length farther along—certainly selected each other because *writing a joint script together* was a viable possibility for these two particular people. That doesn't mean, however, that they will find it easy to do so. The power struggles that go on in many intimate attachments—most particularly when the new relationship is crystallizing—frequently involve a contest about *whose ideas about reality* will be the stronger ones, the ones that hold sway in their shared emotional territory.

Accusations flung at the partner can, therefore, be seen as power moves, efforts to force the marital plot to move in its "correct" and natural direction. Laura Brett, by merely introducing the name "Karen" into the marital conversation, defined herself as a vulnerable, emotionally open innocent in a relationship with a cold, feelingless Lothario.

Tom, struggling against her characterization of the marriage, countered with accusations of his own. Since his ex-girlfriend was, in fact, long gone from his life—and had been since he'd become involved with Laura—the truth of their attachment was a different one entirely. He was a faithful, committed individual, being falsely reproached by a pathologically jealous partner—a woman who was in passionate competition with a phantom. Theirs was, as he saw it, a relationship between a reasonable, logical husband and a wife who was irrational and hysterical. So they had argued, interminably, about whose version of the marital scenario most corresponded to objective reality.

The Sharing of Power

The therapeutic behavior assignment had enabled the Bretts to see that the only way that either one of them could gain power and control in the relationship would be if power and control were *shared*. Laura, given undisputed charge of her Tuesday evening hour, could use it to vent (communicate intimately) all of her thoughts about Tom's ex-lover, without his interrupting her or running away. She could complete her communicational broadcast from start to finish, without static and without interference. In this fashion, her concerns about her future husband's ability to be honest and open—not to be deceptive about his past or his present feelings—were able to get a full hearing.

And Tom, in exchange for giving her his full attention, traded that hour of concentrated listening for the assurance that the toxic subject of Karen would not be brought up at *any other time* during the week. It wouldn't be within Laura's power, at any moment when she happened to be feeling tension, to turn up the flame under this particular emotional stewpot. As a result, each partner gained the sense of being securely in charge of a particular piece of the relationship. He would not have to remain on battle alert, ready to defend himself at any moment—or to attack if he suspected that his wife was about to do so.

The pair of them had been working in an "If you win, I lose; if I win, you lose" kind of framework. Each had had, in other words, to seize control of the action because if he or she didn't, the other would take over. But there was an option *other* than "I win/you lose": the option that each would have his or her own territory within the relationship, and so power and control could be shared by means of mutual negotiation. Each partner had, according to the terms of this agreement, time and space that did not have to be wrested from the other one.

What the behavioral task actually demonstrated to the Bretts was that there was a way of being in a close relationship that was different from the "If you win, I lose; if I win, you lose" kind of system in which they had been working. In *that* system, both had been losers, for they'd been in an unresolvable fight to the finish, a finish which could be achieved only by one person's being mashed, or by the ending of the relationship. The homework assignment prescribed by their clinician had forced them into a collaborative situation and put them into a totally different sort of relational framework—one in which it became clear that winning meant winning *with* and not *against* the partner. In relationships, there is never really one winner and one loser; two people either win—or lose—together. But that is the hardest thing in the world for some people (especially people in couple relationships) truly to understand.

THERAPY HOMEWORK

Laura Brett had, as she told me later, actually completed her therapy assignment, in its entirety, on only one occasion. That had been on the first Tuesday after she and her fiancé had agreed to the clinician's odd-sounding deal. On that occasion, she had raged and complained for the entire hour, with Tom's gaze focused upon her. *He* had, as he'd described it to me, found it extremely difficult to remain still! But, because he had succeeded in doing so, he'd actually managed to hear some of the things she needed to tell him—things that he'd never heard, because she'd never quite gotten past the first few sentences without his interrupting her, telling her that he *knew* what she was going to say and that she was totally mistaken! As so frequently happens, in emotionally overloaded circumstances, he'd assumed he *did* know, and yet he didn't, not completely.

There were parts of her recitation—things she needed to say about how she was feeling—that she'd never gotten to tell him because things became so confused and angry so quickly.

Tom had learned, in that first Tuesday evening session, things about how it felt to be in Laura's skin that he had never realized before. She, on her part, having had her full say on that initial occasion, found that there was less to talk about the second time around. It was, in fact, hard to fill a full hour with complaints. By the third week, the therapy assignment had been experienced as burdensome; Laura had stretched it out to forty-five minutes, but then found nothing more that she could say. On the fourth Tuesday, she and Tom had forgotten their clinical homework completely; they'd gone to a concert that evening.

Somehow, though, the issue of his relationship with Karen had been transformed from an ongoing, wild, irrational battle to an occasional and manageable spat.

THE GHOST OF KAREN

In the course of my talks with the Bretts, nevertheless, a figure whom I thought of as "the ghost of Karen" continued to haunt the interaction between them. This figure was a nebulous presence, much more a fantasy than a real person with an existence of her own. But she was there, as I came to understand, for the best of reasons: The Bretts needed to have her be there. Karen enabled them to work on certain conflictual issues, harking back to each partner's past life, in his or her original family.

These issues, which had never been satisfactorily resolved, revolved around several themes which were of deep concern to both of them. It was by no means chance that they, like most people who fall in love, had been attracted by what was deeply *familiar* about the other person. "[T]he reasons for the suddenness and intensity of falling in love," write Lily Pincus and Dr. Christopher Dare, "are usually unconscious. The choice of a marriage partner seems often to have been made very quickly, on the basis of relatively little conscious knowledge, and with, as it turns out, great accuracy of complementarity, fit of personalities and even life experience of the partners."

Most of us know, as if by means of some sonar signaling system, who *is* the person with whom our earliest conflicts can be resurrected and reenacted—and, hopefully, resolved eventually. It is as if we recognize, at some deep level, that other who can aid us in our struggles to put behind us matters that really do belong in the past. In Laura and Tom Brett's case, the nature of the underlying issues (among them, an exciting, vanished partner) became apparent once work on the construction of their family genogram began.

2

Where the Past and the Present Converge: Genograms

As I took out my large, eleven-by-fourteen-inch Strathmore sketchpad and an assortment of red, blue and green pencils, the Bretts watched me in baffled amusement. Was I, they wanted to know, planning to draw their portrait? I smiled and explained that I was going to construct a diagram of sorts—an overview or blueprint of the important relationships in each of their lives, one which would stretch far backward in time.

"It's called a genogram," I said, "and it's like a good old-fashioned family tree—except that, as you'll see, it's also somewhat different."

For me, the discovery of genograms (which I first encountered while studying at the Family Institute of Westchester) had brought a new kind of knowledge, a way of understanding the true nature of the raw materials that couples bring into their intimate relationships. Genograms provide a systematic way of looking at each partner's own natural context—the family subculture in which he or she was reared—and discerning those repetitive themes, issues, myths, patterns of behavior, etc., which have been brought forward from the past and resurrected in the marriage of the present.

Tom and Laura Brett had not, before meeting and deciding to marry, floated around in other space somewhere; neither one of them had existed in a social vacuum. On the contrary, each had come from somewhere—and that somewhere was his or her own family of origin.

Families, *all* families, are intensely emotional social systems (even those that appear to contain no emotionality whatsoever). It is within this highly emotional setting that each of us learns a particular set of rules, regulations, and expectations about our own and other people's behavior that eventually become taken for granted as *obvious matters that everybody knows about.* What is learned includes, among other things, many deeply held assumptions and ideas about what a real adult woman is like, and what a real adult man is like, and how the two sexes relate.

This learning occurs, as a matter of course, from observations of our parents' behavior. We humans are not only mammals, but *social mammals*: Whom we become as adult persons has to do with the environment in which our development takes place, i.e., the social world we inhabit in childhood. Whom we become is profoundly influenced by those people with whom we interact on a daily basis, the significant persons linked to us by blood or by choice. On a genogram, the interplay of generations within a family is carefully graphed, so that the psychological legacies of past generations can be readily identified.

And how *connected* I continually found the structure of early, childhood experiences and later marriage choices to be! I became aware, over and over again, of how tenaciously the past searches for its expression in the present!

The drawing that I was about to construct with the Bretts was simple, nothing other than a blueprint of the two family systems which had been joined together when Tom and Laura had married. This relational road map would, when completed, include people who were young and old, dead and alive, sick and well, loved and hated, and, for that matter, some who were not thought about very often at all.

What intrigues me, always, is the way in which two individuals—who often have emerged from families with very different sets of rules for interacting, behaving, and even *thinking* about life—come together to hammer out a new system of their own devising. This involves not only the merging of two sets of perceptions and understandings, but so frequently, it also involves a largely unconscious collusion, an unspoken agreement to restage some version of a family drama that has special meanings for both of them. I knew, even as I drew my first line on the empty square of paper before me, that a whole universe—the Bretts' individual pasts and the present world they had fashioned together—would gradually emerge around this commonplace mark that I was making on a page.

The genogram, I explained, was a device which would enable me to get to know both of them very quickly. "It will help me to learn some things about your family, Laura, and about yours too, Tom, in a rapid and fairly orderly fashion," I said. They nodded, exchanged a smile, then looked at me expectantly as if I'd proposed an interesting game. Smiling, too, I warned them that they might find filling out this chart to be a somewhat surprising experience. Then, pointing to the line that I'd already sketched in, I told them that that horizontal mark was a symbol representing their relationship.

"Now," I asked, my blue pencil poised above the paper, "how long have you two—" "Six years," said Laura at the same time as her husband answered, "One," and then the three of us laughed. My pencil remained where it was, and I waited. Tom explained that they had overlapped at Princeton, as undergraduates, and had, "technically speaking," known each other since 1974.

"I don't think we were actually introduced until 1976," put in Laura, primly.

The figure I wanted was, I said, the number of months, or years, that they'd been a married couple. It was just a little less than a year and a month.

I wrote, just over the line, "one year" and then added a small plus sign. At the right-hand end of the horizontal line, I drew a small circle, under which I printed "Laura"; at the left-hand end, I sketched a small square, labeling it "Tom."

Tom objected at once, saying that he didn't like being represented by a square. I offered to use some other designation, explaining that genograms are standard tools used for doing research on (and therapy with) families; the symbol used routinely, to designate a male person, is a square. Tom then laughed, shrugged, and said that he really didn't care.

I wondered. Was being a "square" (unmanly? not "with it"?) a worry that Tom Brett had?

I let the beginning of the sketch stand as it was, and it looked like this:

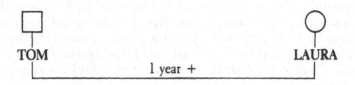

On that empty page, standing by itself, Tom and Laura's relationship seemed to exist as a solitary phenomenon—one planet in an otherwise empty sky. But there would emerge, as we worked on the genogram, a family firmament surrounding it; no marriage exists in isolation from the important people and charged issues in each partner's individual past. I looked up at Laura, then, telling her that I wanted to ask her a few things about her family, but she was frowning and had a preoccupied expression on her face.

DECEPTION

"Did you," Laura asked her husband swiftly, "get to say everything you needed to say about that stuff we were discussing before? About how we got interested in each other, in the first place?" Her intent, intelligent gaze was fixed upon him, but he broke away, glanced toward the picture window to our left for a moment, then finally said, "No."

"Go on then," she urged, and I was taken aback, not only by this evidence of their private system of knowing (a mysterious aspect of the private universe of couples) but by the swift way in which Laura had assumed charge of the proceedings.

"I came away from that discussion," Tom said slowly, speaking to me, "with the idea that Laura was *attracted* by the notion that I could have been in a long relationship with someone without ever . . .well, without having opened myself up to that person in an emotional way." Laura seemed to be challenging him to be open and vulnerable in *this relationship*, he was complaining, while the man she'd initially found attractive had characterized himself as an inaccessible sort of a guy. Which kind of person had Laura actually *wanted*? He couldn't be emotionally open and intriguingly out of reach simultaneously.

"If *that* was what she liked about me, in the first place, then it turns my stomach a bit," Tom continued, sounding anxious. "It—it makes me kind of—" He paused, failed to say the word that would have completed this sentence. Instead, he began a new one. "Because that whole notion she has of me—as this secretive, unreachable guy—as we've talked about it, and fought about it, has turned out to be a *misrepresentation*."

The coldhearted loner whom Laura had been drawn to was, Tom feared, the kind of man whom she really found exciting. There was not only anxiety but anger in his voice. The force of the phrase he'd used, too—"it turns my stomach"—had surprised me, and I said so. "That was a pretty strong way to put it; why is that statement so strong?" I asked. Laura's cheeks had become rosy with emotion, but she said nothing. "It just makes me nervous," her husband reiterated, promptly.

I looked at him quizzically. "What makes you nervous—can you say?"

Tom turned to Laura, answered *her* as if she had asked the question of him.

"That our relationship started off on a false basis," he said. He was telling her that he feared she'd been attracted by the idea of his being an unfeeling man, who'd never opened himself to anyone in an intimate relationship, and that she had, therefore, fallen in love with a person who wasn't really *him*. Was he, in fact, the unavailable, cynical fellow he'd presented himself as being, or was this a role she was forcing him to play, in their ongoing marital scenario?

The conversation faltered, halted, there. Here was a mate, Tom, who in the early stages of courtship was seen as never vulnerable, never emotionally exposed, never even having shared his inner world with any intimate partner, before. And here was a perfectly complementary mate, Laura, whose most important values had to do with "sincerity," "honesty," "making oneself vulnerable" and a sacrificial willingness to make a total commitment of the self. It was as if each of them had found, in the other, a missing aspect of something lacking in his or her own inner being.

Laura said, breaking the tension of the silence, "I don't feel as if— because of that stuff you said about never having opened yourself up, in the relationship with Karen—I fell in love with an *illusion*!" She stared at him for a moment, then explained, turning to me, that the pair of them had developed a big problem having to do with the way Tom described things. "I don't want to say that's our *only* problem", her voice was fervent, "but that has been a big issue."

I nodded my head in agreement. I didn't believe that she'd been attracted to Tom "by mistake." There is just too much communication and meta-communication between lovers. They are reading each other at both a conscious and an unconscious level, and recognize full well who will, or will not, fit into what is a particularized agenda of needs, wishes, desires—that amalgam of what is strange and what is familiar that makes the other person *right*. A single misunderstood statement could not bear the weight of such responsibility; it couldn't have been the sole source of his wife's initial attraction to him. But this, I knew, was what Tom was afraid of.

There was, however, something that Laura was trying to articulate which had to do with her husband's relationship to that ex-girlfriend (or, at least, to the way in which he had *described* that earlier relationship). It had to do, I suspected, with some question about his capacity for honesty and openness—which plugged in, perhaps, to some real fears of her own. I recalled, then, something she'd mentioned having told Tom, on their very first date—something about having just come through a very rough time during which she'd been involved with a man who was faithless and who'd been betraying her, throughout the time they were together as a couple.

"In a way," I said to her, "you seem to me to be worried—or let's say 'concerned'—by values or qualities having to do with 'sincerity,' 'willingness to be emotionally open,' and the like. And these things have, I think, a very special meaning for you. Honesty, in intimate relationships, is something about which there's an enormous amount of concern, on your part. And it brings to my mind something you said earlier—which was that before you and Tom got involved, you were in a long relationship with someone who deceived you . . . 'used you' was what I think you said."

Laura blinked, hesitated before speaking, then nodded. "Yes, and it happened in *another* long relationship, too—before the last one. And that other one went on for three and a half years." She seemed, suddenly, on the verge of crying.

THEMES OF EARLY LIFE

Starting to construct a family genogram is like beginning work on an elaborate puzzle or detective story. The horizontal line which I'd drawn, connecting Laura and Tom Brett, was the single puzzle piece or clue that I had, and yet, as experience had already taught me, many other parts of the puzzle would emerge upon the page in the course of this discussion. The background would fill in, as bits of evidence from each mate's own past were supplied. Surveying the ways in which the two members of a couple fit together—and how the needs, dilemmas, unresolved issues, etc., of their individual pasts have *shaped* that affinity—is always a remarkably sobering process.

For the degree to which mates are, in their present-day emotional relationships, at work on re-creating and struggling to master old family concerns and difficulties is an absolutely striking phenomenon—one which affects every one of us deeply, but which we usually comprehend in only periodic glimmers and glimpses. Emotional themes and sequences which were present in one generation tend to surface in other ones: It's as if family dilemmas that had never found their satisfactory resolutions needed to be resurrected, in the real world, so that different individuals could work on those problems once again.

The tendency (or even *urge*) that people have to replicate themes of early life in the context of later intimate relationships has been commented upon by many marital theorists and therapists. As social worker Lily Pincus and family therapist Christopher Dare, founder of the Tavistock Institute for Marital Studies, have observed, "We all have a tendency to get into repetitive patterns of relationships that are motivated by the persistence of wishes in unconscious fantasy form and derived from the way earlier needs were satisfied. Sometimes, in marriage, the repetitive aspect of sequences of partnership is remarkably literal, as when a woman whose childhood was damaged by her father's alcoholism finds herself marrying a man who turns out to be an alcoholic, divorces him and then gets herself into the same situation once more. Or, a man whose childhood was dominated by his mother's heart disease may marry a woman with congenital heart trouble."

The "repetitive sequences of partnership" to which these clinicians refer is, obviously, that of child to alcoholic (or heart-damaged) parent and then, later, of that grown person to his or her alcoholic or heart-damaged spouse.

Such strange iterations of past family experiences often turn up in something that is going on, very currently, in a couple's relationship. The partners, usually unaware of the fact that their problem is a repetition of one that existed earlier and elsewhere in the extended system, are startled when they see that particular "charged issue" stand out in high relief upon their family genogram. There are instances when the most astonishing thing of all is that the parallels between "what was" and "what is" have not been noticed before! I will cite two such examples—situations in which a family dilemma had been resurrected and worked upon in a blatant and dramatic way while the partners involved were totally oblivious of any connection between patterns of the past and the present.

FAMILIAR RELATIONSHIPS

In the first instance, the couple was, at the time of our interviews, in the midst of a full-blown marital crisis and maintaining their emotionally fragile connection for reasons that seemed to have more to do with mutual hostile dependence than with anything relating to love, satisfaction, or caring. They behaved toward each other, by and large, like an angry parent (mother) and a truculent child. He was her incorrigibly bad boy of a spouse.

The wife, in this case, had had a father who was much loved by her but who had made his entire family's life insecure and difficult. He was a man who had kept shifting jobs, changing careers, owing to restlessness and dissatisfaction on his own part or dissatisfaction on the part of his employers. He had been a musician, at one time, and a teacher of music at another. He'd run a community organization (and gotten into difficulties with the board), tried to start a school, and also worked at a number of other, very different sorts of occupations. The emotional turmoil about this entire issue—for each job that her dad lost or decided to leave tended to involve a move to a new community—had been an important and painful part of this woman's entire growing-up experience. When we talked, she was forty-three years old, and she and her executive spouse had been married for eighteen years.

Her husband, when she'd married him, had had a solid professional training; he had a master's degree in business administration and was moving rapidly up the corporate ladder in a large financial institution. At a conscious level, the wife had done everything possible to avoid a repetition of her earlier difficulties; she'd found a partner who was not only prepared for a stable, well-remunerated career but *interested* in the things that he was doing professionally.

But, as became evident during the course of the interviews, this pair had duplicated, in their own lives, what had happened in the wife's family earlier. Some five years before our conversations got under way, the husband had begun feeling restless in his job, like a cog in a large industrial wheel. He'd felt, as he put it, "trapped on the company's organizational chart" and had decided to take an entrepreneurial flyer—to start a new business of his own. It wasn't working out, and recently it had become clear that this effort (in a field that had nothing to do with his former occupation) was destined for failure. He was now, as he described himself, "in the midst of a male menopause," a crisis of middle life. At a time when their oldest daughter was on the verge of entering college, he had used up a lot of the family's savings and was bringing in no salary at all. As this wife's father had done, so was her husband doing—behaving like a recalcitrant, irresponsible child. Had she herself, at some level, *required* that the past repeat itself in this fashion?

One couldn't know. We all have (as marital experts Pincus and Dare have noted) tendencies to get into modes of relationship that are familiar. This particular wife, like her mother before her, surely *knew* how to be a powerful and competent woman who is in a relationship with an immature, incompetent man. At the time of our conversations, their entire family (which consisted of two adults and two adolescent children) was being supported by the wife's fairly ill-paying job. This, again, was a repetition of a past set of circumstances—her own family had been supported, once upon a time, by her mother's secretarial salary. So she was, in the middle years of her adulthood, dealing with the same painful dilemma that had preoccupied her throughout her childhood.

How had this duplication of an emotionally charged set of circumstances come (or been coaxed somehow) into being? It was as if the entire predicament had—almost like a bar of music—been picked up from a prior generation and transposed down on to the next one. As anyone who works with family genograms (or families in general) can attest, such repetitions of problematic themes, circumstances, etc., tend to recur again and again. And while it seems reasonable to expect repetitions of styles or systems of *being in a relationship* (such as the highly functional female/ powerless, low-functioning male mode of relating that these two had worked out), this restaging of a toxic family situation, in its entirety, does defy rational explanation.

Far eerier are the replications of family problems by couples who have no knowledge of a particular dilemma's existence. And this was true in the second instance that I want to relate, which emerged from a set of interviews that I had with a couple in their fifties (he was fifty-five, at the time, and his wife was fifty). These partners had begun their marriage, now in its thirty-second year, by running off and eloping. It was not until many years later that the husband learned that his *own parents* had eloped, and for an oddly similar set of reasons!

The spouses that I talked with had decided to marry secretly, because they were certain that her family would never give their approval. Her parents would consider her too young for marriage—she'd been eighteen, at the time, and a freshman in college—and they would view *him* as not sufficiently ambitious, for he was not preparing for one of the more lucrative professions. (He'd become a high school teacher, eventually, and they lived in Washington, D.C.)

What neither of them had realized, for many years, was that once upon a time *his* parents had done exactly the same thing. His folks had never told him that, not ever—and the parents had seemed profoundly shaken by their son's elopement at the time of its occurrence. But they continued, at the same time, to keep their *own* earlier elopement a well-guarded family secret.

It was not until after both his mother and father had died that the husband learned that his oldest sister was illegitimate: His parents had run off and gotten married because his mother was already pregnant. This information had come to him by chance; he'd simply stumbled across the dates of his parents' wedding, and of his oldest sister's birth, when he was going through some family papers. Then he had realized what had oc-curred.

What had been told to him, as part of the family lore, was that his mother's people had initially disapproved of her suitor; they'd viewed their daughter as too young for marriage; and they had considered her suitor unambitious, not sufficiently upwardly mobile. (His father, a shopkeeper, wasn't considered to be the equal of the men in his mother's family, who were all academics and clergymen.) His suspicion, confirmed in retrospect by many odd bits of information which he'd hitherto ignored, was that his parents had eloped without his mother's family's consent because his mother was already well along in her pregnancy. But he could not recollect having heard any such story in his childhood and thus was puzzled by having done the same thing, eventually, himself. There it was, however—a very similar sequence of events appearing upon the family genogram.

And it *is* puzzling: How could it have come about that a family dilemma—a secret marriage, made without parental blessings and consent—was repeated, in a subsequent generation, without anyone's having been aware that such a problematic event had occurred before? The answers to such questions aren't obvious. Do we imbibe our family's psychological issues and concerns along with the mother's milk that we drink?

This is, most probably, about as close to the truth as one can possibly come. Families are such affect-laden little social systems that people who live in them can "know" each other's truths in ways that are almost magical; they can know them without ever being told. Because they are the first truths of existence to which each of us is exposed, our families' truths are embedded within us, and in our lives, these truths struggle to make themselves known.

A Way of Being in an Intimate Relationship

Such examples as those I've just cited involve, of course, the literal restaging of core experiences that once occurred in one or both partners' original families. Far subtler—and far more prevalent than is commonly recognized—are the numerous instances in which a *system for being in an intimate relationship* is what is being brought forward, from the past and into the present, by one or both members of the pair.

If, say, a husband's own father had failed in his business or career aspirations—and if his mother was clearly disappointed by the marital match that she'd made—that man, in his adult life, may need to repeat *what he knows about being in a male/female relationship* (and knows well, because he learned it before anything else), which is how to be the inadequate husband of a wife who is fundamentally disappointed by him for some reason, and in some way. Such knowledge about the way in which a male and a female relate can, I might add, remain impervious to any outward successes in the real world that this man manages to attain.

What he *won't* have learned, in his earlier years, is how to be the well-loved mate of a woman who cares about him and is content to be his wife. That he may strive very diligently, albeit at an unconscious level, to re-create that past situation—by means of any number of strategies, including the extreme one of being an inadequate and frustrating sexual partner—demonstrates the great and hypnotic power of past experiences upon the everyday occurrences and happenings of present-day life.

To some large or small degree, when we attain adult status, most of us have not put our childhood things behind us. In the very process of choosing our mates, and of being chosen—and then, in elaborating upon our separate, past lives in the life we create together—we are deeply influenced by the patterns for being that we observed and learned about very early in life and that live on inside our heads. The fact that there may be *other options*, other systems for being in an intimate relationship, often doesn't occur to us, because we don't realize that we *are* operating from within a system, one which was internalized in our original families. What has been, and what we've known, seem to be "the way of the world"; it is reality itself.

Perhaps this is why "the way it was" feels, to so many people, like "the way it has to be." Perhaps this is why, in the process of constructing a couple's family genogram, one stumbles across so many repetitious coincidences. And certainly, when encountering them, one wonders, is it *coincidental* that a man whose own mother was hypochondriacal and depressed has married a woman who *was* warm and outgoing and then, a decade later, found himself the disgruntled husband of a seriously depressed and somewhat suicidal wife? Is that bad luck, or is it the present bending to the will of the past?

THE FAMILIAR RELATIONAL WORLD

It may be that the universal tendency "to get into repetitive patterns of relationships" (to quote clinicians Dare and Pincus once again) is based, more than anything else, upon our need to remain in a relational world with which we are familiar.

One glamorous young wife whom I interviewed, for example, told me that her mother had been a powerful, effective, angry woman who was disgusted by sex. Her father was, in her view, "spineless," and she had always seen him as a man without any rights, who had been "crushed" by his wife.

When I began meeting with this woman and her husband, the pair of them were both thirty-three years old. He was the handsome, gentle heir to a family business; they had a three-year-old son, and they had an entrenched sexual dysfunction. The wife had vowed, she related, that when she grew up she was going to be as different from her mother as she could possibly be. But now, in the seventh year of her marriage, her behavior and that of her mother were indistinguishable.

She herself was in the position of making all the family decisions (the large ones as well as the small choices of movies and restaurants); she dominated her husband and experienced no sexual desire—only great anxiety—whenever he made an approach. Very clearly she had replicated in her own marriage her parents' system of being in a relationship—even though, at the level of awareness, what she'd most wanted was to avoid it!

What was remarkable to me about this couple's history, by the way, was that both husband and wife said they had completely enjoyed their sexual relationship until the time of their marriage. It was as if, once they were married, and no longer involved in an affair, they'd begun to reenact their mutual understanding of how it is that husbands and wives behave—a reenactment with which the husband certainly was colluding, for reasons that derived from his own problematic earlier history. Each had gotten himself or herself into the kind of relationship with which he or she was familiar—and most people are, never doubt it, terrified by what is unfamiliar and unknown.

That is why what is painful and familiar is often preferred to what is new. It is also, in some large part, the explanation for why so many of us get into what Pincus and Dare call "repetitive patterns of relationships": It permits us to stay in a world that we know.

The case that Pincus and Dare cite, for instance—the daughter of an alcoholic who then marries an alcoholic—can be understood in terms of that woman's staying in the only kind of world that she knows. She *knows* what life is like when you live with an alcoholic: What she doesn't know is what it's like when you don't. When it comes to dealing with a mate with a drinking problem, she knows how to behave; she is dealing with the devil she knows.

What she does know may not be pleasant, and may be frankly undesirable at a conscious level; but what she doesn't know (so goes the unconscious reasoning) is alien, and might be far more threatening in ways she doesn't know and can't realize. It is for these sorts of reasons—plus the fact that repeating the past is a way of remaining psychologically connected to the past—that people will remain in uncomfortable yet well-known types of emotional scenarios.

I don't mean to suggest in any programmatic way that each generation is a carbon copy of the one that preceded it. This is obviously not the case. What I do want to say, however, is that there is a tremendous affectivity within families, and that the powerful interconnectedness of each generation to the people of preceding generations is often insufficiently appreciated.

As family therapist Patricia Meyer has written, in *The Family Life Cycle*, a majority of people's "life course is grounded in a likeness of opposition to the life course of the parents. In other words, an individual follows the behavioral patterns that he or she has experienced, or establishes behavioral patterns *opposite* to those experienced in growing up."

That is, the knowledge base from which we operate is what was learned in our original families. We do things, by and large, as we saw them done or as *a reaction to* the way we saw them done, and this tendency to behave in *reverse* ways is especially evident in certain emotionally charged situations. A daughter who, for example, was in a relationship with a mother who was angry and harsh, might—because of what she had experienced as a child—promise herself that she will never display anger or hostility to her own children. One could predict, in such an instance, that *the daughter's own daughter* would one day develop a critical, tyrannical stance; that is, become someone very like her grandmother. Doing it completely differently, in reaction to a parent or parents, often involves turning a behavior inside out. One does the opposite, and in the next generation it boomerangs.

Why? Because going from one extreme to the other, i.e., from total tyranny to inappropriate submissiveness, does not resolve the basic problem—which has to do with how anger is rightfully handled—but instead merely turns it inside out. The system for being in a mother/daughter relationship is no different, but contains the younger female in the one-up position in this particular generation.

It may happen, in some cases, that a charged family issue goes underground, to resurface two generations later. Many marital and family theorists have observed that, in looking over a family's genogram, one often notices an important difficulty that the grandparents were having disappears completely and then reappears as a problem that the grandchildren are experiencing. For instance, the son of an alcoholic father, having seen the havoc that excessive drinking can cause, might become a staunch opponent of the use of alcohol and never allow it into his own home. But *his* children—because drinking is a charged although possibly never openly talked-about concern—are at high risk for eventually developing alcohol problems in their own adult lives. What one finds, with curious frequency, is that a family's difficulty hasn't vanished completely in the middle generation; the difficulty has simply gone underground, into behavioral remission, so to speak.

When, however, the problem mysteriously reappears in the grandchild generation, it indicates that it has been there all the while and that it has remained a toxic, reactive issue for everyone within that family's overall emotional system.

Families seem to have their theme songs, their problematic issues— whether these be "alcoholism," "inappropriate anger," "overclose attachment between a parent and a child," "depression," "difficulties in dealing with separations and losses"—and these songs are sung by differing individuals at different times from different perches on the family tree. But what is astonishing, when one stops and looks at that tree in its entirety, are the persistent ways in which certain core passages or recitativos are repeated again and again. They are passed along from generation to generation, picked up here and there, and then worked on anew.

Sometimes they seem to be almost palpable, these family concerns, myths, fantasies: Inheritances that are as real as the family's rugs, pictures, chairs and other possessions. Like other inheritances, I might add, they are not always equally parceled out; in many instances, a particular child is the recipient of the lion's share of the family's emotional burdens.

That child, for some reason—perhaps because he or she resembles some terribly needed or furiously resented figure from the past; or perhaps because he or she has become "triangulated" into the parent's marriage (that is, become the third party upon which their own disappointments are deflected)—is the object of feelings that are overly intense. In any case, and for whatever reasons, because the "special child" is given, or assumes, the weight of the difficulty, other children in that family are left, relatively speaking, free.

It is fair to say, though, that the more a person has been thus pressed into the emotional service of his or her original family, the greater will be that individual's tendency to replay problematic earlier relationships in the intimate partnership that is marriage. Why is this so? I think it is because we tend to stage the same charged scenarios over and over, as we search for a different ending—for a resolution. But until the issues of the past are truly resolved, the curtain cannot be rung down upon them, so the repetitious efforts to master and resolve them continue.

Shadow Relationships

Laura Brett was the fourth of five children in her family.

This information surprised me. She had that tendency to take a leadership position which usually corresponds to having been in charge of younger siblings (the oldest child) or of never having had one's supremacy questioned (an only child). As I drew her two older brothers and her older sister into the family genogram, I noticed that all four senior siblings were two years apart but that the difference between Laura and the youngest child (a brother) was ten years; he was a full decade younger than she.

So, while Laura was in one sense the junior member in a family of four children, she was in another sense the eldest sibling in a family of two. She had been ten years old when that brother was born—a helpful little assistant mother.

Laura's mother (Harriet) was now almost sixty; her father, (Nicholas) was seventy; there was an eleven-year age difference between them. They had been married for thirty-four years—a marriage that was, according to their daughter's characterization of it, "stable but frustrating." There was, Laura added, very little communication between her parents. "My father simply does not participate in their relationship," Laura said quietly.

I sketched in swiftly, above the marriage line connecting her parents, another line—a lineful of dashes, which symbolizes relationships that are emotionally distant. The genogram that I was drawing looked, at this juncture, like this:

KEY
――― Distant Relationship

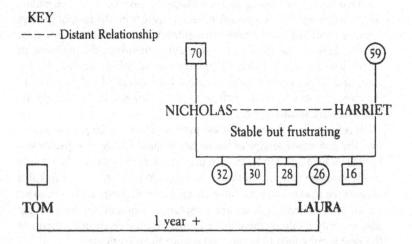

I asked Laura to tell me what her mother was like. "How would you," I asked, "characterize your mother, as a person?"

The descriptive terms that sprang to Laura's lips were "easygoing," "pleasant," "sensible." "She's not sensible to the point of being dry and dreary; she's just capable. A good person in a situation of crisis—she works as a secretary, full-time now. But she didn't work at all when we were little."

Her own relationship with her mother, she said, had always been a good and easy one. But then Laura seemed to retract that statement by adding that they'd always disagreed about a variety of subjects, as long as she could remember.

On what subjects, in particular, had they disagreed?

She laughed. "My mother's always found me a bit unorthodox. Recently, we've been able to talk about this, openly, and with a lot less tension than we used to. . . ." She shrugged. "My mother's always wished that I'd stay in line and play it safe a little more than I do. Or curl my hair and wear makeup." Her voice was not only amused but wistful.

"You mean that she wanted you to be more girlish and feminine?"

A confused look crossed Laura's features, and she shook her head. "Not only that, but more success-oriented. You know, go to law school rather than to seminary. . . . Make it in a big way, in all respects." She drew in a breath. "I just make my mother nervous, I think."

"Does making her nervous make *you* nervous?" I asked.

"Rarely," she responded swiftly, but then acknowledged that when she was in high school she had scared not only her mother but *herself* a bit, too. Tom, following this discussion intently, had no decipherable expression on his face. I wondered what he was thinking.

My own thought was that if a developing young woman made her mother nervous, she would be unable to avoid feeling some nervousness about herself: Mother's feelings are such powerful feedback. I asked Laura whether her mother could be described as a physically affectionate person.

Instead of answering, she turned to look at Tom. He, in the midst of taking a sip of coffee, merely put the cup down on their glass coffee table with a resounding clatter. Turning back to me, she said, "Not very."

I smiled. "So she's not a hugger and a kisser?"

Laura, smiling too, shook her head. "She's what you might call a 'borderline hugger.' But my father is definitely *not* a hugger, and that's the standard for comparison."

I glanced at her father's name—Nicholas—on the genogram, just as she remarked, "It's a second marriage for both of them."

"Oh." I entered those first marriages into the family chart, as Laura produced the following data: "Each was married about a year and a half; neither of them had children." An odd look, partly curious, partly frightened, came over her face. "I don't know what happened in those other relationships. Maybe quick disillusionment."

What an odd parallel, I thought, between a present-day triangle—Laura, her husband, and her husband's ex-girlfriend, Karen—and two similar triangles (mother, father, mother's ex-spouse; and father, mother, and father's ex-spouse). Was Laura concerned about whether her own marriage would survive the year and a half limit?

"Have you ever spoken to either of your parents about their first marriages?" I asked. Laura answered, in an airy, bubbly sort of voice, that she had. "One of the strange things, though, is that I didn't know, until several years ago, that Dad had ever been married before! It just wasn't spoken of in our family! And then someone—I don't know who—mentioned 'Lorraine'. I asked who Lorraine was, and that's when one of my brothers or sisters said, 'Didn't you know that Daddy was married before?' " Her eyes were wide. "I was kind of shocked."

Laura could not remember, when I pressed her to do so, the scenario surrounding this discovery. It had not occurred more than a few years earlier, and yet the circumstances in which she'd made the discovery were a blank space in her mind. Struggling to recover any bits of memory that still existed, she said, stumblingly, "My mother . . . I think . . . she told me actually. I think I found a little insurance form that said 'L.C.' instead of 'H.C.'—Lorraine Constantine, that is, instead of Harriet Constantine—and so maybe I asked her about it, and she told me then. But what I seem to recall with a lot more clarity is the next time it came up—because that was a really strange story."

A SYSTEMIC ISSUE?

Clearly excited, Laura inhaled and then expelled a breath. "We were in the dining room. . . . There was a date with me, someone I hardly knew. And somehow the subject of my dad's other marriage came up; I think one of my older sisters raised it. He got to talking about it—about how he'd gotten married just before the war and then had gone right off into the service. When he got back, Lorraine was fooling around a lot . . . that was the end of the marriage."

She stopped, picked up a strand of her hair, began twisting it round and round. "It's strange."

Looking at the genogram, I observed, "It's our first deception, in that generation," and then, to underscore the comment, wrote the word just above her father's name.

Laura's fears about being deceived were not only a problem in her present marriage, but "deception" had been a major element in two important *prior* relationships of hers—ones which had ended painfully—before she'd met Tom. I was suggesting that deception might be a resonating family issue, a theme that was evident not only in her own life but in the larger emotional system.

She seemed startled by the idea. "I didn't know about my father's first marriage until I was twenty-three," Laura said swiftly, as if in protest, "and all I really know about it *now* are the stories Dad told me! About how clever he was, and the ways he went about it, finding out that Lorraine was unfaithful!"

Leaning forward in her seat, she emitted a sudden laugh. "She was, supposedly, absolutely compulsive and ritualistic about everything's being done the same way, all the time. So one day, before Dad left for work, he put a little crease in the bedspread, at a certain point; nothing that anyone would notice. That day, she was going to work and not expected to be home until a certain hour; but when Dad came home, beforehand, the bed was made and the crease was gone." There was a hint of triumph in the daughter's voice.

"There was another part, too," added Laura, "about her wearing her fur jacket at a time when she ordinarily wouldn't have done it. He worked out some pattern having to do with times when she wore that fur and when there were extra miles on the car's odometer. . . . Something tallied there." She hesitated, frowning. "I can't remember . . . there was more . . . another whole part."

I asked her if she could remember how hearing those stories had made her feel on that evening when her father had told them.

Laura looked awestruck. "The reaction I remember most is being just amazed at how casually and even *jovially* he talked about the whole thing!" Her voice had dropped suddenly; she was speaking in an almost reverent hush.

She had made no connection, it seemed, between her father's "shadow relationship" with a woman (his first wife) and the woman whom Tom had been involved with before meeting her—that is, his ex-girlfriend, Karen.

Nor had Laura noticed that both men—her father and her husband—had characterized a former sexual involvement as unimportant and themselves as having cared little or not at all about it. In that peculiar conversation about his first marriage, her father had talked about the shadowy figure of Lorraine in such a way (Laura had used the words "casual" and "jovial") that it sounded as if she didn't matter. The question was: *Did she?* Was the partner of the present the one who was truly loved— or was it the woman who had vanished?

I looked, speculatively, at Tom.

3

Autonomy and Intimacy

What became clear, at many points throughout the interviews, was that the Bretts saw themselves as very different sorts of individuals—as polar opposites in many respects.

Toward the close of our first conversation, for example, I asked them the following question: "If someone you both know—a friend, say, or a family member—were describing your relationship to a third person, what kinds of things do you think he'd say?"

"Improbable," Tom answered immediately, with a smile.

"Improbable—for what reason?" I asked. "Oh"—he shrugged—"newspaper and church; cynic and believer. . . . I'm pretty logical and reserved, and Laura's exactly the opposite."

He hesitated, looked at Laura, who was shaking her head in agreement, a rueful yet amused expression etched upon her features. "You're the calm and passive one," she acknowledged, "and I'm always freaking out all over the place, for better or for worse." He nodded at her, said to me, "We're different in every way that you can think of. . . ."

They, like many couples who appear to be in marriages of opposites, were actually dealing with that most pervasive of marital problems: distinguishing which feelings, wishes, thoughts, etc., are within the self and which are within the intimate partner.

The dilemma has to do with the drawing of personal boundaries. The prime cause of distress in close, committed relationships is, in fact, a basic confusion about exactly what is going on inside one's own head and what is going on inside the head of the mate.

Many couples, like the Bretts, appear to be polar opposites—*thoroughly different* sorts of people. They are like puppets in a Punch and Judy show: Each plays a vastly dissimilar role on that part of the stage which is open to the objective observer's view, but below stage their strings are entangled. They are deeply enmeshed and emotionally fused, beneath the level of each mate's conscious awareness. For each of them embodies, carries and expresses *for the other* disavowed aspects of that other's self—his or her own inner being.

If one looked, for instance, at what was happening in the Bretts' relationship, a division of emotional labors seemed to be occurring. It was as if the pair of them had taken certain human wishes, attitudes, emotions, ways of relating and behaving—a whole range of feelings and responses that might be integrated parts of *one person's* repertoire—and parceled them out in an "I'll take this, and you take that" fashion.

They had, as couples often do, accomplished this in an unarticulated but nevertheless powerfully operative kind of unconscious agreement. Laura, in their relationship, took the optimism, while Tom took the pessimism; she was all belief, and he was the skeptic; she wanted emotional openness and he wanted to keep himself to himself; she was the pursuer and he the distancer—the individual on the run from intimacy. Together, in fact, they made up one fully integrated, adaptive organism, except that Laura had to do all the breathing in and Tom had to do all the breathing out.

If, however, Laura appeared, onstage, to want total closeness, honesty, integrity and oneness, out of sight she and Tom actually had an arrangement. Whenever she tried to move nearer to him, his autonomy string would be activated, and he was impelled—in an almost reflexive fashion— to make some distance immediately. She depended upon him to preserve the necessary space between them.

For Laura, like other people, needed some autonomy of her own— some personal territory in which she could be an individual in her own right, pursue her own separate wishes and goals. But for Laura, meeting her own independent needs was perceived as something wrong, danger- ous—something a good adult woman didn't do. Her rightful role, as a female, was to concentrate upon staying *close*, in the relationship; she could not acknowledge autonomous needs as anything that existed inside herself, anything that she actually wanted. She was aware only of the needs of the self (the separate, independent self) as they existed *in* and were expressed *by* her mate.

Similarly, Tom's natural desire for closeness to an intimate other was a need he saw *not* within himself but as something existing primarily *in Laura*. The need to be close to his partner, in the context of a trusting, mutually self-revelatory relationship, was seen as *her* need; Tom never experienced it as a wish or a need that originated from within his own being. He was, in his own view, self-sufficient; that is, sufficient unto himself.

But in the same way that Laura depended upon Tom to run when she chased, Tom depended on Laura to try to get closer so that he could feel necessary and wanted—intimate.

Rather than express directly any wish or need for intimacy (or even *be aware of,* and take responsibility for, such wishes and feelings), Tom had to dissociate them from consciousness. Such thoughts and wishes made him feel too exposed and too vulnerable! When he needed closeness, he had to experience that wish as coming from his wife; he had, without any conscious recognition of what he was doing, to make sure that her intimacy string was tugged. One way of doing this was, perhaps, looking soulful and abstracted, so that she would wonder if he was thinking about Karen. Then Laura would pursue him anxiously—for the intimate exchange that he himself desired.

Splitting the Conflict

What was going on, in this couple's relationship, is extremely common in marriages, in general. The conflict both partners were experiencing—a conflict between wanting to meet their own separate needs and wanting to meet the needs of the relationship—had been split evenly down the middle between them. Instead of being able to recognize that *both* of them wanted to be close, and *both* of them wanted to pursue their own independent goals—*that the autonomy/intimacy conflict was a conflict that existed inside each person's own head*—the Bretts had made an unconscious, collusive arrangement.

Laura would never have to take conscious ownership of her need for personal space, and Tom would never have to acknowledge to himself his own desire to be emotionally open, trusting, and close. She carried the intimacy needs (the needs of the relationship) for the pair of them, and he carried the autonomy needs (the needs of each person to pursue his or her separate goals) for them both. Laura, therefore, always seemed to want to get a little nearer and Tom always seemed to want to be more distant and unencumbered.

The upshot was that instead of an internal conflict—something which existed inside each person's subjective world—the dilemma had become a *transpersonal* conflict—one that could be fought out between them, over and over again.

This *shifting of an intrapsychic problem* (i.e., a problem within an individual's mind) *to an interpersonal conflict* (i.e., a difficulty that two people are having) occurs by means of a process mentioned earlier, the process called projective identification.

PROJECTIVE IDENTIFICATION

This term refers to a very pervasive, tricky and often destructive mental mechanism which involves one person's projecting denied and disavowed aspects of his or her inner experience onto the intimate partner and then perceiving those dissociated feelings as *existing in the partner*. Not only are the unwanted thoughts and feelings seen as being inside the mate, but the mate is encouraged—by means of cues and provocations—to behave as if they *were* there! The person can then identify vicariously with his or her partner's expression of the repudiated thoughts, feelings, and emotions.

One of the best and clearest examples of the way in which projective identification operates is seen in the totally nonaggressive and never angry individual, mentioned earlier. This person, who is uniquely devoid of anger, can become aware of angry feelings only as they exist in someone else—in the intimate partner, most predictably. When something disturbing *has* happened to the never angry individual, and he *is* experiencing angry emotions, he will be consciously out of contact with them. *He will not know that he is angry, but he will be wonderfully adept at triggering an explosion of hostility and anger in his spouse.*

The mate, who may not have been feeling angry at all before the interaction, may quickly find herself completely furious; her anger, which appears to be about some completely unrelated issue, is, in fact, anger that is being acted out for her spouse. She is thus, in some sense, "protecting" him from certain aspects of his inner being which he cannot consciously own and acknowledge.

The never angry person can then identify with the intimate partner's expression of the suppressed rage without ever having to take personal responsibility for it—even in terms of being conscious of the fact that he was the angry person in the first place! And, frequently, the feelings of anger which were so firmly repudiated within the self are just as sternly criticized in the mate. The never angry individual, in a projective identification situation, is often horrified by his spouse's hot-tempered, impulsive, uncontrolled expressions and behavior!

In a similar way, the never sad person may see his or her own depressed moods only as they exist in the partner (who can, in such a circumstance, be understood to be the person carrying the sadness and despair for them both).

Projections tend, generally speaking, to be *exchanges*—trades, so to speak, of denied parts of the self, which both members of the couple have agreed to make.

What has happened, Some Enchanted Evening in the early phase of courtship, is that a person like Tom has communicated (without a word's having been said) that Laura is to carry his own suppressed wishes for emotional openness, vulnerability, oneness—wishes he has utterly disowned, because at some point in his life, for defensive reasons, he found it necessary to do so.

And the other half of this bargain, made in the absence of anyone's awareness that a bargain *is* being made, is that a person like Laura will externalize all of her own unacceptable wishes—for emotional distance, perhaps, and even for badness and deception (in which she could identify with her father's first wife)—and experience them only as coming from her intimate partner.

This collusive exchange of internal territories is a bargain that is struck between two interested parties. In marriage, despite all overt evidence to the contrary, there really are no victims and villains; there is a deal that's been made. What is nearer to the truth, in conflictual relationships, is that an underground exchange of denied parts of the partners' selves has taken place. Then each one sees, in the partner, what cannot be perceived in the self—and struggles, ceaselessly, to change it.

THE DREAMER

The door to the apartment opened, almost upon the instant of my pressing the buzzer, on the occasion of my second visit to the Bretts. There stood Laura and Tom. The three of us remained where we were, for a moment, inarticulate: In one sense, we were intimates, and in another, I was a stranger. "Would you like some coffee?" Laura finally asked, breaking the silence. They ushered me into their studio apartment, which, on this late Saturday morning in early February, was bright with welcoming sunlight streaming in through the picture window.

Laura went into a small kitchen alcove while Tom led me to the seating area just off to the left of the large, framed square of cloudless blue sky. I took the old-fashioned rocking chair which I'd occupied last time and which faced the sofa. He, to my surprise, sat down in the other chair; Laura, when she joined us, would be sitting on the long expanse of their maroon sofa alone. I wondered, Did her husband, on the occasion of this second interview, require more space between his wife and himself? He seemed to be saying so, not verbally, but in the language of behavior.

Opening my large sketchbook, I turned to the page which held the Bretts' genogram and then placed the pad, face open, on the glass-topped coffee table between us. Tom and I silently surveyed it.

A favorite expression of Laura's mother's—"Marriage is the amount of work you put into it"—had been written on the paper, just off to the right of Harriet's name. Laura had heard her mother say this often during the years when Laura was growing up. Her mother had said, as well, that she thought her first marriage might well have worked out if only she and her first husband had put that extra bit of effort into it. Right now, according to Laura, her father put *no* work into his marriage at all. He was inaccessible, hot-tempered—out of contact with the family, unless he happened to be blowing up at somebody.

There were many other notes and scribbled comments on the Constantines' side of the page. We had talked, during our last meeting, about Laura's paternal grandparents (emigrants to this country from Greece) and about her maternal grandparents ("hillbillies," she'd said, from West Virginia). We'd talked, as well, about her relationships with her brothers and sisters and the role or "parts" in the ongoing family drama that she and each of her siblings had tended to play.

Family labels or roles—such as the "the good girl," "the trouble-maker," "the bright one," "the spoiled brat," etc.—are a common shorthand that is used to personify the individual members who make up a family group. What they denote, generally, is not so much the reality of the individual being dog-tagged or labeled in this fashion, but rather his or her place in the family's emotional system. That is, "the bright one" may not be significantly brighter than his siblings, but he has been elected to carry the family's intellectual flag forward; this is his role within the group.

Labels may not always be accurate, but they do have powerful effects upon the people who receive them: The "overly sexual" daughter or the "clumsy, inept" son may struggle for many years to free herself or himself from the yoke of the family's characterization. The child who is "the angel" or "mother's savior" may find his wings getting heavier and heavier, and his task of saving a woman more and more impossible, as he plays this part in the later, adult parts of his life.

Laura Brett's family role designation had been, she thought, that of "the dreamer." "They see me as being a fruitcake—an idealist, an intellectual, and all other nonpractical things. But I think that when the chips are down, I'm just as capable as the rest of them." Her own view of herself was as a "combination": at once the inheritor of a strong tradition of sensible, self-reliant women (women like her mother and her two grand-mothers) and someone who was yet, in some important respects, extraor-dinarily needy and emotionally fragile.

Where, I wondered, had this needy woman inside her, so concerned about deception and possible abandonment, come from?

Laura did, during the course of our interviews, veer between these two visions of the self: one of them sturdy and reliable, the other in need of constant support and reassurance. She was, at one and the same time, an admirable, competent person and a wary individual who lived in the expectation of some dangerous knowledge's being brought to light—some-thing to do, somehow, with becoming the victim of a sexual deception about which she was dangerously ignorant.

Tom's side of the page was still, at this juncture, almost completely blank. We'd gotten no further, in the course of the previous interview, than his mother's name (Diana). Where, I now speculated, did he himself fit into this picture, and what, in his own family of origin, made Laura's overriding concern—that a prior relationship of one of the partners would affect an emotionally bonded couple—something natural and familiar *to him*.

Tom cleared his throat, and I became aware—as aware as if he'd suddenly shouted—that he was in a state of intense nervousness.

THE OBSERVER

We commenced work on Tom's side of the genogram. His family, I learned, derived from stock that was half English and half a mixture of Scots, Dutch and German. The oldest sibling in Tom's family was now in his late thirties, and then there were three others (another male and then two females) spaced closely together. Tom himself, six years younger, appeared on the genogram as a sort of family afterthought.

In terms of birth order, he and Laura were, I noted, in positions that were familiar to both of them. He was the much younger brother of a sister who was the youngest in her own group of siblings; that sister was, therefore, both the smallest child and her brother's superior, by far, in terms of wisdom and of years. Laura, in her own family, had been in a complementary place.

The German psychologist Walter Toman, in his book about birth order effects (*Family Constellation*), suggests that the older sister of a younger brother usually takes on the role of the nurturer. "She has to take care of the little one," writes Toman, "has to guard and protect him and will be held responsible for him by the parents, but she also gets a little in return: He looks up to her. He appreciates and loves her and before long learns to do her courtesies and favors, too. . . ." The young maternal caretaker develops, in other words, an adoring follower in the line of duty of helping care for her little baby brother.

The role adopted by the younger brother of an older sister is, observes Toman, an altogether different one: "He is usually allowed to pursue his own wishes and interests in a rather carefree and sometimes selfish or incoherent manner. He is treated more tolerantly and more generously than his big sister, and frequently more so than, say, the younger brother of a brother. The younger brother of a sister increasingly learns to understand his sister better, but he does so ultimately for his own purposes. He tends to take her help and motherly care as a matter of course. If he cannot get what he wants, he finds ways to lure his sister or other girls into acting as a mother on his behalf." The younger brother of an older sister is, thus, likely to become somewhat manipulative in regard to the women in his life.

It is birth order and sibling position which, in Toman's view, affect not only the development of personality—in the most straightforward and specific ways—but the possibility that any two individuals can be happy in a committed, long-term relationship. Two eldest children, for example, are considered a risky marital proposition: Both are accustomed to taking leadership, and they are likely to get into a struggle over who is, like the pope, the "first among equals"—the person with the ultimate power. Two "only" children, according to Professor Toman, are liable to face similar sorts of difficulties.

While I myself, as a reader of the literature on birth order effects, have always remained quizzical, I did note that Laura's and Tom's orientations toward each other often did have a big sister (or big mommy)/ naughty boy flavor about it. And the first thing that Tom said, when I asked him to tell me a bit about his early life in his family, was, "The most important fact that there was a gap of six years between myself and the next oldest—my sister. My mother had a miscarriage in between."

He paused, then added, "That is, I think, what got me interested in journalism and photography; I was always observing all of these other people." I wasn't sure that I saw a connection between that six-year age gap and Tom's sense of being an observer—someone who (like Laura's father) seemed to stand outside the family somehow.

"Watching the world go by, you mean" I attempted to clarify, "instead of being *in* the world—is that what you mean?"

"To a certain extent," he answered guardedly, "I may have."

"Why do you think you adopted that particular strategy?"

He'd been alone a lot, he replied. They hadn't had a television set, at that time, and he'd spent his time out in the backyard, kicking field goals. "By yourself?" I asked, and he nodded and answered yes in a forlorn tone of voice.

Hadn't there been other children his own age in his neighborhood? I inquired. Tom shrugged. "There were kids in the neighborhood, sure, but even at an early age—" He paused, then said, "I played with them, but I was different."

I recalled his concern about being represented on the genogram by a square. "In what way were you different?" I asked. He responded by launching into a tale about how, when he was a small boy, some of the older children in the neighborhood had surrounded him one afternoon and had tied his hands behind him. Then they'd strung him from a tree branch in such a way that he'd hung there, dangling by his heels. Laura gasped.

I turned to her and asked, "Is this story news to you?" and she exclaimed in an amazed voice, "Yes!" Had this tale been excluded from their intimate exchange because it concerned Tom's vulnerability—and, in *their* relationship, Laura was the one who could be vulnerable? Her husband, cutting in, said emotionlessly, "It was kind of fun, in a way."

Fun? Both Laura and I gazed at him, astonished, and I said, in a joking tone, that it sounded like a whale of a good time to me! He, his voice still affectless, conceded that it had been a humiliating incident. "But it wasn't without enjoyment; the physical sense of it, you know— swinging from a tree. How many people get the chance to swing by their feet from a rope?"

He was, I realized, perfectly serious; he was having trouble processing his emotional responses to what must have been an extremely painful incident. I responded ironically, "Gosh, what a golden opportunity!" and he smiled, nodded, admitted that in the wake of that occurrence he'd been a marked person in the neighborhood. "The kids would laugh and say, 'Hey, that's the guy we strung up from a tree!' "

"So the hard part of this was being humiliated?"

"Yes," acknowledged Tom, "it was."

His mother, a schoolteacher, had come home at about four-thirty every afternoon. "You were, then," I asked, "a kid who was alone, after school—kicking field goals by yourself in the backyard?"

Not always, he answered, but much of the time. "Other times, I was with friends from the neighborhood. . . ." And when he hadn't played with the other kids, I continued, what had been the reason? Tom said, "Because I was, supposedly, better than they. They might be stronger, but we were smarter; our family was better off, more intelligent. . . . That was my mother's thinking, anyway, and the rest of us tended to go along with that point of view."

Tom's mother, Diana, had been forty-two years old when he was born; his father, Martin, had been the same age. Diana was now seventy, and Martin was dead; he'd died very suddenly, of a heart attack, the year that his youngest son turned fourteen.

Laura's men, I noted with a quick glance at the family map I was constructing, had been bereft of their fathers early in the course of their lives; her paternal grandfather had died when her father was in his infancy.

There were other similarities in these partners' backgrounds: Both of them, for instance, had had relatively "old" fathers (who were in their early forties when these later children in their families were born); Tom's mother, of course, had been "old" to be a new mother, too. And both Tom and Laura had come from families which were fairly large—in both cases, there were five siblings in the nuclear group and, as it developed, a resident grandmother, too. Tom's paternal grandmother and Laura's maternal grandmother had lived in their homes as they were growing up.

The Bretts' genogram, at this point, looked like page 69.

Such odd correspondences between the His and the Hers sides of a couple's genogram were, in my experience, anything but rare. Whenever I encountered them—which was frequently—I had to pause and speculate, wonder about it. . . . For instance, did a couple *know*, at some meta-level, at the time when they were falling in love, that both had suffered asthma in childhood? Or were they *aware* that there was a maternal parent suffering from depression—which emerged as hypochondria in one mother and frank depressive symptoms in the other—in both of the partners' families of origin?

So often such similar issues—alcoholism, or the early loss of a parent, or even time spent in an orphanage early in life—pop out on both sides of a family tree! We humans must, I think, have powerful ways of knowing about each other and it is this knowledge which draws us, in an inexorable and almost hypnotic way, to the person who is to become the mate. It is the recognition, somehow, of what is familiar—the words "familiar" and "family" derive, after all, from an identical root.

What interested me, at this moment, was the way in which Laura's father (out of contact with the family unless he was angry at someone)

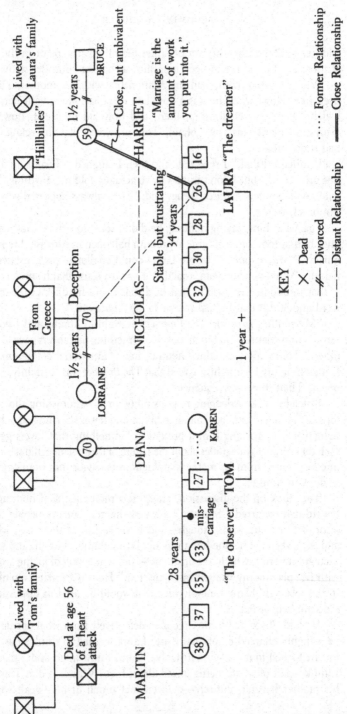

English/Scots/Dutch/German

Lived with Tom's family

Died at age 56 of a heart attack

MARTIN

28 years

"The observer" TOM

mis-carriage

DIANA

KAREN

1 year +

LAURA "The dreamer"

From Greece

Deception

LORRAINE

1½ years

NICHOLAS

Stable but frustrating 34 years

Lived with Laura's family

"Hillbillies"

1½ years

BRUCE

Close, but ambivalent

HARRIET

"Marriage is the amount of work you put into it."

KEY

✕ Dead

⚊⧸⧸⚊ Former Relationship

⚊⚊⚊ Close Relationship

······ Distant Relationship

and her husband (the observer-of rather than the participator-in the lives of those around him) had been identified as having "outsider status".

What, I asked Tom, had his relationship with his mother, Diana, been like? How, when he was a boy, had he gotten along with her; how had he seen that relationship, then, and how did he see it, now? His expression blank, his voice bland, Tom answered that the relationship had been "filial."

I smiled. "Filial," I repeated, and then I laughed. "That is an affect-free answer . . . but I don't think you've actually told me anything." He, with an elaborately carefree shrug, said, "She's always appeared very matrimonial, to me."

I gazed at him, saying nothing; he didn't seem to realize what he had said. Laura, too, stared at him, her mouth half open in surprise. I repeated quickly, "*Matrimonial?*" before Laura could challenge his misstatement herself. "What do you mean, exactly?" I had the sense that he understood, at that moment, the mistake that he'd made, but he did not retract the word and admit that he had meant to say "*maternal.*"

"My mother gave me *The Prophet*, by Kahlil Gibran, and I got the sense—from Laura—that that book was something that lovers gave to each other." Tom's voice remained neutral, free of emotional coloration, and I, matching my tone to his, agreed that *The Prophet* was, certainly, a love poem. Then there was a silence.

Instead of acknowledging responsibility for his astonishing slip of the tongue, Tom had handed it along to his parent: It was *she* who had behaved seductively, in making him a present of "something that lovers gave to each other." Any ambiguities about the nature of their relationship stemmed, in other words, from *his mother's* ambiguous behavior, not from anything to do with himself.

Tom took up the discussion, after a few moments, as if nothing untoward had occurred. "She and I are very different sorts of people. She's a lot of fun to be with, though—and to make fun of the world with—and she's very smart. She has a way of playing dumb, though, and saying men are superior, which sets up *our* act—our whole way of joking around, with her playing my straight man, my foil." He was speaking rapidly yet in the relatively bland tone of voice that would be used in discussion of a distant acquaintance.

He had, it seemed to me, recoiled defensively from what appeared to be a highly charged emotional issue. Laura seemed to think so as well, for she turned to me, saying irritably, "Can I throw in an aside, that is—I think—part of what's being talked about here? Which is that Tom and his mother haven't, entirely—or even that much *at all*—dealt with or accepted the fact that they aren't going to complete each other's worlds. This is, I believe, why his mother keeps a toothbrush for him in her new apartment. The children are all gone—*all of them*—but she keeps a new toothbrush there, only for Tom! Even though he's never lived there at all!"

Tom protested, immediately, that he had once lived with his mother in her new apartment for a three-month period, but admitted that a new toothbrush had been purchased for him subsequently. His work travels were, he added, supposed to bring him to Boston—where she lived—one night a week over the course of the next few months.

"I'd planned, initially," Tom's voice was reasonable, "to spend that night with her, at her place, which is convenient insofar as—"

"That"—Laura interrupted—"made me *furious*. And I just said no, he couldn't! I didn't even say it—I shouted! 'No, you won't; that's not a viable option, your going home and living with Mom!' " Her color had risen and her cheeks were suddenly a dark shade of rose.

Turning to her husband, she said, "You and I started talking a lot, at that point, about the toothbrush—and my feeling that you and your mom haven't really given each other up; you haven't figured it out that you're still not going to come home one day and be hers!" I was startled. In the Laura-Tom-Karen triangle the configuration had been that of the couple and a former partner of the husband's; here was a replication of precisely that configuration, which had similar players, except that Tom's "prior attachment" was the very first love attachment of his life.

4

Love Itself

What is love?

What makes a certain person feel "special," "right," desirable, lovable to someone else? On what basis are our emotional choices actually made—those loving attachments which, once formed, will serve to organize and dictate so many aspects of our lives?

The answers to such questions are, in some respects, so elusive that it seems naive even to attempt asking them! And yet what *can* be said is that each one of us carries within himself or herself a set of deeply held beliefs—a pattern for being in an intimate relationship which is a template of sorts, a set of assumptions about what loving and being loved is really like. This internalized game plan for being in a close relationship (which certainly includes an incompletely articulated, inchoate and yet powerful model of who the close partner shall be) is part and parcel of what British psychologist C. Murray Parkes has termed the individual's "assumptive world."

The assumptive world, writes Dr. Parkes, "is the only world we know [which] includes everything we know or think we know. It includes our interpretations of the past and our expectations of the future, our plans and our prejudices." We predicate our anticipations of what will happen on what *has* happened and not only on what has actually occurred, but on the ways in which we have interpreted and dealt with the material of those experiences.

When it comes to the forming of adult love relationships we work, to some large degree, with assumptions that have been made very early in our own individual histories. For every act of love in mature life, there is a prologue that originated in infancy: In that time, lost to the mature person's conscious awareness, when life's first passionate attachment was slowly forming and emerging into being.

Awakening into Love

Imagine an infant, some two months old, cradled in his mother's arms, nursing. As he feeds, his hand rests upon her bare skin; then, replete, he moves away from the nipple, leans back to gaze upward at her breast.

When will he be able to discern that the small hand which lingers there is his and that the breast is a part of her—to distinguish the "I" that is his own self from all else (which belongs to the world of the "not me")? Adrift in the oceanic, timeless, boundless world of infancy, his being and that of his caretaking human partner are merged.

Before the young baby develops sufficiently to gain a sense of a world that is within him—a personal, psychic reality which his own being encompasses and contains—self and mother, inner and outer space, are commingled and fused. The hunger pain which arises from inside, and the satisfaction of that pain which is initiated from outside, are as one: Life is a haphazard series of intensely experienced feeling states, corresponding to internal and external happenings. The infant has not yet integrated them into a pattern of understanding, and so the source of the need (i.e., intense hunger, arising from within) and the source of relief, (i.e., milk, given from without) are undifferentiated.

It is from this primitive psychological state—of total emotional symbiosis with a responsive, intuitively comprehending, need-satisfying other—that we slowly awaken to the human world. And it is in the context of this awakening that we begin to form assumptions about what the experience of intimate loving is like. For even as we come to know and recognize those who care for us—particularly mother—we develop feelings of attachment that are so intense that it would not be at all exaggerated to term them "the first grand passion of human life."

Mother, most of all, is experienced by her baby as a being who is totally necessary and irreplaceable. Her offspring moves, during the first year of existence, from mere recognition of her as someone special to the discovery that (in the words of child development expert Selma Fraiberg) "she is the source of joy, the satisfier of body hungers, the comforter, the protector, the indispensable person of his world."

Her presence becomes, in itself, the source of her child's feelings of security, satisfaction, contentment. "All love," writes psychologist Fraiberg, "even in later life, begins with a feeling of exclusiveness. 'You are

73

the one who matters—only you.' It's the magic circle of love that in infancy includes the father and a few choice people but not yet the stranger."

FEELINGS OF SECURITY AND SAFETY

Most powerful, early in existence, are the baby's feelings about the primary caretaker herself—the ministering mother. From the very dawn of consciousness, feelings of safety seem to be linked to having her, the "special other person," nearby and readily available. She becomes, for her child, what scientists have come to call an "attachment figure"—i.e., a loving partner with whom the infant can form an intense emotional bond.

If, because of some adverse circumstance, no such attachment figure is available, the developing human will show widespread mental and physical deficits by the end of the first year of his or her life. It is not, in other words, a matter of simply being fed or of being adequately cared for. Infants need to establish an emotional relationship with a loving, protective caretaker, and this *psychologically experienced* need develops, in all its intensity, very early in each individual's existence. (This is true not only in the human instance, but among closely related primate groups; for example, our nearest relatives, the chimpanzees, form strong and enduring mother-infant attachments.)

A study of foundling home infants, a classic in the psychological literature, demonstrated this reality strikingly, if in a somewhat grim fashion. Dr. René Spitz, in research carried out in the mid-1940s, demonstrated that babies who were being cared for in a hygienically isolated environment—with one nurse assigned to every eight infants—showed signs of profound psychological and physical retardation by the end of the first year of life. They cried frequently, never smiled, and had no beginnings of speech.

They were also apathetic, unresponsive and caught infections easily; the mortality rate among those neonates (all of whom had been separated from their prison-inmate mothers at birth or very shortly thereafter) was, in fact, astonishingly high. What Dr. Spitz's work showed, with awesome clarity, was that the availability of a loving partner is a precondition of the immature offspring's normal development and sometimes of his or her very survival.

Prewired for Loving

The inborn need to form a powerful love attachment to the caretaker is probably—as a good deal of scientific evidence, gathered over the course of the past few decades, strongly suggests—programmed into the human species. We humans are, it appears, preadapted for developing strong emotional ties to our parents, as they are psychobiologically prepared ("prewired," so to speak) for loving, protecting and caring for us. The love that grows up between babies and their caretakers does not, in other words, spring into being as a result of happenstance or happy good fortune. On the contrary, seen from the point of view of evolutionary biology, the almost universal tendency to form potent emotional attachments makes the best of adaptive good sense. These bonds promote the offspring's *survival*—an odd way, admittedly, to think about loving!

For the human neonate is utterly and completely dependent upon the parent's protection and care. Baby humans are, in fact, the most helpless newborns in nature. And strongly felt emotional attachments—experienced as *the need to be near to the loved other*—motivate both the nurturer and the needful offspring to maintain close proximity. This promotes the occurrence of a mutually beneficial situation, for the baby cannot possibly survive without a goodly input of protective caring, instruction, often self-sacrifice, on the part of the parents. And it is their own huge attachment and emotional investment in their child that make this effort seem worthwhile to the caretakers.

Thus it is that the bond that develops between nurturers and offspring has important effects in terms of everyone's behavior: It motivates the teachers about life and the apprentice in living to stay close by and to view each other's nearness and well-being as emotionally essential. This keeps the developing individual in a state of relative safety over a long period of time—an adaptive advantage, for the complex lessons which must be learned, prior to his or her becoming capable of independent survival, are immensely difficult, subtle and protracted.

The Human Truth

The baby's psychologically felt need for the caretaker's presence—a predictable development of the early months of life—brings with it, inevitably, feelings of anxiety and fear. For the growing infant, emerging from a state of pure subjectivity, now begins to comprehend his differentness and separateness from the mothering person. The dawning recognition that there is a "me" (which is himself) and an "everything outside me" (which includes not only the food and comforting care his mother brings him but the mother herself) is accompanied by an uncomfortable and novel awareness: Mother, as a separate individual, can go away; one may be totally abandoned.

The developing baby, beginning to differentiate his own self from the symbiotic union with the caretaker, has discovered his ultimate aloneness—and responds with protest and fear. He will now, with all of the primitive equipment that he has at hand, show every sign of his awful dependence and his caring. He will do everything within his small powers to keep his mother close by.

Young babies, as they hatch out of the infant-mother symbiosis, exhibit a predictable range of responses which are called "attachment behaviors." Between the ages of one and three they will, very predictably, object and weep and cling when mother goes away; they will attempt to follow after her, if at all possible. If she *does* leave her infant behind, when she returns, he will greet her ecstatically (in short, his behavior is punishing departures and rewarding returns).

The little child will, if he is playing nearby his mother and wanders away, rush back to her at the least suggestion that there is something to fear. It is in her embrace that security and comfort are to be found; she *is* safety, to her child. This baby behavior is, by the way, indistinguishable from that of our primate cousins in the wild: Monkey and ape juveniles become emotionally attached to their mothers and also experience security as a state that is linked to "having mother nearby."

The primate truth, which is the human truth, is that young babies fall desperately in love. Although there are, obviously, other important people in the little human's world, a great deal of his attachment behavior will be, early in life, focused on the primary caretaker. Studies have shown that babies' smiles (and the smile is the universal greeting sign of our species) are directed at their mothers more frequently than at anyone else and that those smiles—from infant to mother—are wider and more joyous than the smiles directed at any other person.

EARLY SORROWS

Not only do babies fall in love; they also show terrible signs of distress in situations in which the beloved parent has become unavailable. They pass, indeed, through a mourning sequence—an intense grief that has been compared (by British analyst Dr. John Bowlby, in his book *Attachment*) to that of an adult whose mate has been lost to separation, divorce, or to death. The young child's responses to maternal separation, as delineated by Dr. Bowlby, move from "Protest" to "Despair" to "Detachment."

In the initial stage of separation—protest—the baby will do just that: cry, scream, make frantic efforts to get away and to attempt to rejoin the mother. At the same time, there is an excited expectation; he expects her to come back at any moment. He will refuse to be comforted—angrily—for only mother, her own self, will do. This reaction will, according to Bowlby, last anywhere from a few hours to more than a week.

It will be succeeded by despair. Now the little child becomes quieter; he may sniffle, even weep from time to time, but he looks and acts increasingly hopeless. His dejected appearance resembles that of an adult who has been overwhelmed by an almost unimaginable emotional disaster. Finally, the third phase of the separation reaction—detachment—arrives.

At this point, the baby becomes more sociable. If he is in a hospital or residential nursery, he will interact more with the nurses and attendants. Should his mother come for a visit, however, the normal attachment behavior of this phase of life will be completely absent; the little child will merely turn away from his once passionately loved parent, listlessly. He will act as if she'd never mattered to him at all.

If, however, the separation hasn't lasted overly long, his air of detachment will not become a fixed part of the developing youngster's personality. After a while, it will reverse itself and eventually give way to a period of whining and distraught and frantic clinging (which the mother may not find altogether easy to tolerate!). Although he may have been well and affectionately cared for, during her absence, he is telling her—by means of his frenzied clutching—that feelings of security are linked to her desperately loved and needed presence.

THE BELOVED, ORIENTING FIGURE

"Anxiety over separation seems to be a built-in, instinctual mechanism," writes psychiatrist Michael Liebowitz, M.D., in *The Chemistry of Love*. It serves the function, he observes, of keeping helpless youngsters from wandering away from their caretakers. "The more highly developed the species, the later in life separation anxiety seems to appear. Baby rhesus monkeys are said to protest their mother's absence beginning about two weeks after birth, while this is not seen in chimpanzees until three months of age."

It is not clear exactly when separation anxiety appears in human infants, notes research psychiatrist Liebowitz:

> [S]ome studies have recorded crying when mother leaves and attempts to follow her in infants as young as four to six months of age; certainly by nine months many babies will show distress when mothers leave and signs of pleasure, such as a smile, lifting of their arms, or delighted gurgles, when they return. Distress about being left by a particular figure, distinct signs of feeling comforted when that person returns, and resistance to the efforts of others to be comforting are all indications that a youngster has formed specific attachment to one person. Actually, they are pretty good markers for attachment in adults, as well.

Feelings of attachment give rise to a sense that where the beloved other is, there is emotional security—a sense of belonging, of being at home. The mother becomes, for her young baby, an orienting figure; she is her child's home base in the world. She is the first intimate partner—to be replaced one day, as Michael Liebowitz suggests, by the orienting figure who is the lover or mate. But it is in this first love relationship of existence that the immature human will have developed a crude template, or pattern, for being in a loving partnership.

For the very young child (somewhere between six and fifteen months) the movement from believing that the parent is a part of himself to realizing that she is a separate and different being represents a developmental achievement. The cost of this self-awareness has, however, been extremely high: The vision of perfect oneness, of engulfment in a caring, intuitively knowing other, is the paradisiacal dream that has been lost. What will remain, somewhere deep within, will be a dimly perceived yearning for that time of total union, that Garden of Eden almost beyond remembering, when human separation and aloneness simply did not exist.

The Golden Fantasy

It is this Edenic vision that, I believe, is reevoked in the experience of falling in love. Falling in love has to do with the recognition of a haunting melody, a series of notes that one once knew, reincarnated in the being of another. "What is the image the lover sees?" asks psychiatrist Theodore Lidz, M.D., in his book *The Person*. "Some trait produces a resonance of the primary parental love model. It may be quite apparent or because of incestuous fears be hidden under markedly different characteristics such as a different physical appearance or divergence of race or religion."

The person in love is not only "resonating" to something that is reminiscent of the original beloved one, but is experiencing something of that relationship again. What has been called "The Golden Fantasy"—the infant's wish to be merged, in a state of well-being and closeness, to the caregiving other—has been reawakened. And thus, as Dr. Lidz notes, the lover, gazing at the intimate partner, "sees an admiring person, noting in the eyes of the other the devoted attraction which may well relate to the infant's fixation on the eyes of the loving and admiring mother."

What is "right", when it comes to the choosing of a mate, is to some degree what has been and what is familiar; it is what "works" on that inner template, or pattern of assumptions about what an intimate partnership is like. "[T]he reasons for the suddenness and intensity of falling in love," write Lily Pincus and Christopher Dare (in *Secrets in the Family*) "are usually unconscious. The choice of a marriage partner often seems to have been made very quickly, on the basis of relatively little conscious knowledge, and with, as it turns out, great accuracy of complementarity and fit of personalities and even life experiences of the partners. Couples quite often turn out to have striking similarities in terms of childhood experiences, which they only discover after they have married or made a decision to marry." (This is an explanation, perhaps, for the curious similarities on the His and Hers sides of so many partners' genograms!)

What we seek—or at least what we tend to find—in a mate is that someone who helps us contact archaic, dimly perceived and yet powerfully meaningful aspects of our inner selves. The marriage partner is that person who, for obscure reasons, connects us to parts of our beings which are completely suppressed, lost to memory—and yet well remembered, at an almost cellular level.

Falling in love has to do with summoning up inchoate, rapturous feelings of engulfment in a safe and intimate world—one in which two are as one, perfect company, and in which perfect nurturance exists. It has to do with the visions of Eden, buried within, before human aloneness had been perceived. . . . And it has to do, as well, with the expulsion from that dreamlike state of being. For reawakened visions and fantasies bring in their train, inevitably, memories of disappointment and old alarums: fears of separation, and fears of loss, and the worst of human threats, which is the nightmare threat of abandonment.

Marriage is, as psychiatrist H. V. Dicks has observed, the "nearest adult equivalent to the original child-parent relationship." It is in marriage that we resurrect not only the intensity of our first attachment feelings, but the miseries of old frustrations and repressed hatreds as well. And what is so frequently sought in a mate—and then *fought out with that mate*—is some unresolved dilemma about a parent.

By re-creating in the new adult relationship the conflictual issues that existed in the original family, some people manage to leave home without ever really going away.

"I Wasn't There"

Constructing a family genogram is a very simple, straightforward process. The questions are so obvious, so nonthreatening, so seemingly innocuous; all that is involved is a systematic gathering of the historical, factual data concerning each mate's important relationships in his or her original family. Answering these questions ought to be, for everyone concerned, no more complicated than filling in the answers on a tax form. And yet, by simply asking a spouse to give a parent's name and then to talk for a while about that parent, one can often open up a Pandora's box of memories, fantasies, dreams, angers, reflections, anguish; information emerges, at times, which has never been shared with anyone before, including the intimate partner. The process by which this happens is something that has never become quite clear to me; it remains, at some level, mysterious. So much that is pertinent and passionate is, I suppose, encoiled in recollections of early relationships and the ways in which they were perceived.

I asked Tom Brett what his father, Martin, had been like. Had he been an "observing" or a "participating" sort of man, and had they been close to one another before Martin had died, while Tom was still in his early teens? The young husband answered, his voice objectively reportorial, that his father had been "a funny guy sort of a guy." They had not been close to one another—"at least," he amended, in a "touchy, feely sort of a way. But I suppose we *were* close insofar as the American male bit can permit it." Tom sounded, nevertheless, somewhat doubtful.

"And how was your folks' own marriage, would you say?"

"*He* never talked about it; *she* now says the marriage was great." He shrugged, as if to say that everyone was entitled to his or her opinion—including me.

"But you were there, yourself, in the house," I remarked, "and so what was your own impression?"

He had, he replied, never ever seen them have a quarrel. It had, moreover, never occurred to him that there were other kinds of marriages than his parents' marriage, relationships that could be different. "My oldest brother, though, has made the observation that if their marriage was so great, it seems odd that every night—at least in their later years—they polished off a half gallon of wine before dinner."

"And that's what they did?" I asked.

He nodded his assent. "That's what they were doing when I was out in back of the house, kicking those field goals."

It did, I thought, argue against his parents' marriage having been as "great" as his mother had said, for why, then, had they had to anesthetize themselves every evening? "Do you think your parents were feeling some tension, to be drinking like that? A jug of wine is a lot of drinking on a nightly basis."

Tom nodded, frowning. "My older brother talked to somebody about my mother's drinking—to a psychologist—and he thought she sounded like a borderline alcoholic."

"Would you say that she seemed depressed?"

He nodded again. "Yes . . . yes. She was very depressed—maybe not in a clinical sense, but I think she might have been that, too. But anyhow, in a layman's sense . . . After she drank, she'd often start weeping and weeping. It was a—a lamentation directed at the fact that my grandmother—my father's mother—lived with us in the house. And my mother resented that bitterly."

"And where was your grandmother when this was happening?" Had the older woman heard her daughter-in-law's complaining? I wondered.

"She was upstairs and, I think, out of earshot." Tom answered my unspoken question.

I was staring down at the sketch of the Bretts' families. On each side there had been a triangle stretching over into the prior generation. Underneath Tom's family of origin, I sketched that triangle labeled the vertices: "Mother," "Father," "Paternal Grandmother." The triangle below Laura's family was labeled: "Mother," "Father," "Maternal Grandmother." The genogram now looked like page 82.

Laura's mother's mother had lived with their family until her death (when Laura herself was eight). This "hillbilly" grandmother had moved, with her husband, from the Appalachians to Chicago just before her own daughter (Laura's mother) was born; in the course of that move, she had intentionally destroyed all the family records and photographs. "My grandma just took them out and burned them and said we were never going to be hillbillies again!" Laura had told me when we were working on her side

English/Scots/Dutch/German

Lived with Tom's family

Died at age 56 of a heart attack

MARTIN

Never quarreled openly 28 years

"The observer" TOM

miscarriage

DIANA

KAREN

1 year +

Paternal Grandmother

Father   Mother

Lived with Laura's family

"Hillbillies"

BRUCE

Close, but ambivalent

1½ years

59

HARRIET

"Marriage is the amount of work you put into it."

Stable but frustrating 34 years

LAURA "The dreamer"

16

26

28

30

32

From Greece

Deception

NICHOLAS

70

1½ years

LORRAINE

Maternal Grandmother

Father   Mother

KEY

✕ Dead
⫽ Divorced
═══ Very Close or Fused Relationship
━━━ Close Relationship
⌇⌇ Poor or Conflictual Relationship
- - - Distant Relationship
······ Former Relationship

of the genogram. "And we didn't need to have pictures of all those poor people! Her children, she said, didn't have to be burdened with that!"

"Good-bye to the past," I said. And Laura, her face mottled with sudden patches of emotion, had nodded. She had felt close to her grandmother, as Tom—I now learned—had been close to his. "She used to read to me an awful lot," Tom said, wistfully, "especially one time when I'd broken my leg. . . ." His grandmother had, he said, moved out of the family home precipitously on the day of his father's death.

Nobody in Tom's family of origin had (according to Tom) been engaged in any real quarreling. But his mother and father had drunk a certain amount of wine, every evening, while he'd been out in the backyard kicking field goals.

"When you saw your mother weeping about your grandmother's presence in the household, I suppose you yourself felt . . . conflicted? Because it sounds as if you were close to your grandma, and yet her presence was making your mother unhappy."

"But I didn't recognize the conflict as such" was Tom's stolid reply. His father, clearly, had done nothing that might further the two women's working their disagreements out. "His favorite expression concerning all that was happening was 'Hmmmmph.' He would say 'Hmmmph,' and he would slam his hand on the table and click the cover of his glasses' case . . . to pass the time, I suppose. But he would never make a committal answer." Tom shrugged.

Had his father been close to his own mother? I wanted to know.

"He called her Mother, and he'd bring her glass of wine upstairs to her—so I guess they all *did* know what was going on. . . . In fact, I remember that she used to say, 'Well, I'll go up now and stay by myself, as I always *do*.'" He leaned forward, as if energized by having made contact with this memory.

"So the two of them got drunk downstairs," burst out Laura, indignantly, "and your grandmother had to have her glass of wine all alone?" When Tom nodded, her only response was "Phew!"

I asked him, then, what it had been like for *him* when his mother had wept, his father had clicked his glasses' case open and shut, and his grandmother had sat by herself, upstairs.

"I stayed out of it," he answered abruptly. "I wasn't there. I don't know much about it, because my recollections are only snatches. Things I overheard, going by in the hallway—either coming in from the backyard or on my way out." He spoke rapidly, as if trying to outrace me to my next question, or indeed to race past it completely.

It sounded as if he'd been making sure he really wasn't there, wasn't part of the family scene, and so, I mused, an "outsider" had been created. Looking down at the Bretts' genogram, I reflected that the grandmother triangles, on both sides of the page, bore a similarity to the triangle that had caused Laura and Tom so much consternation in the first place. Once again, the configuration consisted of a prior attachment of one of the partners—about whom some anxiety and high feeling were being generated—and a couple who were either distancing or quarreling, or both.

"Where the Future Is More Exciting Than Terrifying"

Noticing, at one point, that Tom was staring worriedly at his own side of the family road map, I paused to ask him a question. What would he like to see happen, in the household that he and Laura were creating, that he had *not* seen happen in the household in which he had grown up?

He replied, without hesitating, "Explicit treatment of conflict would be high up on the list, and along with that, explicit acknowledgment of love."

Tom wanted what he, as a person, did not have: easy access to his own emotions and easiness in communicating about them. His own states of feeling were, in general, more recognizable to him when he perceived them in Laura.

Laura, sitting up on the sofa, straight and alert, observed that in her family, people had been able to get angry, but they had been "shy" about expressing love. "When I think in terms of what I want from a household," she declared, "a sense of *engagement* from Tom is really important to me! I'm terrified at the thought that somebody could be like my father and just pretend that I wasn't there—except, maybe, to bitch. I mean, my dad just won't participate! And that's the one thing that frightens me out of my wits! The idea that somebody would just turn around and say, 'I'm not here' or 'I'm not responsible' or 'That's not my problem; I'm out of it'!"

There was fear in her voice, and, looking up, I saw that fear on her face. These statements—"I'm not here," "That's not my problem," "I'm out of it," etc.—were, most clearly, the very sorts of things that Tom had had to tell himself in order to distance himself emotionally from the situation that had prevailed in his own family of origin.

"Knowing how much this scares you," he now said to his wife soberly, "I get afraid—scared of somehow slipping into it."

But Laura, unheeding, continued.

She had raised her eyes and fastened them upon a corner of the room, as if that bit of ceiling contained "the future." "I want us to have a house, or a home—I mean, *both*—where people don't have to burn up pictures of the past! I don't want to have that happen, and it *has*—there's so much sense of not knowing, in my family! Of not feeling easy about who we are, or where we're going, or knowing what there is to be ashamed of!" Two bright spots of color flamed in Laura's cheeks. "That whole sense of anxiety that was in my house; I don't want that in *our lives* together." Laura's gesture, a wave of the arm, included herself and Tom.

"I'm at a place," she added, fervently, "where the future is more exciting than terrifying. And the past is more appreciated than it is a burden—you can live with it, and you don't have to run! The past can exist, and so can the future, and oh"—she exhaled a sigh of relief—"does that sound good to me!"

This young pair might have their charged issues, I reflected, but the positive, hopeful parts of the relationship were still evident, still clearly in place. Laura, however, added in a somewhat tremulous voice, "I'm still not sure it's possible . . . that it will happen that way. . . . I don't know, but it sounds so good. . . ." She wound down on a note of uncertainty, and I turned to Tom.

Had his own family, too, seemed to be fleeing the past? He shook his head. "No, we're all big photo album makers—I used to be one, too, before Laura and I got together. But then there were problems about my dealing with—with my history. About reinterpreting it, I mean. To the extent where I've had to throw away some of my pictures, which ordinarily I wouldn't have done." The irritation and outrage in his voice were inescapable.

"What part of your past have you had to throw away?" I inquired, and he responded, not unexpectedly, "Relationships with other women."

We had come to the place in our conversations at which we were to arrive, and arrive over and over again: Laura's certainty, experienced as a kind of fate, that she would always be duped by a heartless deceiver whose real desires bent toward someone else—toward a better loved and deeply regretted figure from his past.

Did some part of her believe, I wondered, that if Tom *didn't* burn Karen's photos, then he would maintain some present relationship with her (if not in actuality, then in the privacy of his own thoughts and fantasies)? Laura's grandmother's precedent might have left her grandchild with the barely articulated notion that the only way in which the past can be dealt with—and put behind a person in such a way that it will remain finished and done with—is by destroying the evidence of its existence completely.

On the other hand, this young wife's obsessive concern—about her husband's real, inner commitment tying him not to her but to some loved figure from the past (Karen? his mother?)—might contain some substantial measure of what was their mutual truth. If so, she could chase him forever and never catch up, for he was not, psychically speaking, at liberty to love her.

And if this were the case, then she *was*, indeed, linked to the man who could make love without loving—that unfeeling "monster" who could be in a close relationship without being open to the intimate partner. That man who was, in some real sense, deceiving her, because she wasn't the person he cared about at all. Laura's bad dream, in a way, threatened to become her reality.

5
Happily Ever After

Most couples, when they marry, really expect to live happily ever after: Hopefulness and high expectations usually are prominent in the relationship of *any* newly bonding pair. Hope and optimism are at the surface of the relationship, that is, but doubt and fear often lurk not far beneath them. For the intense attachment of the marriage alliance—from which we expect love, friendship, sexuality, and, in time, shared parenting of the next generation—tends to elicit not only a great many magical and irrational expectations, but distrust and uncertainty about whether those wishes and needs will be met.

Few couples, however, when they marry, entertain the notion that a high degree of distress (much less a breakdown of the relationship) is something that might ever happen *to them*. Most of the spouses whom I interviewed—including some who had married under some highly unusual circumstances—expected to find happiness on the other side of the ceremony. One wife, for example, who was pregnant by another lover, told the man whom she wanted to marry—a junior at Princeton at the time—that *he* was the father of the child. Still, she acknowledged during the course of our talks, she expected to be happy with her husband, and to have the relationship work out well, once the two of them were wed.

People *expect to be happy* once they have paired off, entered the house of marriage and closed the door behind them. Even when, like Laura and Tom Brett, they are having some obvious difficulties in advance of the wedding, the problematic portents are put aside as much as they possibly can be. For getting married is a way of making an old dream come true, of fulfilling a vague and misty promise . . . the promise of living happily ever after in unruffled romantic entwinement.

This is the dream, and most people, when they marry, believe in it to some substantial degree. They look forward not only to "being happy," but to being happier than their parents were, doing better than their parents did, succeeding in ways that they thought their parents had failed, and being better parents themselves, eventually. They will, the partners believe, show the world how a relationship should be made and how you keep an attachment alive and vital. They will create what Christopher Lasch called a "haven in a heartless world," a home of the soul, a place to be one's own self in an increasingly alienating, cold and indifferent environment.

As the statistics on divorce indicate (and these figures don't, obviously, reflect all marital unhappiness), things often don't work out that way. Partners who married expecting to live happily ever after frequently find themselves in dilemmas that bear some eerie resemblance to one or both spouses' earlier experiences in the family environment. The past—matters that pertain to each mate's own personal history, in his or her original family—has a way of surging into the present and becoming a part of the new marital relationship.

It is as if old problematic issues, like jack-in-the-boxes, are continually being pressed back into the containers of memory and continually popping out into the center of the partners' current life once again. The problems that one spouse had with a parent (or that he or she saw the parents have with one another) become the difficulties that emerge in the relationship with the mate. The anger that once seethed between a son and his father (or between a son and his sibling or grandparent) is re-created in a relationship with his wife or perhaps with his own child. There is a half recognition, usually avoided, that what is happening *now* partakes of what has been, but the connection between what *was* and what *is* tends to remain unintelligible, even shunned, by those who are the most deeply concerned.

It is in our intimate relationships that these things happen, "for better or worse." It is in the context of close emotional attachments that what is most secret, and most defended against, and most vulnerable, and most irrational forever threatens to emerge. The nearer one comes to another human being, the nearer one comes to one's own inner self, and for many of us, this feels dangerous. We can learn things that we're unwilling to know. We can be seen for what we are, and be abandoned.

At one level, when we marry, irrational hopes—the hope of giving and receiving perfect gratification—run high. At another level, the urge to resurrect old patterns and conflicts which existed in each of the partners' own family arouses unconscious fears that "something new" will turn out to be "something old"—something very much the same. The mate who was to help one *to improve upon the past* turns out, so frequently, to be the individual who *restores one* to the familiar family system, and the ghosts of old struggles rise again.

"The Less Said the Better"

Throughout our talks, the subject of Tom Brett's ex-girlfriend continued to come up from time to time. Tom and Laura were no longer getting into unresolvable quarrels about Karen; the subject had been, to some large degree, detoxified during their brief stint of premarital therapy. But Karen, as a potential charged issue, had not completely disappeared from the Bretts' relationship either.

Early in the interviews, I asked Laura what had aroused her jealous feelings in the first place. I wondered, but did not ask the question aloud, whether she herself believed that Tom had gone on seeing Karen after their own relationship began.

When it comes to discussing past involvements of one or both members of a couple—or an affair that is current, or recently ended, or supposedly ended—the mental set that I find it most realistic to assume is that of the wary disbeliever. I did not and would not ever take it for granted that one spouse's worst apprehensions—in Laura's instance, the fear that Tom might have continued seeing his old girlfriend for a while or even be in contact with her at this time—could not, in fact, be the reality.

She herself, however, did not appear to believe that such was the case. For while Laura agreed, with a brief shake of her head, that she *had* been jealous, she added at once that she hadn't been so jealous as she had been "offended." "*Offended*," she repeated the word, "about not having been told the truth."

That serene Madonna's smile was upon her lips, and yet I thought I saw a glitter—anger?—come into her eyes. "I just wasn't sure, at one point, exactly *what* it was that I was dealing with," she explained, in a raised, yet controlled tone of voice. "Was she a current girlfriend? Someone who'd never been more than a passing acquaintance? Or what *was* Karen to him after all?" She turned to Tom, who sat next to her on the sofa, and stared at him momentarily, as if she were gazing at a stranger. Then, turning back to me, she added, "It wasn't clear to me whether they were still available to meet together on weekends, to sleep together, or whatever!"

She paused and, when I said nothing, went on. "There was a time when I really felt completely bananas about all of this—and so much so that I just couldn't cope! Anytime her name came up, I'd have to ask, 'Who, exactly, are we talking about? Someone you *cared* about? Someone you care about *now*? Someone who never mattered—or someone who matters to you *at this moment*'?" Sounding both indignant and helpless, she lifted her shoulders in a great, hopeless shrug.

"But what," I asked, "had put the idea that she was a current girlfriend into your mind?"

Laura shot a bitter, sidelong glance at her husband. "The fact that he'd slept with her quite recently—just before we started seeing each other, in fact! And that it wasn't obvious whether it was over, between them, or not! Months and months after he'd reassured me, over and over again, that this was ridiculous—the affair had been nothing, and was completely over, anyhow—her birthday card arrived. And what she wrote on that card was, very simply, 'I miss you.' In other words, you're welcome into my arms at any time, and I expect you to *act*. This implied a whole lot more between them than I had ever been told about. And the creepy thing was that when Tom and I first met and when we first started talking about relationships—"

"On that first evening?" I interrupted.

She flushed slightly, gave me a quizzical look. "Yes, I guess it was that first evening when we got on to the subject of Karen. Tom told me that he'd never had a really close sort of relationship with anyone, but that there was this one woman whom he'd slept with, off and on. Someone who'd never been a romantic interest of any kind—just a person he'd known in the dim past, years ago, and with whom he'd had a bit of a fling, in terms of mixing friendship with casual sex. But that the sex had never been anything like *making love*. And then I find out!"

Laura, turning to look at her husband balefully, continued speaking to me. "It was at his mother's house, going through the photo albums. And then—all of a sudden—*there she is*." I was taken aback. Tom's ex-girlfriend had been discovered in a photo album; it made me think, at once, of the family albums that Laura's grandmother had destroyed. In Laura's original family, the past had been so dangerous that it hadn't even been permitted to exist! Karen's appearance, in Tom's album, must have unleashed a storm of anxiety in his new partner—anxiety about when it is that the past is over and done with, and when it is that it's very much alive.

My next thought was of her father and of that deceiving ex-wife of his—I glanced at the genogram, saw the name "Lorraine"—to whom Laura's father had once been married for just a year and a half. Laura's father, ordinarily remote or angry, had seemed ambiguously "jovial" and excited when discussing the manner in which he'd exposed that faithless woman's activities.

"There she *is*," reiterated Laura, holding up an imaginary album, at which she stared with wide, rounded eyes, as if demonstrating her shock at the sight of those photographs of Karen. She blinked, several times, in rapid succession. "And there are all the captions: 'Tom and Karen, spending Thanksgiving at Tom's house,' and 'Karen and Tom, at Karen's house; Christmas Eve,' and I—I'm taken aback! This isn't the relationship that you told me about, you know!" She was talking to Tom.

When she looked back at me, her cheeks were marbleized with streaks of pink. "She's somebody he went out with for a whole year—and talked about *marrying*—and that's an entirely different matter, in my view!" It could hardly, Laura observed sarcastically, be considered a casual relationship which had occurred sometime in the dim past.

Tom, beside her, sat facing me and did not respond. If, however, a person can draw away without making any visible motion whatsoever, then this is what he did at that moment. His wife stared at him, for a few minutes, and then turned back in my direction.

"Tom has a whole pattern," Laura said, "which I would call his family's pattern, of 'The less said the better.' 'Keep it proper,' 'Keep it private,' and above all, never tell anybody anything that might upset them—even if it happens to be the *truth*."

"It's Been Painful"

Tom's own recollections of what he had said about his relationship with Karen, he said defensively, varied considerably from the recollections of Laura. "I still don't—I mean, she and I have hashed this out a lot—and I still don't recognize my words as she reports them. Even from the beginning, her description of what I said about myself and Karen includes a lot more denials than I remember making! My philosophy about these things *is*, in fact, 'the less said the better,' but I never said that Karen had meant nothing to me!" He met his wife's eyes, said firmly, "What I *did* say to you was that she's just a friend, someone I sleep with, but that it isn't anything romantic."

"I asked you about that, specifically," objected Laura indignantly, "because I was so shocked by the things you'd said! And I never remember her being talked about as anything other than irrelevant—someone who'd never mattered in any way at all! But now you're acknowledging that that wasn't ever really true!"

"I have a question," I intervened, addressing Tom, "and that is: What *was* the status of your relationship with Karen, after you and Laura began going out?"

"Obviously, it changed," he answered readily. "It changed from 'indefinite' to 'no longer a potential romance.'"

In actuality, he stated, Laura had had no reason for being jealous about his possibly seeing Karen—or sleeping with her—again. She had been someone whom he'd liked and with whom he had shared a sexual relationship but to whom he had not been committed.

"After you got together with Laura, what happened between you and Karen?" I asked.

Tom, before replying, cleared his throat. "The week after I met Laura, I wrote to Karen. She'd been trying to arrange to come and visit me in New York—she lives in Brookline, Massachusetts—and she'd written saying that she could come in three weeks. I, by then, had gotten involved with Laura, and I answered by telling her that I'd met someone else. I said something like 'Can't we defer this visit?' . . . I haven't seen her since then."

I waited, after he had stopped speaking, for objections to this version of events, but none was forthcoming from his wife. I looked at her questioningly, and she nodded as if to say, "Yes, I do believe this to be what happened."

"So in reality," I said to Tom, "you canceled out. You postponed Karen's visit . . . and what happened then? Did you explain to her that you weren't going to be seeing her again, and did you explain why that was the case?"

He shook his head. "No, but I did call her about a month and a half later, and I gave her an update. Then the birthday card arrived, so I wrote to her saying that we"—he turned to look directly at Laura—"that our relationship had continued and gotten more serious and that we were considering marriage." He said, then, to me, "After we got engaged, I called Karen and told her."

"So Laura's response to your behavior seems to be irrational?" I asked.

"Well, it's been painful," he said.

"HE WOULD RATHER BE FREE"

Laura Constantine Brett had, before her marriage, been through a series of relationships with men which had ended in a mysteriously similar fashion. She had discovered, in every instance, that she'd been naively gullible and overly trusting and that she had been deceived. Her first long and intense attachment had been with a high school classmate who had turned from a platonic friend into a lover. The two of them had become involved in what seemed an important, durable relationship, one which had lasted for three and a half years.

"I even lived with his family for a summer and it was just *the happy relationship*," Laura recounted, "and in a family which, by the way, was basically much happier than mine." An expression of gloom settled upon her features. "But the fact was that it never really gelled, not when it came right down to making a decision. When it came right down to that, he was able to say no. He could say, 'Well, this is wonderful; but I've got to go out and get some experiences and I've got to live my own life.' And that was always . . . that was my pattern." She drew a deep breath. "I'd give it my best shot, and it wasn't enough. Whatever it was, *I* wasn't what was needed."

She no longer seemed merely gloomy; she appeared to be stricken. I looked at Tom, but his head was lowered. He was staring at his hands, which were joined at the fingertips, suspended just over his lap. "After that," continued Laura, "the next major relationship I had was with this guy who was—oh, so remarkably deceptive! Someone who would make me feel guilty whenever I was suspicious or possessive in any way *whatsoever!* Who, whenever I tried to question him, would say, 'I don't understand you—how can you be so jealous?' And 'How can you not understand that I have female friends?' and so on. . . . I didn't find out, until a year later, that he'd been sleeping with women right and left, behind my back!"

Her voice was scornful. He had, she said, tried to get her to forgive him and to trust him again. "He wanted me to love him and eventually *marry him*," Laura declared angrily.

But a moment later, deflating once more, she said miserably, "So it is, I'll agree, true that I've been through the wringer on this entire issue. And I feel . . . I think . . . susceptible to it, in some way . . . ?" She looked at me, as if for an answer, for what had begun as a statement had ended as a question.

"Perhaps," I responded, my voice tentative, "Tom's version of what has gone on vis-à-vis Karen is just what he says, and he's not another heartless deceiver. It's possible that you're trying to force him into that role . . . so that you yourself can be jealous. But it may not be real, in any other way."

"It's *not* real," she admitted, immediately. "And yet, strangely enough, I believe it." Tears were, suddenly, standing in her eyes. "I believe *him*, too"—she tilted her head toward her husband—"and at the same time, I'm really jealous and angry.

"There's still a little something inside here," she continued, touching her hand to her chest as if to locate that "something" right there, "that says that when it comes right down to it, he would rather be free—or with someone else—than be here, with me." The tears were gone, as suddenly as they'd come, as if sucked backward by a returning sense of control. "It's just an assumption," Laura acknowledged, wiping the corner of one eye with the tip of her finger.

What made it so comfortable and *right*, I wondered, for her to believe that the one she loved loved someone else much better? Turning to Tom, I asked him if he understood what question it was that she was struggling to answer for herself.

He looked startled, like a student listening to a recitation who is suddenly—unexpectedly—called upon to answer. "Something about deception perhaps?" he essayed, a slight tremor in his deep bass voice.

I nodded, but then added, "Her question, as I am hearing it, seems to be along the lines of 'How important am I to you? Am I *the* important person to you; am I number one? Or does this past relationship matter so much to you that you would conceal it from me?' In other words," I turned to Laura, "the question that I think you may be asking Tom is 'How much do I really count?' "

"And do I count enough," she continued passionately, "so that you'd let me know what's really going on? So that, for example, when you're sorting through her old letters and *mourning* for that old relationship—as you did just after we got engaged—you don't just fob me off by saying it's nothing that ever mattered to you!" Did she feel, I asked Laura at that point, that Tom was *guarding* Karen—or his memories of Karen—as something that belonged to him and that she couldn't be permitted to know about?

"He has in the past," she replied, but added nothing further by way of explanation.

I turned to Tom, observing that Laura seemed to feel that he was protecting Karen's privacy. "No, *his* privacy, not Karen's," his wife burst out at once. "I believe he's cherishing that relationship as something that he can still have and that I can't see!" It was as if she were being locked out of any true intimacy with her husband—excluded from the possibility—because his real attachment was to the woman who had preceded her in his life.

"THE SCARY PLACES, IN BETWEEN"

I gazed at Tom, asked him in a light, almost conversational tone of voice whether or not he did actually love Laura.

"*Yes.*" The response, given without an instant's hesitation, sounded both fervent and certain. I turned to his wife, asked her why she was so convinced that he didn't. "It would take an awful lot to convince some people that they weren't loved," I added, meeting her watery gaze. "But for you," I said the words gently, "it's just the opposite, isn't it?"

"I'll tell you what I think." The tears were sliding down her cheeks. "I think this tells me something about how unlovable—just *unlovable*— I actually do feel! I'm so hyper about whether or not I'm someone anyone could really care about!" She turned toward Tom, swinging her legs up on the sofa between them, so that she sat akimbo, facing him. Absently smoothing her wide print skirt over her knees, she leaned toward her husband, stared into his pale, somewhat stricken-looking face. "How can you love somebody who's always questioning whether or not you really *do* love her?" she demanded.

He was silent. "It's a very bitter thing for me that I should be this way," she went on, "and I don't know—I don't understand it."

"What could he do to convince you, Laura," I asked, after a few moments, "that you do come first?"

Laura responded, her eyes fixed upon her husband, in an almost trancelike way. "Bit by bit I *am*, I think, getting more convinced. And Tom is really patient and energetic, trying to help me pinpoint when I'm angry and when I'm scared. And he listens to me and asks questions . . . which makes a whole lot of difference. As does living with me, marrying me, whatever." She lifted her shoulders, shrugged, then inhaled a great wavery breath like someone who has just stopped crying, let the air out in a sigh of relief.

"But I think another thing that would make a *huge* difference," continued Laura, "would be our being able to talk about the scary places, in between. Talk about them honestly instead of covering them up. Because the minute you feel—" Instead of completing her sentence, she stopped talking abruptly. Then she turned to look at me, without having shifted her body's position.

Was it the sideward tilt of her head, or did she now wear an arch, somewhat seductive expression? "Obviously, in some ways *both* of us would like to be single," she observed, in a practical tone of voice. "I mean, everyone wants to have their cake and eat it, too! . . . You know.

. . . You'd like to have a million romances, as well as having one—and what is important, I believe, is being able to talk honestly and openly about it."

"OPEN MARRIAGE"

Laura had turned the conversation inside out. Was she, then, perceiving her own doubts about the relationship as her husband's doubts? Was *she* the one who wanted a prior lover back again—who yearned for the heartless deceiver?

The deceptive person was, in any case, clearly a highly eroticized figure.

It was as if Laura had to some degree identified with that faithless partner in her father's past. Her father's first wife had not (like Laura's own mother) been abandoned, emotionally; instead, *she* had been the successful abandoner. That other woman seemed, moreover—or so the daughter fantasized—to have remained the object of her father's secret thoughts and desires.

Betrayal was, for Laura, something sexy—or at least something necessary in a close relationship. What she appeared to be involved in, at present, was the reworking of old conflictual material. Neither she nor Tom had yet been capable, it seemed, of fully detaching herself or himself from the intense emotional bond to the opposite sex parent. Their earlier attachments, obviously still very highly charged, were being resurrected in the Bretts' current relationship—not a surprising occurrence, considering that they were still fledgling adults, fresh from the family nests in which they had been reared.

I asked Laura if she was trying to *force* Tom to share with her the fact that he wished he were free. "Because," I remarked, "that might not be the real situation, you know."

Oddly enough, both the partners remained silent, and so I asked Tom, directly, whether "being free" was the foremost on his agenda. Or did he, on balance, prefer being in a committed relationship? But he had apparently received a sonar signal from his spouse; he was to make some emotional distance between them, so she could resume pursuing him.

"I'd rather be in a relationship," he said agreeably, "and at the same time, it's important for me to be free."

I smiled, for what he wanted was, paradoxically, a thing (intimate commitment) and its opposite (liberty to form other relationships) simultaneously. "So how do you reconcile two such irreconcilable wishes?" I asked.

"By being free *within* the relationship," he explained, earnestly, "and in that way getting both. We have talked about an open marriage," he added, "which is to say, remaining sexually free within a committed relationship."

"And I'm hard to convince," put in Laura, demurely, "but not impossible." She swung around again to face Tom.

I continued focusing upon him as well. "And is that what you would like—an open marriage?" I asked him. "No," he looked uncomfortable, "but I would like the possibility of it, if we decided that we wanted to do it. If *I* decided that I wanted to do it!" Why did his statements have such an air of unnatural bravado, of his having been forced into a somewhat uncomfortable part?

"I can see," I said equably, "that this is a problem area, because I think your wife is saying that she's going to be a somewhat jealous wife—"

"I don't want to be!" interrupted Laura suddenly.

"And I think you're saying," I said to Tom, "that you aren't sure that you want someone to be jealous of you—is that right?" He responded by telling me that the pair of them had actually played out some role reversals in which Laura had pretended to be the one who wanted to become involved in an outside relationship. They had done so, he explained, in order to practice what their reactions to such a situation might be; Tom had, in fact, found the whole thing extremely upsetting.

"When I heard Laura saying things like 'I still love you, but I want to expand my horizons a bit and explore other relationships,' I felt a gut reaction," he admitted. "A reaction to the whole notion of her going off and sleeping with somebody else." In other words, if she became the distancer, he would pursue.

If they did reverse their roles, the chaser and the runner-away would be different, but the way their relational system operated would itself remain unchanged.

Psychologically speaking, the Bretts had constructed a Rube Goldberg mechanism for working around the basic dilemma—a dilemma about autonomy and intimacy. How can you be intimate without exposing yourself to the terrible possibilities of rejection or abandonment? Laura's answer was that you could do so by running after emotional closeness while always making quite certain that it got away.

How can you, on the other hand, be your own self and be close to another person? Doesn't getting intimate open one to the danger of being swallowed up alive? Tom's answer was that you cannot be a full self, and yet be in a close relationship, so his way of resolving the conflict was to run away while making sure that his intimate partner was not far behind.

THE HEARTLESS DECEIVER

Tom was, I learned, not the first man carrying that name to figure significantly in his mother's life. This information, which emerged in the middle of our final interview (the sixth), struck me as almost ludicrous.

It was Laura who mentioned it. She had been staring at the two triangles—signifying her parents and each of their previous spouses—which I'd sketched in upon the Bretts' family genogram.

Those triangles seemed to intrigue her. "Can I fill in one fact?" she inquired. She had been sitting forward on the sofa, examining my drawing from her upside-down point of view. I picked up the art tablet, turned it around so that she and Tom could see it more easily, and nodded my agreement.

The Bretts were, on that afternoon, dressed to go out. The interview had begun at 4:00 P.M. and was to last an hour and a half; they were going to a cocktail party at Tom's boss's apartment as soon as I left them. Tom, in his gray suit, striped shirt and maroon print tie, looked unusually formal. Laura, in a navy silk dress cut in middy style, had a slightly shy, self-conscious air about her; it was as if she were a schoolgirl, not completely comfortable in her grown-up woman's finery.

"Before Tom's parents married," she explained eagerly, "his father had been proposing to his mother for many years." Having made this statement, however, Laura hesitated and looked uncertainly at her spouse. Tom, with a brief nod of assent, then repeated what she had said. "My father had been proposing to my mother," he echoed her words, his voice as flat and definitive as a radio announcer's.

"For *years*," Laura's voice was rising, "even before she became engaged to Tom Garrison! And she—his mother—kept turning his father away!"

"My mother *was* engaged to somebody else," acknowledged Tom, "and that was—oh, two years, or thereabouts, before she and my father got married. He—the other person—was the one who broke it off."

"Oh," I said, and then just waited.

"My mother laughs about it now," he continued, "and says it was a pretty lucky thing for my dad that he *did* break it off, because Tom Garrison was everything she'd thought she'd ever wanted in a man!" He stopped talking, suddenly, as if startled by the import of what he had just said.

"I don't know whether it was before," he added disjointedly, "but I do know that they—my mother and father—had been going out." It wasn't clear to me what he meant. Did "it" refer to her engagement to Tom Garrison or to her rejection of his father's initial proposal?

"His folks had been going out for *ten years*." Laura leaped back into the conversation, eagerly. "And in the middle of that time," she explained to me, "his mother became engaged to this Ivy League type, this pretty wealthy—I think—Tom Garrison character. Tom Garrison then broke off the engagement, and two years later, she married Martin—Tom's father, that is."

"Right." Her husband accepted her account of what had occurred as gravely as if he were a judge adjudicating the acceptable evidence in this case. "So at least from what I've *heard*," she swept onward, "there was a real strong question of whether she feels she ended up with second best! At least that's how Tom's older brother, who's been thinking about this a lot, sees the whole situation nowadays."

"Yes, that's the way he sees it," agreed Tom, neither his voice nor his expression giving any indication of the way in which he saw it, himself. I asked Tom, at that juncture, why his mother had given him the same name as that of her onetime fiancé.

"My grandfather's name was Thomas—my father's father," he replied. Then he blinked several times, in rapid succession, as if the light in the room had brightened.

"And Tom was also her faithless fiancé's name," I observed.

He made no response.

"I wonder," I said musingly, after a few moments, "if you yourself might have been scripted?" The question hung in the air until Tom's features hardened into an expression that was either wary or angry. "Scripted, I mean, as the ghost of Tom Past—the dream of the past. The one who will make it better, who will bring about the happy ending. The person who will, in some fantasy sense, love your mother as she needs to be loved, by the kind of man she admires." Tom's only reply was a shrug.

But Laura, turning to him, said excitedly, "Your brother Bart went to Oberlin—where your dad went—and that, your mother found okay! But when it came to you, that was different: You had to go to Princeton, and there were no two ways about it!"

"That's interesting," conceded Tom, an uninterpretable half smile hovering around the sides of his mouth.

"It was this whole big important thing!" Laura insisted, sounding anxious. "Remember what you told me, about that big deal your mother made when you were thinking of going to the University of Chicago?"

The memory seemed to amuse him, for he laughed, turned to tell me about it. "I had been thinking about the University of Chicago, but my mother said to me, 'Well, you can do that if you like, but it's not on the most selective list.' She even went out and got a copy of *Barron's Guide* in order to make her point. It *had* to be on the most selective list; she had something against the University of Chicago! Maybe it was just too far away, but that wasn't the reason given. . . . Finally, I said to her, 'Okay, but just pay the fare, or eighty percent of the fare, so that I can get to go out there and look at the stockyards and the trains and the city,' which was really what I wanted to see. If she did that, I promised her, I wouldn't even apply there." He laughed again, a deeply pleased, chuckling sound. "She paid it," he said.

Then Tom added, as if in logical continuation of this topic, "I was telling Laura the other night that I may be my mother's revenge for Tom Garrison."

"Meaning what?" I inquired.

"Meaning that I'm supposed to go out and break women's hearts." To be, I thought, the heartless deceiver that Laura expected and feared.

PART II

LOVERS AND OTHER THIRD PARTIES:
Emotional Triangles

6

Marriages as Systems

The very idea of a couple visiting a psychotherapist together—as the Bretts had done in the period prior to their marriage—would have been unthinkable in the earlier years of this century. For in the early 1900s, and all the way up until the mid-1950s, most clinicians tended to think of emotional distress as problems going on *within an individual's own head.* If, therefore, married partners found themselves unable to cope with the difficulties they were having, they tended to assign ownership of the problem to one or the other member of the pair—frequently, to the wife. She would then go for treatment of the psychological distress that "she" was experiencing.

The clinical avenue to the understanding of marital disturbance seemed to skirt the relationship *between the members of the couple* and lead directly to the individual psyche. For the dominant (Freudian) psychiatric understanding, at the time, was that a person's internal world was always the true locus of his problems and the site at which those problems had to be approached and ameliorated. The difficulty was *within* the individual, and not within his close relationships.

Those people who were closest to the person in distress were, said Freud, "a positive danger, one which we do not know how to deal with." The mate and other family members often, he suggested, served as a pernicious obstacle to a patient's improvement.

The distressed person's relatives, the spouse included, should be excluded from the therapeutic scene as completely as possible, counseled the founder of psychoanalysis. "Anyone who knows anything of the dissensions commonly splitting up family life," he commented, "will not be astonished in his capacity of analyst to find that those nearest to the patient frequently show less interest in his recovery than in keeping him as he is. . . . [T]he relatives," complained Freud, "should not oppose their hostility to one's professional efforts. But how are you going to induce people who are inaccessible to you to take up this attitude?"

A Curious Truth

How, indeed? For years, the mate and other family members were excluded from the treatment process and seen as the potential *cause* of problems, but never as part of any potential solutions. Ideally, in the therapist's view, the distressed individual's intimates would refrain from interfering and would remain relatively quiet. The patient's spouse and close relatives provided, thus, a kind of backdrop—the constant, unchanging context of his life—while he himself was the figure in the foreground. The patient was, in theory, expected to change and improve without encountering resistance or countermoves from anyone around hm.

But in practice, as Freud and many of his followers noted, marital partners, parents, siblings, grandparents and other family members tended to have powerful and unpredictable effects upon the patient's therapy and upon the progress that he did or did not make. A curious truth, moreover—which certainly did not escape clinical notice—was that improvement of one person's psychological well-being and overall functioning often seemed to bring about pathological reactions in another, closely connected individual—frequently, the patient's mate.

A typical instance of such an occurrence (one of many such cases reported upon in the psychiatric literature) was that of a forty-two-year-old corporate lawyer who was admitted to a mental health facility for treatment of his long-standing alcoholism and a deepening depression. This patient had, it should be mentioned, agreed to enter the hospital only because his wife was threatening divorce. Once there, however, he responded extremely well to the therapy, and as he improved, his wife reacted with every sign of happiness and relief.

The husband, vastly better, was eventually discharged and returned to his law practice and to his former family life. He remained abstinent, undepressed and well. But as the months passed, and he remained healthy and confident, his spouse's state of mind deteriorated. Gradually, *she* developed symptoms of a clinical depression and was eventually admitted to the same hospital after an attempted suicide.

Such situations, anything but rare, seemed to indicate that the well-being of one marital partner could be connected, in some mysterious fashion, to having the other partner be ill.

Certain families seemed to resemble a child's toy hammer and peg-board, inasmuch as banging down one brightly colored peg made another one pop right out. When, that is, an identified patient got better, what resulted was an upsurge of disturbance in a different family member, who had formerly been asymptomatic and well functioning.

THE SELF AND THE SYSTEM

Another, equally puzzling phenomenon—which, until the mid-1950s, had never been seriously examined—was the way in which some schiz-ophrenic patients become calm and rational while in the hospital, went home, and then within a very brief space of time (a day or a weekend) regressed and became deranged once again. Were there families, as a few experts working with young adult schizophrenics were beginning to sus-pect, who "required" that one of their members be seriously disturbed or frankly crazy in order to retain the stability and equilibrium of the other members of the group?

If so, this would be a novel way of viewing mental health and mental illness. In the classical, Freudian model, the patient's dysfunction was seen as a disturbance occurring inside his own psyche and not as a dis-turbance of the small social system which he inhabited; that is to say, the family. While the person's current difficulties might be seen as related to reactions to very early life experiences in the family, his symptoms were still seen as stemming primarily from *intrapsychic conflicts occurring within his own internal world*. His symptoms were not *inter*personal in origin, but rather *intra*personal. That which required psychotherapeutic treat-ment was, therefore, the individual patient himself.

As far as the individual's close relationships were concerned, the as-sumption was that recognition and working through of repressed erotic and aggressive strivings—infantile needs and wishes which existed out of conscious awareness and yet created inner turmoil—would inevitably lead to better and more reasonable functioning in his present-day interpersonal world. In other words, as the disturbed, distressed individual improved, so would the nature of his interactions with his intimates.

What could *not* be explained in the individually oriented model was, however, the frequency with which the person's family members behaved in ways that sabotaged the treatment. Nor could psychoanalytic theory provide explanations for why, if the patient improved and maintained that improvement, the mate or a close relative often reacted by developing symptoms of an equally debilitating nature.

A HUMAN SACRIFICE

In the middle decade of this century, a few maverick clinicians and researchers—prominent among whom was the brilliant anthropologist Gregory Bateson—violated the established psychiatric convention which dictated that family members be banished from the therapeutic scene. Almost in concert (although they were largely unaware of each other's activities) experts at such leading university-connected medical facilities as Stanford and Yale, and at the National Institute of Mental Health, in Washington, threw the doors of the consulting room wide open; they invited the families of schizophrenic patients to come and participate in the psychotherapeutic sessions.

Although they did not realize it initially, these early family researchers were beginning what would later be called a "quiet revolution" in psychiatric thinking.

For the new idea at play was that a better understanding of the schizophrenic's mystifying talk and strange behavior might be obtained by looking at him in his own natural habitat, i.e., the family environment in which he was living. And, as things developed, bringing entire families into the therapy sessions was rather like turning a pair of opera glasses around. Instead of focusing on early materials relating to the patient's thwarted strivings to gratify his needs, the researchers were now observing the individual figure *within the context of his own familial ground*. Turning the opera glasses around meant viewing the person with far less detail and clarity, true; but it enabled experts to look at all the other players on the stage—to study the repetitious sequences and distinct patterns which were intrinsic aspects of the family choreography.

Early family workers noticed that the schizophrenic was frequently the spokesman for what was in fact a family-wide disturbance. Having a member of the family be psychiatrically "ill" and dependent often appeared to serve an underlying function—that of keeping the rest of the family "well" and keeping the family system together and operational.

The schizophrenic person maintained the stability of the pathological social structure in which he lived; he expressed *the entire system's disturbance* in his own disturbing behavior. This was, the pioneer family theorists hypothesized, why the patient's close relatives often undermined or resisted his improvement.

It was, some experts began suggesting, futile to return a changed and "recovered" schizophrenic to a disturbed, dysfunctional family setting. The system itself was "ill"; it needed to have a member in the sick role. The schizophrenic, by expressing the craziness and badness of all the "healthy" family members, relieved some of the internal pressures that threatened to blow the entire emotional system apart.

Some clinicians began to think of the schizophrenic as a kind of human sacrifice—someone who, by offering himself up on the altar of the family, was sacrificing psychological growth and sanity itself. The patient was "protecting" the people he loved by keeping their attention on his sickness and away from their own disappointment, anger and suffering.

TREATING "THE SYSTEM"

It followed, from such assumptions, that what required treatment was not so much the individual as the family system of which that person was a part. The dysfunctional system itself had to be altered in ways that would make a sacrificial victim—or self-appointed martyr, depending on how you looked at it—no longer necessary for the family's overall stability. For the early clinical researchers, the emotional system itself had become "the patient" and the problem was that of finding ways to treat it. How did one go about changing the patterns of those ongoing family transactions that tend to produce problems, difficulties and disturbances in their individual members?

In attempting to answer these questions, experts discovered a number of intriguing replies—new theoretical concepts, methods and techniques—and modern family theory and therapy began to emerge. At the present time, almost three decades after the first scouting parties into the unknown territory of the family, a wide variety of sophisticated clinical devices exists and new ones are continually being developed.

The therapy homework assignment carried out by the Bretts was, for example, only one among the many behavioral "tasks" which have now come into widespread clinical usage. (Laura was, it will be recalled, given one hour per week when she was *required* to rant and rave about Tom's ex-girlfriend Karen, and this proved effective, in terms of detoxifying the difficulty they were having.) There are numerous other such problem-solving techniques and strategies, useful in special or very general types of situations, which are now available in the therapeutic marketplace.

The particular assignment carried out by the Bretts is especially effective in situations involving an extramarital involvement—whether that involvement is real or, as in Laura's case, imaginary. It helps the "betrayed" partner to vent her anger in an orderly fashion and in a way that promotes her chances of being *listened to*. This task is also useful in keeping other parts of the relationship uncontaminated by the anger and outrage that threaten to erupt at any and every moment. Finally, by assigning the innocent mate a special time in which to express her (or his) fury, loss of trust, sense of devastation, and the like, the possibility that *she will not want to do her homework* is promoted. Having said her say, in the course of a few (or a number of) sessions, she will usually be readier to let go of the "hotter" part of her anger and bad feelings and to begin work on improving the healthier aspects of the relationship.

But this therapeutic device is, as mentioned, most effective in circumstances involving an affair. A far more generally applicable and remarkably effective sequence of behavioral exercises—designed to put intimate partners into different situations and give them different kinds of experiences—is that described in Chapter Eleven ("Tasks"). Couples should, however, not attempt to make use of these exercises before having gained some understanding of what they are about and the direction in which their relationship will inevitably be channeled.

THE MARRIAGE IS THE PATIENT

As clinical interest in "the other side of the opera glasses" grew, not only did an assortment of new concepts and techniques emerge; but also several important family models were developed. One of the earliest of these, currently called Bowen Family Systems, focuses upon the ways in which the past experience of the extended system affects the lives of family members in the present. It was psychiatrist Murray Bowen, M.D., the originator (during the intellectually explosive decade of the 1950s) of this powerful, multigenerational approach to the understanding and treatment of families, who devised the genogram as a therapeutic tool.

Several important (and a number of less important) schools of family theory and therapy now exist. They differ in certain ways, but have one thing in common: All systemic theories are theories about close relationships. If, therefore, a couple comes in to see a family-oriented therapist, it will be the marital unit—not the wife alone or the husband alone, but the particular relationship that they have, in combination, created together—which will be viewed as "the patient." It is the *interpersonal system*, not the separate individuals involved, which will be seen as requiring assistance.

THE TROUBLE IN THE SYSTEM

If, therefore, an entire family comes into systemically oriented treatment with what they consider an "individual" complaint about a single member's behavior—such as the delinquency or school phobia of a child or the depression of a parent—the person with the "problem" is not considered to be the only person with a problem who is present. On the contrary, the ill or disturbed member of the group is seen as the spokesman elected to express the pain that everyone in the household is experiencing.

The difficulties and distresses which bring a couple or an entire family into therapy are understood, by the systems-oriented clinician, as something occurring within an intimate, transactional network. The individual's complaint can, as Professor Froma Walsh points out, often have a poetic, metaphoric quality which serves to symbolize a worry that exists in the system at large.

"A mother's concern about her sixteen year old daughter's sexual promiscuity may be, in large part, a displacement of anxiety about a current sexual problem in her own marriage," writes Dr. Walsh. Or, adds Walsh, it may "signal the reactivation of unresolved issues from parents' families of origin, as when it is learned that the mother, above, became pregnant out of wedlock at the age of sixteen. It may even be that grandmother, at sixteen, gave birth out of wedlock, to mother, and a multigenerational repeated pattern of expectation is in operation."

ENLARGING THE CONTEXT

In brief, the family therapy approach to individual problems is to enlarge the context—to remove the therapeutic spotlight from the single individual and to see what function or role or relationship that individual's "symptoms" or disturbing behaviors might have or might be playing in the wider system. What would be happening, for example, to the delinquent and promiscuous girl's family if she were *not* acting out?

Would one of the parents become depressed? Would the marriage itself be in jeopardy? Where symptoms serve a function in a family, suggests Froma Walsh, "change in the symptom bearer will have a reverberating impact on the system. As a patient begins to improve, family members will react to preserve the homeostasis. The family may resist or counteract the improvement, or another family member may become symptomatic as the system is destabilized.

"Such complementarity in a marital relationship becomes overt," she adds, "when [for instance] a recovering alcoholic finds his spouse tempting him to drink, becoming depressed at his improvement, or even getting a divorce." What are considered the individual's own psychological or behavioral problems (in this case the husband's alcoholism) are often highly contextual in nature. They are problems which exist in an intimate, interdependent relational system rather than within the distressed person's own psyche.

And if the system's rules and regulations decree that the alcoholic husband must continue drinking or take the chance of sending his spouse into a total tailspin, he will know, at some subliminal level, that becoming dry is *not* the behavior that she really requires. The pair of them are in a relationship in which he expresses for her everything that *she is not*: undisciplined, "bad," impulse-ridden, uncontrolled, dependent, and the like. She can see, in him, those disreputable aspects of the self which are nowhere evident in her own self-reliant, "good," sturdy, controlled self. If he changed, she would have to take inner ownership of these suppressed aspects of her own internal being, and so she, unaware of what she herself is doing, becomes the system's enforcer.

SPACE WITHIN THE SYSTEM

This is not meant to suggest that necessary changes in a marriage can only begin at the relational level and that improvement can never be initiated from the other direction. Quite the contrary: Individual change (such as improvement in a person's sense of self-esteem and ability to function effectively) leads inevitably to marital change, which leads to further changes in both spouses, in a never-ending cycle. What is crucial, though, is that the relational system *allow for changes to occur.*

When the system does not do so, each mate's ability to grow and elaborate upon his or her own themes and goals is—like the growth of a Japanese bonsai tree—altered, diminished and stunted. When, however, space *is* provided within the system—space for changing, growing, being different over the course of the time—marriage can be the most therapeutic of relationships, the fertile terrain which permits both partners to expand, flourish and attain their full potentials.

7

An Intimate System: The Caretaker and the Wounded Bird

The house, a yellow-painted clapboard, sat well back from the street. The grassy lawn was well tended and, as I came up the curved cement path, I smelled the heavy scent of roses before I saw the large bush that flourished right next to the front door. Inside, in the Kearneys' living room, there were roses, too; a vaseful, haphazardly arranged, sat on a colonial-style maple table, near a copper lamp with a pale green shade.

There was also a clear glass bowl, filled with an abundance of the same flowers, on the maple and leather cocktail table in front of a chintz-covered sofa. As I sat down, I picked up a fallen rose petal absentmindedly. It was still a deep and perfect red, so undiscolored that its fall from the blossom seemed surprising. There was, I realized suddenly, an almost unbearable tension in the atmosphere.

I took out my large sketchpad, tape recorder, blank cassettes, and several drawing pencils of different colors, moving slowly and methodically. The Kearneys, watching me with nervous interest, were both silent, but their baby daughter, gurgling nearby in a playpen, seemed happily oblivious of whatever it was that was happening (did I imagine it?) between her parents. She was cooing at her toys.

It was close to seven o'clock, and the twilight of a June evening was descending, dimming the visibility within the room. As I readied myself for the interview, Jo Ann Kearney went around switching on the lights. The scene she illuminated was pleasant. A sea-green rug, with a high pile, stretched off in every direction.

I realized that I had, at the outset of this discussion, a choice that would have to be made.

I could either ask a question that would elicit conversation about the anger and pain that I thought I saw before me, right now—in Gordon

Kearney's set, hardened jaw and in Jo Ann's widened, pleading eyes—or I could (to use the jargon of the family therapy trade) "cool the system down" in the initial part of our conversation by directing our attention elsewhere. My decision was to take the latter route. Although there were, I sensed, some immediate issues clamoring for attention, it seemed important to me to become acquainted with these two people as *individuals* before becoming acquainted with whatever argument was going on between them.

We spent the first hour working with the genogram, and during that time, the Kearneys relaxed somewhat, although they (most especially Gordon) could not be said to have calmed down completely. He did, however, become absorbed in his wife's—and then his own—responses to the questions that I asked each of them in turn. The harsh, infuriated expression on his features softened as we discussed what life in their original families had been like.

How does it happen, so routinely, that we ignore the organic connection between a couple's present relationship and the individual history of each of the partners? Jo Ann Kearney, née Farrell, had been the daughter of a beloved father; he had died when she was in her early adolescence. This was one of the critical facts of her existence; it emerged, as it had to do, not too far along in the fact-finding mission which is the filling out of a family genogram.

Jo Ann had already told me, in her calm and yet curiously hurt-sounding voice, that she and Gordon had been married for eight years. Their one child, Susannah, was just seven and a half months old. Jo Ann was a registered nurse; she worked in a small hospital close to the Connecticut suburb in which she and Gordon lived. She had taken a few months away from her job just after the baby's birth. Now she *had* to work, because her husband had left his former job (as a psychiatric technician) and had entered law school.

THE MODEL OF A MARRIAGE

Jo Ann was the middle child of three sisters in her original family. "I also have some stepsisters," she told me, "but I never lived in the house with them after my mother remarried. I was married, myself, by that time."

There were, I observed with a smile, a plenitude of females in the family in which Jo Ann had grown up. "Before we go on to talk about your mother's new husband and children," I added, "what happened to her marriage to your father? Are your parents divorced?" She shook her head, answered in a voice that had dropped almost to a whisper, "My father is deceased."

I asked her what his name had been, and she said, softly, "Michael." He had been dead now for eighteen years; the cause of death had been cancer, a brain tumor. What had her father done for a living before becoming ill? Jo Ann answered that her dad had been a chemist. "And where did he work?" I went on, matching the low pitch of my voice to her own.

"Ah, I was just trying to reach back. . . ." She sighed, ran her hand through her light brown hair. "The last job he had was with a large chemical firm in Stamford—the name's just gone out of my mind—but he got sick very shortly after our move to Connecticut." The family had, she explained, come to Connecticut from Pennsylvania and had been strangers to the region at the time that her father had first fallen ill.

Her mother's name was Elizabeth. For some reason, when I asked what her mother's age was, the young wife responded with a sarcastic laugh, "I'd say she's around fifty-six." Jo Ann, shrugging, turned to Gordon, and he, for the first time, smiled—a sarcastic grin.

I asked about the ages and present circumstances of Jo Ann's sisters and of her stepsisters. Then I asked her how old she had been at the time her father had died.

"I was in seventh grade," Jo Ann replied, "and I'm not sure what age that puts me at." Pausing, she counted back from her present age—thirty-two years old—and realized that she had been turning fourteen.

And what, I went on, had her relationship with her dad been like?

"A close one, I would say," she answered readily, leaning forward in her chair. Her expression was dreamy. "Most of the prime time that I remember having with him was when he was already sick. A lot of the earlier years are hard for me to recall. I just don't remember that much—except that he and my mother did a lot of fighting. I remember, about that, only that I always took *his* side in the arguments. . . ." This was, I reflected, in capsule form the model of a marriage that Jo Ann (Farrell) Kearney had internalized during the apprenticeship years of her childhood.

I wonderd what, if anything, it would have to do with the hurt expression that lingered in the back of her eyes and the rock-hard anger that I'd seen on Gordon's face when I had entered their house this evening. There certainly was no link that was apparent to me, at this time. "So," I murmured, "you were much closer to your dad than to your mother?"

She nodded. "Very close." There was a silence, which I broke by asking Jo Ann what her mother was like, as a person.

"Domineering." She laughed the same brittle, sarcastic laugh. "A little overbearing, I would say."

A CROSS-GENERATIONAL COALITION

"So your father was under your mother's thumb, in your view—and you sided with him?" I asked. Jo Ann nodded. It raised, in my mind, the suggestion that what has been called a "cross-generational coalition" might have existed in her family of origin.

This is a situation in which individuals from differing generations (in this instance a father and a daughter), both of whom feel relatively powerless, join forces against a third person who is experienced as being overly strong (the mother in this case).

Such an alliance involves, of course, the psychological breaching of a generational boundary. The appropriate and natural partner of a parent is the *other* parent; the spouses are at the top, or "executive" level of the family hierarchy, to which no member of the offspring generation should be offered entrance as a peer. The covert joining of a parent and a child *against* the other parent, as many systemically oriented experts have noted, leads to distress and dysfunctional operation of the family organization as a whole.

What is involved is, in fact, a classic two-against-one power play—one in which two less strong individuals, acting in concert, are able to exert enough strength to override that of the one individual who would be stronger than either one of them, if each of them stood alone.

In the emotional microcosm which is the family, it is not at all unusual to see a weaker marital partner and a child (who is, by definition, a needier and more dependent member of the goup) join forces against the marital partner/parent who is perceived as having the lion's share of the family power. This two-against-one coalition, involving members of differing generations, obviously leads to the serious undermining of the legitimate authority of the initially more powerful parent. Also, it makes the authority of the parent who is *in* the cross-generational coalition dependent on his offspring's continued support.

"So," I asked Jo Ann, after a moment's pause, "did you and your mother quarrel a great deal?" She nodded her agreement at once. "I remember quarrels with her, after he died. All of the time I was growing up, to be honest . . . But after my dad died, she was working hard, at a couple of jobs, and we children were left pretty much on our own. And there were lots of arguments about restrictions that she put on us. She's not one to let go."

Jo Ann's voice was growing increasingly hard and bitter. "Let go of her children, I mean. Even now, when I'm married, she doesn't want to let go. But there were a lot of arguments, back then, about restrictions—about her not being very trusting of what we were doing while she was at work. And she worked most of the time. We really didn't see her that often."

The Perverse Triangle

"In a way," I observed, "it seems as if you lost two parents at once."

Jo Ann stirred in the chair, in which she now sat with her legs curled up underneath her, and sighed, saying that yes, she agreed; that was true. I wanted to know who had been in charge of the children.

It had been her older sister for the most part. She was now in her mid-thirties, and she was divorced. "My older sister was also very close to my father, and now that he is not here, she's allied to my mother—definitely. But I would say that she had an even closer bond with my father than I did."

"Was she closer to your dad, before his death, than she was to your mother?" Jo Ann thought that she had been. I observed that her father, during the time of his illness, had made everyone—all his daughters, at least—feel very, very close to him.

"Yes," Jo Ann was thoughtful, "and yet, you know, it was a very strange relationship. When he was sick we had, at certain points, to take care of him—physically—because obviously he couldn't take care of himself anymore. And that bond in itself was an extremely close one; I think we all felt it. Before he was taken ill, I really don't remember much. I'm sure my older sister was close with him, but we don't talk much about that time—when he was so sick, I mean." She'd gotten slightly confused, and her skin, as smooth and white as that of a porcelain figure, was suddenly, almost magically flushed.

"You don't?"

"No."

"Why is that?" I asked. Shaking her head, Jo Ann replied, "I don't know; I think it's just something that devastated all of us, and we just pushed it aside." She had, she'd said, pushed it aside and put it behind her, and yet it did not seem to me to be unrelated to the fact that she had gone on to make a career for herself as a nurse.

What, I wanted to know, had her parents' fights tended to be about? Jo Ann wasn't sure. "I can remember the fights themselves, but what they were fighting about . . . ? I don't know. Money, I think; my mother's a very demanding kind of person, and it was probably money. Money, or maybe not getting enough attention—I still don't have it clear in my mind."

She must, I persisted, have speculated about her parents' fights a great deal, when she was a child. Jo Ann hesitated momentarily, staring off into space, then said, "Yes. The money was an issue, for sure, because he was laid off at one point. I just don't think she felt that he was ever ambitious enough, even though he always did what needed to be done, except for the time he was laid off. . . ." Jo Ann was defending her father even now.

"Somehow, though, your father wasn't being the kind of person your mother wanted him to be?" I asked.

"No." Her voice was frankly angry. "He should have made more of himself. I guess he should have doted more on *her*!" The sound of Jo Ann's raised voice must have startled the baby, for she began, suddenly, to cry. Guiltily, the young mother stood up, went over to the playpen, and scooped her small daughter out. But when she returned, patting Susannah's back, the furious expression was still on her face.

That family triangle which clinician Jay Haley has called "the perverse triangle"—a triangle involving an ongoing covert alliance between two members of differing generations *against* a third party—still existed in Jo Ann Kearney's mind. She was taking her father's side, carrying his standard in the battle against his demanding, domineering wife. And yet her mother was now remarried, and her father had been dead for the past eighteen years!

Jo Ann herself was, moreover, no longer a fourteen-year-old girl, but a married woman in her early thirties with a little daughter of her own. Still, insofar as the important triangle of her early years was concerned, time itself appeared to have remained motionless.

Fixed emotional triangles have, as many family clinicians have noted, a persistent and enduring quality—a way of keeping people curiously stuck in old family situations even when those situations no longer exist.

MIDDLE SIBLINGS

Gordon Kearney, like his wife, was the middle child in a family of three. He had an older brother and a younger sister: Gordon himself was thirty-three. Both his siblings were married; his brother John and his wife had a child.

Middle siblings, observes Walter Toman, in *Family Constellations*, often feel overlooked or excluded even when they are still in the family. "They think they notice that they matter the least among the siblings. Hence they may long to leave the family earlier in life than their siblings would. They may move out, move far away, or opt for a professional career quite different from that of the rest of the family."

And psychologist Lucille Forer, in a doctoral thesis entitled *Birth Order and Life Roles*, also considers the middle child to be in a less favored family position. "Under customary circumstances," she writes, "he must from the beginning of his existence share the good things of the family with another child or with other children. He does not tend to develop a feeling of omnipotence as often does the first child of a family. He never feels that he owns the parents and his relationship with them is usually not as close and intense as that of the only or oldest or even the youngest child in the family. It is not that the parents do not love him as much; it is just that everyday contact with them is usually divided with other siblings."

When the child is in a middle sibling position with just one person above and one person below, the birth order placement is, in Forer's view, even less desirable. "On the basis of the information I have been able to obtain," she comments, "I am going to make the categorical statement that the middle child seems to be in the most precarious situation for his comfort and development, if he is the middle one of only three children, and that the difficulty of the position is increased for the middle child if all three children are female."

Although the literature on birth order and its influence on later life adjustment is (as some detractors have pointed out) full of what often appear to be overly general statements, I always like to take note of which position, in his or her own family of origin, each marital partner has occupied. I observed, aloud, that the Kearneys were both middle children in their original families, and the two of them, looking mildly surprised, said that they hadn't ever noticed it.

The remark did, however, lead Gordon to say, "In my case, though—which may make a difference—the three of us are adopted. Apparently," he added, "my sister is genetically my half sister. My brother is my complete brother. As far as my growing up is concerned, that made no difference. I didn't find that out, about my sister, until I was twenty-five. I always assumed that they were both genetically full-blooded relatives." His voice, as he gave me these facts, was instructional and without emotion.

AN ADOPTED SON

I was amazed. What had happened, I wondered, that had led to three children from the same family having been adopted at the same time? And what was the "secret" surrounding his sister's (that is, his half sister's) birth? I looked at Gordon, who is a compact, well-built man, with a head of fine brown hair and a fine brown mustache to match. "So you believe," I asked, "that you were really all adopted at once?"

"I *know* we were," he responded. "All at the same time. Apparently, though, my sister has a different father than my brother and I." I questioned him then, for a while, about how close his relationships with his siblings had been when they were children and about whether they were close, now, as adults. "We don't see them very often," Gordon said.

"Not very often, but I speak to Kathleen—his sister," put in Jo Ann. She was rocking the baby in her lap.

"I used to be very close to my brother, when we were younger," Gordon explained, "but he's a policeman and he works bizarre hours. I did, too, when I was working as a psychiatric technician: I worked three day shifts and two evening shifts every week and every other weekend as well. So we began tapering off. And besides, we'd drawn very far apart in a lot of our views. My politics are probably on the radical side of liberal, and my brother moved further and further to the right as he became more of a policeman." He laughed a mocking, uninvolved-sounding laugh.

Gordon's mother's name was Irene, and she was sixty years old. "No, not sixty," objected Jo Ann. "She's fifty-eight or fifty-nine." He made no reply, merely shrugged.

When I asked Gordon what his mother was like, as a person, he shrugged again and said—almost as if giving me his qualifications for holding the opinions he wanted to express—that he had been a psychology major as an undergraduate. "She is, I would say, a real classic. The typical oldest child, female, of a very successful, self-made man. Very autocratic, domineering—she is all of those things. German background. A very powerful woman." His voice was firm and his answers were clear; but what he said was said with an icy dislike.

"The daughter of a self-made father," I commented, "but not a daughter who was repressed or kept down by him?" He answered that his mother had run the home, and her father—his grandfather—had run the business; his mother had taken over what would ordinarily and expectably have been *her own mother's* duties. "My grandmother didn't take care of the day-to-day stuff, handling the household accounts. My mother grew into that role, because *her* mother had no head for figures."

Instead of the alliance between husband and wife which was so typical of that time, earlier in the century—i.e., He ran the business; She ran the home—the division of labors had been made between father and daughter.

Had there been the same kind of triangle as existed on Jo Ann's side of the map—that is, an overclose father-daughter coalition, with the mother (incompetent and with "no head for figures") pushed into the excluded, outside position? It sounded, in any case, as if Gordon's mother had been promoted into an executive, decision-making role in the family hierarchy, while his grandmother had been demoted downward.

Gordon said that his adoptive ancestors had come to America from Germany as highly skilled workers, and they had prospered enormously. "My own grandfather, by the time he was twenty-six, had made his first million dollars. He went from a position of working in the textile mills to owning his own mills—you know, the Horatio Alger American success story." There was less pride than distance and disaffection upon his relatively immobile face. Did he, or did he not, consider himself to be a member of this adoptive family in which he had grown up?

I asked him what his adoptive father was like, as a person, and Gordon answered, "My father is deceased. He died about twelve years ago."

"When you were how old?"

"That would make me twenty-one, twenty-two—somewhere around there."

His father's name had been Russell, and he had died of leukemia. "So you both had fathers who died of cancer," I observed.

Gordon answered, without missing a beat, that his father had died within a month of being diagnosed and that he himself had not been part of that dying process. "I was in basic training in the army. I heard he was diagnosed, flew home, saw him once, and then—not even two weeks later—got a call that he had died. So I wasn't around for much of that." The little boy who had, for some mysterious reason, been moved from one set of parents to another set of parents had learned well how to deny feeling pain.

MOTHERS

"What do you know about your natural parents?" I asked Gordon.

"Nothing," he replied.

"Nothing," I repeated. "Have you ever tried to find out anything about them?" He shook his head, moved restlessly in his seat. "No, I know where I was born. I know what my name was before I was adopted. But I've never really had any interest in finding out about my biological parents."

"And has your brother or sister done so?"

He blinked, as if startled, then shook his head. "They've never expressed any interest to me. I was four at the time, and my brother was six. My sister was a year and a half." He had, Gordon assured me, no memories that stretched back beyond the age at which he had been adopted by the people he considered to be his parents.

Would he, I asked, describe himself as having been close to his adoptive father? "I would say that I was closer to my father than I was to my mother, but I don't think back to being very close to either one of them," he answered stolidly. His voice sounded unmoved, despite the distressing things being discussed: his adoption, his father's death, his lack of real connection to either parent. "My father was certainly less threatening," he observed with a somewhat supercilious smile.

I looked from him to his wife and then back again. "You sound as if you both have rather threatening mommies," I said.

"My mother is a dragon." Gordon laughed.

I turned to Jo Ann. "Is your mother a dragon, too?"

She seemed taken aback. "Well, it almost sounds like we're talking about the same woman, but we're not. They are totally different. *His* mother is just totally obnoxious, and my mother—"

"*Her* mother will manipulate while mine will just hit you head-on," cut in her husband, with another laugh. "Their styles are totally different." He turned to Jo Ann. "Your mother uses emotional weapons and makes everyone feel sorry for her. Mine is more of an emotional icebox."

"Manipulation . . ." She gazed at him. "Yes, that's a good way to put it."

WHAT A MOTHER IS LIKE

I asked Gordon, at that moment, to picture himself at the age of ten or twelve trying to ask himself the question "Who loves me?" What would the answer have been?

"Probably my father," he replied. "I remember my mother most strongly and dynamically as a disciplinary figure. Very, very cold. My classic childhood memory is of being run off the road and going over an embankment—getting scraped and cut and what not—and coming home and being told by her not to bleed on the carpet!" We laughed; I accused him of having made up the story as a joke!

"No." His large gray eyes were serious behind the rimless frames of his glasses. "Although *she* might look back and say that it was a joke. She's a very cold and distant woman, who's never really learned how to reach out. She grew up in an authoritarian household."

His father, on the contrary, had been an easygoing person, an optometrist with a good independent income of his own.

Gordon and Jo Ann were, then, people who were both used to occupying the same space in the family structure: Each had had a sibling below and a sibling above, and the older sibling was of the same sex. Both had had difficult relationships with their mothers and either softly absent or actually tender relationships with their fathers. "I would suppose," I said to the Kearneys, as the three of us looked at the genogram I was sketching in, "it would be likely that everybody in this family would think it inevitable that mother would become a virago or dragon. And now you, Jo Ann, *are* a mother. Do you worry, ever, about becoming a virago, like these other women here?"

I pointed to the page.

"Am I becoming like my mother?" Her blue eyes grew wide, and Gordon said, "It's what you say you're afraid of."

"Yes," she admitted.

"You talk about that," he continued, as if accusing her. She looked at me and said quietly, "I have said to Gordon a number of times that if I started to act like her, I wanted him to stop me dead in my tracks."

I asked Gordon if he ever worried about that. "I mean, do you worry that a woman will turn into somebody like your mother?"

"I won't tolerate it!" he snapped, and the expression that he'd worn when I first came into the house turned his features back into stone. "I won't tolerate it from anybody else *except* my mother! And on occasion I have to point out to Jo Ann that I think she is acting *like* my mother!"

It was when I inquired, in specific detail, about what those occasions actually were—when his wife behaved in ways that reminded him of his mother—that I first heard about the extramarital affair.

THE CARETAKER AND THE WOUNDED BIRD

Gordon Kearney thought, in retrospect, that he had probably been "close to psychotic" throughout the course of the summer that he and Jo Ann had first met. "I had just been thrown out of Villanova, where I was a student, for radical politics, and to make it even worse, I had had a really bad LSD trip. I mean, looking back, I *know* I was psychotic, but nobody else seemed to be aware of it. And that really bothered me: that I realized I was crazy and no one else knew."

He had stayed a little bit drunk all day long, throughout that summer, because he'd discovered that alcohol was a good antipsychotic medication. "I would just keep up this general level of—" Gordon halted in mid-sentence, then added inanely, "It was a lot of fun."

A moment later, however, he said, "It was probably a fear reaction, to the psychotic episode I'd had when I took the LSD."

He and a friend had, apparently, taken identical dosages, but their responses had been totally different. "I was tripping my brains out eight hours after he'd gone to bed and was peacefully sleeping. That got me pretty nervous. And I was going through feelings of being totally deper-sonalized—looking at my identification with my picture on it and won-dering who I was in relation to that ID."

"That must have been terrifying," I agreed, thinking about how foreign the story sounded in this wall-to-wall-carpeted colonial-style room.

"It was, and then it was just as terrible to come down enough from it to know that there was absolutely no one in the world that I could turn to. I was in Hartford, and I couldn't go home to Wallingford, where my parents lived—they had no idea I *was* in Hartford! So instead, in very ragged shape, I had to turn around with my friend and hitchhike all the way back to Philadelphia, over two hundred miles. It was a pretty weird, disconnected kind of experience . . .impossible, almost, to describe."

In which year of college had he been, I wanted to know, at that particular time? Gordon said that he had been a freshman.

He had, it occurred to me, very probably, been acting out around the trauma of separation. "It sounds," I remarked, "as if you, as soon as you got out from under the virago's watchful eye, were really taking off for the moon. . . ." Gordon's smile was the guarded, coolly rebellious "you can't reach or hurt me" smile that must have been the protective mask he'd worn habitually at that time.

He had clearly been a rage-filled adolescent.

"It was also a reaction to having spent two years in a very restrictive Catholic prep school," he said, his voice becoming flatly explanatory, pedantic. He had left home to go to boarding school during his junior year in high school. It was the same year, I believed (and a glance at the Kearneys' genogram confirmed it), that Jo Ann's father had died. Both had, oddly enough, become "abandoned babies" at a relatively similar historical time.

Gordon, describing his boarding school experience, spoke in tones that became ever drier and more drained of emotion even as the content of the words grew angrier. "My brother went there before I did; he'd gone there for four years. The prep school was, in fact, full of people like my brother and myself; they guaranteed your parents that you would get into college even if you'd just been thrown out of five high schools." He laughed. "It was a school for rich delinquents, as restrictive as being in the army."

"So when you went to college and there weren't those restrictions— you really just spaced out?"

"Yes," he replied. I turned to Jo Ann, asked with a smile, "So what attracted you to this radical, way-out guy?" She laughed somewhat rue- fully. "I don't think," she answered, in a tone that grew increasingly serious as she spoke, "that when I first met him I realized the problem with the drugs that he was having."

Addressing her husband directly, she added, "Even when you de- scribed your behavior at Villanova, I didn't really see it *in you* when we first met!" I asked them how long they had known each other before Gordon had described the problem he'd been having in the wake of taking LSD. It had been within a relatively short period of time—probably, they agreed, within a week.

Gordon had, he believed, been attracted by Jo Ann's sanity and sta- bility. "I knew that I was feeling crazy, that summer, and that nobody else was really noticing. And I needed somebody who was together, de- pendable, who was not, essentially, part of a drug scene or a wild crowd."

He'd been, in other words, a wounded bird that was desperately in need of a caretaker.

THE ROLE OF THE CARETAKER

Why, I asked Jo Ann, had she been so ready and willing to take on that particular job—to take responsibility for someone who was in such turmoil and so unable to take responsibility for himself? She hesitated, for a long while, and then blurted out several possible hypotheses. "I knew he was doing a lot of things that I wished, perhaps, I'd been able to do. It was a difficult time, remember, in the late sixties and early seventies— lots of drugs going around in school. And I was never, myself, able to experiment; I was too afraid of losing control. So here"—she glanced at Gordon, looked awed, and then turned back to me—"I saw a person who was able to do it, and I wanted to know more about it, I guess."

In other words, hypothesis number one was that she'd been the good girl who needs to get the inner badness out into the external world—to contact "badness," in somebody else, who could then carry and express for her those denied parts of her own inner reality. She could say, looking at Gordon, "The rebellious druggie is in you; it's not in me." By seeing and experiencing, in him, projected aspects of her own internal world, she could say *not* "This is what I am" but "This is what I am not." *Gordon* was the uncontrollable, rebellious person that Jo Ann was, at a conscious level, completely unable to be.

She was, however, not unaware that such impulses existed within her.

"Also," she continued, her voice speculative, "here was someone whom I could *take care of* and help. I like that, being able to do that." Her tone of voice was wistful. "But that part of our relationship, as time went on, went out the window . . . because eventually he didn't need that anymore. After he got—" She stopped, and I was unable, mentally, to complete the sentence that she had had in mind.

Hypothesis number two was that Jo Ann felt comfortable taking care of somebody who was "disturbed," "troubled," "sick."

She had, after all, received intensive early training in the role of caretaker of a beloved man who was desperately ill. She was experienced, in terms of knowing how to deal with a dysfunctional male.

An Emotional Deal

Jo Ann and Gordon Kearney had, when they'd married, entered into what could be viewed as an emotional deal—one of those unconscious marital contracts of which psychiatrist Clifford Sager has written so eloquently. She would be the caretaker, or all-giving nurturer, and he would be the inept wounded bird.

What is being agreed to, in such a situation, is that the "doctor" or "nurse" on the partner's case (Jo Ann *was* a nurse!) will be endlessly patient, long-suffering and parental as long as she or he remains the party in control. And, it must be emphasized, the partner who is far less self-revealing and openly known.

Jo Ann's Vow

If, in the marriage ceremony, Jo Ann had verbalized this agreement openly, she would have said, "I promise to care for you, my maladjusted, drug-ridden and disturbed partner, as long as you remain extremely needy and emotionally unwell. But you, on your own part, must agree to *be taken care of* and never to become competent enough to look at your caretaker too closely."

Why does the caretaker of the wounded bird wish, in this fashion, not to be seen? The answer, which is crucial to the understanding of this kind of couple's underlying dynamics, is that the nurturer's self-esteem is usually so low that she is certain that no one in the entire world would ever be able to love her for her own self alone—not, that is, if she ever were to expose her inner self and let her terrible deficiencies and vulnerabilities be realized by the intimate partner.

What the caretaking partner is actually selling—his or her emotional wares, so to speak—is an often exquisite awareness of the needs and sensitivities of the mate.

But an underlying demand, put upon that mate, is that he or she must never get well enough or competent enough to examine the caretaker closely.

The nurturer/endlessly needful person contract is, by the way, common among members of the so-called "helping professions," and very much so among psychiatrists and their wives or husbands.

GORDON'S VOW

If Gordon Kearney had recited his own half of this marriage vow, he would have said things such as the following: "I, in exchange for your love and care, promise always to remain a crazy guy, who spaces out on potentially dangerous and sanity-threatening drugs and who will very probably never be able to live a normal life and hold down a decent job."

What threatens the caretaker/wounded bird relational system—endangers the couple's relationship at the very root of its being—is, paradoxically, the fact that the nurturing person often does so well that the "disturbed" person becomes increasingly functional. The wounded bird is, in other words, not wounded anymore, and the internal stability of the partners' emotional system thereby becomes unbalanced. The very rock upon which the marital agreement has been founded starts to tear loose from its moorings and to look as if it will come tumbling down, taking the entire edifice of the relationship along with it.

For if a caretaker has no wounded bird to care for, she can't be a caretaker anymore. For her the dilemma is: "If I can't take care of this other person, why should he [or anyone in the world, for that matter] ever want me at all?" The ability to nurture is, she (or he) deeply believes, the only attractive thing about her.

And for the wounded bird, the directly opposite question is posed: "If I am no longer wounded, why do I need a caretaker?

"THE BEGINNING OF ONE OF THE WORST YEARS OF OUR MARRIAGE"

Gordon Kearney was, in fact, feeling far better in the summer of 1980 than he'd felt for the previous ten years. A full decade had passed since he'd taken the LSD, and he and Jo Ann had been married for seven years. "My self-image was the best that it had been in a very long while," recounted Gordon. "It was the tenth anniversary of that horrible drug experience, and I hadn't lost my mind. Things were going well: I'd been accepted to law school and graduated magna cum laude from college. I had my act together, and that was the beginning of one of the worst years of our marriage—that time when my self-liking was at its highest."

It was the time of his meeting Nina and the time when the affair began.

8
Marital Infidelity

In the late 1940s and early 1950s, when Kinsey and his co-workers published their landmark findings (in *Sexual Behavior in the Human Male* and *Sexual Behavior in the Human Female*), the statistics on adultery took most people by surprise. In that era of "togetherness"—well before the development of relatively safe, effective contraceptive procedures, the sexual revolution and the women's liberation movement—extramarital experiences were, apparently, not at all uncommon. Kinsey's data indicated that one out of every two husbands, a full 50 percent of the married males surveyed, had engaged in sex with an outside partner before the age of forty. And so had 26 percent of the wives, which is to say one out of every four married females queried had had an extramarital sexual experience by the time they'd reached the same age.

While becoming involved in an affair was widely viewed as shameful and dishonorable behavior (recent surveys indicate that most people's opinions about this haven't changed; they disapprove), many spouses seemed to go ahead and get involved extramaritally *anyway*. Intercourse with a person other than the mate, as all subsequent studies of marital infidelity have demonstrated, is by no means a rare and isolated occurrence; sex outside marriage *happens very frequently*.

The current research on EMS (extramarital sex) suggests that the chances that any marriage will be touched by this issue are very high indeed. For in the decades following the publication of Kinsey's data not only have rates of infidelity among males risen slightly; rates of infidelity among females have also risen *significantly*. In a recent overview of the research on extramarital sex, psychologist Anthony P. Thompson observed that while the incidence of extramarital coitus appeared to be "at least 50% for married men," the "figure for married women is rapidly approaching the same level." This represents a steep increase from the 26 percent infidelity rates among females that the Kinsey workers found in the early 1950s.

All estimates of extramarital sexual activity tend, moreover, to be on the conservative side. For statistics on marital infidelity are notoriously difficult to gather, given the secretive nature of adulterous behaviors. Most experts do, however, consider the "educated guess" of sex researchers G. D. Nass, R. W. Libby and M. P. Fisher—that at the present time some 50 to 65 percent of husbands and 45 to 55 percent of wives become extramaritally involved by the age of forty—to be a relatively sound and reasonable one.

Considering that, in many cases, only *one* of the partners is the philanderer, the number of marital relationships affected by this issue is clearly enormous—on the order of two out of every three marriages, at the minimum! One would imagine that, given the widespread existence of marital infidelity, and the fact that it is the statistical "norm" rather than the isolated exception, many couples would anticipate such problems emerging in their own relationships. By and large, however, they don't.

The discovery, by one partner, that the other is involved in an affair is usually experienced as a totally unexpected and catastrophic event. It is a disaster, like a death—which, in an important sense, it actually is. It is the death of that marriage's innocence, the death of trust, the death of a naive understanding of what the relationship itself is all about.

THE EXTRAMARITAL CRISIS

The vows of emotional and sexual exclusivity have been broken, and the reactions, on the part of the betrayed mate, are shock, anger, panic, and incredulity. The marriage, as he or she knew and understood it, no longer exists, and suddenly, the "haven in a heartless world" feels frighteningly insecure and exposed. A fire storm of fierce emotionality—accusations and anger, on the part of the faithful partner; guilt and defensiveness on the part of the extramaritally involved person—rages throughout the entire relationship.

"By far the largest part of extramarital activity is secret and furtive, violative of the emotional entente existing between the spouses," points out sex researcher R. N. Whitehurst, in summarizing the results of his study of 982 husbands and 1,044 wives. Affairs are "productive of internal conflict and guilt feelings on the part of one engaging in such acts, and anywhere from infuriating to shattering to the other if he or she discovers the truth."

The crisis generated in the marriage, upon the discovery of a partner's extramarital activity, is—like other crises—one characterized by intense psychological strain and profound emotional disequilibrium. Many individuals find it extremely difficult to concentrate, and even to think; they ruminate, and are distracted by thoughts of the affair and the betrayal. One wife whom I interviewed said, for example, that in the week following her discovery of her husband's extramarital affairs, she'd found herself standing in the middle of a department store with no idea why she had gone there or what she had intended to purchase! "I felt," she recounted, "as if the very floor I stood on were moving, waving and buckling underneath me. It was as if I myself, and the world around me, were completely unreal."

The stress experienced during an extramarital crisis can, according to expert Anthony Thompson, result in "physical and behavioral changes. . . . [D]aily living and work routines may be disrupted; some sleep and appetite disturbances may occur [and] depression and suicide can be a risk for fragile personalities."

We may, in this culture, have experienced a revolution in our sexual mores, but most spouses continue to feel intensely afflicted and distressed by a partner's violation of the boundaries around the marital relationship. This is true even in situations in which the deceived mate has himself been the deceiver at an earlier time in the relationship. One husband, who had had a long affair several years before he discovered that his wife was now extramaritally involved, described his own reactions in the following manner: "I felt furious, betrayed; I felt as if I couldn't *trust* her! I felt that there was someone else out there who knew all about me, and who had, for that reason, *triumphed*! He had—even though I didn't know who he was—*bested* me, taken away something that was mine, exclusively!"

This man was angrier at the unknown lover than he was at his wife. His experience was that of having been defeated in a contest with the other man involved in this three-person relationship—and his reaction was by no means atypical. For, as a study carried out by J. L. Francis demonstrates, males do tend to associate their jealous, angry feelings with the rival male in the emotional triangle. Females, on the other hand, tend to associate their feelings of jealousy with a more global, generalized sense of loss—the loss of the partner's attention, caring and concern.

The very existence of the affair has, plainly, transformed the couple's relationship from a two-person into a three-person system—and this triangle is affected by pressures emanating from the third person who has entered the marriage and become part of it. "The identity of the extramarital partner, the degree of emotional involvement, and the nature of the sexual practices are matters of major impact," reports sexual researcher Anthony P. Thompson.

"There is often," writes Thompson, "a tenacious interest in the disclosure of endless details and many spouses exert pressure to know everything. This process is stressful for both partners as queries and disclosures are likely to hit upon areas which are most sensitive and threatening for the married couple. . . ." Kissing and telling can be extremely painful to the betrayed mate, who *needs to know*, and yet finds it hard to tolerate hearing about what actually did happen.

In the wake of the affair's revelation, the comparative status of the two marital partners inevitably changes. The partner who has been involved extramaritally is, to some degree, the one in the more powerful position. For while his spouse feels staggered, helplessly enraged, overwhelmed, and the like, he feels—amid whatever guilt feelings he may be experiencing—victorious and attractive.

His sense of self-esteem may have been enhanced by the relationship, making him feel more likable and confident, while his partner's self-concept will, as a result of the affair's revelation, inevitably be deflated and diminished. The faithful spouse is thus, because she feels hurt, one down and inadequate, at a power disadvantage in the relationship. This may, in fact, have been among the betrayer's motivations for having become involved in the affair in the first place.

WHY DID IT HAPPEN?

One of the most difficult issues that a couple has to deal with, when the infidelity of a partner becomes known, is the whole question of what actually "caused" the affair. Did it have to happen, and if it did, which spouse is the one who is truly to blame? These are the sensitive matters that both partners are struggling to answer for themselves—and often fighting about interminably—in the unsettled weather following the storm of the extramarital affair's revelation. The faithful mate wonders, "Is my partner a sick, disturbed individual, or am I myself sexually inadequate?" She or he also wonders how much the spouse cared (or, worse yet, *cares*) for the other person in the emotional triangle.

Most painful to deal with, though, is the fundamental uncertainty about *why* the affair occurred in the first place. What was going on, inside the marriage, that made going outside it seem to be necessary?

The reasons offered by adulterous spouses, in explanation of their behavior, are bewildering in their multiplicity and variety. They may range, as sexual researcher Frederick Humphrey has reported, from "conquest" to "rebellion" to "combating depression" to "getting promoted" to "being drunk or otherwise under the influence of drugs" to "creating jealousy and gaining attention"—to name just some among the many rationales for marital infidelity that have been offered.

Among the multitude of "causes" cited, however, certain common themes tend to emerge and predominate. In a retrospective study of 750 case histories, clinicians Bernard L. Greene, Ronald R. Lee and Noel Lustig found that sexual frustration, curiosity, revenge, boredom, and the need for acceptance and recognition were the "reasons for the affair" most frequently given.

And researcher Anthony Thompson, in his elegant overview of the literature on extramarital sex, condenses the explanation for marital infidelity even further. The major findings in the field, he observes, consistently demonstrate that the lower the evaluation of the marriage, and the lower the frequency and quality of marital intercourse, the more likely is the development of an affair. There is certainly, he comments, far more fantasizing about extramarital involvements among those people who are less satisfied with their marital relationships.

"It is possible that marital satisfaction and coital satisfaction are the two major variables and that the influence of many secondary marital characteristics are incorporated in these broader evaluations," concludes Thompson. In short, if sex is to be viewd as an important medium of emotional exchange in the relationship, then finding another sexual partner is a way of devaluing the spouse's currency and perhaps rendering it totally worthless. This is what the dissatisfied partner does by going outside the relationship—for adultery *is* a form of communication. It is a way of acting out a message, in the language of behavior, and that message is: "For me, this marriage isn't working."

INTIMACY AND INFIDELITY

An affair may be thought of as an emotional distance regulator. The very existence of a third person in the marital system indicates that the couple is having trouble handling problems of separateness and closeness. According to clinical psychologist Betsy Stone, it is generally the case that in a marriage where one partner is having an outside relationship, the other partner has *also* been fantasizing about becoming involved extramaritally.

What that implies is that there are no real "innocent victims" and "vile offenders," but that who happens to go outside the marriage first has to do with matters of opportunity and timing. Both members of the couple are lusting in their hearts for—or at least dreaming of—other partners, because both are feeling profoundly alienated and disappointed.

An affair is, in this sense, not something that happens *to* somebody; it is something that happens *between two people*. And often it is the weaker spouse who acts first; he or she makes a strengthening move by getting into a coalition with the extramarital partner. Becoming involved in an outside relationship is, for this person, an adaptive maneuver—a way of dealing with the problems in the relationship. The affair itself is a symptom, the symptom of a global marital disturbance; it is not the disturbance itself.

The affair's very existence does, however, indicate that the intimacy in the couple's emotional system is out of balance. Someone is frightened about getting too close, or someone is overly frustrated—hungering for an intimacy that is lacking. Let me say, right away, that the word "intimacy" is not meant to imply candlelight, a table for two in a small bistro, a violinist playing gypsy melodies as the absorbed couple engages in mutually fascinating, intensely romantic conversation. What is meant by "intimacy," in this context, is something different, closer to each person's ordinary reality. Intimacy is, as understood here, an individual's ability to talk about *who he really is*, and *to say what he wants and needs*, and *to be heard by the intimate partner*.

This involves, for instance, a person's being able to tell his mate about how rotten and defeated he happens to be feeling rather than having to pretend to be always masterful and adequate. Or, to take another example, it involves being able to make his sexual needs and friendship choices explicit, rather than remaining inarticulate about them—and then feeling exploited by and angry at the spouse.

If, however, the fear of getting too close (so close that the mate will see and condemn his weakness and failings) is the husband's problem, an affair provides a pseudosolution. For if he has another, secret partner, he is not as close to his wife as he feared he was becoming; she does not know something important about *who he really is*. The furtiveness, secrecy and time constraints upon the outside relationship, moreover, set certain external limits upon the degree of intimacy that can be achieved in the extramarital relationship.

THE UNFAITHFUL WIFE

When, on the other hand, it is the wife who is extramaritally involved, it is usually—though certainly not always—due to a *hunger* for emotional intimacy rather than a wish to avoid it. The wife is someone who, hopelessly outdistanced in her emotional pursuit, has given up the chase and gone outside the marriage to find what the husband will not give her—acceptance, validation of her worth, the willingness to listen to her talk about *who she is, as a person*, and learn about *what she needs and wants*.

For her, as for the emotional distancer, sexuality is not really the primary motivator for the affair. Just as he became involved in an outside relationship in order to avoid the demands of real intimacy, she has gotten into an affair in a desperate attempt to achieve feelings of closeness. With her lover she can, at least, get the physical sensations of touching, hugging; she can be *attended to*. And she can, at the same time, give up the endlessly frustrating pursuit of her endlessly frustrating partner.

When intimacy, in a marriage, is an impossibility—when talking about one's fears, needs, desires, sexual requests, etc., to the partner is out of the question—the unheard person begins feeling powerless, resigned, alienated. The extramarital affair develops as a way of finding a comforter and ally.

The failure of trust, closeness, mutual attentiveness to each other's needs and wishes, inevitably gives way to a desperate struggle between the partners—a struggle for power and control. What the spouses cannot get from each other, by a process of mutually satisfying collaboration and negotiation, each tries to *extract* from the other by means of manipulation and/or force. It is as if the lack of intimacy has created a vacuum at the center of the relationship—and the power struggle rushes in to fill it.

MOTHERS AND LOVERS

Gordon Kearney's mistress was a woman eight years older than he (it did not surprise me to learn this) and a person who was an experienced mother. She—her name was Nina—had three young children and a marriage that was disintegrating at a rapid and frightening pace. (She and her husband subsequently divorced.) It was, however, a certain maternal, wise, warm and comforting quality that I suspected this young husband must have been seeking in another woman—the mother, I mean, who had vanished from her little boy's life and about whom he still denied having feelings of grief, yearning or despair.

It did not surprise me that a child who has had his "real mother" suddenly replaced by a "substitute mother" might, at some point in his life, begin to act out a similar drama regarding a real and a replacement wife. For Gordon, whose natural mother had vanished so bewilderingly when he himself was four years old, any close attachment must have seemed to be provisional. Staging a repetition of the circumstances, with himself as scriptwriter and director, was a way of asserting control over a situation that was, internally, experienced as extremely dangerous.

This time he himself was the abandoner of the intimate other—and perfectly capable of selecting her successor himself. He could, therefore, feel reassured about his own self-sufficiency; he was not dependent upon Jo Ann and could manage and survive without her caretaking.

It was, nevertheless, in the course of our discussion about the ways in which he saw his adoptive mother and Jo Ann as similar that the story of Gordon's love affair suddenly emerged.

Speaking in a dry and somewhat pedantic tone, he'd observed that both his mother and his wife "had a capacity for authoritarian behavior." Did he mean, I responded by asking, that they displayed their anger easily? Instead of answering, he merely smiled. I reworded the question and asked it once again, addressing it not to him alone but to the pair of them. "When somebody in this family is going to get angry, who is that person most likely to be?"

Jo Ann was the one to reply, sounding tense. "If you're talking about being openly angry, then I feel it's usually me. Gordon does not say that he's angry—a lot of times I don't know when he's angry—but *I* show it!" I wondered, Did she mean that she showed it for herself or for the pair of them?

It was almost as if I'd asked the question aloud, for Gordon said coolly, "I don't get into the state that I would describe as 'angry' very often." There was a silence, followed by his amendment to that statement: "On the occasions that I *do* get angry, I get very angry."

"What could get you very angry?" I asked.

"Invasions of privacy," he said.

It was at this point that the story began to spill out—the story of an affair with a fellow student which had, Gordon said, broken up some seven or eight months earlier. The liaison's ending had been brought about by an invasive act: Jo Ann had read about it in a daily journal that her husband kept at that time.

He was infuriated by her having read his journal; it was private territory, in which she had no right whatsoever to venture.

I wondered what had made Jo Ann suspicious enough to think that she might find something worrisome there. "What made you read his journal?" I asked Jo Ann, wanting to know what had been happening between them *beforehand* that might have led her to her discovery. Had he been signaling to her in some subliminal—or obvious—way?

"Well, it wasn't—no, I can't say it wasn't intentional," she answered, sounding guilty. "He had left it out on the table, on top, with a bunch of books, and I went to grab one of the books—"

"The table being my desk," intervened her husband, laughing a brief dismissive laugh.

"Yes, his desk. Oh—no—I didn't go to grab a book; it was my calculator, which was stuck underneath it. And when I pulled it out, the books all fell. Picking them up, I saw a picture of a woman—the diary had opened to that page, because it was heavier with the picture—and she was someone whom I didn't know. At that point, I couldn't close it, put it back, and just say, 'I'll let this go.' So I read it." She sounded strained and deeply embarrassed.

It was my own opinion that she wouldn't have been human if she hadn't done so, given that particular set of circumstances. "Gordon feels, to this day," said Jo Ann, "that I should have closed the book and put it back."

I turned to him and said, "Suppose—" but his wife interrupted, saying forcefully, "I still say, if it happened again, I would do the same exact thing!"

"Suppose," I asked him, "the same thing had happened to you? I mean, suppose that Jo Ann's journal dropped, fell open, and you saw a picture of a man you didn't know? Would you have shut the book, put it away and forgotten it?"

"Yes." He didn't hesitate before replying. "I have memories of my childhood—my mother would sometimes open my mail—and privacy is something so deeply ingrained in my being that it would never *occur to me* to read somebody else's diary. Jo Ann leaves her own journal all over the house. On occasions I've had to move it to get it out of my way when I was doing something, and it would never occur to me to open it—not even after having had my own journal read. I just would not do that."

"So you both keep daily journals?"

"I haven't," said Jo Ann in a low voice, "since all this began." I asked her why, and she replied, "Because it would be too painful. I just can't write it down."

"And I no longer keep a journal," put in Gordon, his voice outraged. "In fact, I burned ten years' worth of my journals! And I don't keep one now, even though I often wish that I could—because I found it such an effective means of charting my course and of seeing how I was responding to the things going on in my life. But now, I don't—I can't—because there's an overwhelming fear of her reading my journal again!" There was, I realized, a hint of panic or outright hysteria lurking in the back of his voice.

To what extent, I wondered, was his rage at his "real mother" (whose abandonment of her four-year-old son did not seem to be a matter of interest or concern to the adult Gordon, now married and a father himself) being displaced onto his "real wife" in this current relationship?

The Injured Party

The conversation had, I thought, gone off in a bizarre and unexpected direction. Instead of talking about Gordon's marital betrayal and its subsequent effects upon each of the partners, we were talking about Jo Ann's invasion of his diary! And of his subsequent inability to keep one! The whole thing had an inside-out, Alice in Wonderland quality.

"You seem," I observed, my voice somewhat wry, "to be as injured by her having read your diary as she is by your having been unfaithful. . . ."

Gordon, though, did not hear the wryness in my tone. "I *was* as furious about her reading my journal as she was about my having the affair," he agreed, his own voice high and charged with emotion. Jo Ann was, technically speaking, "the injured party," but he sounded more injured than she did.

I looked at his wife—or attempted to—but could not meet her lowered eyes.

Although Gordon had obviously been the transgressor in the accepted sense, there seemed to be some mutual acceptance, on both their parts, that what had happened was *her* fault and her responsibility. How had it come about that the guilt and blame that were actually his, for having gotten involved in an outside relationship, were less than the guilt and blame that were hers, for having discovered it in the particular way that she had?

Caretakers and Wounded Birds

I wasn't sure what the answer to that question might be, but suspected that it had to do with her caretaker status. Caretakers, after all, do just that: *take care and take responsibility*, including responsibility for events that are utterly beyond their control. Jo Ann Kearney, by taking on the blame for what had gone wrong in her world, was maintaining the illusion that she was in charge in ways that she really was not. Caretakers think that nothing happens without their having allowed it to or made it happen—and they assume guilt easily. Wounded birds, on the other hand, tend to externalize blame, and instead of feeling guilty they find fault. Thus, with one partner taking too much, and the other too little responsibility, the relationship finds its skewed—and all too uncomfortable—equilibrium.

"I KEPT GETTING THE FEELING THAT HE WAS STILL SEEING HER"

My conversation with the Kearneys, that first evening, went on for an unusually long time and became almost painfully brutal at one point.

Jo Ann was describing her discovery of Gordon's affair.

"I'd just learned, two weeks earlier," she said, "that I was pregnant—something we'd been trying for, and even seeing a *specialist* about, for the past two years. So there were a lot of emotions running around in my head. I guess one of my first impulses, after finding out about his"—she halted, suddenly, in mid-sentence, then went on after inhaling and exhaling a long breath of air. "After finding out about Gordon's other relationship, my first impulse was to want to go off and have a fling myself—almost for revenge, more than anything else! But I was pregnant, and I couldn't see doing *that* while I was pregnant. Then I even considered terminating the pregnancy. I don't know how serious I was, as a believing Catholic, about actually having an abortion. But I definitely *did* give it some thought.

"Because," she murmured almost as an afterthought, "I didn't know if we could continue the marriage after that. It came down, finally, to my saying, 'Either you break off total contact with this woman, or I leave. And that's the only way it's going to be!' "

Gordon had, apparently, urged his wife to permit his relationship with Nina to continue "on just a friendship level," but Jo Ann had not been able to tolerate the idea. "I just couldn't deal with that," she said.

The position Jo Ann had taken was that if their marriage was to endure, Gordon had to break off all relations with Nina—a condition to which he had finally acceded. "Throughout the next year, though, I kept getting the feeling that he was still seeing her. It was . . . oh, little things that were left around. I kept accusing him, too, of doing it—of continuing the affair—but I always ended up feeling guilty after our blowups, sorry that I'd ever raised the subject. Then," here Jo Ann paused to draw in another long, jagged breath of air, "after that had gone on for *an entire year*, I found out that all along I'd actually been *right*. And there I was, with a three-month-old infant. I felt totally lost."

There was an extended, heavy silence. I turned to Gordon, and asked, "So what are your feelings about Nina now—at this moment, I mean?"

He looked at me, stared at me, but he offered no reply.

Changing tactics, I asked him to tell me what Nina was like as a person. He responded as if to an interview survey, repeating some and adding a few new superficial details: She was now divorced, forty-one years old, and had two children; one of them had a learning disability, a serious case of dyslexia. "She is working on her M.B.A. [master's degree in business administration] and her main interest is in organizational psychology," Gordon added stiffly. "I'm not sure what other descriptive terms you want."

I wanted, I repeated, to know what she was like as a person.

His voice, when he spoke again, was altered; he sounded much more engaged and alive. "She's a very compassionate, empathic person—*very* intelligent, honor society, and all that; a very attractive woman." I looked swiftly at his wife, who'd leaned back in her seat, white-faced, as if she'd just been struck a blow. We passed a terrible few seconds before I asked Gordon quietly but directly what his feelings about that relationship were, right now. "Is it in the past, or am I mistaken when I get the impression that it's all still very much an issue in your mind?"

He, by way of an answer, explained that just about the time Jo Ann had discovered that the relationship had continued, Nina had been in the process of filing for a divorce. "She—Nina—became furious with me over my carelessness, because she was afraid it might impact on her pending custody suit. So I—well, it left a bad taste in my mouth that a friendship that had gone on for a long time, in spite of a lot of problems, would end on that kind of bitter note." The only warmth in his voice at this moment was provided by the small flame of outrage it contained.

He had, by means of some strange sorcery, transformed himself into the injured party once again.

"How Was I Inadequate?"

I said nothing and merely sat quietly, waiting for his wife to respond. When she did, however, it was clear that she'd not heard a word he had said after that description of his ex-mistress.

Almost as if in a trance, she was staring fixedly at Gordon. "Those words you used to describe her . . . when you were talking before, I mean . . . 'empathic,' 'compassionate,' 'intelligent,' 'attractive' . . . they're the exact words you've used, at times, when you were describing *me*."

It was not so much a statement as a cry of protest.

Gordon looked at her, saying nothing; his expression was at once quizzical and frightened. Jo Ann's voice, when she resumed speaking, was lower and sounded slightly muffled. "And that makes me wonder . . . it confuses me. Because if we're so *similar* in those ways, how was I inadequate—unable to satisfy your needs, emotionally, myself? What is *wrong* with me that I couldn't do that—be enough for you, I mean?" Her voice continued dropping, as she spoke, so that I had to lean forward to hear.

"And there's a lot of anger in me, too," she added, turning away from him to address her words to me, as if this part of her message to her husband had to be delivered indirectly. "Because I feel that I am—less of a woman somehow, since he had to go out of the marriage and find someone else." I believed her when she said that she was angry, but realized that the energetic, assertive force with which hostile emotions are usually expressed was completely missing from her posture, expression and tone of speech. She sounded more ashamed than anything else.

The Party at Fault

Driving away, much later, I thought about the manner in which these partners handled guilt and responsibility—i.e., he handed it to her, and she took it over completely. It hadn't even been necessary, in the interchange about who bore the ultimate blame for Gordon's affair, for him to ask his wife to be the party at fault; Jo Ann herself had actively campaigned for the job.

But it wasn't these thoughts that preoccupied my mind primarily. It was, instead, a visual image of that frozen tableau in the Kearneys' Colonial-style living room—particularly of the devastated expression on Jo Ann's face when Gordon had described his ex-lover. Fixated, mentally, upon that image, I had a sudden illumination. I felt, irrationally and yet with utter certitude that Gordon Kearney and his mistress were still very much involved at this time.

I knew it, for reasons that I could not fathom, and yet hoped against hope that I was mistaken.

9
Emotional Triangles

As everyone knows, a triangle is a simple three-sided geometrical form. But for those who study the ways in which small emotional systems operate, this configuration has assumed a special importance. Although I have, in the discussion of the perverse triangle, already described a particular *type* of triangle, let me say more about what triangling is all about.

An emotional triangle is an ongoing, repetitive cycle of interactions that involves three people. Triangles develop, as a number of systemic theorists have noted, when a problem that *two* people are having cannot be talked about (much less resolved); the focus of their attention needs to be diverted onto something outside the dangerous area—outside their own tense relationship. Triangling in a third party (a lover, a child, an in-law, or even a therapist) offers a means of deflecting or detouring, but in any case *lowering the intensity* of the primary conflict.

Emotional triangles come into being because they offer a disaffected and distressed couple a way of *not* confronting the problems and disappointments that one or both of them are simply too scared to think about, much less talk about openly. By enlarging the conflict in such a way that *three* people are involved, the tensions in the relationship can often be successfully obscured from every one of the people involved. And while getting into a triangle inevitably commits the pair to a series of endlessly repeated skirmishes, it helps them stave off the all-out battle which might well end in the total defeat of one of them or the destruction of the emotional system itself.

FAMILY TRIANGLES

The mere mention of a triangle usually evokes the notion of the "eternal triangle," the romantic threesome involving a couple and an intimate other (who, once she or he has made an appearance, is usually seen as the cause of all the painful dilemmas in the original relationship). But love triangles, as I mentioned earlier, are just one among the various kinds of triadic situations that exist. Less noticeable and dramatic, but nevertheless ubiquitous, are the emotional triangles that develop within ordinary, everyday families—among mothers, fathers and children, for example.

Dr. Murray Bowen has postulated that because two-person relationships are so inherently volatile and difficult to maintain in a balanced state, triangles inevitably occur within any emotional system (and an emotional system is what every family *is*). In his view there are always, in triangular situations, two closely involved players and one person in an outside position.

"Patterns vary," writes psychiatrist Bowen, "but one of the most common is basic tension between the parents, with the father's gaining the outside position—often being called passive, weak, and distant—leaving the conflict between the mother and the child." Although the original difficulty was in the parents' relationship, the father can remove himself from the battle and hold the coats while his wife and child fight it out.

This trilateral pattern of relating is described as the "family projection process" by Dr. Bowen. The difficulty has been removed from the arena of the couple's relationship and is now, by means of projection and displacement of the conflict, seen as friction, strife and contention between a parent and child. "Families replay the same triangular game over and over for years, as though the winner were in doubt," he observes, "but the final result is always the same. Over the years the child accepts the always-lose outcome more easily, even to volunteering for this position. A variation is the pattern in which the father finally attacks the mother, leaving the child in the outside position. The child then learns the techniques of gaining the outside position by playing the parents off against each other."

WHY TRIANGLES FORM

What are the underlying advantages, to the distancing and disaffected marital partners, of having gotten into a triangle in the first place? The answer to that question is that when anxiety rises, in a two-party relationship, the couple's possible responses are otherwise limited in nature. The partners can: (1) resolve the issues by confronting and dealing with their relational dilemmas or (2) be forced, as the emotional pressures escalate beyond endurance, to end the relationship completely. Bringing a third person into the interaction allows for a variety of responses other than these two polar extremes (i.e., settle it or break up).

A three-person group allows for a number of different coalitions. Any two of the individuals can join together, covertly or overtly, against the third member of the triangle. The perverse triangle—which involves a covert alliance between a parent and a child, who band together to undermine the other parent's power and authority—is just one among many triangular configurations that might develop. Another was described in the example above, in which the original conflict between the parental couple was being detoured in such a way as to become an ongoing quarrel between the mother and the child. A couple's distress, when handled in this roundabout manner, can find expression in fights that don't threaten the existence of the marriage itself.

PARENTS AGAINST CHILD

In still another kind of mother-father-child triangle, the marital partners are able to unite around the problems they are having with their "bad," incorrigible child. In this sort of circumstance, familiar to most therapists, the couple usually sees themselves as lovingly in unison; they have no difficulties aside from the ones that they are having with their unmanageable offspring.

"One may find," writes clinician Lynn Hoffman, "an unalterable pattern around the 'bad' behavior of a child." Hoffman's schematic rendering of such a repeating cycle is given in the following example: "Stage one: Mother coaxes, child refuses to obey, mother threatens to tell father (father-mother against child). Stage two: When father comes home, mother tells him how bad child has been, and father sends child to his room without supper."

Then, however, mother sneaks up after father has left the table, bringing the child a little food on a plate. The new and second configuration of the triangle, notes Hoffman, is now mother-child against father. The next part of the sequence, she continues, is Stage three: "When child comes down later, father, trying to make up, offers to play a game with him that mother has expressly forbidden because it gets him too excited before bedtime (father-child against mother)." Finally, at Stage four, mother scolds father while the child, "overexcited indeed, has a tantrum and is sent to bed; and the original triangle comes round again (mother-father against child)."

In the above instance, while the mother and father appear to be in harmony, there is covert dissension between them which is being worked out through the ongoing struggles with their "misbehaving" child. The parental couple need not, I should mention, be deflecting any particular and specific conflict onto the offspring: Their distress might have to do, more globally, with underlying feelings of futility and emotional impoverishment which both of them are experiencing. There may be a sense of deadness within the relationship that neither partner would dare to talk about—or perhaps even to think about, consciously. Getting into a triangle helps the pair to relieve some of their latent, suppressed emotionality without approaching the Pandora's box of their unmet needs or confronting directly their own feelings of disconnection. Fighting with their child also adds some excitement to an atmosphere that has become lifeless and flat—because the unsayable and the unsaid have a way of sucking up all of the available energy and vitality.

Getting into a triangle with one of their children enables the marital partners' underlying uncertainties and anxieties to be contained for a period of time. Eventually, though, the developing child will—owing to the biological and psychological push toward separation and individuation that increasing maturity inevitably brings—struggle to get out of the repetitious three-person game. The other parties involved, whose own conflict is being handled and rerouted through that particular child, will experience alarm and will frequently react by attempting to block their offspring's self-differentiating efforts. This occurs *not* as part of any manipulative plan but at an automatically reactive level.

For, should the third member of the triangle manage to leave the field, the tense pair's preexisting problems and difficulties would predictably return and intensify. *Their* conflict, which the triangular situation has served to cover over, will now have to be confronted and resolved, or the family system itself may be destroyed. At such a juncture, the offspring—whose natural impulse toward increasing independence is running counter to his parents' need to keep him in his special position—is highly likely to develop "symptoms" of some sort.

The triangulated child becomes involved in either destructive or self-destructive behaviors, and lo and behold, it is not the spouses but their *offspring* who is deeply troubled and perturbed! What's more, the couple can often unite around caring for their depressed, or phobic, or anorexic offspring—or, alternatively, unite around fighting with their promiscuous, drug-taking, thieving or otherwise delinquent child. The marital problem, whatever it may be, remains well underground and out of sight.

The existence of the triangle enables the pair to avoid facing the ultimate questions that concern them, and this is, of course, why the triangle has come into being in the first place. It is often easier for marital partners to discuss (or fight wildly about) the intolerable behavior of a child than it is to discuss feelings of rage, grief, disappointment and discontent about the relationship they share. Such feelings, because they're perceived as so threatening to the emotional system as a whole, tend to be avoided—for they are experienced as unbearably dangerous.

THREE-LEGGED TABLES

Triangles develop as a self-protective reflex on the part of the emotional system itself—the system which is struggling to maintain its own ongoing integrity, equilibrium and balance. One way of thinking about triangles, suggested to me by marital therapist Stuart Johnson, is to visualize them as three-legged tables. A three-legged table is, obviously, easier to keep in a balanced state than is a two-legged table—or relationship—which is far less stable by nature. A tripod provides a far sturdier and more secure base.

Thus it is that when a couple's distress barometer happens to be on the rise, adding on that third table leg is a most understandable response. Getting into a triangle is part of a natural effort to preserve the emotional system as it is—to counter changes which may menace it or lead to its eventual demise. But triangles do prevent the system from changing in *either* direction—prevent things from becoming better and improving as well as from getting worse.

TRANSIENT TRIANGLES

Triangular situations, of a transient sort, obviously abound in the everyday world. If, for instance, two friends were experiencing tension in their relationship and preferred not to discuss that tension, they might easily fall into a discussion of a *third* person in which all their negative feelings and anxieties could be vented. They would thus be adding a "third leg" to the table of the relationship between them, stabilizing it by drawing closer over the issues related to that third, outside individual. What they would *not* have achieved is, however, any direct resolution of the problems between them.

In this kind of situation, the creation of a triangle—which helps the tense twosome to circumvent their difficulties—might be eminently adaptive. There are certainly many circumstances in which navigating around the difficulties is the most astute and wise thing that both people could possibly do. But in the triangles that emerge among intimates who are connected by blood or marriage, the individuals involved tend to become stuck in repetitive, rigid and painful relational roles.

FAMILY LIGHTNING RODS

The triangle involving a set of parents and a child is one that is extremely common. Children become, in an emotionally reflexive fashion, the small lightning rods that bring down upon themselves all the electrical charges that exist in a particular family environment. So, very commonly, do in-laws. As family therapist Monica McGoldrick has written:

> Among the problematic triangles for the couple, the one between husband, wife and mother-in-law is probably the most renowned.
>
> In-laws are easy scapegoats for family tensions. It is always much easier to hate your daughter-in-law for keeping your son from showing his love than to admit your son doesn't respond as much as you wish he would. It is easier for a daughter-in-law to hate her mother-in-law for her intrusiveness than to confront her husband directly for not defining a strong enough marital boundary to keep his mother from interfering. In-law relationships are a natural arena for displacing tensions in the couple or in the family of origin of each spouse.

The triangles that develop between the parental couple and the new couple may mean trouble in the senior twosome, in the younger twosome, or in both.

THE STABILIZING LOVER

It may seem odd to think of the "eternal triangle" in the way one thinks about the triangles that have been discussed above, but it is not fundamentally dissimilar. The Other Woman or the Other Man is, frequently, introduced into a situation as a means of handling otherwise unbearable tensions that exist within the marital relationship itself.

The lover, although one doesn't tend to view his or her presence in this fashion, is often brought into the picture as a way of *keeping a shaky twosome together* when they're in danger of flying apart. Becoming involved with someone outside the relationship is, at times, similar to adding that third leg to a table that's about to fall over with a resounding crash. The third person provides a middle alternative—a way of dealing with the difficulties other than the starker options of facing the problems and dealing with them directly or of ending the marriage completely.

The lover, curiously enough, often serves a stabilizing function (at least in the early phase of the affair); the involvement keeps the couple's relationship in place by diluting its emotional intensity. What has happened is that, psychically speaking, a third person—invisible to one of the partners—has been brought into the room. The person involved in the outside relationship is now in a secret coalition with the lover, and this permits him to distance himself from the painful pressures being experienced in the relationship with the spouse.

He can, no matter how problematic the interaction with the partner, console himself with thoughts of his unknown alliance. He can say to himself, "I don't have to care about what goes on in this place," and "I am not really involved here." He is thus able to avoid or forestall confronting the troubles in the marriage directly; the third person has rendered the difficulties with the mate bearable because the mate no longer matters so desperately. The existence of the triangle, even though one participant is unaware of it, often buys some time for a distressed relationship in which the basic issues are being scrupulously avoided.

BEFORE NINA

Gordon Kearney observed, in the course of our discussions, that the most immediate effect of starting the affair with Nina had been a damping down of the escalating pressures that he was experiencing in the relationship at home. And both he and Jo Ann had acknowledged, in the course of our conversation, that their "communication had been extremely dysfunctional" (i.e., they had stopped really talking to each other) long before Nina had ever entered their lives. Gordon's mistress represented both a problem for the young couple and an effort to circumvent the problems that already existed. Getting into a triadic situation made it possible to discuss "the problem in their relationship" (his affair with Nina) without discussing "the problems in their relationship" which came from within and which had preexisted Nina's appearance.

The hardest task they faced would be, I suspected, getting Gordon's mistress out of the center of their relationship, because then the Kearneys would have to face their difficulties directly—an idea which, it seemed to me, was terrifying to both of them.

"HE'LL NEVER BE RESPONSIBLE"

The next time that I met with Jo Ann Kearney it was a hot summer afternoon, and the two of us were alone. Susannah slept in her bedroom throughout the early part of the interview, and Gordon was not (by prearrangement) at home. Had it not been for my tape recorder, sitting on the cocktail table, it might have been a meeting between two neighbors; we sipped tall glasses of iced coffee as we talked. Jo Ann was dressed in white shorts and a white T-shirt, as if, even when she was away from work, her leisure wear had to be that of a nurse.

One of the troublesome things about her marriage was, she told me, the fact that so many of the everyday household responsibilities were hers. "This summer has, especially, brought it out; it's been hard to keep up with things. Gordon may be getting a job. . . . It's up in the air . . . but it disturbs me that he doesn't work and I carry the main brunt of the financial dealings. He does have—he *relies* on his trust funds and draws allowances from that source, but as far as his being responsible goes, I don't know if he ever will be! Will hold down a job, I mean, when he graduates from law school." She pursed her lips disapprovingly, shrugged to indicate that her man was an impossible child.

"What makes you think that?" I asked, and a doubtful expression crossed her face. "He procrastinates so much that I don't think he'll ever—" She stopped, shrugged again. "He wants to go into business for himself, and if he does I don't think he'll get much done, because he *is* such a great procrastinator."

I took a sip of coffee and wondered if it were her fear (or hope) that he would never become a competent adult. "He would love to stay in school for the rest of his life," she continued, after a brief pause, "if only he could. And he relies a lot on the money that his family has, which we will eventually, I suppose, inherit. But as far as the responsibility of even running the household finances goes—budgeting and so forth—it's all my job, and he doesn't even know the first thing about it!" She laughed. "If I were in the hospital for a week or so, and he had to take care of the finances, he would be *stuck*. He just wouldn't be able to handle it!" She laughed again, but she sounded annoyed.

"So," I said musingly, "you are having to be supercompetent and he's having to be not quite competent, and that's the way things have settled down in this relationship?"

"He lets things slide a lot," she agreed.

"And you can't do that?" She nodded; for her, letting things slide was an impossibility. They were fighting a lot these days—about money as well as about Gordon's affair.

Picking up on that last remark, I asked her if she was worried that he might still be in love with Nina. Jo Ann nodded. "I think he is, and I suppose I can't expect him to get over it this quickly," she replied. "It only ended a couple of months ago, and it *does* worry me a lot. I suspect"—she met my gaze for a frightened instant—"that even now he is seeing her. But I suppose"—a quick shake of her head was a negation of that thought—"that I'm going to have those sorts of suspicions for a while. . . ." Her cheeks were bright pink under the light brown coating of her tan.

"HIS WILLINGNESS TO LISTEN"

The two of us were quiet for a few moments. A quietly whirring floor fan played across her face and hair and then played across my own. "That feels wonderful," I remarked. I thought about some of the things that had been said in the course of our first, very long interview. Jo Ann, in discussing those qualities in Gordon that had drawn her to him initially, had dwelt upon his "sophistication" and his "willingness to listen without making judgments."

Making judgments about what? I had inquired. "Nothing dramatic" was her reply. But she'd gone on to say that she had told him about the whole situation in her home, during her father's long terminal illness—something that she'd never discussed with any other man she'd dated. "That was a very traumatic time for me, and yet I could talk to him about it from the very beginning." Gordon had been empathetic. He would listen and was able to hear her tell him what that long dying, that death and its aftermath had been like.

I reminded Jo Ann now about this part of our earlier conversation. "When the three of us talked, you mentioned that what had attracted you to Gordon most were his sophistication and his ability to hear you out about a very painful period of your life. How do you see each of those aspects of your relationship, having been married for"—I glanced at the genogram on my lap—"for just a little over eight years? His sophistication and his ability to listen, I mean. Are they still there, and are they still as important?"

"He still listens to me," she answered, "but the painful parts of my life are what he has done to me—and he'll listen to other things, but not to that part." He was not, she added after a moment's reflection, as empathetic as he once had been. "The sophistication is there, perhaps even more than it *was*. . . ." There was such ruefulness in the way that she uttered this last remark that I asked her at once whether that sophistication made him seem more out of reach. "Does he use it to make distance between you?" I inquired.

"Distance?" She gave me a startled look, then said, "*Yes*. I never looked at it like that, but it's definitely something that he does!"

An Adult, Not a Daughter

I waited for a moment to see if Jo Ann had something else to say, but she didn't. Then I asked her if, when she'd married, the timing of the marriage had been influenced by a desire to leave home. She smiled, shrugged a shrug of admission: "I wouldn't say that it was the main objective, but it had something to do with it."

"What was going on that you wanted to get away from?" I asked, and she said, "Just that my mother is very domineering. Just that I wanted to get out from under her thumb." She had wanted to set up a place of her own where she could be an adult and not a daughter. "Couldn't you have moved out and done that without being married?" I asked.

She shook her head. "Looking back, I wish I had . . . lived on my own before I got married, but my mother would not have accepted that." I pointed out that she had been over twenty-one years of age and had had a profession of her own, but Jo Ann merely shook her head again. "What you say is true," she acknowledged, "but all of us have had trouble breaking away . . . all the children. And living by yourself before you marry is something that she doesn't see as being necessary. So it's either stand up and do it or stay at home and avoid all the grief!" Jo Ann had not been brave enough to do the former and still wasn't sure that the latter course would have been the less painful one to take.

"In other words, then," I commented, "getting married was the solution to a certain problem called 'I would like to leave home.' " Yes, she admitted, that had been part of it. At the present time, she was embroiled in a furious quarrel with *Gordon's* mother. "I just don't get along with her, and I have a very hard time dealing with her when I have to be there! We were just in Florida, where she lives during the winter, and the plan was that Gordon would drive her back to Connecticut, and Susannah and I would fly home. On the way out to the airport, she—my mother-in-law and I—had one big blowout of a fight. When I got on the plane, I was *crying*. I've seen her only once since then, and it's very proper and cool. *I* feel as if I've tried to talk with this woman—gone out to lunch and to plays with her—but we just can't communicate with one another!"

Jo Ann was in touch with her anger at this moment.

I wanted to know whose side her husband tended to take. "He sides with me, although he does tell me that I should stand up to her more."

"And does he stand up to her?"

"No," she answered with certainty.

Gordon wanted her, I thought, to do for him what he could not do for himself: handle all the suppressed hot stuff between him and his domineering, emotionally unavailable parent.

The three of them were, in other words, in an emotional triangle in which Jo Ann and Gordon's mother were to carry on the quarrel while Gordon himself became the referee or onlooker—the person in the outside position.

The triangle involving the Kearneys and Gordon's lover, Nina, was—like the above relationship—a triangle comprised of two females and a male. And although Nina was not a member of the older generation, she was Gordon's senior by almost a decade. The familiar story had to do with the tension in a marriage becoming transformed into a quarrel between a younger woman and an older woman, who were competing for the love of a man.

If the Kearneys' marriage endured, one could predict that the triangle involving two fighting females—and a male in the more distant, remote position—was very likely to emerge once again. It would, in its new incarnation, involve strife between Jo Ann and Susannah, perhaps, with Gordon serving as the unemotional, eminently objective and logical umpire.

But in the meanwhile it was Nina, the other woman in the triangle, who occupied the center of their lives.

"THE SEXUAL PART HAS BEEN AMAZING"

Gordon and his lover had become acquainted some two years earlier, when they were students in a course on psychiatry and the law, a subject in which both were extremely interested. Gordon's ambition was, in fact, to become a lawyer working on behalf of mental patients who are involuntarily incarcerated.

That same summer, Gordon and Jo Ann had been seeing medical specialists about her failure to become pregnant; they were, however, having very little sex. At that time, and for the couple of years which preceded it, they were making love infrequently. And after the affair with Nina began, the Kearneys often went for an entire month without having sexual relations. "I would be aggressive from time to time, but I was always being pushed aside. Looking back, I believe that when he *did* sleep with me, it was with the thought 'I'll do it just to get her off my back.' " At the present time, she added without meeting my eyes and with a small, nervous giggle, their lovemaking occurred several times every week.

"It's a very drastic change," she commented. "Since this whole thing has been happening—but especially after the second time I found out—the sexual part has been amazing. It hadn't been like that for years and years. And it's continued. . . . I'd made him move out for a few days, when I discovered that he was seeing her again, and when we got back together, I didn't expect—well!" Jo Ann gave a great shrug, as if to say that this newfound physical fulfillment gave her great happiness but was completely beyond her understanding.

Such honeymoon experiences, following the revelation of an affair, are not at all unusual. For, in the wake of the emotional volcano that erupts, the tensions in the marriage become readily apparent. And despite the damage that has been done, there are often feelings of relief; things are, at last, out in the open. A great many molten resentments, which simmered deep within the relationship, have been released, and the partners are often talking as they have not talked for months, years, or—in some cases—decades.

A lot of mutual sexual interest seemed, I remarked, to have been kindled by Gordon's affair. Jo Ann nodded, said that she'd been unable to explain this to herself. "I expected the opposite to happen. I don't understand it. But as I said, previous to all of these blowups, I was usually the aggressor, sexually, and now it seems that Gordon usually is. It's turned around a lot."

It had, I thought, in one important respect: He clearly felt more powerful and in charge.

So there had been a few diamonds under the pile of horse manure that had been dumped into the center of the relationship! Nina's appearance on the scene had shifted the power balance in the Kearneys' system—had turned it upside down, completely. Now Jo Ann was the wounded one and Gordon was the person in command; and this new situation had, it seemed, unleashed a surge of mutual sexual feeling. His mistress was, in a way, the ace that Gordon held over his wife's head—that let her know that he could survive if he ever did choose to leave the relationship. ——

LIES

Jo Ann was, she told me, more disturbed and upset by the lying than she was by anything else. "I don't know how to trust him now," she complained. He had begun the affair in the summer before she'd found out that she was pregnant, and she'd found out about that relationship two weeks after discovering that she and Gordon were going to become parents. "He wanted to continue seeing her as a friend, and I said 'No!' I said, 'It's either break it off completely or it's Out!' He said he'd break it off, and from what I can gather, he did so for about three weeks. Then they started seeing each other again."

She glanced at me, a strange, quick glance whose meaning I couldn't interpret. "He says that the past year was purely platonic," she murmured in a flat, expressionless voice.

"Do you believe that?" My voice was equally expressionless.

She didn't answer for a few moments, and when she did, her voice was doubtful. "Maybe they did not have sex, but . . . a platonic relationship is a friendship, and I think that—in their feelings and emotions—they were more than just platonic."

I repeated my question, this time more explicitly. "Do you think that they were, or were not, having sex?" Jo Ann shrugged; she believed that it *hadn't* been a sexual relationship during the period dating from her reading of Gordon's journal to her recent discovery that the relationship with Nina had continued. I was surprised that she could believe that.

"I'm not so clear about what was going on in her life during this time," the young mother was saying, "aside from her having started proceedings for the divorce. I don't know when she separated. . . . From one thing of Gordon's that I read, I got the impression that if she'd given him the opportunity, he would have moved in with her, but this is something he denies. It's just that—oh!—being pregnant, and having a child, and all the lies surrounding the whole thing! It's very difficult to get over . . . you would think that your first pregnancy and your first child are something so special to share!" She leaned forward, as if in supplication for my understanding. "And so, to ruin all of that with this other nonsense going on all the time!"

BIRTHDAY PRESENTS

As if to do something with her hands, Jo Ann lifted her glass of iced coffee to her lips; her hand trembled slightly and she put the glass down without having bothered to sip. "I blame him a lot for that—for making my whole pregnancy a disaster. Full of suspiciousness, because I kept finding odd things. If I borrowed his car, I'd find a bottle of wine in it, and a bag of stuff for a picnic. . . . If I confronted him, though, he'd deny up and down that he'd ever seen her again."

I shrugged. "It's funny, clues left everywhere, messages for you to follow up."

"He denies that!" She leaped eagerly on what I had just said. "I've said it myself, but he denies it completely!"

The message that she *had* received, ultimately, had been literally left for her at their front door. Jo Ann, returning from work one evening, had tripped over a small airline bag in which Gordon carried his books and heard a strange clinking noise; it was the sound of breaking glass. She had opened the bag, found it full of wrapped presents and two wineglasses (one now broken) and a bottle of liqueur. Gordon had been inside the house, asleep.

"I opened the presents, and—this is one of the reasons why I'm suspicious about the platonic relationship—one of them was a teddy." She looked at me assessingly. "Do you know what that is? A camisole, with snaps down the front? *Her* birthday and my birthday are actually just a week apart, and Gordon had bought me a very lacy, sexy one; I'd asked for it. Her present was the same camisole, exactly the same style . . . understand?"

I nodded that I did.

There was a rat-tat-tat sound coming from outside, and Jo Ann jumped up and went to look out the window. "Firecrackers," she said. "The neighborhood kids are setting them off, for the Fourth of July." It was July 3, and Independence Day was tomorrow. "There was more," she continued. Another present, wrapped to give to his lover, was a small picture that Gordon himself had painted. "The week before this, my baby had been in the hospital with an intussusception. The bowel telescopes on itself, and if it's not corrected within twenty-four hours you begin to develop gangrene of the bowel, and there's a high mortality rate connected with it if it's not picked up immediately. The bowel dies . . . and the two of us were frightened and under a lot of stress. Understand?" she asked me again.

Again I nodded my head, urging her to continue. "Susannah had been at Stamford Hospital for almost a week, and this same painting—which had mushrooms, a little house, a tree—was something that he'd put in her crib for her to look at, so she would be able to enjoy the colors. And he'd wrapped that up to give to *her* as a gift—which upset me." Jo Ann's voice didn't, I thought, sound as upset as it should. She was continuing to catalog the gifts she had discovered in the bag.

There had been another painting, about which Gordon had solicited a lot of his wife's advice. "As he was doing it, he kept asking me, 'How do you like this part?' and 'What about the blackness on this side?' and kept wanting my opinions—and then he gives it to her! He had wrapped it as a present to her!" Now she sounded good and angry. The expression on her face was fierce, but it turned, within the next few moments, from fierce to speculative and uncertain again.

"There were also a lot of other little things—a T-shirt that he had given me for my birthday, but in a different color for her." She paused, and the fierce, belligerent expression returned. "When I found all of this, I woke him up and told him I wanted him out of the house by the next morning! It was—oh, unbelievable, a crazy night! There was so much yelling, and he kept trying to explain, saying he didn't know what had happened to him this past year! That things had gotten very crazy in his life, and he couldn't explain why he was doing some of the things he was doing!"

MESSAGES

There was another burst of firecrackers, from outside, and I half jumped out of my seat. "It's all right . . . just kids," Jo Ann assured me. "It's very difficult for me to accept his buying this other woman the same things that he would buy me," she went on, her voice losing its angry energy and becoming more distressed and helpless-sounding as she spoke. "Or that he would give her something that he'd put in my daughter's crib. *Do* it, and leave it all out there, wrapped and waiting . . . sitting right next to the front door." She shook her head, as if indicating that it was all beyond her comprehension.

Then she sighed, a long intake and expulsion of breath. "To me, it was absolutely crazy. But he still denies, to this day, that he didn't leave things around hoping that I would find them! He says that I invaded his privacy, and that's why I found the bag. . . . I am, at this point, fearful of touching anything in this house; I'm so afraid of what I'm going to find!" As if on cue, there was a long howl from the bedroom; Susannah was magisterially awake and commanding her mother's attention.

"Just two weeks ago, for instance—" Jo Ann started to add, but her daughter's cries informed her that the baby would brook no further delays. Excusing herself, Jo Ann left, and returned a few minutes later with a smiling little girl in her arms. Susannah, consoled, looked interested in her mother and in me, but much more interested in her bottle. "Two weeks ago"—resumed Jo Ann, as if the subject had not left her mind for a moment, "Gordon brought home a book for me—a book about career changes, which is something that's on my mind at this time. The other night I brought that book in to show to someone I work with—she's also thinking about leaving nursing—and I opened it up and a piece of paper fell out."

There was dread in her eyes, and I myself dreaded what she might say. "Obviously, Gordon had taken the book to school with him, and on the paper bag was—I think it was a dream. I read the first paragraph and then put it away. I said, 'I'm not going to read this; I know how upset he'll get if I do.' "

I asked her what the dream had been about, and she answered that it had involved herself, the other woman, the other woman's husband, and Gordon himself. "I think her kids were in it, too. . . . I didn't read the whole thing," she assured me in a guilty-sounding voice. In the beginning, however, everyone had been at Gordon's mother's house. "Something— I'm not sure what—was about to happen, but I don't know the rest of the story. But why would it *be* there, in a book that he'd brought home for me?"

Because, I thought, he is sending you messages, and working hard to make sure you receive them. Although I hadn't said these words aloud, Jo Ann responded immediately. "He, when he realized the book was gone from the house, called me at work. He told me that there was something in it that he didn't want me to see and that I was to put it in an envelope and seal it. I said that I'd already seen it and read the first paragraph— because I didn't know what it was. I told him that it had obviously been something he wouldn't want me to read and that I'd known that and put it away immediately. . . . *He* says that he didn't leave it there with any great underlying purpose in his mind!" Scorn and disbelief accompanied these last words, trampling down the fear and confusion that had gone before them.

Adultery is, it merits repeating, a powerful form of communication, but while Gordon Kearney's transmissions were being delivered loudly and clearly, his wife's receiver was jammed. The messages were too painful and threatening for Jo Ann to hear.

BABY MAKES THREE

It might be said, and with some justification, that a crisis in the Kearney household could have been expected or even *predicted* at around the time of their first baby's birth—or even earlier, at the time that they had begun trying to get Jo Ann's pregnancy started. Choosing to have a child together is an extremely intimate venture; it links the couple in a permanent bond that is irrevocable. The decision itself can be alarming for someone who is fearful about commitments, emotional ties, being close. But even more problematic, for someone like Gordon, would have been the anticipated loss of his wife's exclusive attention. Jo Ann was, after all, the only intimate partner he had ever really owned; she was his alone. That would change, inevitably, when she had someone else—their new baby—to lavish her affections upon and to care for.

The arrival of a first child, even in the best and most benign of circumstances, inevitably presents a profound challenge to the intimate twosome. "Exclusive ownership and love, an often cherished fantasy, has (sic) to accommodate to sharing, and to limits," observes family therapist Kitty La Perriere. "The child's needs at times take absolute precedence. The ensuing disappointments are at times blamed on the marital partner. Many parents experience acute jealousy of the time their partner spends with the child and of the pleasure the experience brings."

Fathers, especially, are prone to feelings of rage, abandonment, profound envy of the attention being lavished on the new personage who has come into the house. "Husbands may not be able to tolerate their wife's breastfeeding," notes La Perriere, "and mothers may get their sexual and maternal feelings mixed up. Nursing the baby may [by the mother] temporarily be preferred to sex with the husband."

Making emotional space for the demanding little newcomer requires a degree of patience and forbearance on everyone's part, particularly that of the father who is feeling—and may *be*, in reality—temporarily deprived of those marital perks which were part of the earlier relationship.

Not infrequently, new fathers—guilty and distressed about their own manfully suppressed and yet still simmering rivalrous, rejected feelings—begin to overwork, overeat, drink, develop symptoms (such as ulcers) or become involved in an affair. Given Gordon Kearney's own special history, a tantrumlike reaction to his wife's impending pregnancy—and Susannah's eventual birth—might have been viewed as something completely foreseeable. He himself had, after all, been abandoned by one mother and then parented by a substitute who was a "bucket of ice."

THE LATEST BETRAYER

Jo Ann, moreover, in becoming a mother herself, was very likely to be seen as the latest in a line of betraying, ungiving or otherwise emotionally unreliable females. For she, instead of remaining the quasi parent who was Gordon's alone, would—by giving birth to a real child—become someone else's loving parent *in reality*. Not only would this new situation be likely to arouse unaccountable, unwelcome feelings in a person so deprived as he had been; it would also stir the embers of ancient remembrances pertaining to himself as a young baby and to that first, utterly vanished human partner—she who existed beyond the shoreline of Gordon's conscious memory, which stretched no farther back than the age of four (his age at the time of the adoption).

In their book on the family life cycle, authors Elizabeth Carter and Monica McGoldrick note that the flow of anxiety in a family is both "vertical" and "horizontal." The vertical, or transgenerational, stresses are those which have to do with unresolved emotional issues derived from the early experiences of one or both partners and/or with toxic dilemmas inherited from the original families (such as a problem with alcoholism or with overclose mother-son relationships, etc.). The horizontal stresses have to do with the normal challenges posed by life cycle transitions as well as with unexpected demands placed upon the system (for example, Jo Ann's father's illness represented a heavy horizontal demand which was placed upon the family unit as a whole).

Where vertical stress and horizontal stress happen to intersect, the couple's tensions may escalate to a level at which they overrun the dikes and can no longer be contained. "If . . . parenting was a *cause célèbre* of some kind in the family of origin of one or both spouses, and has not been dealt with, the birth of a baby will produce heightened anxiety for the couple in making the transition to parenthood," Carter and McGoldrick write.

It is around important life cycle events involving *entrances* of new family members (through birth, marriage, etc.) or *exits* and losses of family members (through death, divorce, departure of grown children, etc.) that physical or psychological symptoms, or relational crises, tend to emerge. In Gordon Kearney's case, it was clearly true that a major move away from the marital relationship had occurred in tandem with his and Jo Ann's efforts to get a pregnancy started. The affair with Nina had begun during the very summer when he and Jo Ann were seeing specialists about their inability to have a child.

Had a warning bell, to the effect that he would need a new intimate caretaker of his own, already sounded in the young husband's head? Or was his emotional defection far more connected to his having come to a point in his life at which he felt unusually well, competent and "together"—less in need of Jo Ann's sanity and stability and able to act out some of his rage at all of the bad, controlling nurturers whom he'd had to deal with in his life?

REBELLION

"A frequent dynamic behind marital infidelity," suggests psychiatrist Stanley Willis, "is that [unfaithfulness] has become, like stealing money out of 'mommy's' purse, a displaced form of an otherwise reasonably normal activity. We frequently see grownups who act like a 'child' to effect a mutinous rebellion to a spouse who is seen as acting like a controlling 'parent.' "

Many spouses, notes Dr. Willis, come to be seen by their mates as nagging or controlling surrogate parents. In the marriage, old scenes with the "parent" are replayed, and the angry "child," in the course of time, misbehaves by finding an extramarital relationship. "To engage in forbidden activities is at the very least an implicit rebellion against prohibitions," Willis writes. "We resist the role taken by the prohibiting person. The injunction is resisted because it has been laid on us by someone who has adopted or assumed a power role over us, which we resent."

A BREACH IN THE MARITAL CONTRACT

Perhaps foremost among the many factors at play, at the time of the affair's beginning, had been Gordon's own state of increased confidence and well-being. This, undoubtedly, had challenged the unspoken rules of the Kearneys' emotional system and thrown it completely out of balance. For the collusive, unspoken arrangement they had made involved his being a disturbed, drug-taking, sometime-alcoholic deviant and Jo Ann's being his steady, responsible caretaker. Those were the rules of their particular marital game, the unacknowledged yet powerful tenets of their emotional contract. Married partners find themselves, on occasion, like members of a club whose regulations have been drawn up to meet the requirements that exist at a particular point in time. It sometimes happens that when those needs seem no longer so relevant and important, a member of that system tries to change—and finds that the established rules simply will not allow such changes to happen.

Was it possible that Gordon had, in that critical summer of their lives, been struggling to alter certain aspects of the marital relationship—to become more competent and less dependent upon his wife, for example? If so, Jo Ann would very likely have—in the unconscious, reflexive manner with which individuals in an emotional system react—automatically tried to block those moves toward independence which would have made her less necessary for his emotional survival.

Her underlying fear, rooted in a profound lack of self-esteem, would have been that she could never be loved for *being herself* at all; she could only be needed for her caretaking function. A nurturer in a relationship with someone who *isn't* dependent upon her for nurturing is, as she sees it, in no viable relationship at all.

What, I wondered, was Gordon's own view of what had been happening between him and his wife that summer when they'd been so disaffected and he had wandered out of the relationship? I meant to ask him about that, in great detail, at our next meeting: Gordon and I were to meet alone. But when he arrived, he was distracted and perturbed—naturally. Jo Ann had suggested that they separate and that he move out of their house as soon as arrangements could be made.

NINA, AS A PERSON

He was about five feet eight inches, a couple of inches taller than my own five-six, and not so tall as I'd remembered. It was as if during our last talk the cold anger he'd communicated had inflated him to an unnatural, menacing size. Now he was a man with a problem, but not someone in a rage. He was dressed in a neat striped cotton shirt, open at the collar, and faultlessly pressed khakis—an almost dapper man, on this hot day late in the month of July. We met at my office on the third floor of Jonathan Edwards College, one of the residential colleges at Yale.

There had been, he explained, a lot of pressure in the marriage recently. "Things are coming out into the open, in terms of us saying the things that are really on our minds, but Jo Ann, I think, finds this very threatening." She behaved, added Gordon, as if she were afraid of finding out something that she didn't want to know.

I responded by asking Gordon where he was, psychologically speaking, in terms of that other relationship. Had he found himself able to give it up, or was it still an important question in his mind? He gazed at me, unblinking. "What do I feel about Nina at this point in time? Is that what you're asking?" I nodded by way of reply.

He still considered her a very close friend, despite his not having seen her. "Obviously, you run into her at school occasionally?" I asked. He shook his head; he didn't. "You never communicate with her?" I continued, allowing surprise and doubt to sound in my voice. Gordon shook his head, in the negative, again. "Then she's in your mind as a friend— and as a fantasy or dream. . . . A dream of the way things could have been or might be someday?"

He paused. "I don't think there's much fantasy involved here," he objected. "I have a pretty good idea of who she is and what she's going through . . . she's in the process of going through therapy right now. There is, I think, some question of a reconciliation with her husband. . . ."

His information seemed to be fairly current. "Is she in individual therapy or marital therapy?" I asked. Gordon, however, retreated into the past tense immediately. "When I had last talked to her she was, I believe, doing both." He stirred restlessly in his seat, looked out the window and down at the statuary in the sculpture garden at the Yale Art Gallery; this is the view which my office, fortunately, overlooks. He was gazing at a Henry Moore statue without seeing it.

After a few moments, I said, "Who is she as a person? You said you had a pretty good idea." Gordon turned back to me, looking startled. "I'm not sure what you're asking." He had told me, I replied, that he saw Nina without fantasy, and I wanted to know what he saw. For a moment, he turned away again. "I guess the thing that usually comes to mind is that we have a lot in common—a lot of the same intellectual, creative areas of interest." He faced me and continued. "We like a lot of the same music, the same art. We're both interested in psychology; we have that in common. She's a warm, compassionate, very attractive woman." He repeated the words he'd used when describing his ex-lover in the first interview we'd had.

These comments were, I said, all in the positive range; Nina seemed

LOVERS AND OTHER THIRD PARTIES

to exist in his mind as an ideal. "I don't hear any remarks to the effect that 'Well, it wouldn't work out between us for such and such a reason.' . . . Is that because no negative aspects of the relationship exist?"

"I wouldn't fantasize about our both divorcing and marrying each other." Gordon answered my unspoken question. "That's just not the fantasy I have."

I asked him why that was so, given the superpositive feelings that he had expressed? Gordon shrugged, said that Nina had some very real problems in her life: She had two children, and one of them had a serious learning disability. "Anybody who has children knows that they present a lot of competition for emotional and spiritual sustenance," he remarked. Nina's children would present him with rivals for her attention. "That's a reality," he added flatly.

Did he mean that had these real-life external difficulties not existed, Nina would have made a more suitable partner? "I believe so," admitted Gordon, and I felt pity for Jo Ann. I suppose it was this that led me to say that Nina remained, in his mind, the unachievable ideal, which Jo Ann certainly was not.

"I don't really look at her as *the ideal*," he protested, an indignant note in his voice. "I really *like who she is*. I accept it—the problems with us having a relationship—those being, mainly, that we had one and we were both married. And that that hurt everyone involved. But that's—" He stopped in mid-speech, for I was shaking my head.

I was, I explained, thinking in terms of what their relationship would be like if none of those external realities impinged—if he and Nina could just wander off into the sunset and live the rest of their lives together. Gordon found that line of thought disturbing. "A lot of why I like her has to do with the way she handled that very bad time!" he exclaimed. "So I don't see, as far as those externals are concerned . . . You can't say what it would be like had they not been there! You can't say, 'If she had never been married and we met,' and that kind of thing, because we wouldn't have been the same two people!" It was useless to speculate, he insisted, because they and the entire situation would have been different.

It was clear to me that he found the idea of his ex-lover, as a real partner in a shared life, something that was unaccountably alarming. I observed that he seemed to like Nina, very much, as a person. "Do you like Jo Ann as a person?" I asked. Gordon answered that he liked her more, now, than he had in quite a while.

The Warp and the Woof of the Relationship

He had come to realize, Gordon added, that even if his wife didn't meet his needs, that was not intentional on her part. "I think she wants to and is willing to try very hard," he said coolly, "but there are a lot of interests that we don't, in some very natural way, share. Interests in music, in art. I, for instance, really *enjoy* spending time in galleries, strolling around, not saying too much but taking it all in. . . . And Jo Ann tries, but you can't just *pretend* to like what somebody else likes." There was a note of superiority and scorn in his voice.

"It's unrealistic," I agreed.

"It's like watching people who pretend to like cats," he continued. "It just doesn't work. The cat knows, and everyone else knows; you just can't pretend. And while you can feel a certain amount of compassion for somebody who is caring enough to try to do that, it doesn't succeed." He thought, he added, that Jo Ann had been trying hard just recently.

So his "sophistication" was a real issue in the Kearneys' marriage. Gordon might have signed on as a wounded bird, but as a bird of a rare and exalted species. As wounded bird, he was one-down in the relationship, but as intellectual superior, he was one-up, rightfully dismissive of his clod of a caretaker. They had polarized in the one-up, one-down (or "If I win, you lose; if you win, I lose") positions, as tense married people do. Thus, while the warp of their relationship had to do with the wounded bird/caretaker dimension, the woof of it involved the sophisticated, creative individual married to the plodding, limited dunce.

I asked Gordon why it was that when he and Jo Ann were courting, the question of their differing tastes and affinities had not really emerged. "I think," he answered uncomfortably, "that we spent most of the time doing things with other people. And the idiosyncrasies, or individual needs, don't really come out in the same way. Everybody is so busy accommodating their own desires to that of the group. You don't—to a certain extent—realize that the incompatibilities are between two people instead of between two people and the rest of the group." It sounded unconvincing, as an argument, and he appeared uncertain and embarrassed.

Maintaining Space

We sat there, saying nothing, for several moments. "Of course," I resumed, "the other aspect of all of this is that in an extramarital relationship, a lot of distance is maintained by the constraints of the situation itself. And people who are concerned about having space—as you are, I think, concerned about having space. . . ?" I paused, asked, "Am I correct in thinking that?" He smiled wryly, nodded his agreement. Then, to my surprise, he added, "Yes, it's a good way of getting your intimate needs met on a part-time basis."

People do, so frequently, have a remarkably good understanding of what is problematic in the self and what issues and tasks have never been mastered—in Gordon's case, a deep concern about the dangers of ever getting close. For an individual who has (for whatever developmental, historical reasons) problems about being intimate, the romantic affair is a wonderful device. It sets boundaries around the relationship which are relatively clear-cut; the limits are set because, after making love and being close, everybody has to go home to his or her own home and family. The external constraints mean that the lovers can be as open and vulnerable as they like and then leave to rejoin their own separate realities.

There is no danger of one's separate space's eroding; each person's autonomy is built into the very structure of the relationship itself. When your partner is, on the other hand, someone who inhabits the same territory, a request for intimacy can come at any moment—an intolerable notion, for some people, who may experience the request for an intimate exchange as an invasion of the inner self.

"If you were to imagine," I asked Gordon, "living in the same house with Nina—" I stopped, because he had leaned forward in his seat, a reproving, almost horrified expression on his face.

"No, this is just a fantasy game," I reassured him. I waited to see if it was all right to resume and then continued where I had left off. "Do you think, given the interests that you say you share with her, that living with her as your partner would be much easier and more pleasant for you?"

He answered, in an anxious voice, that it would be different, but not necessarily easier. There would be different sorts of problems—divorce, custody issues; his daughter, her two children—but problems would certainly be there. "Susannah wasn't born when we were first having the affair, but I never look at that and say to myself that things would be better or different without thinking that she *does* exist and she's now part of the picture," he asserted.

LYING AND AUTONOMY

I smiled, told him that I was asking him to play another kind of game entirely. "Forget the external difficulties, for a moment, and think about what kind of psychological, interpersonal dilemmas might exist if you and Nina lived in the same house. Imagine that the rest of the blackboard, around you two, is erased; it's just you two, inhabiting the same space, as partners. What, in your heart of hearts, do you really think that that would be like?" I leaned toward him, as if to urge his words from him, because his expression had become reserved and doubtful.

He didn't respond for a short while, and after a certain time had passed, I thought that he wouldn't. But finally, he cleared his throat. "I think there would be tension surrounding a certain intellectual competition," he admitted.

As things stood, in an affair, he could be as intimate with his lover as he wished to be without ever having his autonomy threatened. If she crowded him, he could go home.

And at home that meant less intimacy, too, for he was telling lies. Telling lies is a way, when one thinks about it, of maximizing autonomy: Not telling your partner what you are really thinking and feeling is a way of shutting her out of your inner reality. Lying, in this way, augments distance and space; only the liar knows the truth of the situation, and he is alone inside with his own special knowledge.

But Gordon, strangely enough, had been behaving as if he'd wanted two opposite outcomes at one and the same time. He had, by involving himself with Nina, been acting as if he wanted to increase that area of his own life which concerned himself alone and had nothing to do with his marriage. But, in leaving "messages," he was engaging in behavior that reminded me of the Hansel and Gretel story. He was setting off through the dark woods of the world that existed outside the relationship with his wife, and yet leaving a trail of glaringly evident crumbs in his wake that Jo Ann could not fail to find. While he appeared, at one level, to be disengaging and seeking his autonomy, at another he was begging her to pursue him and to bring him back home where he belonged.

SHE PUTS THE BLAME ON THE AFFAIR

Even though the Kearneys were, at the present time, discussing separation, there was a sense in which neither one of them seemed to believe that the relationship could, indeed, come to an end. "We've been arguing about being supportive, and who is supporting whom, and that's a pretty murky issue at the moment," Gordon complained, that afternoon in my office, sounding irritable and anxious but not ultimately threatened. "I think that Jo Ann feels that she's been very supportive of my being in law school, while I see her as being just—tolerant at best."

He was currently, he explained, working at a summer job, sharing in the care of Susannah and taking a demanding course in ethical philosophy. "I'm under a lot of pressure and I just don't have any energy left over to explain why I need to be in the library until eleven-thirty at night," he said in a controlled yet belligerent tone of voice. Jo Ann, he added sarcastically, saw her own behavior as "supportive" and himself as "unappreciative," yet she had, in his view, no idea of what the intellectual pressures and demands upon him really were like.

"She looks at the last two years and attributes all the difficulties that we've had to my having had an affair." He shrugged, as if this notion were ridiculous. As he saw it, she didn't appreciate the strain he was under and the energy drained away by the schoolwork and the schoolwork alone. He had, a few days earlier, just returned from the funeral of a favorite cousin, when Jo Ann had begun talking about how supportive she was— and that had led to an argument. "I would never choose the hour right after a funeral to start such a conversation," he stated, looking ever angrier as we spoke.

It was that particular conversation, or argument, that had led Jo Ann to suggest that it might be better if he moved out for a while. "I don't have a job," Gordon said, his eyes bright with scorn. "I essentially have very little money. So she wants me to move out—God knows where!— with no money and job! And this, according to her, is going to reduce the pressure and anxiety! I have," he added, "a paper due this week. There is something *wrong* with her logic!"

SOMETHING FROM THE PAST

He'd had, Gordon told me, no chance to cope with his grief about his cousin's death before getting into that quarrel with his wife. "The day after that was rather bizarre as well," recounted Gordon, sounding less angry but now speaking with an Olympian objectivity. "I had decided to make an effort to smooth things out with Jo Ann, so I asked her to come down to the campus for a drink or something, after classes. Which she did. We went to the bar opposite the law school, and after that I gave her directions for getting back. I was going, on foot, to the library, and she began questioning me about the route that I would take."

He paused, briefly, gazed at me with an assessing, enigmatic expression. "I was walking down the street, and at the corner where I would turn in order to head toward the library, I stopped. I stood there, and I was looking at the Psychology Department building, which wasn't all that absurd because the paper I'm writing is on informed consent for certain psychiatric procedures. I was thinking about the fact that that was now a taboo building, because of Nina's being in there, and it seemed to me—it still does—that it wasn't unreasonable for me to stop and ponder about the fact that I could not go inside. And I turned around and saw that Jo Ann had followed me in the car. I was *absolutely furious*." His lips had, suddenly, become a thin band of white.

His voice, with each word that he spoke, was rising. "Furious that in spite of her claiming to have gotten over her suspicions, she would follow me around! It was like having your worst paranoid delusion come true! And in that setting . . . a foggy evening . . . and I turn around and see this car sitting in the fog, thirty yards down the road."

Had he, I wondered, dropped some suggestion in their conversation that would have alerted Jo Ann's suspicions? I would have asked him had I not realized that along with the indignation and the fury, there was something almost frightened in the expression on his face. I realized, with the same electric shock of knowing I'd experienced after our first meeting, that this situation aroused in him an ancient rage.

"There's something from the past here," I found myself speaking aloud, "and it's almost a sense of being dependent on a person whom you don't really want to be linked up with. Is that something that rings a bell for you from a time when you were a young child—say, seven, eight or thereabouts?"

He looked at me as if I'd asked him a question in a language he didn't understand.

"Was there a problem, in terms of your not feeling the things you were supposed to feel for your mother? For instance, did you love her enough?"

Gordon opened his mouth, but said nothing, for the carillon of the Harkness Tower bells suddenly commanded the attention of the world around. In the wake of their melody, his voice was sober. "I can remember getting strange messages from my mother. Like 'If you weren't adopted, where would you be?' And those, not unreasonably, were interpreted as 'I must not be a good person' or 'I must be doing something wrong.' "

His voice was no longer angry-sounding. He sounded dispirited or even depressed.

He had, he said suddenly, tried very hard to please.

"You tried hard to please?" I repeated his words. He nodded. "Yes, and I never felt that I was doing quite well enough at it."

He had had, as a child, the "wrong caretaker", and—since he himself did not have the right feelings about her—his survival in that situation was precarious. For if he didn't really love his mother, she might realize it and respond by not caring for *him*. He was, moreover, undoubtedly not only fearful but deeply guilty about his true feelings toward his parent. Now, the same things were happening in the *present* situation with the new caretaker who was his spouse.

How often, in the dawn of life, are we presented with certain kinds of problems which we attempt to re-create and to work upon, subsequently, with our mates! We seem to be uncannily *efficient* when it comes to choosing partners who will help us get into situations that recapitulate earlier dilemmas that have never been successfully mastered. It is as if we were guided by a dizzyingly complex and yet remarkably precise inter-nalized radar.

"There are elements of my mother's personality in Jo Ann," observed Gordon. "I guess a lot of that dependability and nursing. . . . She is solid, and you know she will be there; she won't run out doing flighty things." The early, frustrating relationship with his adoptive mother had been replicated in the present, frustrating situation with his wife. He himself could not be in any *other* kind of marital system, for this was the only kind of intimate relationship that he really knew about—one in which he felt dependent for nurturance upon a person for whom he did not have the correctly affectionate feelings.

HONEYMOONERS

I ran into the Kearneys, in a restaurant on the main street of Westport, Connecticut, a year after our series of interviews had been completed. I saw them before they saw me; they were feeding Susannah, at a open table in the center of the room, and the pair of them looked healthy and content. I greeted them and asked how they were. "You look wonderful," I said, as if answering my own question.

They exchanged amused glances. "Are you?" I asked. Jo Ann, with a wry smile, told me that they had recently separated; Gordon was no longer living in the house. She herself seemed, however, to be perfectly composed and self-assured. He, while he wore a somewhat sheepish expression, seemed less taut and anxious than I had ever seen him be before. I could not understand why they were together and looking so satisfied and relaxed if their relationship was, in fact, falling apart.

"Gordon wants to come back," Jo Ann said calmly, "and I am thinking about whether to let him." They were seeing a marital therapist in order to clarify matters and to help her in making this decision (they had just come, in fact, from their second session). A great many things had happened since I had last seen them, she explained. Then she glanced quickly at her husband.

He nodded slightly, and she went on. Gordon had, she told me, been involved with Nina throughout the time of our interviews; he maintained, now, that it was only a friendship, but she, Jo Ann, did not believe him. For once again the relationship had been discovered by her reading "some notes he had made—or maybe it was a letter—which had to do with him living with her, someday." Jo Ann had insisted, then, that he move out.

Her sister had come to live with her, at that point, and Gordon had gone to live with his sister and brother-in-law. He had as well, begun using drugs again, going to bars, and doing some serious drinking. Two weeks before our meeting he had, she went on, plowed into a tree and totaled his car. "I almost killed myself. I was lucky," he said, in a voice that was at once ashamed and proud. No wonder they were looking so contented and had such a honeymoon air! He had almost destroyed himself, and she, when she took him back—which she would—could nurture him as she'd nurtured him before. In other words, as his accident had demonstrated, he needed her for his very survival. He was her wounded bird, and she was his necessary caretaker.

They'd returned to the original collusive bargain, the exchange of projections with which the relationship had begun. He was the other half of a relationship in which she could give to a loved partner who depended upon her for his emotional survival, and she was the other half of a relationship between an all-powerful female and a male who is not loving her in the way that's truly required and yet is dependent upon her care. "My mother has disinherited me," stated Gordon, at that moment—an apparently random remark.

I asked him why she had done that, and a glint of the old anger shone in his eyes for a moment. "I guess," he said finally, sounding coldly contemptuous, "that she doesn't approve of our being separated and"— he paused, looking at his wife—"thinking about maybe getting divorced.

No son of *hers* would ever be involved in such behaviors!" He shrugged, as if to say that it mattered not a whit to him; his membership in that family had been tenuous anyway.

He was now, I realized, even more dependent on Jo Ann's support— and in some very practical ways—than he had been before.

At that moment Susannah, now a pretty, active little girl of some seventeen months, picked up a potato chip and put it between her daddy's lips. Gordon, making an exaggerated face, chewed the morsel in such a way that his daughter laughed excitedly. Jo Ann laughed too, but then, her lips slightly pursed, she leaned over to wipe the crumbs away from their baby's mouth. She had regained the illusion of control once again.

PART III

THE COUPLE IN MIDSTREAM:
Marital Problems, Marital Solutions

10

What Marital Problems Are Made Of: Couples in Collusion

In trying to understand couples and the ways in which they put their relationships together, I have found no tool more powerful than the concept of projective identification. This important theoretical construct provides an explanation of just why it is that marriages—seemingly, paradoxically—become stronger and more intimate to the degree that the overall "rules" of the interactional system permit the partners to be separate and different people. The basic idea of projective identification, once grasped (not only intellectually but emotionally) by the members of a couple, can literally alter the fundamental nature of their transactions and turn their shared relationship completely and surprisingly around.

For once a member of the pair has had the experience of *taking back a projection*—accepting that, for example, the craziness, hostility, incompetence, depression, anxiety, etc., that is being perceived in the partner may be emanating from the self—everything has to begin to look different.

Or, alternatively, once a mate has *refused to accept a projection*—to behave crazily, angrily, become depressed, or the like in order to express the spouse's suppressed and dissociated feelings—changes have to start occurring in the relationship.

When the unconscious trading off of mutual projections slows down or ceases, the emotional system itself shifts about. The familiar, constrictive, inflexible, rigidly demanding yet never consciously acknowledged rules of the game can be changed. Things can be different, in ways that would have been impossible before.

Because I consider the mechanism of projective identification so fundamental to the understanding of marriage (especially conflict between intimates), I will return to this subject again and again. The ideas involved are at once easily intelligible and complicated—difficult to discern at work in one's own life *by definition*, because the exchange of projections is a psychological barter which occurs at an unconscious level.

But the concept itself (a rose which is called by many another name in the clinical literature—for example, "irrational role assignment," "externalization," "trading of dissociations," to name a few) is often hard to comprehend at anything short of the "Aha, now I do see it!" level. Once truly taken in and understood, however, it is—like the understanding of how to ride a bicycle—knowledge that will never be completely lost or forgotten.

For once a person knows how to ride a bicycle, he cannot *not know*; what has been learned has become part of his repertoire. And similarly, once a person experiences being in a relationship in which few or no mutual projections are being exchanged, he or she cannot *not know* that this better, more separate and yet more intimate kind of relationship exists.

The Primary Intimate Relationship

The concept of projective identification was introduced into the psychoanalytic literature by one of Freud's early followers, Melanie Klein. Klein was the forerunner of what eventually became known as the "object relations" school of analysis, a deviation from strict or "pure" Freudian thought. For Freud conceived of human development as a lengthy, sequential unfolding of instinctually based inner imperatives. His theory focused upon the internal, intrapsychic world of the growing child as it underwent successive changes—as the infant and then toddler shifted from primarily "oral" concerns to the "anal" and then "phallic" stages of psychosexual growth and ultimately confronted the Oedipal calamity.

This is, of course, the Oedipus complex—that pained renunciation of the opposite-sex parent as a possible erotic partner, which Freud viewed as the central tragedy of every human being's early life. Freud emphasized the internal struggles of the developing, changing child, whose inborn sexual drives were opposed by the civilizing demands of the society which inevitably overwhelmed and tamed them (often producing neurotic symptoms along the way).

The object relations theorists, while not in essential disagreement with this model, still came to see human personality development as less determined by instinctually based sexual forces (and, as Freud later added, aggressive forces) than by the neonate's crucial experiences in the context of the primary intimate relationship. There was no such thing as an internal world, they suggested, which existed independently of what happened in that magical first human attachment between parent and child. Theirs was and is a concept of the self as an organizing, experiencing system into which the "other" is inextricably woven.

The blueprint of the personality comes into being, according to these thinkers, far in advance of the Oedipal crisis (which occurs somewhere around age five); it emerges, within the first months of life, in the caretaking duet between the nurturer and the dependent child. It is within the setting of the utterly needful baby's powerful first attachment to the protecting, caretaking parent that his or her internal programming develops, here that the basic instruction manual for living comes into existence and is set down in its earliest, most primitive form.

Object relations theory is, clearly, a far more *interpersonal* than *intra*personal, individual approach to the understanding of psychological growth and development.

What this branch of Freud's intellectual descendants tends to emphasize is the importance of what happens *between emotionally bonded people* in the long-lasting attachments which characterize human life. The earliest, deepest wish of every newborn individual, according to W. Ronald D. Fairbairn, M.D. (whose series of brilliant papers, published in the 1940s and early 1950s, established him as an important founder of the object relations movement), is for a loving, satisfying connection with the nurturing parent. The forming and maintenance of this crucially important connection—rather than the mere gratification of instinctually based sexual tensions—is the ultimate goal toward which the infant's powerful libidinal strivings are directed.

THE INNER IMAGE OF THE BELOVED

Here let me note that the strange word "object" refers to "love object"; the term "object relations" connotes the emotional attachment between the one who loves and the image of the beloved as *this exists in the lover's own mind*. The term is used, in other words, to differentiate between the inner picture of the love object and the *actuality* of the person who is loved.

The subtle distinction being made—which the term "object" is meant to underscore—is the distinction between *an internalized image* of the loved and needed other (an image which is colored by one's own experiences and fantasies about those experiences) and a reality which is external to the self.

The object relations theorists suggest that we have all internalized mental representations of people and relationships about which we have felt deeply. These internalized objects (Melanie Klein termed them "imagos") have become incorporated into our mental landscapes; they are part of our subjective terrain.

Our inner pictures of the world, formed in childhood, provide the framework for perceiving "objective" reality in adulthood. If, for example, *my vision* of my father was of a distant, unapproachable human being, then I will be predisposed to view intimacy with a male as virtually impossible. My "inner father" will incline me to see all other men as cold and emotionally unreachable.

We relate to our inner objects—old intimacies, shards of intense emotional relationships that once existed—as if they were "real." And why should that *not* happen, given that our first human attachments are at the deepest strata of the personality and are the stuff from which our internal, subjective reality has been formed?

Difficulties and confusions arise, however, when such mental images affect our perceptions so profoundly that it becomes difficult to discern the *differences* between the inner object from the past and the real attributes of the intimate partner in a relationship in the present—that is, to disconnect an old fantasy from an actual person out there, now.

The Fantasy and the Facts

Let me give a brief example of how an early fantasy could affect the way in which a person came to see his world, in adulthood.

A young toddler's attachment to his mother may have been disrupted by an illness that she suffered, which took her away from her baby for a period of time. If her absence occurred during the critical stage when separation distress can be overwhelming (say, at around age one and a half), the small child would predictably respond with terrible anger and fear. She who was experienced as magically omnipotent would be perceived to be vulnerable; instead of being kind and loving, Mommy would be absent, sick, ungiving.

Because something has greatly disrupted his small world and his sense of its safety and predictability, the small child would be likely to take in (or "introject") an internal picture of a relationship between himself and an object of his powerful feelings who is frustratingly *not there*, although she is so desperately needed. This mental representation of the intimate other—from whom his own sense of self is still poorly differentiated—may be an inner picture of a vitally wanted and loved being who is frustrating, rejecting, and perhaps experienced as full of hatred and rage.

This image of the mother is, clearly, only the dependent child's frightened imagining; his own feelings of loss and rage, because he lacks the capacity for self-reflection, are hard to differentiate from those of his caretaker. The boundary between self and other is still, at this stage of development, so uncertain that he is unclear about what the source of the hostile feelings actually might be. Is the anger within himself, or is it in the beloved mother upon whom he is so utterly and completely dependent? No matter. That helpless fury, which threatens to overwhelm him, must be thrust out of the mind's sight—or, as the object relations theorists would phrase it, "split off" and repressed from the needful youngster's conscious awareness.

The bad, frustrating love object, and the internalized picture of the relationship with "her," are suppressed—because the possible loss of the relationship is experienced as a threat to survival itself. And survival, as I remarked earlier, is the evolutionary bottom line of this first, intensely important human attachment. Also, in the magical world of the child's thinking the wish to hurt and the capacity to do harm are not clearly separated, and so there is a lurking fear that his hatred and negativity could destroy the beloved other completely. For these powerful reasons, the internalized image of the evil, ungiving intimate partner must be swept under the carpet of the mind.

The real individual who is Mother was, all the while, merely ill and in the hospital for a necessary stay. But this depriving, frightening episode, albeit long lost to her child's conscious memory, may leave a residue in terms of irrational fears of being abandoned by the needed other to whom he is emotionally tied.

Thus, while later experiences with the good and loving mother might eventually overlay the "bad object" (the internalized image of the evil, frustrating and withholding intimate partner), they may never fully eradicate the child's horrendous experience of believing that he has been abandoned—or the expectation that it will happen again.

Often, in our adult relationships, active yet unconscious efforts are made to shape the intimate partner to a model that exists within. That inner model, which is an image of a once-loved and desperately needed other, can override and preempt our capacity for seeing a partner in what are appropriate and realistic ways. Melanie Klein, when she first defined projective identification, spoke of it as "splitting off parts of the self and [then] projecting them on to another person." Later she added that it also involved "the feeling of identification with other people because one has *attributed* qualities or *attributes of one's own to them* (emphasis added)."

In other words, in the example given above, the adult who once felt forsaken—and who had internalized an image of a rejecting, rageful, untrustworthy intimate partner (the mother)—might have no conscious contact with his own anger at having felt deserted, and yet he may struggle to incite hostility (or even the wish to abandon the relationship) in his otherwise nonangry, nonabandoning mate.

In this respect, Gordon Kearney's behavior—leaving that airline bag full of presents to his mistress in the front hallway "mistakenly," as a provocation to Jo Ann—certainly does spring to mind.

THE SELF AND THE OTHER

According to psychoanalysts John Zinner and Roger Shapiro, projective identification is a defensive activity of the ego which serves to *modify a person's perceptions of his intimate partner* while—in a reciprocal fashion—*altering his own image of himself.*

The individual who is seething with unconscious hostility can, for instance, remain utterly out of contact with those feelings and experience himself as completely without anger—as long as he is assisted by a collusive, obliging mate who will act out his anger for him.

In other words, it is not enough to have one person project his repudiated and disavowed qualities or emotions—such as his angry feelings—onto the other. The spouse must then conform to the projection, by behaving or feeling in just the ways that she or he is supposed to! It is, in short, a deal; if there is to be a game, *two* players have to agree, albeit unconsciously, to play it.

It would be useless, clearly, for the perennially nice guy husband to project his angry impulses onto his wife if she did not *accept* those impulses and feelings—and proceed to express them (for him) as if they were really her own. If the wife did not collude with him by becoming enraged about something (thereby providing vicarious gratification of her spouse's denied and repudiated emotions), the entire defensive maneuver would fail. If the projection were not taken up and acted out by the partner, it would fail to find any expression at all. Like a rocket spinning out of the earth's orbit and heading for the distant reaches of the universe, it would be lost, gone entirely. The always equable, never unpleasant husband would be in danger of experiencing his hostile feelings *as his own*—as negative emotions which are inside him, about which he is (for some reason) painfully conflicted and therefore unable to express for himself.

Intimate partners, all too frequently, become engaged in the exchange of mutual projections of denied, disavowed feelings and attitudes. They collude and take over aspects of each other's inner world—things one person cannot tolerate as real aspects of his or her own psyche.

Needless to say, when this kind of exchange of internal territories is taking place, the communications between the parties involved become extremely confused. As clinicians Ellen Berman, M.D., Harold Lief, M.D., and Ann Marie Williams, Ph.D., point out, "The person doing the projective identification will simply refuse to hear communications which do not conform to the projection. For example, a woman who states that she would like a loving, kind man, meanwhile projecting all of her disavowed aggressiveness onto her husband, will only remember and acknowledge his harsh and aggressive communications, steadfastly refusing to recognize any kind words." Because the wife does not experience her anger as existing within her own self, she can recognize it only as she sees it in her partner *whether it happens to be there or not.*

An example that they give (which is reminiscent of Laura Brett's situation) is that of a woman who has internalized a conflict with her explosive, judgmental father. She may, in such a circumstance, "repudiate the aggressive, critical component in herself and project it onto her husband. She will then interact with her partner *as if he had those characteristics* [my italics] as a way of externalizing, while maintaining, the conflict."

EXTERNALIZING WHAT IS INTOLERABLE

It is, as these clinicians observe, a commonplace for men to accept the role of the logical, unemotional member of the married twosome. Many males do so, very naturally, because it fits in with their intrapsychic needs and with cultural expectations as well. But when this occurs, the husband's own dependent wishes and vulnerabilities are repudiated and dissociated; vulnerable emotions and feeling states can be perceived only as they become manifest in the mate. Wives, in such marriages, carry the dependency and neediness of the pair. But the projection of disavowed elements of the self onto the intimate partner does not really resolve the husband's own inner conflict (which is a conflict between his own warring needs to be vulnerable and close and yet—seemingly irreconcilably—to be emotionally independent, completely sufficient unto himself). The site of the struggle has merely been moved. It is no longer a conflict going on inside the husband's internal world; it is a conflict *between* the marital partners.

Instead of having to deal with the threatening emotions that exist within himself, the husband can externalize them and make contact with them only as he experiences them in his unquenchably needful, anxious and intimacy-demanding wife.

One woman patient, quoted in the clinical literature, phrased her own reasons for wanting to fight out an *inner* conflict in her marital relationship in the following way: "I feel better when my husband hates me," she said, "than when I hate myself."

This, in my opinion, is a succinct and clear statement about just why it is, and how it is, that people tend to put outside themselves—and onto the mate—feelings, wishes and behaviors which cannot be "owned" as anything that exists within and is radiating outward from the self.

But where such projections exist, it is inevitable that the marital relationship will become suffused with the intense emotions that a person has been unable to accept (or perhaps even experience) as her or his own. Until the wife, in the instance given above, becomes able to accept responsibility for her own self-critical, negative feelings, the couple is doomed to fight out *her past in her own family* (where her repressed, negative images of self originate) in the relationship that they currently share.

A Projective Trade-off:
An Example of How an Early Attachment Can Affect a Later Intimate Commitment

Therapists Berman, Lief and Williams cite an intriguing example of the ways in which an early emotional attachment can affect an intimate commitment forged at a much later point in time.

"A woman who before her marriage had competently lived alone for a number of years, proud of her total independence, married a rather lonely, isolated man," they report. The wife's perception of her husband was that he was a strong, powerful man—someone like her father—and she projected onto him all of her competence, allowing her hidden, helpless, dependent self to surface. Soon, they recount, she found herself so dependent that she was unable to drive or make a shopping list. She insisted that she did not know why this was happening but felt that she had simply "lost her nerve." She had, in fact, given over into her mate's keeping all of her former competence and assumed the burden of carrying his dependent needs for him.

The husband, in turn—because such projections involve a mutual "deal"—gave over to his wife all of his own unmet and disowned dependency needs; she expressed these needs for him by means of her own utterly needful behavior.

Therefore, while objecting verbally to her dependency demands, he drove her everywhere, smiling indulgently about "my helpless little wife."

In effect, a projective trade-off had taken place. She took charge of the helplessness for the pair of them, enabling him to be in charge of the mastery and the competence. At the level of conscious awareness, the partners appeared to be very different people, but each held, for the other, a repudiated part of the self.

"The polarized relationships resulting from such projections have many problems," the authors point out. "It becomes difficult to share feelings, to 'own' one's own ambivalent feelings, or to produce collaborative behavior." The mates tend to *fight, in each other, the disallowed and denied aspects of the self.*

A Conceptual Bridge

The object relations way of thinking is a conceptual bridge between "pure" psychoanalytical theorizing—with its focus on individual, intrapsychic experience—and systemic (which is to say, transactional and interpersonal) modes of understanding human behavior. For a couple *is,* after all, a system—a two-person social and emotional system—and the concept of projective identification provides a powerful means of understanding the ways in which certain two-person systems form and how the individuals involved in them interrelate.

Since, however, the exchange of certain aspects of each person's internal world is involved, the theory also has to do with the intrapsychic experiences of the intimate partners (be the partners infant and mother, or husband and wife, or, for that matter, partners in an intensely powerful intimate friendship).

The object relations approach to the understanding of two-person relationships, which emphasizes the concepts of projective identification and collusion between emotionally bonded pairs, combines a way of understanding both the individual person and the behavior of the person in an intense, intimate relationship. It is here that the subjective world of the person and the objective world of the couple overlap—where the older, individually oriented, and the more recent, systemic kinds of theories meet and converge.

COUPLES IN COLLUSION

When partners collude to express disavowed, dissociated aspects of each other's beings, an inner conflict that *each* of them is experiencing soon becomes the quarrel between them. As psychiatrist David Berkowitz points out, each member of the couple seeks to feel better about himself or herself by seeking to bring about improvement and change in the mate.

"How frequent is the opening gambit of the patient in either individual or marital therapy that a change in the spouse, who is being blamed for the difficulties, would be the answer to his or her problems!" writes Dr. Berkowitz. "*As is well known, many marry precisely in an unconscious effort to resolve underlying intrapsychic difficulties* [my italics]."

People often choose and use their mates, Berkowitz observes, as part of an ongoing effort to resolve and master internal issues that have grown out of early significant relationships in their original families.

We humans often try to get our mates to act out our disavowed, repudiated, dissociated feelings—to play out the other side of what is an internal conflict of our own.

I think, in this regard, of a couple who were in their early thirties at the time of our interviews, David and Virginia Palmer. The Palmers provided a striking example of the ways in which a couple's mutual projections tend to fit together like the proverbial hand and glove.

Virginia Palmer had been the daughter of an alcoholic father, a man whose career in filmmaking had been demolished by a drinking problem by the time he'd reached his fiftieth year. This disaster was being experienced by her family, and—although she only realized it, consciously, when she became an adult—her parents' marriage was also a miserable failure. No hint of anger or untoward feeling, however, was ever expressed by anyone in the family. The household was sinking beneath a weight of defeat and grief, but no one talked about what was actually happening.

Virginia, during her late girlhood and adolescent years, lived through all this without ever becoming consciously aware of the extent of her own hostility. She had learned, in her stoically nonexpressive family, to suppress, and not to feel, anger.

Her husband, David, a successful architect, came from a southern lower-middle-class family with a brawling and violent history; his outbursts of rage, from the very outset of their marriage, had horrified and frightened his wife. She had, she said, not seen anything like his behavior ever before in her life! In the wake of each emotional explosion, Virginia drew back from him with feelings of loathing and dread.

Eventually, she began to feel overwhelmed. She sank into longer and longer states of depression, which were characterized by intense helplessness, dependency and neediness. What was absent from her conscious experience was, however, *any sense of the hostile emotion within herself, which she could experience only as she perceived it in her husband and identified with in his eruptive behavior*. All the rage—rage enough for *both* of them—was in him. She was uniquely without any angry feelings whatsoever. He was powerful, she was weak; he was capable, and she incompetent; they had, in short, polarized around a variety of human attributes, attitudes and feelings.

When people polarize in this fashion, they behave in ways that transform their distorted perceptions of both self and other into a distorted and uncomfortable mutual reality.

Marital treatment, in the Palmers' case, had held the relationship together long enough for their powerful mutual projections to be teased apart. Virginia had, in therapy, become able to "own"—take responsiblity for—the very real fury that she felt, a fury that was *inside her*, and that related to feelings about her father and the long misery of having grown up in that household. These feelings had been simmering within her since she could remember, but she had *seen* them as existing only in her spouse.

She no longer needed to see *all* hostile emotions as external to herself; she had no need to make contact with them *only* as she experienced them vicariously, by means of her husband's angry behavior. It became possible for her to *be angry*—know she was angry and express her angry feelings—something which had been unthinkable in her own original family.

David, on the other hand, had eventually been able to make contact with the side of himself which was terribly needy, dependent and babyish—with the vulnerable feelings which had been suppressed in the tense and dangerous atmosphere of his own family of origin. These helpless, overwhelmed, frightened, wounded aspects of his own inner being were states of feeling that he had been able to experience only as he recognized them *in his wife*.

Each had had to be either needy, anxious and scared—or assertive and furious—for two people instead of for one.

What had been necessary, in order to bring about change and improvement in their mutual relationship, was for both partners to take conscious responsibility for the part of the ambivalence (never dependent/always dependent; never angry/always quick to anger) which he or she had suppressed. David could be needy, vulnerable and intimacy-seeking as well as demanding; Virginia could be competent, autonomous *and* appropriately angry without having to externalize her rage and see it in her terrifying husband's irrational behavior. Only when the projections of past relationships were peeled away did it become possible for each of them to connect with the other person's real attributes and feelings.

The Palmers' story, sketched out here in the broadest and briefest fashion, illustrates a human truth: It is only when we are *not* projecting aspects of our inner world onto our partner that it becomes possible to connect with that other person's reality.

THE REFLECTION IN THE MIRROR

Until present attachments have been unhooked from earlier experiences, the projections from the past can be like mirrors—mirrors in which we can find, not our mates, but disavowed aspects of our own inner beings. This is very different from real intimacy—which involves that wonderful, satisfying exchange of messages from one subjective world to another—for, in the mirror of our projections, we don't see our spouses; we see ourselves.

COLLUSIVE ARRANGEMENTS

There is no such thing, outside the realm of romantic fantasy, as a marriage which is completely free of conflict. Such a relationship is, as psychiatrist A. G. Thompson, M.D., of the Tavistock Institute of Marital Studies in London has written, not in the nature of human beings. "In the depths of our minds we never, throughout all our lives, succeed in freeing ourselves fully from the hates and resentments that first arose in infancy, or from the excessive and unreal demands and expectations of those earliest years. These emotional forces are part of the essential dynamics of our personalities, and they operate intensely in marriage as they do in any deep emotional relationship, and lead inevitably to some measure of conflict, frustration and aggressive reaction against the partner."

The question is, thus, not one of whether discord, contention, feelings of hostility and the like will be present in a marriage—they *will* be, overtly or covertly, and more or less intensely at differing phases of a couple's journey through time and past each station of the family life cycle—but of how readily can the members of the couple negotiate around their differences and disappointments once they have sprung into view. In marriages marked by constantly simmering resentment or continual outright warfare, negotiations have frequently become an impossibility—and collaborative behavior out of the question—because certain aspects of the partners' internal beings have become so confusingly intertwined.

When a man has, for example, been struggling with an underlying, denied and dissociated depression, he may have found himself attracted to—and have married—the very woman who can give expression to this aspect of his internal world *for him*. He may then play out the role of the logical, nonemotional, nonneedy husband of the openly vulnerable, dependent, moody, often frankly despairing wife. The problem is, however, that the same underlying motivations which led him to select that particular mate—as part of an effort to relieve his own anxiety—will inevitably result in his wanting to have her remain depressed at the same time as he finds her recurrent depressions unbearable! This is the equivalent of his wanting her to be tall and short, or fat and thin, at the same time!

Predictably, the more he projects his repudiated, intolerable feelings of dejection and sadness onto his wife, the more he is likely to dissociate his own self from them—and from her—as well. She will, then, not only be carrying the depression for the pair of them, but the more she does what he, at an unconscious level, *wants her to do for him*, the more their mutual estrangement and their tension will grow. For the husband, both in flight from and wanting to connect with his own internal experiences, will not only induce her to express his dissociated feelings and emotions, but also criticize her roundly for doing so.

It may be assumed that the wife, in such a projective identification system, has not only agreed to carry those aspects of her mate's inner experience which he cannot consciously tolerate, but has also given aspects of *her* internal world into *his* safekeeping. Perhaps it is her competence and independence which he must hold for her—*because she learned, early in her life, that it would be impossible to be both independent and nurtured in an emotional relationship, and so it was necessary to choose one or the other.* It is only when one becomes aware of the collusive arrangements that couples make that it becomes apparent that there are no victims and villains—or saints and devils—in marriage. There are, instead, only active colluders, each carrying a disclaimed area of the spouse's internal territory as part of what is a mutually agreed-upon, unconscious arrangement.

SPLITTING

Although it is true that projections of the internal self (and identifications with those projections) are probably always going to play some role in close, emotional attachments, the degree of mutual gratification that a couple experiences will depend greatly upon how much of the personality of each partner is being disposed of in this fashion. It will also depend, as clinicians Pincus and Dare observe, upon "the degree of violence with which the mental act is carried out, and the rigidity with which it is maintained."

They write: "The hardworking wife, who keeps herself, her home and her children meticulously clean and runs [around complaining] about her dirty drunkard of a husband, may well be worried about the bad, dirty aspects of herself, perhaps her 'bad' sexuality. It may be this anxiety about herself which makes it so important for her to keep all the 'bad' things firmly fixed onto the husband. Her demands for help may express, on one level, an unconscious striving to relieve her of her guilt about herself which has been intolerably increased by her destructiveness towards her husband."

Similarly, they add, "the rigid man with high moral standards who is desperately anxious about his slovenly, promiscuous or delinquent wife may need her to express similar drives of his own which he has never dared to face and has repressed into the unconscious." What is notable, in the above examples, is how strikingly different the marital partners appear to be, so different that one would question the reasons why they ever married in the first place! One mate is all cleanliness and order, the other totally dirty and disreputable.

Once one realizes, however, that in such situations a trade-off of projections has occurred—an unconscious deal worked out in which one partner has agreed to carry the "badness" and one to carry the "goodness" of the couple, as if they were parts of an undifferentiated whole organism—what needs to happen becomes apparent. Each member of the couple must reown and take responsibility for those aspects of his or her internal world which are being put onto the partner.

This means *learning to experience ambivalence*—the good and the bad within the other and the good and the bad within the self.

It involves, in plain words, seeing both one's goodness and one's badness, one's craziness and one's saneness, one's adequacy and inadequacy, one's depression and one's happy feelings, etc., as aspects of internal experience rather than *splitting off* one side of any of these dichotomies and being able to perceive it only as it exists in the mate.

THE ALL-GOOD SELF, THE ALL-BAD PARTNER

Projective identification is, according to psychiatrist L. B. Feldman, M.D., a defense mechanism which occurs in two steps. Step one, he explains, "consists of dividing or 'splitting' intrapsychic self and other representations, one of which is experienced as 'all bad' [frustrating, rejecting, cruel, etc.] and the other as 'all good' [nurturing, gratifying, kind, accepting, admiring, etc.]." The second step then "consists of projecting one or more of these 'split-up' images onto one or more external others, thus altering one's preception of those others and of the self. In other words, instead of seeing both self and other as partly good and partly bad, one frequently sees "self" in the white shirt and "other" in the black shirt—and deserving to be run out of town!

"The 'all good' self-representation is retained," continues Dr. Feldman, "leading to an experience of self as the innocent victim of the 'all bad' spouse. The 'all good' representation is often projected in fantasy, leading to the thought that someone other than the spouse (a fantasied other) would actually conform to the (unrealistic) 'all good' image."

What is good is seen in the self and in the imagined perfect partner— he who will arrive on the white charger (or its female equivalent). *What is bad is projected onto the spouse and seen as existing in her or in him ineradicably.* When two people are engaged in polarizations, one can be either a perfect person or a louse; it is hard to be anything in between.

Learning to contain one's ambivalent feelings about the self and about other people is a part of growing up; it is a developmental achievement. Many individuals cannot, however, acknowledge the badness, weakness, inadequacy, incompetence, anger (or certain other proscribed feelings) within. Or, as I noted earlier, it may be that it is strength, competence, or other positive qualities which must be kept out of conscious awareness, for (so the person has learned) these qualities and attitudes will threaten the existence of a vitally needed emotional relationship. Because, at some point or another in that individual's early life the push for independence and self-sufficiency produced so much anxiety, his or her autonomy needs had to be suppressed—pushed down out of sight of the mind's inner eye.

In conflictual marriages, it is usually the case that each partner is defending himself or herself against intolerable (often negative, self-critical, self-deprecating) thoughts by keeping them out of conscious experience completely. Instead of "owning" certain discomfiting thoughts, images, attitudes, feelings, etc., each individual rids his or her own self of them by projecting them onto the mate and then making contact with them only vicariously.

Many of us do, it must be reiterated, choose marital partners who will help us recapitulate old conflicts which never were successfully mastered. Using the mate in this fashion—i.e., to play out the other half of a dilemma one had with a parent—serves, suggests marital theorist David

Berkowitz, a dual sort of function. In the first place, by fighting the battle out with the spouse, one does not have to experience it as what it is: a painful internal conflict which is actually taking place within one's own psyche.

And in the second place, Berkowitz explains, the mutual exchange of projections "serves to recapture and restore through reenactment important conflictual early relationships. Projective mechanisms are, thus, both defensive and restorative: They defend against internal conflict and they are object conserving at the same time." The original relationship with the object of one's powerful feelings—i.e., the parent—is (in the internal world) thus maintained. One does not have to make the internal separation from the earlier, problematic, unresolved attachment; one can, instead, reproduce it with the partner and go on fighting the eternally unresolved battle.

THE ALTERNATIVE: CHANGING THE SYSTEM

Then one can fight that battle again, and again, and again in the familiar vicious cycle of repeating interactions that therapists call "the game without end." Or, alternatively, one can work actively and resolutely to tease those interlocking projections apart. When it becomes possible for partners to take up the unfinished work of childhood and to reown parts of the self that once had to be disavowed and discarded, then marriage becomes a therapeutic relationship in the best, most gratifying sense of that word. It becomes a place in which old wounds can be healed.

What this often requires, however, is the dismantling of the old projective identification system and the formation of another kind of relational system entirely.

II
Tasks

When it comes to loving, we all do it in the ways that are familiar and find it hard to imagine that there may be *other options*, other ways of being in a close relationship. In many instances, though, the familiar ways of loving are painful. If, for example, the members of a couple have begun to polarize—so that each is disavowing certain parts of the self, projecting them onto the other, and then condemning those qualities *in the partner*—the entire marriage becomes suffused with misunderstanding and conflict. The mates feel trapped, for their way of relating to each other is extremely ungratifying, and they have no idea about how to change things.

How, in fact, can changes in the relationship be brought about? Opinions on this subject differ. Some experts believe that in order to improve a troubled marriage, the problems of each partner must be addressed individually. In other words, in order to have a healthy relationship, the partners must be in tiptop psychological shape: Clear up the individual problems, and the problems of the marriage will resolve themselves.

Other marital experts disagree. They believe that the individual issues of each spouse are far less important than is *the way in which the partners interact*. The couple has created, as every couple does, unspoken rules for regulating their existence together—but the rules they have created cause them pain. It is the dysfunctional rules of the relationship which must be addressed, according to this point of view, and not the individual partners themselves.

But *can* the rules of the marital system be changed? And if so, how might one go about doing it?

Doing Things Differently

According to marital therapist Stuart Johnson, M.S.W., the use of behavioral tasks can prove enormously helpful in initiating positive change. For while there are many couples who are well aware of the ways in which they are replicating unhealthy patterns of the past, they simply don't know how to behave in different ways. What these partners need to experience, according to Johnson (who was for many years the director of family therapy at the Yale Psychiatric Institute and now maintains a flourishing private practice) is what being in a different kind of emotional system actually *feels like*.

"What the couple generally needs," says Johnson, "is a taste of the honey of what being in a far more functional, more differentiated relationship is like. Because," he adds, "they *don't know*. How could they? If you've never been in that kind of emotional system—or even *seen* anything like it—how could you possibly know of its existence?"

What the behavioral tasks do is to get couples into this new kind of relational world—one in which being a whole, separate and autonomous person, and being able to remain close to your whole, separate and autonomous partner, are not perceived as incompatible states of being.

For those couples who are capable of carrying them out (and many mates are *not*, because the power struggle between them is too intense to permit collaboration) these structured exercises can provide an entry into a new way of being together, an utterly transformed kind of intimate partnership. I must warn the reader, however, that while they seem deceptively nonchallenging, the tasks are constructed in such a way as to make shifts in the emotional system inevitable. These simple, innocent-appearing exercises are, in fact, remarkably effective stratagems for initiating change—for sorting the self, the other, and the entire relationship out. They should, therefore, be handled with care.

Talking and Listening: Task One

The directions for carrying out the first task are the following: The members of the couple are asked to select a particular hour, during the forthcoming week, and to agree that this time is to be spent together with no interruptions allowed. They are then asked to decide, perhaps by the flip of a coin, who will be entitled to the first half hour of that segment of time. The mate who goes first (let us say, the wife) is then in charge of the family microphone and is instructed to talk *about her own self only*. She is not permitted to say anything pertaining to her spouse, or about their relationship, at all.

The other partner is enjoined to listen attentively, but to make no verbal response whatsoever. After this part of the task has been completed (i.e., when the half hour is over), the speaker and the listener positions are switched. The second partner talks, and the first one gives him her complete attention with no interruptions allowed. Any discussion of the mate or of the marriage is, as before, forbidden.

He, during his half hour, is to talk about himself as a separate person—the things he thinks about; his life; his joys; his hurts. The rules ordain, in short, that each spouse take a period of time to talk about his or her own needs, desires, wishes, frustrations, fantasies, and so forth—so long as what is said involves the speaker alone. They ordain, as well, that the listener remain quiet and give an attentive hearing to whatever it is that's being said.

At the end of the hour, when both partners have talked and both have listened, the homework is complete. (The following week they may want to reverse the order in which they speak.) A final and very important part of the instructions is, however, that when the task is finished, *no discussion of it is to take place*. The members of the couple are, simply, to resume their lives without saying anything further on the subject.

What is critically important about this exercise is that *the partners cannot respond to each other*. The jobs of talking and of listening are rotated, and then further conversation on the subject is disallowed. (If the mates were in treatment, their "homework assignment" would be discussed during the next therapeutic session. For those couples who want to try carrying out these tasks on their own, therefore, the best approximation would be an agreement to postpone all discussions of the exercise for at least three days after its completion.)

Because the rules of the homework game prohibit the usual ongoing, back-and-forth interchange between the spouses, the usual operation of the projective identification system is (for that one hour, at least) blocked. For in a projective identification situation, it takes both members of the couple to tango—it is almost impossible for any mate to tango alone. If, for example, a wife perceives her own feelings of inferiority and inadequacy as being her husband's thoughts and feelings *about her*, she needs to sustain that projection by experiencing her own self-accusations as accusations and reproaches which are coming from her mate. She must (albeit she does so quite unconsciously) provoke him to treat her like an incompetent dodo, thus enabling her to *fight the bad feelings as they exist and become manifest in him* instead of experiencing them as painful feelings that exist within.

"The collusion between the partners," points out Johnson, "has to translate into *behavior*. The husband must accept the projection, in response to the unconscious cues that she's sending him, and then he must act accordingly. He has to behave in ways that fit her perception that these painful, horrible self-accusatory ideas are not anything emanating from within her own head; they are all coming from within *his*. One way of looking at this is, by the way, to see him as behaving protectively—helping her to turn an internal conflict, which she finds intolerable, into a fight that is going on between them." Most of us can appreciate the reasons why a person might find it easier to fight an enemy outside than to confront the enemy within.

So long, however, as the pair of them continues to operate within this kind of relational system, their interpersonal difficulties cannot—almost by definition—be resolved. The rules by which they're operating won't permit it. She, in other words, must continue to provoke him to provoke her to provoke him to provoke her . . . to go round and round in a vicious cycle in which neither person can possibly connect with the other because his or her own repudiated, dissociated feelings stand directly in the way.

The agreement that when one is committed to speak, the other is committed to listen interrupts the usual interaction between the partners and impedes the continuous flowing together of what is self and what is other—that blurring of personal boundaries which takes place in projective identification situations. "What the talking and listening task does is to increase the likelihood," explains Johnson, "that each individual will actually get to *hear* what the partner is saying! Because the exchange of projections is, at least during that period of time when they're actually engaged in *doing the exercise*, being obstructed—which forces them into a different kind of relational system, entirely."

The task compels the members of the couple to face each other as separate, autonomous people. "If," points out Johnson, "a person has to listen to his spouse, and cannot speak, he is respecting her autonomy. He is allowing for her separateness, rather than responding to a confusion of what's inside his own self and what is really out there, in his partner." Merely *being* in such a circumstance can, for both participants, be experienced as something surprisingly different and gratifying.

Imagine, for example, the impact that this assignment might have upon couples who are in pursuer/distancer relationships. She who chases (I use this pronoun because it is, more commonly, the woman) is dependent upon he who runs away to express autonomy needs for both of them. Similarly, he who is in flight from emotional connectedness must be assured that someone is still after him; otherwise, he might have to accept responsibility for his own intimate needs and feelings of vulnerability, which she expresses for both of them. As I mentioned earlier, they have divided the ambivalence—the needs of the individual self and the needs of the relationship—right down the middle seam of the emotional attachment that they share.

The pursuer has split off, denied and dissociated any self of her own; autonomy needs are perceived as selfish and bad and can be recognized only as they exist in the mate. The distancer obliges by needing ever-greater areas of individual turf—and the more she chases after him for closeness, the greater is his need for space. Intimacy is, as he perceives it, something which could swallow a person alive—a state which, moreover, only *the partner* desires! The distancer cannot experience the wish for emotional communion as his own, for it would make him feel so much at risk, so vulnerable to rejection and abandonment.

The rules of this couple's system command that the pursuer chase after the distancer forever, but that she (or he) never catch up. They enjoin the distancer, moreover, to keep on running—so long as he (or she) never really gets away. What the partners achieve, by their mutual enforcement of these regulations, is a way of modulating the needs of the self and the needs of the relationship in a balanced, predictable fashion. She tries to get closer as he runs off, so the space between them is maintained. This is a somewhat crude way of modulating autonomy and intimacy—i.e., "You handle all of the closeness, and I'll handle all of the personal space concerns"—which generates great anxiety and tension. But it is the only system that the pursuer and the distancer have been able to work out, the only one that either of them *knows*.

Clearly, maintaining the polarization requires a collusion, on the part of both members of the couple, to express those thoughts, feelings, qualities, attributes, etc., which are being so strenuously denied by the mate. When, therefore, the pursuer is forced (by the rules of the task) to talk *only about herself*, she is compelled to stop chasing and focus upon the person she is, inside. She cannot continue recycling her usual remarks, which tend to center on the partner (particularly his shortcomings) and on things that are happening in the relationship.

She must, in complying with the rules of the exercise, concentrate on trying to be an autonomous person and on doing so in the presence of her mate. What she will hopefully learn, while carrying out the task, is that it is being one's own self (rather than continually pursuing someone who continually eludes you) that makes closeness to the partner possible.

The distancer, halted in his headlong flight from intimacy, is made to learn what happens when he does give her his attention—for he has been commanded to listen to her for that full half hour and not to run away. And he, when it is his turn, gets to do what he knows how to do best—i.e., behave autonomously—but *to do so in the company of the partner* this time around. What the distancer experiences (perhaps for the first time ever) is that he can talk about himself and his own concerns without feeling guilty about excluding or rejecting the intimacy-seeking spouse, or that he's in danger of having her engulf him.

Her intimacy wishes have often, by the way, tended to be one-sided. She has, generally speaking, set the subjects around which their intimate relating is to take place. And often it is true that on those occasions when he's tried to talk to her about matters that don't concern her or the relationship—which have to do with him alone—she has in fact, cut him off rather quickly. Although she desires closeness more than anything else in the world, the pursuer wants it in her own fashion, in her own time, and in her own way. She needs to have him be there for her, but has trouble hearing things that remind her of his separateness and independence. They both, it might be said, have a similar sort of problem—the great problem, which we all find so difficult, of *dealing with human aloneness*.

Part of respecting a person's autonomy is, according to Stuart Johnson, being willing to really *listen* to him or her, to hear all that the individual has to say. "Since the instructions for the task include that prohibition against talking about the partner and about the marriage," he notes, "the one who speaks must focus on his or her own self alone. The assignment is, in other words, framed in such a way as to get each person to talk autonomously—and to have the spouse *honor that autonomy by giving it his or her complete attention*."

What the members of the couple often discover is that while the entire exercise is autonomy-enhancing, the process of going through it makes them feel unaccountably *intimate*. Being separate persons, in each other's presence, promotes a sense of closeness. This experience contravenes the unspoken rule that people in a projective identification system live by. Which is: If you are autonomous, you cannot be intimate, and if you are intimate, you cannot be an autonomous person. "It puts them," Johnson explains, "into a kind of emotional system which neither one has, usually, ever seen before—one in which independent personhood and closeness to the partner are synonymous."

Having been there—if only for the hour of working on the task—the couple begins to realize that such a relational world actually does exist.

ODD DAY, EVEN DAY: TASK TWO

The instructions for the second exercise, when one first hears them, may sound eccentric and peculiar. Couples who have, however, successfully weathered an initial time of working with the Talking and Listening task will undoubtedly be motivated to move ahead and try this one. They will, moreover, probably choose to add this assignment to the last one—rather than replace the old task with the new—because that one hour per week of exchanging information about *where one is as a separate person* has been found to be so individually gratifying and so good for the relationship as well.

If, however, a particular set of partners feels that they have milked the first exercise for all that they needed or wanted from it, they can drop it as they proceed with the second or "odd day, even day" task.

The instructions to be followed are these: At the outset, the couple agrees to divide the weekdays between them. The wife may, for example, take Monday, Wednesday and Friday, while her husband takes Tuesday, Thursday and Saturday. On Sunday, their day off, they are free (in Johnson's words) to "practice their pathology," i.e., to let the tried-and-true, old recurring cycle run its familiar course.

On the odd days of the week (one, three, five) the wife is, then, the person who is in charge of the intimacy in the relationship. On the even days (two, four, six) the husband is given control of the intimacy wheel. How, one might ask, is "being in control of intimacy" actually supposed to manifest itself in one member of the couple or the other?

The answer is that each partner, on his or her day, must make *one intimacy request*; the mate has preagreed to meet it.

Beyond that, while the person in charge is certainly permitted to express other intimate needs (as can her spouse, even though it is not "his day"), it is with the express understanding that the other person is under no obligation to respond positively after that one intimate need has been satisfied.

On the wife's day, to recapitulate, the husband is to meet a single intimacy request—clearly labeled as such *by* her—and on the subsequent day, control of the intimacy in the relationship passes into *his* keeping. According to the stated rules of the game, he then must ask her to meet one intimate need of his, and she, by prearrangement, will meet that request on the day when he is in charge. That is all there is to it. These are the relatively simple, nonthreatening rules of the second assignment.

It is, though, important to add that each mate's intimacy requests must be noncosmic—that is, *not* "Love me forever"! The intimate need communicated should, suggests Stuart Johnson, be on the relatively modest side. "The request ought to be something readily achievable," he advises, "which can be performed on that same day and not carried over to the next one." It should be clearly describable in terms of something behavioral, something that a partner can *do*. How, if one mate asked the partner to love him or her forever, could the spouse go about meeting so impossible a demand?

There is no straightforward way that a husband can respond to his wife's intimacy need if she says to him, "I want you to adore me." If she makes such a request she is not only asking him to control something which is not volitional, but she is putting him into a destructive, paradoxical bind: She is commanding him to behave spontaneously. It is illogical to ask him to "have" certain feelings which, by their very nature, can only be spontaneous and which, furthermore, *cannot* be spontaneous in this situation (because she has requested that he have them!). Paradoxical communications of this sort—"I want you to tell me about how much you love me"—tend to place the other person in a highly uncomfortable position and usually bring little satisfaction to the person making the request . . . who, naturally, wonders if that expression of love really did come from the other's heart!

What is vitally important is that if one spouse says to the other, "I want you to be particularly tender and loving to me," he or she must also give the partner clear directives about what *action or actions* "being tender and loving" would translate into. One individual might, for example, put "being tender and loving" into the following behavioral terms: "I want you to spend the next hour talking with me about some of the things that are on my mind." Another might say, "I'd like to go out for a walk, just the two of us." Still a third might say, "I can't think of anything else I'd like more at this moment than having you give me a five-minute massage."

Requests such as "Rub my back," or "Help me to think through the problem that I'm having with my office mate," or "Let me choose the movie that we go out to see tonight" are the readily fulfillable ones that Stuart Johnson has in mind (as opposed to "I want you to be committed to this relationship until the end of time"). The person in control of that day's intimacy must, in short, state his or her own realistically meetable intimate need and the preferred way in which the partner is expected to respond. Needless to say, it would be self-defeating to make requests that will produce untenable conflicts in the partner. It would be unwise, for example, for a husband to ask for fifteen minutes of his wife's time just as she is rushing out the door on her way to an important appointment.

Along these lines I should add that in many instances couples will want to define certain problem areas in their relationship as off-limits and taboo even before work with the odd day/even day task commences. Such proscribed topics will, most frequently, have to do with sex or money—the two most highly charged marital issues, around which power struggles are very likely to be taking place. When, by prearrangement, a particular subject is put under ban, intimacy requests relating to it are not allowed to be tendered. The sensitized, explosive material, whatever it might be, remains out of the bounds of the assignment.

It is, generally speaking, counterproductive to approach a control battle by attacking the distressing, painful issues directly. Instead of charging, head-on, into the heavily defended front door of the relationship, it is far easier to enter (one small, relatively nonthreatening step at a time) through a less scary, more accessible side entrance.

The odd day/even day task is, I should note, a variation on a therapeutic assignment first used by the famous Italian analyst Mara Selvini Palazzoli. It was developed by Palazzoli and her Milanese colleagues as a device for breaking up control struggles being waged around the parenting of a child. The feuding adults, locked in a power struggle, were each certain that he or she *knew* how a child should be nurtured and disciplined; each believed that the mate, blind to the real facts of the rearing process, was interfering in misguided or downright malevolent ways. As a way of dealing with this impasse, the Italian clinicians put *both the mother and the father in complete control of parenting*—not simultaneously, but on alternating, odd, even days.

What this rotation of command served to demonstrate to the parents, by means of their own *experience*, was that they could coexist in a system in which neither one of them was in perpetual and complete authority. Instead of having to compete continually for the role of acknowledged winner in what was an unresolvable and destructive (to their child) contest, control of the parenting process could be shared between them—by shifting the leadership position on a daily basis.

The rules of the odd day/even day task, as adapted for use by couples (by replacing "parenting" with "intimacy" as the major concern to be addressed), serve to block the desperate power struggles which are so ubiquitous in troubled relational systems. In such unhealthy systems, the partners are usually working with the underlying assumption that there is only a single option for being in an intimate attachment: You can be the controller or you can be the one *who is under the control* of the mate.

The carrying out of the therapeutic assignment, however, puts the couple into a different kind of emotional framework entirely. They cannot, while working with their new operational regulations, maintain the on-going, determined battle for ascendancy—for the rules of the task decree that control of the intimacy in the relationship will oscillate back and forth between them. The partners are, thus, able to achieve by mutual agreement what neither could ever quite attain on his or her own: a sense of being in undisputed charge, at least during certain designated time periods. Taking turns, on an alternating, daily basis, gives to *both* what neither person could manage to get separately.

Many people take the position that they can be intimate with the spouse as long as they are totally in control of that intimacy. "In other words," Johnson says, "they are willing to be intimate so long as they're not vulnerable—which is an absolute impossibility." Real connection with another human being involves vulnerability—opening oneself to the other person and not trying to maintain control over what it is that he or she does or has to say. Intimacy requests, which are simple statements of small personal needs, are small steps in the direction of letting mates know that this is safe.

It is easier, obviously, for a partner to make an intimate request when he knows that his mate has committed herself to *meet his need* in advance and by prearrangement. It is easier for her to satisfy his request when she is aware that on the following day *her own turn* is coming. Good stroking produces good stroking. Playing by the new rules involves being in a system in which control is *shared with* rather than *wrested from* the partner—a relational world in which each individual remains in charge of his or her own self and then works out a mutually agreeable arrangement with the equally empowered mate.

If, moreover, the pair is to function within the guidelines of the task, their closeness needs and their separateness needs must be modulated by them in what are new and novel ways. The partner who, for example, forever runs away from intimate exchange is now expected to look within, ask himself *what he wants from his partner*, and, in the simplest terms possible, request that she meet his need. For him, in the past, such behavior would have been—literally—unthinkable, for he is usually someone who has difficulty experiencing such needs and wishes as anything that *exists within himself*.

The autonomy-seeking distancer has, by and large, denied wanting or needing much of anything from anyone else. One might suppose that his difficulties in experiencing his own intimate wishes stem from an underlying assumption that it's better not to have such needs at all—if one *did* have them, they would be compromised, misunderstood, or otherwise unmet by the intimate partner. He has come into the relationship believing that it's better not to *have* intimacy wishes, because the other will so certainly deny them. This somewhat crude defensive tactic (which frequently involves infantile feelings that the partner should, somehow, meet his needs even if he himself is not quite aware of their existence) is accompanied by an underlying rage, for the needs *are* there, within him, and they are not being met.

Unless she reads his mind (which the partner is, of course, unable to do), the distancer's mate will have to deal with his unaccountable, illogical and often very subtly expressed anger *at her*. He, naturally, doesn't know what he's angry about either (if he knows that he's angry at all). His intimate needs are being short-circuited—suppressed before he can even take conscious cognizance of their existence. He assumes, without ever questioning his assumption, that it's better not to have such needs at all; he is so certain that they will not be gratified. His fear is that if he makes his real wishes known, they'll be frustrated by the partner, or she will simply swallow him up (in her needs) alive!

Experiencing an intimate need as his own, and making a request of his partner which is related to that need, are the new things that the emotional distancer must (in order to play according to the rules of the task) now begin doing regularly. This puts him into a new position not only vis-à-vis the spouse, but vis-à-vis his own inner self. Owing to earlier frustrations of his normal desire to have his emotional needs satisfied by another person, this is something which the distancer has hardly ever attempted! But now, every other day of the week, he is called upon to dredge up and openly recognize an intimate need *from within*—which, frequently, he finds to be a surprising experience. The therapeutic assignment requires, moreover, that he not only recognize his inner wish or need, but communicate that need to his partner—who has preagreed to meet it.

The pursuer, on her part, has no such problem in owning or conveying her emotional needs to the mate; this is her area of expertise. It is, however, frequently difficult for her to recognize that *he* might have symmetrical wishes and desires of his own—emotional matters that he needs to share and that both have colluded to push out of sight.

In the projective identification world which they inhabit, he provides the space, and she is in charge of the intimate sharing in the relationship. His needs, when they do surface, are something that alarm her; she usually doesn't know how to contend with them. For while she is very adept at sharing her own intimate life, she has problems in acknowledging that he *does* have feelings and that these need a hearing as much as hers do! A more subtle way of understanding her behavior might, however, be that of seeing it as "protective"—by taking on his neediness, emotionality, anger, upset, depression (or whatever), she assumes responsibility for feeling and expressing the affect that both individuals believe the distancer is incapable of handling. In any case, by alternating who makes intimate requests and who fills intimate requests, the mates get intensive training in that aspect of the emotional exchange in which each of them is deficient.

In the process, as the alternation of the odd, even days provides an ebb and flow of emotional exchange—experience in recognizing intimate needs and in getting them met—each partner's inner concerns become, inevitably, much more apparent to the other. What the mate wants and needs are often so unaccountably *different* from the wants and the needs that are one's own! The mate, as an independent center of motivation— a universe unto himself or herself—swims more and more clearly into view. And just as the autonomy-enhancing first task produced an unaccountable sense of closeness in the couple, so this intimacy-enhancing second task brings with it a sense of the profound separateness and individuality of each of the members of the pair.

Adding Requests: Task Three

The directions for carrying out this task are the simplest in the sequence: What comes next is more of the same. Once the pattern of alternating control of the intimacy in the relationship has become established and familiar, the requests allotted to each partner should begin to increase. Instead of the one permitted at the outset of the second assignment, the couple might move up to two or three or four per day.

It is, I hope, clear that there will be intimate wishes and needs expressed throughout this process which are *not* presented as formal requests and are not part of the task. To such informal bids, the spouse may react as he or she pleases, with a "yes," "no," "maybe," "later, if possible," etc. But when an intimacy need is presented and identified as such (i.e., as part of the assignment), the mate is obliged—by preagreement—to respond positively and to meet it.

Insofar as timing is concerned, spouses would probably do well to move ahead with due caution and deliberate care. It would be prudent to become completely accustomed to and familiar with the give-and-take of intimate gratifications before increasing the pressure in the relationship by assuming more and heavier emotional burdens. And as to the ultimate number of requests to be honored on a daily basis, there is no outside limit on how high any pair should think of going—other than whatever the system seems able to tolerate. Some couples may want to ascend slowly and allow the number of intimate needs permitted daily to grow by just one per week; they may, moreover, decide that they've reached their desired total when they get up to four or five or eight.

Others may want to increase the figure exponentially—to go up to two, four, sixteen, etc., as high as they can count to, and even remember, on a given day. Couples ought, while working on this third assignment, to monitor their own performances. When they feel they have gone high enough and worked on this task long enough, it will be time to move forward to the fourth assignment. But the process ought not to be hurried. It is wise to get very comfortable with how it *feels* to negotiate the intimate exchanges in the relationship with the partner before beginning the next task.

One small addendum: If the first (talking and listening) exercise is still in use—or even if it's not—variations upon it can be useful as intimate requests. If, for example, a quarrel erupts, a partner may state an intimate need which involves taking ten minutes to discuss his side of the story and then asking for ten minutes in which to listen to the mate. This is an extremely effective way of preventing fights from escalating because it halts the exchange of projections that can so easily get under way.

CONTROL AND METACONTROL: TASK FOUR

The rules of the fourth task will—take warning—sound odder and more artificial than anything encountered thus far! They are a variant of the odd day/even day task, in which the partners learned to share control of the intimacy in the relationship by agreeing to take charge of it sequentially. In this fourth task, they move in the direction of sharing control in such a way that they are *both* in control of the intimacy in the relationship simultaneously.

This is how healthier emotional systems—in which covert or overt power battles are not being endlessly waged—actually function and operate.

The structure of the assignment is this: The overall schedule, for each partner, remains unchanged. If, for instance, the wife has Monday,

Wednesday and Friday as her intimacy days, and the husband has Tuesday, Thursday and Saturday (with Sunday off, for old pathology), their weekly agenda is unchanged. Except for several important details, the first one being that the person who is in charge for that day—say, the husband—can make as many requests as he wants and there is no limit on the number of needs that he may ask his wife to meet. She, according to the newly revised regulations, must respond positively to all of his intimate requests—with one important exception allowed: If she reaches the point at which meeting a particular need feels like too much of a demand, and she either cannot or doesn't want to honor a particular request, she has the power to announce to her partner that she is *canceling out of the entire game for the rest of the day.*

She cannot, in other words, say no selectively. If she responds negatively to one of his intimate needs, that day's assignment is over; the rules decree, furthermore, that the partner cannot argue with this decision. Once she has said that the intimacy is over, for that day, she is under no obligation to meet her husband's needs or to say yes to the intimate requests that he puts forward subsequently. The task is finished—until the following day, when the game resumes with both players in the reversed positions.

At this point, the wife is in charge of the intimacy in the relationship, and she may ask her husband to meet as many of her intimate needs as she wishes to have met—while he, of course, now has the power to stop the game entirely.

What the new instructions enable the spouses to experience is the sense that both can feel in charge *at the same time*—if each person's control exists at a level which is noncompetitive with the other's. Both spouses can negotiate their intimate needs from positions of strength and entitlement, because each maintains control of a differing yet important domain.

A wife may, in this system, meet fifteen of her husband's intimate needs on a given day, but she retains the capacity to cancel out of the agreement entirely. She is, ultimately, not trapped in their relational system, for she can choose to go outside it—to say, "That's enough; I won't play anymore for today." Thus, while he retains control of the intimacy within the emotional system, she has metacontrol: She can decide whether she wishes to exit or *to stay in the game* (a metaphor for the ongoing intimate interaction) or to take a breather for a while. This option—i.e., that of choosing to go outside the system when necessary— combats the terrible feelings of being trapped and powerless which are so endemic in polarized marital systems.

What the rules of the fourth task introduce the partners to is a system in which the possibility of saying no to the mate's need, in a given circumstance, exists as an available and viable option. This is of particular importance to the inveterate yea-sayer in the relationship, who is often in a simmering burn about feeling manipulated and controlled by the spouse. (Frequently, *both* partners are certain that they are under the control of the partner; both experience themselves as the controllees in the relationship, without comprehending that it is the system itself that regulates the behavior of the major participants within it!)

It is the realization that saying no to the spouse is both acceptable and possible which renders saying yes a real act of freedom. The capacity to refuse a request permits a person to grant those that are granted voluntarily so that when the mate does say yes, it is because he really means it. It is a volitional act, and not something that he's been manipulated into doing in such a way that he's left feeling robotized and furious.

When this small set of new rules is introduced into the homework, interesting things usually do begin to happen in the relationship. As might readily be imagined, each partner is a bit reluctant to refuse one of the partner's requests (thereby canceling the game for the rest of the day) because it is so clear that she or he can, on the following day, retaliate in precisely the same manner. And what has been learned about the partner, in the course of carrying out the preceding assignments, is now found to be astonishingly *handy* information to have.

Each person knows (from the talking and listening task) what matters are foremost on the partner's mind, what are the things which preoccupy him. Each person knows as well (from the odd day/even day homework) which particular intimate needs and desires are of critical importance to the mate. Negotiations with the partner are, as a result, far more easily manageable, for such information makes it easier to trim the sails of one's *own intimate needs to the winds of the relationship's reality*. Going too far, on a particular day, would tempt the partner to cancel out of the game entirely—and so requests are usually phrased more empathetically, i.e., with the knowledge of what emotional burdens the system and the intimate other can tolerate.

The sequence of exercises, in its entirety, is directed toward blocking the tendency to polarize around vitally important issues—such as who has the power and control, and who is actually feeling which feelings, and who should give those feelings expression. These are large dilemmas, which many bright and good-hearted people—people who really are committed to their marriages—struggle blindly and fruitlessly to resolve. The tasks, which are to be recommended heartily, can and often do serve to resolve these issues so simply and readily that the members of the couple are at a real loss in attempting to comprehend the nature of the wonderful thing that has hit them. Their relationship may change profoundly without either one of them being able to explain what has happened, or exactly why.

12

A Classic System: The Silent Husband and the Hysterical Wife

There is no clearer, more commonly encountered example of a projective identification system than that seen in the relationship of the nonexpressive husband and his voluble, highly emotional wife. In this kind of marriage, each spouse has his or her own area of specialization. One partner carries all of the expressivity, warmth and feeling in the intimate system, while the other is in charge of cool rationality, attention to detail, and logic.

Angie and Bob Carrano, in their mid thirties at the time of our interviews, happened to be from a working-class Italian background. But theirs was a type of relationship that I saw over and over again, in every social, ethnic and economic class and group. Marriages much like that of the Carranos are particularly frequent in academic families and among executives, lawyers, and scientists; the husbands, in these relationships, have a propensity to the obsessional pursuit of order, detail and knowledge, while their wives take care of "feelings" for the pair of them.

Often, in such marriages, the male partner is someone who is extremely successful and highly functional professionally. In his intimate life, however, he is patently *dys*functional—as is his spouse—for they inhabit a system which is emotionally unhealthy and deeply ungratifying for both of them. These partners are caught in a mutually collusive, projective identification arrangement, involving a husband who cannot be emotionally expressive and a wife who cannot be anything *but*.

"HE NEVER ATTRACTED ME"

The Carranos, married fourteen and a half years, had two children: Cathy, age ten, and Robert, almost seven. They had, as well, a tall, trim semidetached house in the Elkins Park area, just outside Philadelphia's northernmost city limit. Bob Carrano, who'd changed jobs during the previous month (October) in order to avoid the night shift, worked as a printer. He was employed, at present, by a large suburban newspaper. The disadvantage of the new job was that it was located an inconveniently long distance away. Getting back and forth involved a grueling hour-plus drive, with bad traffic in both directions.

Angie Dinelli Carrano had been a secretary and managed a small insurance office before her marriage, but now worked part-time as a waitress. When I asked them what had, initially, attracted them to one another, the wife laughed and the husband smiled. (Such responses to that particular question were so common that I was far from surprised.)

But then Angie said that she could not remember *ever* being attracted to her husband at all.

"I was . . .", she hesitated, then shrugged, "I didn't *like* him! I wasn't, I mean, drawn to him in the slightest." She had, she explained, been "sort of preengaged" to someone who was in the army and away in Germany, and she had been feeling empty and lonely and sad. "Two of my girlfriends, who'd met Bob previously to me, said, 'Oh, you've got to come out!' " she explained, automatically mimicking the breathless, excited way in which the invitation had been given. "They said they'd met these real nice guys . . . and I was feeling so *depressed* at that point. I'm very depression-prone," she added, in a suddenly subdued, almost whispering tone of voice.

But the depression that she'd been in, when she'd met Bob, had been the first really *bad* one ever. "I was sixteen, at the time—or was I seventeen?" She turned, appealed to her husband, who sat next to her on the sofa. He shook his head, shrugged, but made no other response. "Well, regardless," she said.

"Sixteen," he muttered, after a moment, but Angie, sweeping ahead, did not stop to react to his statement. "So I'd been feeling down at that time, just staying home and brooding, and he wanted to go out with *me* right from the beginning—I think?" Again she turned, looked at Bob for confirmation. "When you first met me, isn't that right?" She didn't pause long enough for him to answer.

"But because he was extremely introverted and shy—my husband is *extremely* shy"—she stopped to observe, as if describing an absent third party—"it took him a long, long time to ask me."

Bob Carrano laughed, a short bark, though I was at a loss to understand why.

"At that point, I went out with him just to kill time," his wife was saying, "and that lasted for three and a half years, and we got married."

She stopped. I waited for some reaction, on Bob Carrano's part, to this annihilating historical account, but none at all was forthcoming.

"What had you been depressed about, before meeting him?" I asked, finally. "Before meeting *Bob*," I amended hastily, for I had almost fallen into Angie's manner of speaking about her spouse as if he were somehow not present and with us in this comfortably furnished basement family room.

"Oh, it was *him* I was depressed about! That other fellow—the one I'd been seeing! I just couldn't cope with that whole relationship and yet was so very, very *involved* with him! When I say 'very involved,' " she rushed on, "I don't mean 'sexually involved'; things weren't the same, fifteen years ago, as they are now; a nice Italian girl didn't *do* that! I just mean emotionally . . . very, very involved. . . ." Her voice level had fallen precipitously, in the course of these comments, so that I had to lean forward to hear her. "We'd been going out for three years, and it had started when I was thirteen—twelve or thirteen?" Again she looked around at her husband questioningly.

It seemed an odd question for her to be asking him to answer. He was her mate, not her parent, and had not even been part of her life at that juncture. This mixture of anger and dependence would, I thought, inevitably be confusing and difficult to deal with. But Bob, a patient expression upon his features, looked as if he were trying to make the calculation for which she'd asked.

"I think, in retrospect—because of my horrendous relationship with my parents, and my home life—that I'd taken a very, very strong attachment." Angie, after a brief pause, had decided that the point of fact she'd queried Bob about did not really merit her halting the drive of her discourse.

"There was a very, *very* strong attachment to this man," she repeated the same words but with an added intensity. "Because he showed interest in me and because I *cared* about him! When he got drafted, I was devastated. As if—oh, it was like having the rug pulled out from under my entire life! And I just brooded and brooded and got into a very severe depression." She was speaking, now, in a melodramatic whisper, like a little girl telling a ghost story.

What, I asked her, in a practical tone of voice, had eventually become of that man who'd gone off to the service and left her pining so unhappily behind? "He's no good," Angie replied, her facial expression shifting from sorrow to contempt. He was, she continued, addicted to drugs—"a total loser"—and she'd been aware of this throughout the three years during which the pair of them had been involved. "I knew he was a druggie, and that was partially . . ." She left the sentence unfinished. "The thing was," she began anew, "I didn't know what love *was*, at that time! I was very, very confused."

"I KNEW HE WOULD BE MY DADDY"

She probably *had*, she went on disjointedly, cared for her husband when they'd gotten together, more, perhaps, than she herself had realized. "I believe, in retrospect, that I married Bob because I *knew* what he was," she stated, in a tone that bespoke pride in her choice. But then she went on to say, "I *knew* he would be my daddy, so to speak, and he would provide for me, and I would never hurt and never have to worry about taking care of myself." What had begun as an affectionate-sounding statement became mocking and sarcastic as she continued. It wasn't clear, however, whether this sarcasm was directed by Angie at herself or whether it was directed at Bob.

"I have *told* my husband many times," she added, in an imperious, almost declamatory tone, "that he's lived up to *his* bargain; he's been just everything that I expected him to be, or wanted him to be, at the age of nineteen! But what has occurred is," her voice was dropping, again, to the lowered, muted levels of grief and disappointment, "that what I wanted at nineteen, as I've found, fifteen years later, at age thirty-four, is not—" She stopped there, as if stymied, and merely threw her arms wide as if to indicate that no words could suffice. What was happening in her life could not be contained by speech.

"Naturally, people change." Angie sounded, all of a sudden, completely objective and reasonable. "I myself have changed drastically, and he has remained what he was when I married him—the guardian, the overseer and the provider." Bob sat there, quietly, beside her—a well-muscled, dark-haired, dark-bearded, athletic-looking sort of man. "But as far as me seeing him in the role of man, lover, husband, it has become very, very difficult for me," his wife said.

She talked easily, fluently, but seemed to take little responsibility for what had been said a moment earlier. "So you were not really totally unattracted by Bob," I pointed out to her. "You were attracted by the idea of a partner who was stable and who would be able to take care of you?"

"Yes!" She leaned forward in her seat, as if intrigued by such a notion. "Because I had never been with anybody *like* that before." "Never been with anybody stable?" I wanted to ask, but she did not give me the opportunity to do it. "I have, unfortunately—maybe because of my up-bringing, or what I am, genetically—never been able to acknowledge my sexuality. I never have. So, when I married my husband, I was not sexually attracted to him. . . . I was still a baby, sexually and emotionally, and I hadn't any notion about what to expect! I just thought, because of being a virgin when I got married, that 'Wow, everybody talks about how great sex is' and that this would happen to me!" Angie, laughing bitterly, slapped herself across her own forehead. "Not having any sexual feelings for him, what in God's name made me think they were all of a sudden *going to happen?*"

A HARD DECISION

She had not, repeated Angie, been sexually attracted to her husband at the time of their wedding. There was, she stated it again, "no physical attraction to him whatsoever." But that, she observed, "had nothing to do with *him.*" I stared at her. "My husband is a very—well, that's another whole story that we can get into later on. . . ." She shrugged her narrow shoulders, ran an impatient hand through her gently wavy shoulder-length hair, which was blue-black and as glossy as a raven's feathers. She was narrow-featured, almost birdlike in the intensity of her stare as well, and her physique was small, slender and compact. But when she began speak-ing, she seemed to enlarge almost visibly and to dominate everything that transpired.

I asked her if she had been sexually attracted to that former boyfriend, the one who had been drafted and then sent off to Germany just before her meeting Bob. Angie replied, huskily, that she *had* been. "Very *much* so," she added, but then said immediately, "He, of course, was a lame-brain.

"I knew that I was intelligent enough," her voice was thoughtful and speculative, "and had a high enough IQ, though emotionally, I've had *many* problems. . . . And I knew that if I ever ended up with him, my life would be horrible—absolutely *horrendous.*" She rolled the r's of the word with an almost eager relish, like a spinster discussing the disasters that had followed an ill-advised sexual liaison. "He quit school at age seventeen, and he could never hold a job; he was just a *loser,*" Angie ended by stating emphatically.

But then she resumed again at once. She had had, on her own part, a difficult decision to make. "Do you marry someone who attracts you physically," the question was being asked in a somewhat oratorical, rhetorical tone, "but who will give you a difficult life—and you *know*, by the way, what will happen to the physical aspect of it in those kinds of circumstances? Or, do you marry someone who you can depend on to *be there* for you, given that you're as nervous and wired-up and emotional as I am?"

I didn't know whether or not she expected me to respond. The answer to this question was that it *had* no answer—at least none that an outside person could possibly supply. I merely shrugged, then remarked, "If you had married that other person, you'd have had to be there for *him*."

"Oh definitely, definitely! I would have had an awful life!" agreed Angie, at once.

"But perhaps had more power and control in the relationship?" I essayed. "Right," she concurred readily but at the same time shook her head in the negative, so that she seemed to be both agreeing and disagreeing at the same time.

SEEKING AUTONOMY

"Ours is a strange relationship, because *I* have—I really do—" Angie hesitated, turned to Bob. "I do have control as far as making the decisions is concerned?" Before he could respond, she swiveled around in her seat, tucked her wool-trousered legs up beneath her, and was looking at me once again. "My husband is a very laid-back person. He is not a decision maker. I don't think he's ever made five major decisions in the fourteen years that I'm married to him." He moved, restlessly, beside her. "I'm sorry." Angie turned to him, her voice honeyed with regret. "I don't mean to speak for—" "No, it's okay," Bob said.

"I'm the family decision maker," his wife went on to explain. "*I* bought this house. I was still into the marriage scene at that time," she put in parenthetically, her voice heavy with irony, "so I always came to him with anything I was planning to do. In these latter years, I just make decisions and carry them out," Angie added, lips pursed in angry disapproval.

But then an embarrassed expression crossed her face, and she amended her last statement by adding piously, "Which is not right, of course, and I *know* it's not right; but I don't even bother consulting him. What's the use? He's always going to say, 'Whatever you like,' 'Whatever you want,' so I just don't bother asking and do it anyway!" Her wrathfulness, an ever-present current of emotion, was carrying her away from the subject at hand; she seemed, suddenly, to realize this. "I'm sorry, I'm getting off the point. . . ." Angie blushed slightly, sounding contrite.

"So you feel that *you* are the one who's in charge of the show here?" I asked her. "You *are* the show, in terms of who can make the decisions, since Bob, you say, doesn't even get into the act?" I spoke mildly, and smiled too, in order to temper the frankly political, undeniably aggressive aspects of these questions, but she didn't smile back. "Yes," her voice was aggrieved, "but in terms of ultimately being able to be autonomous . . . can I?"

This question was, like the previous one, not to be responded to by me; it was to be answered by she who had posed it, herself. "Definitely not" was Angie's reply. A moment later she added, as if reacting to an objection coming from myself or from Bob, "Never. It would be impossible."

That word—"autonomy." What, I inquired, was its meaning to *her*? She had, perhaps, been giving this matter some thought, for she answered without hesitating, "Being able to run my life, run the whole show, on my own."

"It sounds as if you're doing that already," I observed.

She nodded. "I know."

"But," she went on, sounding doubtful, "when I fall . . . and I fall often . . ." Her unfinished sentence trailed off into the implication that she needed, when she fell, to be sure that someone would be there to catch her. "Four years ago, Bob had to literally *carry* me in to see a therapist," Angie resumed. "That was the position I was in, at that point. I do have a tendency to become—emotionally—totally nonfunctional and inadequate."

This was said with so much flair and drama that I asked her whether or not Bob had actually *carried her there, in his arms* when she'd needed to go and see a clinician. Angie shrugged. "Well, not literally.

"But I was a vegetable, a total vegetable; you can't imagine what I was like!" So she was, I commented equably, either the supercompetent decision maker, taking complete charge, or in the baby position—totally needy and out of control.

"Yes." Angie nodded her wholehearted agreement. I turned my head slightly to gaze directly at Bob. "What attracted you to this lady?" I asked him, in a slightly jocular tone that made them both smile. Bob, slow to answer, filled a space of time with a brief, gruffly masculine laugh. Finally, though, he did speak. "She was, oh, attractive, vibrant. . . . And of course, being young, you want to meet a young girl and take her out. So it went from there; it just grew rapidly. It went from one night to every night with Angie, and nothing with the guys. . . . They used to kid me about it and say, 'We don't see you anymore; what's happening?' " There was happiness in his voice. "You know what it's like," he met my eyes, directly, "seven days, seven nights a week. . . ."

"So you just fell in love?" I asked.

"I just wanted—" he began to reply, but Angie interfered.

"I think it important that you know," she started, then turned to Bob, asking with elaborate politeness, "if you don't mind my telling her this?" He said nothing, stared at her without answering.

"Last Thursday night I asked my husband for a separation," she turned back to me to say, "and I think it was the first time he was ever aware of how strong I feel about being alone and about needing time alone! I thought—I *believed*—it was all settled, but yesterday he informed me that he is not leaving! Maybe I didn't stress the importance of this to him enough!" Her position, as stated, was one of pathos and weakness, yet she sounded passionate, triumphant and strong. "Maybe I didn't get him to understand how, having gone from a helpless child under my parents' rule to a helpless child under *his* rule, I never became a self! I never found myself . . . and I still haven't!"

I glanced down at the Carranos' family genogram on my lap. There was not very much information sketched on the page, and very little more, I realized, would be added during the course of this afternoon's interview. Angie was, by the sheer force of her anxiety and emotionality, taking over the proceedings entirely. It was a form of theater, and I could either attempt to ring down the curtain and conduct the interview as planned or settle back and watch matters develop. I decided upon the latter course and closed the art tablet in a studied and obvious way. The young matron, whose intense gaze overlooked no detail, apologized to me immediately. I answered that we could, quite easily, return to the genogram at a later date. Bob followed this exchange, his expression affable, but he added no comment to it.

AN UNRESOLVABLE CONUNDRUM

"I felt, and I tried so hard to get this across to my husband," Angie went on to explain, her expression agonized, "that if I could struggle alone for a while, with the children and really know what it was like to be in control of myself—not know that he'd *be there* if I fall—it would be so *important* to me! . . . It *is* so important to me!" She'd changed tenses as if to change her statement from a wish to an act in the present. "So very important to me," she insisted.

It was, I thought, an unresolvable conundrum, a self-contained paradox from which there was no obvious escape. Angie had married Bob so that he would, in her own words, *be there* for her; she considered herself emotionally needy and subject to periodic "falls" during which she required help in getting back on her mental feet, so to speak.

The problem was, however, that she now perceived this neediness as springing from a lack of maturity; she saw herself as never having grown up into a self-sufficient adult person. In order for her to do so, it was necessary for her to develop psychologically—to grow up into an independent and separate human being who is capable of surviving on her own. This was, of course, not really going to happen so long as she knew that Bob was there to catch her if she "fell" emotionally. If, on the other hand, she were *really* on her own, she might fall apart completely. Suppose, when she became "a vegetable"—a dysfunctional human being who had, furthermore, two young children to care for—she found herself unable to cope?

She could grow up only discovering that she could make it without Bob's being there for her, and if he was *not there* when she "fell," she feared she could not survive. Angie was, therefore, in an untenable position, and so, obviously, was her partner. "I just felt—I just *feel*," she was insisting, playing spokesperson for one side of the ambivalence about independence and dependence, "that if I struggle alone for a while, with the kids, and really find out what it's like to be in control of myself and now know that he's there if I stumble— It's so *important* to me!" She was on the edge of her seat. "But *he* feels," her expression grew stony and contemptuous, "that if we separate there won't be any going back."

"*Is* that what you think?" I shifted my body completely, concentrating my total attention upon Bob. It was proving almost impossible to contact him directly. Given the diversions being offered by his wife, he withdrew into the scenery very easily. But he, after a few moments during which no distractions occurred, shrugged his muscular shoulders and said briefly, "I don't think it's going to help matters by separating. I just feel that sticking together and trying to fight this thing, one more time . . ." His voice trailed off, and he merely shrugged once again.

"Fight this thing?" I shook my head as if to say I wasn't sure, precisely, what he was alluding to. "Well, you know, I have my hang-ups and my problems, and she has hers, and it's something married couples have to work on—" His voice, I thought, sounded bland and uninvolved.

"With my husband," intruded Angie, "what you have to understand is—" She stopped, for Bob suddenly shifted his position on the sofa; the gesture was, unmistakably, meant to convey a sense of anger and impatience. "I'm sorry," she apologized, with demure and exaggerated courtesy.

"If you *don't* work on the marriage," he then proceeded stoutly, but he seemed to have nothing further on that subject to say. "These things happen, you know," he observed vaguely, after a brief silence. Angie swooped in again. "I have not ever tried to blame him for my condition," she declared.

She had known that she was prone to depression when she'd married him, she continued, but in the course of therapy she'd realized that the marriage was affecting her in ways that were profoundly destructive. "I was a total vegetable when I went into treatment—and I do have the capacity to become one again," she declared. "It took me a long time, working with my therapist, to realize how dead the marriage was! And I've been able, only recently, to come to the point of being able to say, 'Well, this is dead; let's bury it.' So I didn't come to this decision lightly," she assured me.

I believed that she meant what she said. I suspected, however, that if Bob Carrano really did go upstairs and pack his bags, his wife would become utterly terrified—and do everything possible to prevent his going.

"He Does Not Communicate"

It had, Angie was saying, taken a great deal of thinking and of lying awake at night to bring her to ask him for a separation this past Thursday. "Without taking all the blame on myself, as I may sound like I'm doing right now," she told me, "you must know that my husband is totally, totally introverted; we will go *weeks* without speaking! He does not communicate with me in any way!" Bob cleared his throat at that moment, and I hoped that he would interfere.

He didn't.

"Whatever communication is going on now, at this moment, is the most that will happen in the next five years!" I looked at Bob, but he turned away, looked over at the far left side of the room. Automatically, my gaze followed his. That area was furnished by a Leatherette bar and some barstools, and the walls behind it were decorated by Heineken and Budweiser Lite Beer signs—copies, I supposed, or perhaps the real thing, which had come into their possession in some way. That end of the room looked like a cozy small café, while the area in which we sat was clearly designated for family sitting, reading, and watching TV.

"My husband is just very—he has a lot of self-hatred," Angie was explaining, "and it's to the point where, if we go to a restaurant, he thinks that everyone is watching him *eat*. I don't want to go into all that—." She waved an arm airily, as if to brush Bob's personal difficulties away. "But consequently, because of the way he feels about *himself* . . . I know he loves me dearly, but he cannot, *cannot* give of himself emotionally, affectionately; he just can't do it! And now," she was clenching her fists in her lap, "he wants to try!"

FRIGID

Angie had escalated into a full-fledged tantrum, and yet, as if she'd reached the very top of a Ferris wheel, her mood seemed to turn and to begin shifting downward. When she spoke again, she sounded much less agitated; her mien was objective, even calm. "Unfortunately," she observed, like a physician discussing a patient with an interesting but incurable illness, "this rage and this anger that I have felt about his ignoring me for so many years have rendered me totally frigid. *Frigid*, completely! That's how I feel; it's 'Don't touch me; don't come near me; don't!' " Bob, a frightened look on his face, moved slightly farther away from her on the sofa. "So it's a very big problem," said his wife.

"I know that I will never, never find anyone like him, and I wouldn't leave the marriage to find anyone else," she added, in a burst of unexpected, passionate loyalty. "Because there is no one who is as *much a man*—as loyal and honest as this man *is*—but on the other hand, I'm growing into a *woman* now, too. I have a *woman's requirements*, and what he's always given me (which is what I've always wanted) is a father/daughter kind of pampering!"

Bob jumped up from his seat at that moment, and for an instant I felt frightened—I didn't know why. But he merely went across the room to where the Leatherette bar stood and opened a refrigerator behind it. When he returned, he had a frosty can of Coca-Cola in his hand. Angie and I had cups of strong tea on the cocktail table before us; she picked up her cup, sipped from it, then replaced it in its saucer with a nervous clatter.

As he sat down and began to pry open the metal tab on the Coke container, I asked Bob, "How long have you been living without sex?" "It's not easy," he answered, concentrating on the task at hand. "It's been an awful long time." His head was bent over, but the skin on his neck looked mottled and flushed. "But, like I said, I don't think that separating now would do any good. *She* feels she needs the time to help herself out, emotionally, but then what would *I* be doing in the meanwhile?" He looked up at me, and met my gaze, but didn't see me; he seemed to be staring into a future alone.

"Okay," he muttered as if to himself, "I could be thinking, day in and day out, about getting back together and working out certain problems in the marriage, but then why go through all that aggravation? Explaining to the children why we are doing this . . . I just don't want to hurt *them*, emotionally, either," he added. This last remark, undoubtedly his interpersonal trump card, was delivered with a certain authority and force.

"Where do you stand on that one?" I turned, immediately, to Angie. An uncertain expression crossed her features, but she shook her head as if to shake that uncertainty away. "Where *he* feels we will hurt them more by separating," she declared, "I feel I am hurting them so much more in this way—I don't have the patience, the understanding *for* them! It's just come to the point where the rage—and my daughter is getting the most of it—because he is so totally unattached to me, emotionally—" She stopped, blinked, looked around as if assessing her whereabouts. "I say *she* gets most of the anger, because my son and I mesh more easily. But Cathy really gets the brunt of the rage, and I am very afraid of becoming physically abusive, because I was an abused child myself." Angie, out of breath, paused. I turned to Bob.

"That's why," she began anew, "I've always been very cautious in that area, and I haven't been lately! I've found myself throwing her around and doing things I'd never have thought of doing previously! He gets very angry with me without trying to get to the root of what all of this rage and this fury is about!"

THE ABUSER

"Tell me your side of all of this, Bob." I asked him quietly. "How do *you* see what's happening in the family right now?"

"How do *I* see it?" He repeated the question blankly.

"The things that Angie has been saying," I prompted him. "What is your own view of them?" He shrugged, sighed, said that he agreed with much of what she had said. "I realize that I'm the kind of guy—that some of my hang-ups have caused a lot of the problems in this marriage. And I would like to work on that. We've talked this over, time and time again, in the past. It's just—we have to *do* something about it! Instead of just talking, and then what does all of it end up meaning anyway? You settle it, two weeks go by, and you're just in the same old rut! I mean these are things you have to fight and to work on every day . . . every day. Take each day as it comes, and try to work on them. I've talked about this in the past, and she has the right to not believe me anymore. That's her *right*," he stated, a message couched in confusion and vagueness.

He sounded as if he were not really involved so much as saying garbled things which might include something that his wife would like to hear.

Angie Carrano had, I reflected, admitted having married her husband because she needed to have someone *be there* for her, even though no real emotional connection existed. Bob seemed, at present, to have very similar requirements: He wanted to have his wife *be there* for him, even though he didn't actually seem to need or want a true affectional relationship. He wanted the marriage, he was clear about that, but did he, I wondered, *want her?*

Perhaps it was the possibility of abandonment, not the loss of a loved partner, that he feared?

"I'm taking all the blame here." Angie, nervously extracting a cigarette from a pack, repeated the remark that she had made a short time earlier. "But he has been genuinely cruel to me, genuinely *abusive*, in a way! I do think—and have come up with the feeling—that to ignore someone completely can be very, very abusive!" She picked up a lighter on the table, inhaled, coughed slightly, blew the smoke out.

"Just like beating someone or mentally or verbally abusing them," she continued, and coughed lightly once again. "When I became pregnant with our second child, I was scared because I hadn't handled the first pregnancy very well. And the subsequent birth . . . well, he totally ignored me throughout. He chose not to even acknowledge the baby that I was carrying—this baby which was his and mine!" Eyes glaring, Angie's body was rigid as she spat out: "He was very abusive to me throughout."

The word "abusive," having entered this conversation, was, I noted, returning again and again. I asked her to be more specific about what she meant. "Verbally abusive," she replied. I asked her for an example, and she turned to Bob. "Oh, he just . . . ?" But nothing came, at that moment, to her mind. She gazed at him as if prompting him to help her.

"I can't really remember," he said, mildly.

"I guess I've blocked it out," Angie said, sounding somewhat deflated. There was a long pause, broken at last by Bob. "I don't know if all of that stems back to the fact that we were trying to have a second child, for about a year, and she wasn't getting pregnant. So we had made up our minds that we'd just have the one child, and that was going to be it— period. And then all of a sudden she found herself pregnant, and it really did a number on both of us. And I think that carried over into the pregnancy . . . maybe." He sounded doubtful. "Maybe," he added dutifully, "I didn't acknowledge it like I should." He was rushing forward to take the blame and be the bad boy. When she, in other words, failed to handle his self-reproach for him, he could do the work by himself.

His rescue had, however, now restored his wife's momentum, and she was able to take over the conversation again. "This really all goes *much further back*, to when we first got married, and I wasn't allowed to have my mother and father over." Angie sounded victimized and aggrieved. I looked at her in surprise, and she assured me that what she'd said was true. "He wouldn't let them come; it was all very strange! You see, he had—"

"I've mellowed, believe it," Bob intervened to assure me. "Oh, he's mellowed," his wife agreed. There was a moment of friendly silence.

"But the anger and rage, I never got rid of it," Angie broke that silence to say.

"She's right, you know," put in her husband. "But now I've mellowed in certain areas, and I have to work on . . ." The sentence trailed off into a shrug.

I turned to Angie. Had she not, I asked her, noticed any of Bob's dictatorial tendencies during the three and a half years during which she and Bob had courted and become engaged?

Martyr or Tyrant?

Yes, Angie replied; she certainly had. "But I didn't know any better," she explained. "My mom was abused. I didn't know, at that time—" She mashed out her cigarette in the ashtray. "I have a tremendous amount of self-hatred, and I never felt worthy of being treated any differently. I never thought that I—that anyone would want to treat me good! I never thought of myself as deserving it. So it was okay; he didn't beat me, and he didn't drink, and he didn't cheat—so that made him a marvelous person! And I just accepted this abuse," she added, tears springing to her eyes.

She was, it seemed to me, using "abuse" where "bossy" would have been the more appropriate word.

"I mean, I would get into his car," Angie continued, "and if I got a crumb of dirt on the floor of the car he would go berserk! I was not allowed to drink tea or hot cocoa or anything in that car—his idiosyncrasies were so *strange*! He used to spit-shine his shoes, and if you accidentally—I mean *accidentally*—hit his shoes, he would go absolutely crazy! And then, when we got married, I wasn't allowed to have my sister, friends, my mother or father come visit; that *wasn't allowed*. When I had my children, he wouldn't allow my mom to come and help me!" The tears were now running unabashedly down her face.

"Why was that so, Bob?" I asked him.

"You have to understand her mother," he said. "I mean, believe me I love her," he added hastily, "and think she's a good woman. But . . ." He left the sentence there.

"She's overprotective," admitted Angie, smiling wanly, as she wiped the tears from her cheeks with her fingers.

There was a moment of calm and resolution, as if a musical movement had just ended, but a new one (the same one) would clearly begin very soon again. An "abused child," Angie Dinelli, had married an obsessive, overly controlling—in her mind, "abusive"—man. But now, fourteen and a half years later, which one of them was the abuser and which one the abused, which of them the martyr and which the tyrant of the pair?

The Hysterical Marriage

No connubial relationship is, I think, more celebrated in the clinical literature than is that of the remote, unavailable husband and his desperately frustrated, perhaps frankly depressed wife. Should either partner in such a marriage seek psychiatric attention, the male partner is very likely to be diagnosed as an "obsessive-compulsive" and the female as suffering from a "hysterical personality disorder."

Actually, the label of the latter complaint has recently been altered (although the content of the diagnosis remains pretty much unchanged). It is now known as "histrionic personality disorder," because the word "hysteria" (which means "of the womb" or "suffering in the womb") was recognized as having a somewhat sexist ring; it implied that this disturbance was earmarked "for females only." The ancient Greek physicians did indeed believe that the symptoms of hysteria were caused by a woman's uterus having come loose from its moorings and gone meandering off throughout her bodily frame.

In the most recent version of the standard psychiatric reference book, it is nevertheless stated that histrionic personality disorder "can be viewed as behavior that is a caricature of femininity" whether it happens to manifest itself in a woman or a man. The histrionic person is "superficially warm and charming," but also "ego centric, self-indulgent, and inconsiderate of others." She or he is, moreover, "dependent, helpless, constantly seeking reassurance" and may be given to indulgence in frequent "flights into romantic fantasy." She is a love addict, in need of a continual supply of affectionate attention. (Let me say, at once, that although this person sounds like a negative feminine stereotype, I have interviewed a number of couples in which the emotive, self-dramatizing partner is the husband and the relatively detached, more rigid and controlling person is the wife.)

THE LOVE ADDICT'S MATE

The histrionic individual has poor impulse control and tends to say and do things which might more wisely have been left undone or unsaid. The partner is, however, her polar opposite—overly orderly, somewhat inflexible, and often lacking in any spontaneity whatsoever. He is always apprehensive lest something unexpected happen, and his anxious sense of mastery over himself and his environment be endangered. While she is sick for love, he has very little to give her; the more she craves affection, the more she threatens to overwhelm him.

In an article entitled "The Hysterical Marriage," Dr. Jurg Willi notes that the mate of the "hysterical" woman is himself most usually "unre-markable, taciturn . . . shy, and almost overly well-adapted or respectful. In contrast to his often extravagant wife, he is pedestrian, pale but sturdy, the 'good guy' type."

The "hysterophile" man, as Willi calls the male who is attracted to the emotionally expansive, attention-seeking female, is frequently some-one who is quiet, introverted, and somewhat insecure with members of the opposite sex. "In contrast to their wives, most husbands of hysterical women rarely dated because they feared rejection," he writes.

These men, he notes, seem to adopt a submissive attitude toward women; their own exhibitionistic and aggressive tendencies are so strongly suppressed that they themselves are not aware of their existence. They cannot, in other words, allow themselves to be aware of their own resentful and angry feelings; such feelings, if they had them, would be profoundly dangerous and destructive. To experience one's own hostility could lead to harm, either to the self or to someone close and important. All anger (and much healthy assertiveness) has, therefore, been purged from the marketplace of consciousness to a dark storehouse where that which is "uncivilized" is kept.

The mate of the histrionic woman would, as Willi comments, "like to see himself as a totally unique and absolutely incomparable creature who stands above and beyond all normal requirements." His wife's responsibility, in the relationship, is to express all of the emotionality that exists in the two of them (and to bear the guilt and the responsibility when her hostility and aggression have gotten beyond her control). He stands aloof, uniquely without feeling and may deplore her overly emotional, somewhat exhibitionistic displays.

THE KNIGHT-RESCUER

The story of their marriage, very frequently, begins with the rescue of an unhappy maiden—from her miserable home life or from a disastrous involvement with a difficult, rejecting (but exciting) lover or boyfriend. The wife tends to *need* the man she marries, in some way, and this lends him a sense of great importance; he wears her ribbon on his visor. He is the knight in her service, not fully loved for himself perhaps, but willing and ready to save her. The mission that he undertakes is that of assuming responsibility for her existence and providing her with stability and security. He vows to be her good parent, in short.

Content with their marital bargain, the couple may live quite happily for a period of time. But eventually the husband, who has suppressed his own dependent, vulnerable feelings—satisfying them vicariously by giving his spouse the devoted maternal caring that he himself actually desires—begins to feel more and more depleted. He wants to placate his needful partner and meet her never-ending demands, but he experiences himself as running short of his own emotional provender and not really having that much of a surplus that he can spare.

After a while, having warmed himself initially at the fires of his beloved's expressivity and emotionality ("She was attractive and vibrant," Bob Carrano had begun to recount happily), the husband finds himself unable to provide her with the constant validation and feedback that she so desperately requires. Although he denies his own needs for attention and affection, he actually wants and needs some of the emotional goodies and supplies for himself. But he cannot ask for anything, often cannot "know" about his own dependent needs and his own wish to be the center of attention—the loved child, who is admired and cared for.

THE COLLAPSE OF THE ARRANGEMENT

One thing that he *is* aware of, and has always known, is that he can be self-contained and can meet his own, very modest emotional requirements. He can take care of his rather limited needs, handily enough, if only he can be rid of the incessant burden of having to deal with *hers*! The symbiotic fusion, in which she was the good, needful child and he the perfect, boundlessly caretaking parent, gives way when, inevitably, he pulls back and creates some distance between them in order to give some nurturance and attention to himself.

His behavior is experienced, by his uncertain and needful spouse, as an awful narcissistic blow and an almost unbearable disappointment. Her profound sense of herself as an unlovable, thoroughly ineffective person has rendered her an emotional hemophiliac; she needs a stream of self-esteem-enhancing affirmation from outside herself, on a fairly regular basis. And although each affectional infusion that she receives suffices for a period of time, she soon experiences the same need for validation, the same terrible craving for assurances just as strongly again. Her partner, having promised to be an unstinting and reliable provider, has now inexplicably refused to continue in his cherishing, caretaking function. She feels dismissed, ignored—as she has felt so many times previously in her life.

THE TERROR OF EMPTINESS

"Hysterical patients," writes psychiatrist Anthony Storr in *The Art of Psychotherapy*, "are defeated persons. They do not consider themselves capable of competing with others on equal terms. More especially, they feel themselves to be disregarded, and, as children, were often disregarded in reality." For such a person it is clearly true that the opposite of love is not hate but indifference.

The histrionic wife cannot tolerate her mate's turning away and is hypersensitive to any signs of his withdrawal. She is deeply convinced that she doesn't quite exist, when she is alone, and fears being by herself and facing her own terrifying emptiness. In the beginning of the relationship what had been promised to her (or so she believed) was that her mate would always *be there* for her and provide her with admiration and attention. He would replace her own low self-opinion with his inflated estimates of her beauty, intelligence and value. She would receive from him the unstinting parental love which she had never been accorded before.

When, however, her spouse reneges on his part of their marital bargain, she experiences it as a terrible violation. He, who was accepted into her service because he had promised to care for her tenderly and without qualification, has instead reopened a badly healed old sore. Is it possible that he, like those others whom she had wanted to love and be loved by—and who had so disregarded her rightful needs—doesn't actually *care* that much about her well-being? She turns upon the betrayer the full high-speed spray hose blast of her lifelong fury and resentment.

STRUGGLING FOR CONTROL

The mate, who had once so reveled in his expressive wife's open emotionality, now desires nothing more than that he find some way to shut off the flow at its source. He, who rarely or never experiences anger, is appalled by the depth of his spouse's; he is appalled, too, by the vicious, almost unbelievable cruelness of the things that she says. Her wild over-statements are viewed as disordered, "crazy," too devastating to merit his forgiveness ever. *His* reaction is to withdraw even further—and she then pursues him with her stream of endless woes, complaints and accusations.

Each partner in the marriage sees the other as behaving in a painfully rejecting fashion. He, who had committed himself to *be there*, for her, has remained with her physically but is emotionally absent. Unable to stanch her suffering, he attempts to placate her while actually keeping himself as uninvolved as possible.

She, who had once been the lady in distress, has now become the ogre to be skirted and avoided. He tries to fend off, as well as he can, her laments and grievances about her life, his behavior, their children, their relatives, her lost opportunities, and so forth. But even when he does consent to hear her out, he does so with little or no empathy; what she says rarely penetrates the self-protective armor that he wears. They are in an interactive cycle in which the more she emotes, the less he listens; and the less he listens, the more strident and emotive she becomes.

She struggles to take charge of him and of the relationship, to turn it into the marriage that she yearns for—one in which both partners are perennially and completely intimate and always emotionally expressive (especially around the subject of her own ongoing difficulties). He struggles just as hard, but in the opposite direction: to control her behavior and the entire relationship in such a way as to ensure the preservation of his own personal space and his autonomy. If he did permit himself to really *listen* to her, he fears, he could get swallowed up in her uncontrolled and uncontrollable affect.

What he fears is not only her emotionality but his own.

THE WILD BEAST WITHIN

"Obsessional personalities, for a variety of personal reasons, have an especially strong propensity toward control both of themselves and of the environment," remarks Anthony Storr in the book mentioned above. "For them, as for the child who fears the dark, both the external world and the inner world of their own minds are places of danger. Only perpetual vigilance and unrelenting discipline can ensure that neither get out of hand."

Such individuals, as Dr. Storr observes, live in fear of an unspecified yet imminent disaster: the emergence of a barely controlled yet wild beast that is straining at the leash within. This beast is, he suggests, "principally an aggressive animal. . . ." Often the most compliant, outwardly pleasant-seeming people, obsessives are sitting on tinderboxes of unacknowledged, unprocessed, unimaginable (to themselves) rage. Like ventriloquists, they often communicate that anger only through the medium of their more expressive, "histrionic" mates.

He has trouble feeling his feelings; he may never perceive that he is having feelings at all. She cannot *not feel*; she can experience her emotions, all too well, but doesn't have any idea about how to limit or control them. Between them, in fact, they contain the qualities that one might expect to find in a single healthily functioning individual—i.e., the ability to perceive and experience emotionality and the ability to set reasonable limits upon emotionality in order to keep it within bounds and relatively manageable.

OBSESSIONAL SOLUTIONS

The obsessional person, although he has chosen a radically different form of psychological defense from his histrionic partner, has suffered from difficulties that are similar in kind. He, too, has been badly nurtured and has had problems getting his legitimate developmental needs duly recognized and met. In his earliest adaptation, his way of dealing with the parents was to become unusually attuned and highly sensitive to what they (or a particular one of them) were feeling. He developed methods of placating the parental authorities—who may have "parentified" him by demanding that he care for and comfort one or both of them—but avoided facing up to them directly or expressing his rage at never having gotten his *own* growing needs attended to.

Full of suppressed resentment himself, the obsessive fears confronting the resentment of others. In adult life, as Anthony Storr observes, such individuals tend to "be authoritarian . . . or else unduly submissive. . . . Faced with possible hostility, one either conquers or submits. In neither case can one achieve equality and respect." Such a person can relate to someone else in an superior-to-inferior mode *or* in an inferior-to-superior mode, but has great difficulty relating to another individual on the *same* level of power and authority. This need for hierarchy makes the formation of an intimate relationship with a cherished peer an impossible, if not unthinkable, dream.

The obsessional person, disconnected from his own negative thoughts and feelings, usually finds it difficult to deal with those situations which *do* elicit his anger and which are inevitable in everybody's life. Frequently, rather than experience and become aware of his own hostile emotions, he will alter his inner reality—that is, act upon his own mental processes rather than upon the real challenge which has come to him from the environment.

He may, for instance, deal with the disturbing situation by pretending to himself that whatever upset him is actually unimportant (and therefore requires no reaction). Or he may question his own manner of looking at the incident so strenuously and meticulously that it becomes impossible to deal with it in a direct fashion. It is as if when someone had stepped on his toe, he were unable to respond with a straightforward "Get off!" but instead pondered the legitimacy of the other person's being there (even though he himself was suffering in the meanwhile).

Still another method for handling his anger might be that of massively repressing it—failing to process the disturbing occurrence and thrusting it out of his conscious awareness completely. He might then react as if nothing whatsoever had happened; this, of course, would preclude his making the appropriately assertive or angry response which might bring him some recompense or satisfaction. This head-in-the-sand strategy, like the other ones, is a device for stifling the obsessional person's own recognition of the intensely rageful feelings against which he is so anxiously defended.

The underlying assumption he is working with seems to be that if certain thoughts are avoided, the painful emotions associated with them will miraculously disappear. But alas, trying to control emotion by exerting control over one's cognitive processes doesn't really result in the bad feelings going away! Anger, like nuclear waste, is nondegradable. Unprocessed and therefore undischarged, it simply remains where it is—but the threat of its emergence is constant.

THE COLLUSION

Even though he may have no conscious awareness of his own enraged state of feeling, the obsessive perceives the existence within of an obscure, vaguely dangerous force—something disturbing, fighting for recognition and expression. His way of finding some partial resolution of his problem is to release some of that anger through the conduit of his wife's emotionality. By seeing all the hostility, distress, and the like as it exists in *her* (and identifying with her expressions of the denied, prohibited feelings), he can at least make some connection with that aspect of his humanity which he has so completely discarded.

She, in turn, having repudiated and disavowed her own needs for mastery, self-control, limit setting, and the like, allows him to take over the experiencing and expression of these aspects of human functioning on her behalf. She is, then, all emotion and intuition; he behaves as if the logical, rational, cognitive parts of himself were the only inner reality. While she has no control, he has nothing *but* control; each seems, in a way, to have brought to the other a dowry which is a missing segment of his or her personality.

Mix together what *she* lacks and what *he* is deficient in and the blended compound contains exactly what each of them entered into the relationship needing: access to emotionality and the ability to set reasonable limits upon it. The pair ought to live happily ever after . . . or so the observer would imagine.

POLARIZING

Two individuals cannot, however, merge into one single, undifferentiated being and remain in that state of fusion indefinitely. The two people may feel extraordinarily close, at first, and their needs may fit together like the interlocking pieces of a puzzle. But inevitably, in the course of time, that initial sense of relief—at having found the very person who makes it possible to establish contact with unacknowledged, repudiated and thoroughly unintegrated aspects of one's own personality—gives way to a feeling of alarm. There is a sense of not only fitting together but of actually being *glued* there.

The bower of contentment, when the exit doors appear to have closed, starts feeling very like a small, claustrophobic cell. The need for personal space, not provided for in the initial merger, inevitably asserts itself as a reaction to the twosome's state of symbiotic fusion. In an effort to assert their individual separateness and distinctness, the mates begin to exaggerate those attributes and qualities that set them off and differentiate them from one another. Each moves in the direction of becoming as much *unlike* the partner as he or she possibly can—in technical terms, they polarize.

The rift between them yawns ever wider as she becomes more attention-seeking, childish and theatrical and he becomes increasingly withdrawn, unavailable and isolated. Soon enough he begins to criticize, in her, the expressions of open feeling (especially angry feelings) which he had once criticized severely in himself—so severely, in fact, that he had repudiated and disavowed them completely.

She, in turn, criticizes in *him* the independent strivings and the self-sufficiency which in her view make intimacy impossible—her underlying reason for having disowned such needs and wishes and cast them out of her internal world entirely. What had, once upon a time, been unacceptable within the self is now what is so intolerable and unacceptable in the partner. The war within each member of the couple has now been transformed into the war that is going on between them. And each believes that peace and harmony could be achieved if only the *other* one would change!

BECALMED

Angie and Bob Carrano, in that phase of the marital cycle called "productivity and parenting," were not experiencing the second wind of commitment to the relationship that is usual during this period; they were, instead, feeling becalmed upon a timeless expanse. Nothing beckoned, changed or stirred upon their marital horizon—what stretched before them, in the future, looked as flat, motionless and dissatisfying as that which lay behind. It was as if they were marooned, together, in mid-voyage.

Their ongoing exchange of projections, the unconscious yet very real foundation upon which the Carranos' relationship was based, kept both partners in touch with a past from which neither had ever been emancipated; the pair of them were at a standstill. It was as if each had thrown down an anchor, one linking him or her to the original family, and the ropes of those two anchors had become entangled.

As a result, Angie carried—for her husband—the emotionality which he had felt forced to discard very early in his own lifetime. For Bob's mother had been abandoned and then divorced by his father when her small son was just three years old, and Bob, her only child, had assumed (as the children of divorce so frequently do) the burden of guilt and the responsibility for his grieving, somewhat depressed parent's welfare. He had, throughout the subsequent years of his growing up, manfully suppressed his own emotional needs in order to care for and nurture the caretaker who should have been caring for him.

Similarly Bob, as his part of the marital bargain, carried—for Angie—the logic, rationality and ability to set reasonable limits upon emotional displays that had been absent from a stormy household in which her parents constantly engaged in verbal assaults and sometimes even wild physical battles.

In order to raise anchor on the relationship—to move forward, not only in the marriage they shared, but in their own individual development—the underwater lines that connected the two partners would have to be patiently unbraided. For only if their mutual projections were teased apart and disentangled would Bob be able to make conscious contact with his own split-off emotionality and Angie get in touch with her own rational, limit-setting capacities. As things stood, the rules by which their emotional system operated would not permit this to happen—and it was the *rules themselves* that needed changing if their life together was ever to be different or better.

PART IV
SEXUALITY

13

Sexual Symptoms: Psychology, Biology, or Both?

In a distressed marriage, the "causes" of sexual difficulties might appear to be obvious. Mere common sense does suggest that being sexually close and loving is impossible where tension and negative feelings exist in the *non*sexual aspects of a couple's relationship. Angie Carrano's "frigidity," for example, would seem to be easily comprehensible—even expected— in a marriage so disturbed and mutually ungratifying.

But had the sexual issues in the Carranos' marriage, I wondered, actually resulted from their other problems, or were the problems in their relationship *due* to their ongoing sexual difficulties? What, in other words, could be seen as "causes" and what could be seen as "effects"?

Sexual dilemmas, in a marriage, are in the nature of true chicken-and-egg dilemmas: A negative cycle is in motion, and its point of origin is often difficult to isolate. In the course of my interviews with Angie and Bob—and with a number of other couples who were struggling with a variety of differing sexual problems, including lack of desire, impotence and premature ejaculation—I came to realize that very frequently this question has no simple, clear-cut answer.

What *is*, however, patently clear is the poisonous effect that sexual symptoms can have—not only upon the partners' relationship, but upon each person's basic sense of self-worth and integrity.

Angie Carrano, for instance, worried a great deal about whether or not she was "abnormal," deficient as a female human being. For, as she acknowledged during the course of the interviews, she had never experienced orgasm—not in any sexual situation whatsoever. She had never reached a climax during youthful petting experiences, or by means of masturbation, or during intercourse with her husband. She wondered if there was something very basic *wrong* with her.

Why had it never happened—or *had* she, perhaps, attained orgasm without having been aware of it? Was it so unremarkable an event that a woman could actually *have* a climax yet not really know it had occurred? Angie, like many anorgasmic women, was not only anxious and confused about her capacities as a feminine individual, but also feeling deprived of the reportedly wonderful, ecstatic experience she was missing. This was among the many woes for which, ultimately, she held her "abusive" husband responsible.

Bob himself, as I learned, was also anxious about his sexuality; he suffered, periodically, from a sexual dysfunction called "retarded ejaculation"—that is, he sometimes (though not invariably) found it impossible to achieve orgasmic release. This was a problem which had plagued him from the outset of the marriage, and it was, he believed, connected with his use of condoms at that time. The condoms had, Bob explained, decreased his ability to feel sensations; they had, he said, "turned me off." Many of the Carranos' early sexual encounters had, because of this, ended with his feeling tense, angry and irritable—feelings which, he now admitted, had sometimes been discharged in ill-tempered, autocratic behavior toward his wife.

Ten years ago, just after their second child's birth, Bob had decided to have a vasectomy. This made the use of condoms unnecessary, but his sexual problem hadn't disappeared completely. He still, at times, found it impossible to reach a climax, but these days, it happened only infrequently.

The partners' dysfunctions, although apparently very different, were in a way somewhat analogous. Both individuals found it difficult to surrender themselves to sexual, pleasureful feelings, to cease maintaining control and watchfulness. Their lack of trust existed not only at an emotional level; they lacked trustfulness at the level of the body itself.

Each person's need for self-protective vigilance felt, moreover, as if it had been "caused" or created by the other person's behavior; thus, wariness and the need to be wary were re-created and reinforced in a self-perpetuating, repetitious cycle. Neither one was, given the emotional system within which they were interacting, capable of surrendering to the enjoyment of erotic feelings—able to stop monitoring what was happening sexually, relax into the experience and let down his or her guard to the degree which would render the natural triggering of the orgasmic reflex

highly likely. So lovemaking, instead of culminating in relief and resolution, often ended in intense feelings of frustration for one, or for both
of them.

THE PSYCHOLOGICAL APPROACH

In practice, a number of therapists do work with the assumption that
sexual problems are not generally the cause of marital disturbances so
much as they are the result of them. Disorders of sexual functioning are,
in other words, merely a reflection and extension of the other, often deeply
pathological interactions in which the members of the couple are engaged.

For this reason, many couples' therapists avoid dealing with sexual
symptoms in a focused, explicit fashion. Instead, they work with the
interpersonal issues—competition, power struggles, fears relating to intimacy, disturbed communications, and so forth—which are making it
impossible for the mates to behave in more collaborative ways. Clear up
these basic relationship difficulties (so the thinking goes) and the strictly
sexual dilemmas will resolve themselves on their own. The spotlight of
attention need never be fixed upon the sexual complaints directly.

Sex, from this vantage point, is seen as merely *one* troubled area of
an overall relational system that is dysfunctional in a number of other
aspects and dimensions. Tinkering with the couple's genital functioning
is, it follows, far less relevant than is teaching the partners to negotiate,
helping them to unscramble the garbled messages they are sending to
each other, and reducing the psychological distance which separates them.

AN EMOTIONALLY DEMILITARIZED ZONE

Often, when there is trouble in a relationship, the members of the
pair have withdrawn to positions of defensive security, thus creating an
emotionally "demilitarized zone" between them. Each of them then finds
this area increasingly hard to traverse—for purposes of sexual gratification
or for any other purpose. It is the slow coaxing of each individual out of
his or her own security space, and into a place which is more open and
vulnerable to the other, which is the vital therapeutic task. Therapy goes,
in other words, beyond mere treatment of sexual symptoms (which may
be totally ignored during the clinical sessions). It involves, more important,
fostering the mates' capacities for getting close and for experiencing that

closeness as safe and satisfying rather than as potentially exploitative and dangerous.

And in practice, it frequently *is* the case that as the spouses become less mistrustful and afraid (many couples learn, in the course of treatment, just how *scared* they are of each other!), their need to maintain a self-protective distance seems less urgent, less necessary, less vital. Somehow, some way, in the course of working on *other* aspects of the relationship, the specifically sexual aspects of the marital problems disappear. Resolution of their interpersonal difficulties is, in such instances, truly the only "sexual therapy" that the pair requires.

But a problem with this therapeutic model—i.e., "Work on the relationship and the sexual symptoms will resolve themselves"—is that it can sometimes prove overly naive and simplistic. For while it is true that in the case of the Carranos Angie's sexual dysfunction probably *was* of psychological origin, and embedded within a hostile, dysfunctional marital system, there are other situations in which this rule of thumb can be a foolish and misleading one to apply. There is not only a psychology; there is a *biology* that underlies sexual functioning as well.

BIOLOGICAL CONSIDERATIONS

There are a number of reasons quite *apart from his marital relationship* which might serve to explain, for example, why potency problems in a male spouse have begun to develop. A husband's erectile difficulties could actually stem from subtle physiological sources; his impotence, or partial impotence, could actually be related to the emergence of a chronic disease, such as diabetes mellitus. This illness affects some 5 million men in the United States and causes erectile problems in about half of them. Impotence is, in fact, often the advance signal of an impending diabetic illness.

The individual in questioin could, on the other hand, be responding to the side effects of a medication that he happened to be taking. Difficulties with getting or maintaining an erection are frequently associated with drugs that are used to treat high blood pressure (such as reserpine, methyldopa, the beta-adrenergic blockers, etc.). It is estimated, writes Carol Botwin in *Is There Sex After Mariage?*, "that a third of treated male hypertensive patients suffer from potency disturbances" as a direct result of the use of a medication.

Yet unless the individual is forewarned or at least carefully monitored by his physician—as often he is *not*, either because the doctor knows too little about sexual medicine himself or because he fears "causing" erectile difficulties by means of the power of suggestion—an increasingly dysfunctional spouse may fail to make the association between his antihypertension drug and the increasingly upsetting problems he is experiencing each time he tries to make love to his wife. If, as a not unlikely sequel, the distressed partners eventually consult a marital therapist for treatment of their sexual problems—and if that therapist views such problems as ones which emanate from underlying disturbances in the relationship—the confusion could easily be compounded even further than it already has been!

For obviously, given the organic influences at play, the therapist could work upon restructuring and improving the marital relationship until the last trump sounded; the resolution of the pair's interpersonal conflicts would *not* result in the disappearance of the husband's sexual disturbance! What could, on the other hand, prove marvelously effective might be a change in the form of high blood pressure medication that the man was taking. But this might, unfortunately, not happen before very real and palpable consequences had been suffered.

SEXUAL SIDE EFFECTS: THE LOCKES

One set of partners whom I interviewed, for example, had enjoyed a good sexual relationship until the husband was given a diuretic in treatment of his high blood pressure condition. Diuretics cause the body to lose salt and water, thereby (for reasons that are still not fully understood) promoting relaxation of the blood vessel walls. It is as if the vessels were like garden hoses that had been widened and—because the volume of plasma coursing through them is unchanged—the pressure created in the system is lowered. One might think of diuretics as a "hydraulic" form of medicating mild hypertension.

The Lockes were in their late forties at the time that Elliot began taking the antihypertensive medicine. Elliot was a personable, highly placed executive who worked at a computer technology firm located just outside the city of Boston; his wife, Jessie, was a realtor, energetic and attractive—a co-partner in a successful business that she and a friend had founded.

When the diuretic was prescribed to Elliot Locke by his physician, he received no warnings about the potential sexual side effects of the drug. For the six months that followed, Elliot struggled with increasing problems in attaining and maintaining an erection, yet he connected this to his getting older; he never associated it with the medication. As his anxiety and fear of new failures intensified, his relish for sex—and his interest in being sexual—seemed to diminish progressively. He had felt ever more reluctant (as he could admit only much later) to place himself in so exposed and vulnerable a position and to "humiliate" himself in front of Jessie. Eventually, his intimate approaches became very rare and usually negatively charged events for both of them.

Her interpretation of what was happening was that he no longer found her attractive or perhaps didn't care for her, or both. Jessie Locke, so capable of negotiating effectively with a wide variety of people in her professional life, was nevertheless without any interpersonal skills whatsoever when it came to speaking to her husband about the painful subject on both their minds. She simply could not talk openly of the desperate feelings of rejection which their bedroom scenarios were eliciting within her; she assumed that he understood those feelings anyway and that the messages being sent to her via the genital communication system were the ones that he intended to send.

Words, spoken aloud, would be much more dangerous, she had believed. Words could turn what remained unsaid—that he did not want her, sexually, and could barely get through the act, despite heroic efforts—into the new facts of her life. He was abandoning her, as a lover, and this could portend his eventually abandoning the entire relationship. She chose the rabbit's strategy and froze in position, doing nothing and saying nothing about what was so patently happening between them.

But the steadily escalating tensions in the relationship could not be suppressed indefinitely. She felt unloved, he felt unworthy of respect and unmanly, and they landed in a couples' therapist's office in a full-blown marital crisis.

Too Dangerous an Enterprise

The Lockes' story could, perhaps, have had a happier ending if the therapist they consulted had immediately made the proper inquiries—about prescription drugs that either partner might be using—and then suggested that Elliot return to his primary physician with his high blood pressure medicine in hand.

For, as mentioned earlier, it often is the case that substitution of one form of antihypertension medication for another (one that is equally effective in controlling high blood pressure) can do away with sexual side effects and restore effective functioning rapidly—frequently within one or two weeks. Unfortunately, in this case, no questions about the use of medications were raised by the marital therapist. Instead, long-term treatment of the Lockes' relationship was undertaken and continued over the course of the subsequent several years. And although they did, as both Jessie and Elliot readily acknowledged, actually profit from the therapeutic sessions, their sexual relationship continued to deteriorate; it became, in fact, completely nonexistent.

When, at last, the connection between Elliot's potency difficulties and the antihypertensive drug he was taking was made clear (which happened only as the result of a chance remark made by a friend), their primary physician was consulted and did prescribe another form of drug at once. But although now he was theoretically capable of becoming erect and of maintaining his erection, Elliot's anxieties about whether or not he would be able to perform could no longer be assuaged. What is known as "secondary impotence" had been engendered by the long months of sexual inadequacy and failure.

His wife had, moreover, developed a sexual dysfunction of her own, one called "inhibited sexual desire." For her sexual appetite, long unfed, had now completely disappeared; she had adapted her pattern to that of her spouse. The calm of abstinence had followed the agitating and ultimately useless and hopeless episodes of trying; she now preferred leaving well enough (if not perfect) alone. The feelings provoked, during their last sexual encounter, had been so intense that she never wanted to find herself in so hurtful and exposed a situation again.

Sex had become, for both of them, too dangerous an enterprise to deal with. But in all other respects, I was assured, their relationship was a functional, healthy, and an immensely caring one. At present, the Lockes told me, they were unmotivated to consider sexual therapy; the entire "problem" (as they called it) was one they had simply put behind them.

So sex, that wonderful aspect of their humanity, had been abandoned by them in the middle of their lives.

CAVEAT EMPTOR

This is, I might add, by no means the only instance of its kind which I encountered in the course of my interviews with couples—and so a small caveat is very much in order at this juncture. Many physicians are uncomfortable talking with their patients about sex and sexual difficulties and neither bring up nor welcome mention of the subject. And even marriage therapists—who routinely encounter a large number of people with varying sorts of dysfunctions and complaints—can be averse to focusing upon these symptoms directly or may lack the basic sexual knowledge and information which would enable them to do so effectively.

My word of warning, therefore, is this: Therapists who are skilled or even *gifted* in psychological forms of treatment are sometimes just as ignorant about human sexuality and its discontents as are their desperately confused and sorely troubled clients. Because, moreover, many marriage therapists do tend to view almost all sexual disorders as stemming from psychological sources, the possibility that physical factors may be being overlooked or discounted is one that is unfortunately very real.

And organic difficulties may, as recent advances in sexual medicine have indicated, actually be far more prevalent in the development of sexual symptoms than anyone has previously realized. Up until this past decade it was accepted doctrine that almost all (90 to 95 percent) of sexual disorders were purely psychogenic in origin, but at present, the effects of illness and drugs upon sexual functioning are being recognized with ever-increasing clarity. The results of a study published in the *Journal of the American Medical Association* (1980) suggest, for example, that *up to 40 percent of erectile disorders may be caused by diseases or the use of drugs!* (Prescription medications are, by the way, not the only "drugs" involved here. Recreational substances such as alcohol and marijuana can, in certain dosages, affect sexual functioning profoundly.)

The symptoms produced by biological factors are, in any case, readily and frequently mislabeled "Psychogenic in Origin"—and then treated with what appears to be the appropriately psychologically oriented therapeutic care. This is why it seems wise to repeat, in one final refrain, that the buyer of clinical services should beware. The possibly *physiological* causes of a sexual complaint should not be overlooked—especially in persons over age forty, who are especially likely to develop problems which have an organic component.

The necessity for a comprehensive evaluation, carried out by a physician who has made sexual medicine his or her area of expertise, should not be postponed while purely psychological forms of therapy are undertaken. Organic factors *must be ruled out*; otherwise, the marital therapist may be leading his clients off on an extended journey with only the crudest of therapeutic compasses in hand. It may be the case, I might add, that some *basic information about human sexual functioning* is one of the major forms of treatment that is needed by a particular pair.

The Price of Ignorance: The Franklins

According to the well-known experts William Masters, M.D., and Virginia Johnson, it is, in fact, just plain lack of knowledge about human sexual physiology which sets the stage for the development of many or most sexual symptoms and disorders. What people *don't know about normal sexual functioning* can, in some cases, cause them an enormous amount of psychological suffering and pain.

What happened to Sara and Bruce Franklin provides a disquieting illustration of just how costly sexual ignorance can be. The Franklins actually underwent a year of marital counseling, during which they separated briefly, because they were unaware of some basic facts about the way in which human sexuality is affected by the process of ordinary aging.

Sara and Bruce, who had been married for twenty-five years at the time of our interviews, had two sons; the older was a medical student, the second boy a sophomore at Stanford. The Franklins' relationship, a closely involved but in certain ways problematic one, had always had a wounded bird/caretaker flavor. Sara, the dependent, needy partner, required a lot of her husband's attention, validation and feedback on a regular basis. Bruce, the nurturer, prided himself upon his ability to care for his mate; what he required, by and large, were her admiration and respect for his accomplishments and his competence.

But in the period just before their sexual and marital problems erupted, Sara's career (she was a poet and had recently been promoted to a coveted professorship) had taken a dramatic upturn while her husband's had moved in the opposite direction. Bruce, having left his job as a well-respected editor in a Manhattan publishing firm, was working on a book of his own, and that project was not working out in the ways that he'd hoped it would. He was feeling dispirited, isolated, at a dead end; he felt, in a word, like a failure. His own self-esteem was at so low an ebb that he found himself unable to offer Sara the stream of steady, satisfying reassurance that she required.

Bruce needed some caretaking himself; *he* felt like the needy one. He began saying to his wife, "It's my turn"—a phrase which Sara didn't understand. When she tried to get him to explain what that phrase meant, Bruce, so unaccustomed to articulating any needs of his own, was unable to tell her in any way that she could find comprehensible.

The rules of their emotional system, which decreed that she carry the neediness and he carry the adequacy, were being violated—and the system itself was unbalanced. It was into this interpersonal situation, a waiting petri dish in which new and destructive organisms might grow with frightening rapidity, that the ordinary physiological changes associated with getting older had been introduced. These changes were then misinterpreted and freighted with negative symbolic meanings by both members of the pair.

Bruce's erection was less prompt and certain; Sara took longer to lubricate and was more vulnerable to vaginal irritations and infections. These normal changes in sexual responsivity, *expectable in the late forties and early fifties*, had been interpreted by each of them as having distinctly personal (hostile and rejecting) meanings. Their relationship, stressed to a point it had never been earlier, had almost come apart over what was, to some large degree, sexual naiveté and a huge misunderstanding.

"I Was Impotent"

The Franklins' problems had begun, as both reconstructed the situation, around the time of Sara's promotion to a full professorship. She had been forty-seven then; she turned fifty during the course of our interviews. Sara Franklin (the name is, of course, pseudonymous) is a poet whose work has achieved some renown. Immediately prior to the development of the Franklins' sexual and marital difficulties, she had, in fact, won a prestigious award; she was also being invited, at a steadily increasing pace, to give readings and lectures at campuses across the nation.

"I'd been working on a writing project of my own," explained Bruce, "for which I had a good contract, enough to support us—with some other income that I have from my family—reasonably well. But just about the time that Sara's promotion and award came—which took us both by surprise, I think—I realized that my book wasn't going anywhere; it just wasn't going to *work*. For me it was . . . the floor of the world dropping out. I'd left the city, so Sara wouldn't have to keep commuting, and, in a way, left my whole support system behind me."

For Bruce, initially, leaving his editorial job and starting work on his book had meant freedom—a new and refreshing beginning. But his life in the academic community to which they moved (to be closer to Sara's workplace) lacked structure; he was without connections, and the writing was proving more difficult than he had ever expected. "Sara was *part* of the life here and getting all of this acclaim, being congratulated everywhere we went. Many of our closest friends are, in fact, her colleagues. And it isn't as if I don't like them. . . ." The end of his sentence was a shrug.

"Still, I had a secret feeling deep down in my soul: 'Maybe the book I'm doing will take off, and then I'll have my share of the adulation.' "

Shaking his head, blushing slightly, he added, "At the same time I knew that what I was producing didn't merit it." Bruce Franklin, who has curly light brown hair with silver streaks in it, shook his head and straightened his rimless glasses on the bridge of his strong, aquiline nose. "I became impotent," he said.

"I had trouble getting erect," he explained, as if he weren't sure I understood his meaning, "and then I'd lose it in the middle of sex. An important aspect of this, which certainly neither of us realized, was that I was getting *older*; my fiftieth birthday had just passed. I'd begun having these mild physiological changes associated with the aging male—namely, that I needed more direct stimulation of the penis in order to attain an erection and to keep it. That's normal," he added swiftly, "but we didn't know it. Not then."

This was, almost ludicrously, information that Bruce himself eventually discovered when he happened to start leafing through a book piled on a table at a local bookstore's inventory clearance. The book was *Human Sexual Inadequacy* by Masters and Johnson, and it included a brief section on the physiology of aging. The decline in erectile responsiveness, a biological characteristic of the aging man, was what he had started to experience. But the facts of mid-life sexual responsivity—that the penis frequently doesn't become erect without direct stimulation and that ejaculation is less forceful and demanding—were matters about which he'd known nothing whatsoever. The conclusion that he had leaped to—in part because of his chagrin about his failed writing project—was that he must be "losing it" completely. Not only was he an incompetent, nonproductive worker, but he was depleted, or perhaps finished, as a functioning human sexual male.

"Sara and I were both," he recounted, "under the impression that if the erection was lost, it was gone; it would not return again. It was *ignorance*, but we were pretty ignorant—and this was stuff that never actually did get talked about, even when we got ourselves into treatment. We talked about some important things with our therapist, most of them having to do with the relationship. But what we *didn't* discuss was the fact that if you lose an erection, all you need is a bit of stimulation—which you can relax and enjoy—and it will come back again. At that time, though, we were in a state of . . . well, we had the most limited sorts of foreplay."

His wife had, he said, scrupulously avoided ever touching his genitals. "She thought that if she got me excited, I'd get impatient and want to have sex immediately . . . and then I'd come right away. She felt—and she may have been right—that it would all be over before she'd even got near reaching satisfaction in terms of the number and quality of orgasms that she'd experienced."

"I am," put in Sara Franklin, with a small half smile, "an extremely orgasmic female." But their sexual life had become, at that phase of their lives, very stereotyped, and their sexual play too brief for her to be responsive. "I didn't know then," resumed Bruce, nodding his agreement, "that I could be stimulated and almost come, and then Sara could stop touching me, and it would go down, and this could go on and on, for a long, pleasureful period. . . . So I think we were both *frightened*. We didn't realize, somehow, that it's the foreplay—the kissing and caressing—that sex is really all about."

"MY TURN"

Sara's expression, I noticed, had become strained and anxious. She took up the narrative and reiterated that, around the time of her award and her promotion to a full professorship, they had begun having huge fights about what Bruce had kept referring to as "my turn." "I am still not sure what he meant by this," Sara admitted, looking almost guiltily at her husband. He shrugged in response, then shook his head as if uncertain of the answer himself. "My turn," he repeated the phrase speculatively, "now what was that all about?" A sense of tension, relating to what was obviously a marital buzzphrase with intense private meanings to this pair, had been elicited; I felt myself picking it up.

But Bruce, instead of responding to his own question, began talking about how wonderful their sexual life had been in the year prior to his work crisis. "The sex just kept on getting better and better," he said. Sara had had a favorite position, a kind of reverse bundling, with her back to her husband, nestling in his arms. He would enter her from that position, he said, and she would have a number of orgasms; it was an explosion of erotic fireworks.

Sara laughed, then said in an embarrassed voice, "I think the fabled G-spot is there. It is, at least, for *me*. . . ."

Bruce paused, waited a moment, then resumed evenly. "When my work crisis struck I became unable to maintain an erection in that position. I mean it was difficult for me to get one, in the first place, but impossible to keep it *there*. So I said to myself, 'Oh, I've been doing it this way for her, during this past year, when the book seemed to be moving along, but now that everything's crashing around me, it's *my turn*. She should turn and take care of me."

He raised his shoulders in a large shrug, laughed briefly, seemed embarrassed himself. "I don't know that this made much sense," he acknowledged. But he had not been capable, he added, of divorcing career issues from sexual issues. "My self-esteem was really *low*, at that point, and this had consequences in terms of potency. And we didn't seem to know how to deal with potency other than to fight about it." There was anger coming into his voice, even as he used the word "fight," and his expression grew stony and self-protective.

"ALL I COULD DO WAS WATCH MYSELF FAILING"

"We would have long, screaming quarrels about potency," continued Bruce, his voice low and husky, "about whether my penis was erect or not. Sara, I think, saw it as an attack on herself; she thought I didn't love her, or that I was crazy, or that I was jealous and furious about her success . . . I don't know. Maybe I was, to some extent; but it threw her into a panic, and it became terrifying to me—that if I couldn't get it up, this would happen; we'd be screaming and raging at each other for the next several days." His eyes grew wide with apprehension even as he talked of this possibility now.

"I couldn't stand it; I became very spectator-oriented, and all I could do was watch myself failing in this area . . .and have this—this entire, pervasive sense of incompetence and failure reinforced." They had begun marital treatment, he added, when his feelings of guilt and anger—and Sara's reactive panic—had become intolerable; they'd both known that the relationship would end disastrously unless some kind of therapeutic cavalry arrived and miraculously saved the day. But their treatment, while useful to them in other ways, brought no improvement in their sexual relationship at all.

Looking back, Bruce believed that their clinician should have discussed sexual matters in a far more direct and open manner. It should have been suggested that they spend an entire session discussing just how the pair of them engaged in sex—and what each partner's feelings about the sex act were—and what kinds of things tended to happen. The therapist ought, moreover, to have elicited very precise information about what was bothering each partner and about the ways in which they, as a couple, were attempting to deal with these issues. Then it would have been possible to educate them about matters which they truly did not know about—"especially about getting older and the male's need for more direct stimulation in order to become erect." Bruce, frowning, shook his head in the negative as if to underscore their clinician's mistake.

"We could also have gone over the changes in the quality of my orgasm, which felt *different*," he went on, "and which I felt bad about, but was unable to discuss with Sara. . . . And he could have talked, too, about the aging changes in a woman, of which I knew nothing whatsoever." Bruce said this almost as an afterthought.

"Yes, I've been amazed by your not mentioning the vaginitis I had," put in Sara at once, "which to me is where so much of this started."

Her husband turned to her, opened his mouth as if to speak, but then closed it without saying anything. He seemed bemused, as if slightly distracted by her remark. Bruce was, clearly, the caretaker in their relationship, and caretakers assume full guilt and responsibility for everything in their world that occurs. It was for this reason, it seemed to me, that he had difficulty even *remembering* those problems for which he could not be blamed or at least in which he was not implicated directly.

"THE SENSITIVITY OF THE VAGINAL WALLS"

I asked the Franklins, after a pause, what else—in terms of sexual information—they thought their therapist could have told them. "What would it have been helpful to know?" I opened both hands, palms forward, as if to say the floor was open to responses from either of them.

Bruce cleared his throat. "Well, about the sensitivity of the vaginal walls and the difficulties of lubrication, which, as you get older, takes longer to happen, like an erection. They are equivalents, as I've learned, because I've now done a lot of reading on the subject." He laughed, as if acknowledging the somewhat pedantic manner in which he had spoken. "And the desirability," he continued, his tone earnest, "of using a lubricant. Most important, though, the whole notion that orgasm is not the goal, the end goal that you run for as fast as you can. That the real point is in simply being there: the mutual caressing—stimulation—the slowly mounting sense of excitement."

He hesitated, gave me a speculative glance, then added, "He could, too, have told Sara that oral sex is okay and not a dirty or humiliating act. He could have told her to relax and not be alarmed by the loss of an erection—not even if we didn't have intercourse on a given day, but just took pleasure in stimulating each other. To just have fun, enjoy each other's bodies, stroking, massaging and caressing, being close."

He inhaled, let out a deep breath, said, "He could have told her not to be so *frightened*."

A HUGE MISUNDERSTANDING

What, I asked, did he think his wife had been so frightened *about* at that time? Sara drew in a small, sudden breath; eyes narrowing, she was staring at her husband intently.

"I guess that was part of the relational problem we had," he answered, sounding controlled and objective. "She had a tendency to see me as a potentially evil person, manipulative and hostile. She could see that in the sex—that it was an expression of willful anger—and she said that 'the limp penis was the ultimate weapon,' which was being wielded on herself. In other words I was having sexual problems because I was *angry* . . . and she may have been right to some degree; that may have been a component of what was going on at that time."

He had, said Bruce, certainly been frustrated by a number of things, but "who got angry first is a moot point; I don't think that it was *me*. Because my nature is different: I tend to try to please other people, to think more of what's coming to the other guy than of what is coming to myself. So I think there was a big misunderstanding about who I *was* which grew up between us and landed in the bedroom somehow. . . ." His wife had, he explained, seen him as powerful and rejecting, when he had been feeling very weak, vulnerable and frightened.

But he himself, I reflected, *had* admitted to some feelings of intense competition—and a degree of frustration and anger—about the accolades that Sara had been receiving at that time. Her hypothesis—that the jealousy he was feeling was being communicated sexually—didn't seem to me to be so farfetched as he was making it sound.

Bruce was, it appeared, having trouble acknowledging and "owning" such negative, unloving emotions. If he'd been angry at anyone, he asserted, it had been *himself* most of all. "I was in despair, my self-esteem gone; that's what the phrase about 'my turn' meant. Sara's always needed a lot of caretaking and being listened to, but I was flat on my back now, unable to do anything or to perform. I needed to be attended to. 'It's my turn' meant 'Take care of me'; 'I'm in pain'; 'It's my turn now.' "

"To be solaced?" I asked, and he nodded. "To be solaced," he nodded his head again in reply. A moment later, he commented quietly, "I don't think the fundamental cause of the problem was anger at *her*, but just some jealousy, a lot of feelings of despair and depression and then anxiety about not being able to perform sexually and the obsessive self-observation that set in. . . . I wasn't having sex so much as I was watching my penis and feeling scared about whether it would go down and she would get angry and upset."

THE FACTS OF SEXUAL AGING

Their marital therapist had, according to the Franklins, never realized that just plain *lack of information* about some relevant sexual matters had been an important issue in their case. Had they merely understood the facts of sexual aging, Sara said feelingly, they might not have had to live through months of quarrels, bouts of drinking, broken sleep, and the prolonged crisis that had nearly brought their relationship to an end "as much from exhaustion as from anything else," in her opinion.

"I now realize—but I didn't know it at the time—that I, too, was experiencing physical changes related to getting older." Sara shrugged, tapped her forehead lightly, as if pointing to the site of what had been her own astounding ignorance on the subject. "Which meant that our sexual behavior ought to have changed, in terms of . . . well, foreplay."

At that phase of female existence, when estrogens are dramatically lowered, a woman requires more stimulation in order to become fully lubricated and moist. If coitus is attempted before she is in a state of full readiness, intercourse may be painful because the partners' genitals are rubbing against each other like parts of a machine that are unoiled. This not only hurts, but can be damaging to the female, for it leads to vaginitis—that is, irritation and/or infection of the vagina. "I had, at that time," reported Sara with a slight grimace, "more vaginal infections than I'd ever had in my entire life."

What she had been unaware of, in terms of normal sexual physiology, was that at this climacteric phase of a woman's life the vagina is undergoing changes. Its lining, formerly thick and ridged, is becoming thinner and atrophic; this is due to a change in hormonal status—her estrogen levels are pronouncedly lowered. As the female moves into and past the menopause (i.e., cessation of menstrual bleeding), she will also produce less of the natural vaginal lubricant which serves to make intercourse comfortable. Episodes of vaginitis tend to develop when the ability of the tissues to self-lubricate has been diminished and special care is not taken by her partner to ensure that she is fully aroused and very ready for coitus.

Attempts to penetrate the highly sensitive vaginal canal without adequate moisture present can lead to pain—and *pain is a sexual turnoff.*

What may be confusing to a woman's longtime partner, though, is the fact that the time required for her to become ready for sex may now have been substantially changed. Because she used to be well lubricated within seconds and might now take four or five minutes (or more) to produce adequate moisture, he could interpret this as sexually uninterested behavior. Frustrated by his mate's "coldness," he may attempt to move along anyway. He hurries her, as if believing that the butterfly of mutual desire must be netted rapidly, lest it fly out of his grasp and the sexual opportunity disappear entirely.

As Sara saw it, it was her vaginal problems, not Bruce's troubles getting an erection, that had gotten the whole negative cycle into motion. For she had criticized his sexual behavior, claimed that he was *hurting* her . . . after which, he'd begun having problems getting hard. "We had, of course, other difficulties at that time." Sara grew silent, momentarily, and that same apprehensive expression settled upon her features again.

INVENTING RETRIBUTION

Sara Franklin, who is tall and slender, has fair hair, with handsome streaks of gray at the temples. She picked up a lock of hair from the back of her head, began twisting it round and round with her finger. She had, murmured Sara, been having a lot of success at the time that Bruce was having what felt (to him at least) like a huge failure. "I was receiving so much attention and recognition, all of a sudden, that I think I was getting really *upset* by it."

"Upset by which aspect of it?" I asked her.

"Oh, by *receiving* it," she replied, her face suddenly reddening slightly.

But then she drew in a long, anxious breath, let it out in the form of a sigh. "I didn't realize, at first, the bad effects that all of this would have—upon our relationship—and yet at some level I think that I *expected* punishment. That, really, is true." The flush upon her cheeks had grown darker. "I think this thing called 'fear of success' was very much operative here." Sara's voice was low, almost shamed and conspiratorial. "A feeling that success will generate envy and that those who envy you will seek retribution and retaliation. That *real disasters* will follow . . . and that is, of course, exactly what happened. Punishment came."

The punishment had arrived, as she saw it, in two forms: her problems with vaginal pain and her husband's growing impotence, which made their sexual relating ever more unsatisfying, swift and clumsy. "I think I *scared* Bruce when I told him that he was *hurting* me," said Sara, looking nothing if not scared herself.

She had tried to ask him for things that she liked: more kissing; more embracing; more *time*. He was, she'd kept complaining, doing everything too fast; he was rushing her and bypassing foreplay. What neither of them realized, of course, was that the time she required in order to become physiologically ready for sex had undergone *objective change*. Bruce, accustomed to a timing which was familiar to both of them, was proceeding at rates which were not different but which felt, to Sara, as unusually *hurried*. She perceived him as hastening her into sex too rapidly, as being self-centered and inconsiderate.

"I think Bruce believed, at that time, that the moment I was lubricated I was ready for intercourse. . . . But that's like saying that if a man has an erection he's ready to go ahead and have sex immediately, which is, of course, not true." Erection is, in fact, just the beginning of a male's sexual response; so is lubrication in the female, and the two are comparable events. Both are signs that an individual is beginning to respond, sexually, but they are by no means reliable signals that he or she is ready to move directly into coitus.

Sara felt that Bruce was putting pressure on her—"pressure to perform, actually," she said. "I didn't have . . . feelings of readiness. And I couldn't *will* such feelings, not any more than Bruce could will an erection. The worst part of it was, for me, that when I did start moving toward a climax, he often reacted by going limp; I felt that he was trying to say something to me, via his penis, and that was 'I'm really *angry* at you!' "

Sara's face reflected, at one and the same time, the hostility she had felt coming from her husband and the sense of menace that she had experienced. Her own interpretation of what was happening had been that he was angry and jealous; he was trying to punish her for being so threateningly successful. "To me, this was treason—just treason—from the one person I trusted wholly and needed to depend upon . . . I depend *a lot* upon Bruce." She glanced over at her husband, almost timidly, then turned back to face me again.

"This felt to me," she went on, "like abandonment—panic. 'He doesn't love me'; 'It's the end'; 'He's crazy'—these were the things that were going through my head!" Bruce was, she'd felt, full of bad, crazy feelings about himself—feelings that he was taking out on her. The anticipated disaster was happening.

What ought to have been a wonderful success had, Sara added, felt like *anything else* to her at the time when it had all been occurring.

"You seem to have known in advance that retribution would come," I remarked in a light, slightly wry tone of voice.

"And I may have been *inventing* that retribution," she acknowledged, with an answering small smile of her own.

It was her belief, nevertheless, that had their marital therapist focused directly upon their sexual problems immediately—and provided them with the kinds of information and reassurance that they needed—then that particular aspect of their difficulties could have been resolved within a few weeks after they'd begun treatment. This was Bruce's opinion, too, and certainly there was evidence to support it. For, within days of his purchase of that remaindered book, the strictly *sexual* issues in the relationship were being worked out. And after that sex continued to get better—less predictable and stereotyped, more affectionate and collaborative—than it ever had been before.

FEAR OF SUCCESS

Certain individuals are, as Freud noted long ago, uncomfortable with the feelings of pleasure and happiness that attend reaching a valued, important goal. Instead of feeling joyful about their successes and triumphs, they feel that to succeed is to do something that is obscurely bad, wrong or harmful.

Being victorious is experienced as dangerous, because symbolically, winning is equated with defeating an inner opponent (the same-sex parent) toward whom deeply conflictual, rivalrous feelings are directed. The underlying fantasy at play is that the vanquished one will be destroyed at one's hands, completely—or, if not, that he or she will retaliate in some terrible way. To succeed is, therefore, a threatening, negatively charged experience; harm to the self or to someone else will predictably and inevitably follow upon it.

Inner fears of this sort are, of course, total distortions from the past which exist at an unconscious level. Such internal taboos about success are based on old, unchallenged fantasies; they can be dealt with, therapeutically, by being brought to the person's awareness—recognized as being totally irrational in nature. But a woman's fear that her partner will be dismayed, angry or rejecting if she begins surpassing him in distinction, achievements and/or earnings is frequently not irrational or unrealistic at all.

For shifts in the marital power structure, brought about by the tra-

SEXUALITY

ditionally less powerful partner's triumphs, can usher in a host of repercussions in a couple's relationship. Sara Franklin's anxiety about her
success—those obscure feelings that "real disasters" would follow in its
wake—were, it seemed to me, linked to particularly *female* kinds of fears
about being overly victorious. Her fears were, moreover, even more comprehensible when considered against the backdrop of Bruce's evident despair—his feeling that his world was "dropping out from under him" and
that he himself was a failure.

COSTLY LESSONS

The Franklins were, undoubtedly, dealing with some difficult individual and interpersonal issues at that particular point in their lives. Bruce
was struggling with a real sense of inadequacy and disappointment in
himself; he was also, it seemed to me, feeling jealous of his wife and angry
about her job's having caused them to move away from his more familiar,
accustomed surroundings. He was, moreover, guilty and conflicted about
these feelings, for he was, in many ways, *proud* of Sara's accomplishments,
and he'd participated in the decision to come to the new community and
been extremely pleased (initially) by the prospect.

Sara, too, was feeling guilty and conflicted—about her recent successes
and about her appearing to have surpassed her husband. Being more
recognized and lauded than Bruce made her feel, in some obscure fashion,
deviant—as if she were being too aggressive, too competitive, too unfem-
inine. At some level of her being, she awaited his wrath and fully expected
him to revenge himself upon her. She, the former wounded bird in their
emotional system, had moved ahead of her caretaker in the most flagrant
manner, and now their world was unbalanced. "Disasters" of all sorts
were inevitable.

The individual and interpersonal issues with which the Franklins were
struggling were obviously complex and serious. The changing circumstances of their lives called for substantial renegotiation and change in
what was a polarized wounded bird/caretaker system. The task confronting
them, during this phase of their marriage, was to work out a new way of
being in a close relationship—a system which would permit both of the
partners to be nurtured *and* to take care of each other whenever such care
was necessary.

But the *additional* challenge presented to them, at that juncture—the
normal changes in sexual responsivity associated with getting older—had
transformed what was a difficult situation into one that was totally un-

250

manageable. For both Sara and Bruce tended to see these changes in behavior as clear signals of anger, hostility or withdrawal instead of what they were: ordinary aspects of human sexuality, attendant upon the process of aging.

The Franklins had simply assumed, as most people tend to do, that being sexually experienced and functional is synonymous with being a sexually educated individual. But there were vital matters about which these two intelligent, sophisticated people were completely and utterly ignorant—and the costs of their ignorance were enormous.

14

What, Precisely, Happens During Sex?

What does actually happen during sex? What physical and behavioral changes—in the female, in the male—occur between the outset and the completion of the sexual act?

Beginning in the early 1950s and continuing for the next eleven years, Masters and Johnson carried out a series of remarkable laboratory studies of a daring and unprecedented nature. What these researchers did was *watch people* engaging in a variety of sexual activities and gather meticulous data about their responses—information about sexual physiology which had simply never existed prior to this time.

The sexual behaviors observed and recorded by Masters and Johnson included sexual intercourse in a number of different positions; masturbation, with fingers or with electric vibrators or massagers; and also what the researchers termed "artificial coition"—a woman copulating with a clear plastic artificial phallus. The "penis," ingeniously equipped with light and a camera, made it possible to study carefully, while recording on motion-picture film, the internal changes that occurred during a female's cycle of sexual excitation, orgasm, and return to an unexcited state.

Masters and Johnson's subjects were 694 normally functioning volunteers—men and women ranging in age from eighteen to eighty-nine years. There were more females in the group (382) than there were males (312); 276 of the participants were married pairs. Although, according to the investigators, no ongoing effort was made to keep an accurate accounting of the number of male and female orgasms experienced in the laboratory setting, they write (in *Human Sexual Response*) that "a conservative estimate of 10,000 complete cycles of sexual response for the total research population could certainly be supported."

For the first time in medical history, the anatomy and physiology of human sexual response were being observed and scrutinized in the same careful, methodical, objective fashion in which the kidneys, the cardio-vascular system and the other great organ systems had been studied. Masters and Johnson, working initially within the department of obstetrics and gynecology at the Washington University School of Medicine and later under the auspices of their own Reproductive Biology Research Foundation, had voyaged into the terra incognita of genital functioning and they returned with a vast amount of novel data about the biology of sex.

The ways in which men and women responded to what the investigators termed "effective sexual stimulation" were expectably different in certain ways, but there were some fascinating *similarities* between male and female sexual functioning as well. These had to do, primarily, with two important physiological phenomena: *vasocongestion*, or engorgement of blood vessels, tissues and organs, and *myotonia*, or increasing tension in the body's musculature. Vasocongestion and myotonia are, as shall be seen, fundamental to sexual responsivity in both women and men.

THE FIRST PHASE OF THE SEXUAL
RESPONSE CYCLE: EXCITEMENT

The first physiological reaction to erotic stimulation—whether the stimulus be a touch, a memory, a film, the sight of an alluring person, a perfume or other odor which carries arousing associations, etc.—is a heightened blood flow, which occurs within a matter of seconds in males and females alike. Blood rushes to the tissues of the body, particularly to the genital organs, far more rapidly than it can be drained. This dramatic vascular redistribution leads to erection, in the male, and to lubrication, in the female—both resulting from the engorgement of the genitalia.

The male's erection (which occurs in the young adult within three to eight seconds) is brought about by the rapid filling, with blood, of three cylindrical "caverns" within the penis (two called the corpora cavernosa, and one called the corpus spongiosum). Erectile tissues within these co-lumnar structures, which run throughout the length of the organ and extend behind the scrotum, become suffused and congested; at the same time, valves in the penile veins close down reflexively, like floodgates, so that little or no fluid can escape.

A high-pressure condition is thereby created.

What erection involves is, in effect, the functioning of a hydraulic system. The penile cylinders, distended by the inrushing blood supplies, strain hard against the unstretchable outer sheath of the male organ, which has now become stiffened, enlarged, and protrudes from the body at a higher angle. What has literally "gotten it up" is the fact that under conditions of sexual excitement, more blood rushes into the phallus than is able to leave it.

This might appear to have very little to do with vaginal lubrication, in the female—a reaction which, during her early years, will occur promptly upon stimulation (within some ten to thirty seconds). But in fact, *her* lubricatory response and *his* erectile response are identical neurophysiological events; both are brought about by the rapid influx of blood to the genitals. He has responded with penile erection; in her case, the engorgement and distension of vaginal blood vessels bring about the "sweating" phenomenon first observed by Masters and Johnson.

A watery, viscous substance, they report, appears on the vaginal walls, oozing through its mucosal tissues. This transudate, which *is* the lubricatory fluid of the female, is actually the same plasma that ordinarily courses through the blood vessels of the vaginal lining. Under conditions of arousal, however, these vessels have become so congested and distended that part of their contents is literally squeezed out under pressure. The liquid "sweats" forth from the interior surfaces of the vagina, providing the smooth, glistening inner coating that will make sexual intercourse comfortable.

This female lubricatory reaction is, it should be emphasized, one that occurs at the very *beginning* of the sexual response cycle described by Masters and Johnson—at the outset of the first phase, which they term "excitement." It is the prelude to a number of important vaginal changes that are yet to occur. Becoming moist and wet is not, although it is often assumed to be, *the* signal that a woman is ready for intercourse—which should now proceed without further delay. Lubrication should, instead, be thought of as the counterpart to male erection, and a man is not necessarily ready to proceed directly to coitus by virtue of becoming erect.

Erection and lubrication, which are vasocongestive reactions, are soon accompanied by the increasing muscle tension—myotonia—which lags not very far behind. Myotonia is, as Masters and Johnson note, "second only to vasocongestion as physiologic evidence of eroticism" and involves not only heightened muscular tautness but the clenching and unclenching of the body's voluntary and involuntary musculature as well. In the excitement phase, for example, involuntary contraction of muscle fibers in the female's breasts cause her nipples to become erect and to grow in length and diameter.

During this same phase, her clitoris—a small, cylindrical erectile structure located just above the vaginal entrance—is becoming swollen and engorged. It is tumescent, in the manner of the male phallus, and the two organs are, in certain ways, comparable. The clitoris has, like the penis, a shaft which contains erectile structures, as well as a head, or "glans," richly endowed with nerve endings and exquisitely sensitive to tactile sensation. As erotic tension grows, the female's clitoral shaft thickens, and its head may grow so enlarged and congested that it actually doubles in diameter.

The clitoris and penis are similar, in terms of appearance, but insofar as biological functioning is concerned, they are very different indeed. The female organ appears to have no task to perform and no clear-cut reason for existing—except, perhaps, that of "rewarding" the woman for engaging in reproductive behavior.

The penis, while also an organ exquisitely adapted for receiving pleasurable sensation, delivers sperm into the female partner's uterus and carries urine from the male's body (via the urethra) as well. In terms of reproductive function, it is the vagina and the penis which are most alike and which fit together in a complementary lock-and-key fashion.

The vaginal lips, both inner (labia minora) and outer (labia majora), are also affected by sexual excitement. In a resting, unaroused state the outer lips meet primly in the center of the vulva ("covering") to cloak the entrance to the vagina. But, in response to erotic stimulation, they become engorged and swollen—so much so that they almost seem to push each other apart and tilt upward slightly, toward the top of the vaginal entryway. The inner lips, also progressively more engorged as sexual tension heightens, are opening outward as well. It is as if the female genital were spreading its portals and inviting its phallic guest to enter.

Within the vagina, in the meanwhile, complex preparations for intercourse are under way. In a sense, what is occurring is almost the inverse of the male erection: Extra space is being created. The female genital was, in its quiescent state, a pale, pink, slightly moist cylindrical barrel whose walls were relaxed and collapsed. But now, in response to mounting excitement, the furthermost two-thirds of the vagina expand like a balloon that is slowly filling with air.

At the same time the uterus, also congested with excess blood content, begins to rise and to rotate in a backward direction. This produces what Masters and Johnson call "a tenting effect"—a stretching up of the vaginal walls which serves to create an even larger inner dimension. The surfaces have now lost their typically wrinkled appearance, the wrinkles are stretched and smoothed out, and their color has darkened. They are deep purple in hue, owing to engorgement of the vasculature of the vaginal walls.

PHASE TWO: PLATEAU

In the subsequent phase of the sexual response cycle—"plateau"—these extraordinary changes in the female genital continue. There is, it should be said, no clearly defined, discrete border between these two phases. Plateau can best be understood as a continuation of the excitement phase, but one which occurs at a heightened level—on the floor above, so to speak. During plateau, that astonishing phenomenon to which Masters and Johnson gave the name "the orgasmic platform" appears.

The orgasmic platform is just that: a cushiony platform of moist, fluid-swollen tissues. It is created by the dramatic engorgement of the nearest third of the vagina—i.e., the area closer to the organ's entryway. The surfaces in this part of the vaginal barrel become, as sexual excitement mounts, so congested that its internal diameter is reduced by as much as 50 percent. As a result, the entering penis is gripped and surrounded, enormously increasing the erotic enjoyment of the male. While this third of the vaginal canal is decreasing its inner circumference, the furthermost two-thirds are continuing to balloon upward and outward, so that a spacious receptacle for accommodation of the lengthened penis is being industriously fashioned.

The male organ, during the plateau phase, is as distended and engorged as it can become; it is stretched to its utmost capacity. A small penis may, at plateau levels of arousal, actually become doubled in length. A large penis tends to expand less, for erection is a great equalizer. There is far less variation in the length of erect phalluses than there is in phalluses in the flaccid state. The male's testes have, too, become fluid-swollen and enlarged; their diameter has doubled in size, and they have been pulled upward and nearer to the body.

The so-called "sex flush," a patchy, measleslike rash, may now appear on the face and upper chest if it has not made its appearance earlier. It is much more common in women than in men. Both the male and female partner, in the plateau phase, are breathing rapidly; their blood pressure is higher and their pulses are quickened—the heart rate rises from 60 to 80 to 100 to 160 beats per minute. Muscular tension has increased to such a degree that certain voluntary and involuntary sets of muscles (in the face, ribs, and abdomen) can begin contracting in what looks like an almost spastic fashion.

PHASE THREE: ORGASM

As the third phase of the cycle—"orgasm"—approaches, the woman's clitoris (both shaft and head) suddenly disappears from the scene. It has risen from its usual position, overhanging the pubic bone, turned up 180 degrees and then retracted—withdrawn under its small foreskin, or hood. This sometimes confuses the sexual partner, who is uncertain about exactly where it has gotten to and who may think that the female has abruptly "turned off." The retraction of the clitoris during late plateau, while clearly open to misinterpretation, is, in fact, a sign of *increased* rather than decreased sexual arousal.

The physiological correlate of orgasm, in both sexes, is nothing other than a series of muscular contractions which are explosively pleasurable in nature. These are most evidenced, in the case of the female, within the "orgasmic platform"—i.e., the overfull, padded third of the vaginal barrel which seems to grasp the penis, enveloping it and stimulating it to a luxurious, voluptuous climax.

This highly eroticized corridor will often, just before the onset of orgasm, appear to shudder lightly or go into a mild spasm. Then a series of rhythmic contractions, occurring at 0.8-second intervals, begins . . . and endures for a brief period of what are eternal-seeming seconds. It is these convulsive contractions, involving the orgasmic platform and the pelvic floor muscles—as well as the uterus, which also clenches and unclenches at the designated 0.8-second intervals—which are accompanied by subjective feelings of intense, almost unbearable delight.

After a matter of moments, the initial contractions slow down and manifest themselves at longer than 0.8-second intervals. These latter squeezes and releases are highly pleasurable but not as acute as the rhythmic set (usually between three and fifteen) that has preceded them, for it is during those first contractions that volcanic vasocongestive and muscular tensions erupt and find their ecstatic release.

The male's orgasm, while remarkably similar to that of the female, nevertheless occurs in not one but *two* very distinct subphases. "Emission" is the first of these, and "ejaculation" is the second. During emission the liquids that will become part of the male's ejaculate are being collected together. These are pumped in, from differing sources, to a dilated bulb at the base of the urethra. Here sperm, carried through the vas deferens by a small volume of fluid, mixes with the secretions of the seminal vesicles, while prostatic fluid pours in from the prostate. Subjectively, this pooling of the reproductive juices is accompanied by an awareness of impending orgasm—what Masters and Johnson termed "the moment of ejaculatory inevitability," when the climactic onrush can no longer be halted voluntarily.

Ejaculation, the second subphase of male orgasm, follows within a matter of seconds. This consists of vigorous, rhythmic contractions—*occurring at precisely 0.8-second intervals*—which, in his case, are generated in the prostate bulb and the powerful musculature at the base of the penis. The strong, undulating contractions that result are associated with subjective feelings of great euphoria and intensely pleasurable excitement; they serve, too, to pump the "bolus," or seminal fluid, upward through the penile urethra—from which it is expelled, under high pressure, into the partner's vagina. After the first three or four strong contractions, at 0.8-second intervals, the muscular compressions and decompressions slow down and are spaced more widely apart. Whatever semen remains within the penile urethra is released in small, gentle squirts.

PHASE FOUR: RESOLUTION

Finally, the phase of "resolution" begins. Orgasm has brought relief of muscular tensions throughout the entire body, and blood is swiftly leaving the congested, distended reproductive organs. The body does not, however, return to its resting, sexually unaroused state immediately. In the male, the penis remains semierect, for while fluid leaves two of its erectile structures (the corpora cavernosa) at once, it takes about a half hour for the third one (the corpus spongiosum) to empty. After orgasm, men enter a refractory period, which may last minutes, in young males, or hours or even days, in older males, during which they are unresponsive to stimulation and are physically incapable of becoming sexually aroused.

In the female, the puffy orgasmic platform subsides rapidly, so that this third of the vaginal barrel increases in internal diameter. The other two-thirds of the vagina, owing to diminishment of the ballooning and "tenting" effects, are shrinking down to their former, unstimulated size; the uterus, as blood flows away from it, is growing smaller too. The clitoris, having reemerged from its retracted position very promptly after orgasm—within five to ten seconds—nevertheless remains tumescent for a period of time. It will take anywhere from ten to fifteen minutes to a full half hour before the woman's genital-reproductive organs have returned to their basal, resting, erotically unstimulated state again.

Women are not, like men, biologically refractory to sexual stimulation in the immediate wake of orgasmic experience. If effectively stimulated, the female can move directly from the resolution phase to excitement or to the higher levels of plateau, and then return to orgasm again . . . and again . . . and again. Nothing can, theoretically, interfere with this process, aside from exhaustion—either her own or that of her partner.

15
Sexual Cures

Sexual problems—of varying degrees of intensity and of longer or shorter duration—are believed to be very common in the population at large. What happens during sex, as described in the preceding chapter, is, of course, *what happens when sex proceeds in a smooth, integrated, unimpeded fashion*—but things don't always happen in that way. A host of organic factors (such as illness, drugs), psychological factors (anger, anxiety about being able to perform, etc.) and cultural influences (shame, guilt) can intervene, affecting delicate sexual mechanisms and sometimes derailing them entirely. One of the most striking characteristics of erotic life is the relative ease with which it can go awry.

And the findings of a number of disparate research investigations do indicate a remarkably high prevalence of sexual difficulties in virtually every group of individuals or couples surveyed. In one study, carried out at Pittsburgh's Western Psychiatric Institute, 100 couples who considered their marriages either "happy" or "very happy" were queried extensively about many aspects of their lives together.

Among this sample of contented mates, the researchers found, "about half the women . . . reported difficulty becoming sexually aroused and 46 percent said they experienced difficulty reaching orgasm. Fully 15 percent of the wives stated that they were unable to reach orgasm. Among the men, sexual dysfunctions were less common, yet approximately 10 percent admitted to difficulty with erections, and over a third reported premature ejaculation."

The assumption that happily married couples would be free of sexual problems was not necessarily a valid one. Nor, conversely, was the assumption that a sexual problem was synonymous with a marital one. "Perhaps the most significant aspect of our findings," the investigators concluded, "was the discovery that very few people have trouble-free sex lives, even when their marriages are satisfying ones."

WHAT CAN BE DONE ABOUT SEXUAL PROBLEMS?

When sexual troubles arrive or already exist (and most human beings can expect to encounter some such difficulties during the course of their lives) what, realistically, is there to be done about them?

Before the work of Masters and Johnson began providing extensive and reliable physiological information about human sexuality, it was commonly believed that analytic therapy was the best, or only, treatment available. The man whose erection was uncertain or who ejaculated almost immediately after entering his partner needed to explore the profound neurotic conflicts (rooted in very early experiences) that had brought his sexual symptoms into being.

Similarly, the totally nonorgasmic female or the woman who could attain climax only be means of clitoral stimulation—which Freud viewed as a very different and fundamentally "immature" form of orgasm—could struggle, in long-term, intensive psychoanalytic therapy, to uncover the repressed infantile traumas that made "adult," i.e., vaginal, orgasm so impossible a goal to achieve. When the Masters-Johnson studies demonstrated that clitoral and vaginal orgasms are observably *indistinguishable* physiological events, such value judgments about "better, grown-up" and "worse, childish" forms of female orgasm came into question.

Most important of all, however, the sexual researchers were able to show that *even in the presence of unresolved psychological issues*, sexual problems could be dealt with very effectively by means of simple behavioral techniques. For as the clouds of myth surrounding so many aspects of erotic functioning began to dissipate, a clearer understanding of *what could go wrong* during various phases of the sex response cycle began to emerge—and so did some highly focused, specific methods for dealing with differing kinds of complaints.

"IMPOTENCE" AND "FRIGIDITY"

Prior to the laboratory studies of Masters and Johnson, certain global, nonspecific diagnoses had been used to label all male and female sexual symptoms: "Impotence" described a man's problems, whatever they were, and "frigidity" referred to any difficulty that a woman might be experiencing.

But now disorders of the arousal phase—i.e., excitement and plateau—could be carefully differentiated from those of the orgastic phase—that is, orgasm and resolution.

Differing hormonal and nervous mechanisms are involved during arousal (when engorgement of the genitals and muscular tension are building to a crescendo) and during orgasm (when intense muscle contractions, accompanied by pleasurable release of sexual and psychological tensions, take place, followed by deflation of the genital-reproductive organs, which are returning to their basal, unstimulated state). Now the bodywide changes occurring during the sexual response cycle can be understood, described and *treated* in more precise, objective and effective ways than ever was possible earlier.

Dysfunctions of the Arousal Phase
1. Male Disorders During Arousal

PRIMARY IMPOTENCE
SECONDARY IMPOTENCE

In the male the major disorder associated with the excitement phase is the inability to achieve or maintain an erection. A clinical distinction is made between the man who never has become erect enough to engage in coitus—and therefore suffers from "primary impotence"—and the person who is currently experiencing erectile problems, but has been sexually adequate in the past ("secondary impotence"). The number of males in the former category is small, less that 1 percent, but the complaint of secondary impotence is not uncommon at all. Practically *all* men, it must be added, experience some transient difficulty with erection (usually when they are upset or fatigued), which generally passes quickly, unless the person or his partner happens to take it in an overly serious fashion.

When erectile problems are present and persistent—and organic difficulties have been ruled out—then fear, anxiety and efforts to take conscious control of sexual functioning are the usual erotic saboteurs. (If, by the way, an impotent male experiences erection on awakening or during the night or during masturbation, this is good evidence that the problem is primarily psychological and not physiological in nature.)

Generally speaking, the more concerned and worried about his capacities a man happens to be, the less likely he is to function in a natural and spontaneous fashion. For if he is too busy monitoring his own performance—especially the height and hardness that his penis has attained—he cannot abandon himself to sexual feelings. He is too preoccupied by the need to take charge of the erotic proceedings and, most important, with keeping his phallus aloft.

He is attempting the impossible; the male cannot will himself to become erect, for this function is not under conscious, voluntary control. The erectile response is governed by that same subsystem of the autonomic nervous system—the parasympathetic—which controls digestion, respiration, sleep, and other neurovegetative functions. In the same way that a man cannot *will* his stomach to digest its contents, he cannot *order* the erectile structures within his penis to become engorged with blood and thereby ordain that the organ will rise accordingly. If he is relatively relaxed and free of excessive concern, he will simply respond to erotic stimuli by becoming erect.

If, on the other hand, he approaches the partner in a state of apprehension and fear or is assailed by anxious feelings during lovemaking, the *other* subsystem of the autonomic nervous system—the sympathetic—is highly likely to become involved. The sympathetic innervations mediate "fight or flight" responses and, when this physiological warning system is called into play, adrenaline pours into the bloodstream; the body moves into a state of battle alert.

During fight or flight responding, blood flows *away* from the genitals, which leaves them less vulnerable in situations involving threat and danger. The "danger" to which the male is reacting is, in this somewhat paradoxical instance, his own anxieties about his sexual adequacy and his fears about being scorned and rejected by the partner if he finds himself unable to perform. His frantic efforts to maintain his erection are thus, from a biological point of view, the most effective way of causing it to disappear.

It is of course true, and it must be emphasized here, that erections often go down and rise again several times during an extended period of sexual excitement; this happens as a matter of course and need not trouble the male or his erotic partner in the slightest. But this situation is to be distinguished from that of the man who feels compelled to watch anxiously and obsessively monitor the state and condition of his penis—for *his* erection will be the one that is most endangered, uncertain, and liable to deflate and stay down.

2. Female Disorders of the Arousal Phase

SEXUAL UNRESPONSIVENESS

In the female, the main disorder of the excitement phase is called "sexual unresponsiveness"—a phrase which means just what the words imply: She does not react to erotic stimulation. The physiological manifestations of sexual arousal are absent: vaginal lubrication, nipple erection, expansion of the vagina's size, and the like. The unresponsive woman has, moreover, little or no sensuous feeling, and while she is physically capable of having intercourse (which is obviously *not* true for the male suffering from a disturbance of arousal), she is liable to find the experience uncomfortable or even painful. Her genital organ is not lubricated, enlarged or swollen and "padded" within; she is tight, dry and uninvolved.

Dysfunctions of the Orgasm Phase

1. Male Orgasmic Disorders

PREMATURE EJACULATION
RETARDED EJACULATION

The male, in the subsequent, "orgasmic" phase of the sex response cycle, can suffer from one of two possible types of dysfunction. The first of these, "premature ejaculation," is considered to be the most prevalent of the sexual disorders affecting men—fully a third of the happily married male partners in the Pittsburgh study suffered from this problem—but different experts have defined, in somewhat differing ways, what is meant by orgasmic prematurity.

When Is Ejaculation "Premature"?

Some authorities have, for example, stated that ejaculation is overly rapid if it occurs before the male has penetrated or anywhere from two to thirty seconds afterward. Others have suggested that the number of pelvic thrusts that the male can execute without moving directly into climax is the definitional key to whether he suffers from premature ejaculation or not.

Masters and Johnson's criteria for diagnosis of this dysfunction are relational in nature. As they see it, the man who cannot control his ejaculatory process long enough to satisfy his partner at least 50 percent of the time is indeed suffering from this disorder. But the noted sex expert

Helen Singer Kaplan views the matter from a somewhat different perspective.

Controlling Ejaculation

All other definitions, states Dr. Kaplan, miss the essential point about prematurity—which is that it involves *"the absence of voluntary control over the ejaculatory reflex."* A male, in Dr. Kaplan's opinion, is ejaculating prematurely if he is reaching orgasm before he *chooses* to; the choice is actually one that is his to make. It is possible to learn how to take charge of ejaculatory release, just as it is possible voluntarily to control the reflexes governing the release of urine and feces.

If a man cannot decide when he wishes to come but is instead swept away by the need to ejaculate very rapidly, then an important lack in his sexual repertoire exists. Writes Dr. Kaplan: "The effective lover must be able to continue to engage in sex play while he is in a highly aroused state, in order to bring the woman, who is usually slower to respond, especially when she is young, to a high plateau of excitement and orgasm."

A remarkably effective and simple technique for learning to bring the ejaculatory reflex under conscious control has been known about for many years (but not, apparently, in Pittsburgh, where that large group of happily married male partners continued to suffer from problems of prematurity!). This method was developed by Dr. James Semans in 1956, but remained relatively unknown until described by Masters and Johnson in *Human Sexual Inadequacy*.

I will say more about this, farther along, but I do want to note that mastery of this technique involves learning to recognize the sensations just prior to emission, when the fluids that make up the ejaculate are being collected in the small reservoir at the base of the urethra. This is the subphase of the orgasmic response that Masters and Johnson termed the "moment of ejaculatory inevitability." It precedes the expulsive ejaculatory substage of the orgasm by the merest fraction of time.

Retarded Ejaculation

The other malady associated with the orgasm phase in males, "retarded ejaculation," is the clinical opposite of the problem of orgasmic prematurity. For while the individual with premature ejaculation reaches climax too readily and rapidly, the person suffering from what is essentially an involuntary inhibition of the ejaculatory reflex has great difficulty in getting there at all. He is, at times—or perhaps invariably—unable to release his ejaculate into the sexual partner. He can get excited and fully erect and can engage in vigorous intercourse, but he simply cannot come.

Much of what was said about the male who is experiencing potency problems can apply to the individual with ejaculatory inhibition as well. The inability to reach orgasm *could* have a physiological explanation, for ejaculation, like erection, can be affected by disease states, medications and drugs. If the person *is* orgasmic on certain occasions and in certain situations, but finds it impossible to be so on others, then the problem can be assumed to be psychological rather than organic in origin. He is, like the man who obsesses about his erection, anxiously monitoring his own performance and unable to stop trying to control it by the force of his will.

Just as the impotent male focuses on the hardness of his penis, the retarded ejaculator focuses on whether or not he will "make it" to the goal of climactic release. Neither individual can abandon himself to sexual pleasure, sink into the experience, and let what should occur naturally happen in that way. The person suffering from ejaculatory inhibition is overcontrolled and, by attempting to direct his orgasm, fails to achieve it, while the premature ejaculator is undercontrolled in a situation where voluntary control actually *could* be established.

2. ORGASMIC DISORDERS OF THE FEMALE

INHIBITED FEMALE ORGASM
SITUATIONAL ORGASMIC DYSFUNCTION

The analogue, in females, of the orgasmically premature male—i.e., the woman who climaxes rapidly and then has no further interest in coitus—is a clinical rarity. For the female partner, when she reaches orgasm, may go on to further orgasms, or if she does not do so, she can at least accommodate the male until his sexual excitation reaches peak levels and he climaxes too.

But the female equivalent of retarded ejaculation—that is, the inability to reach orgasm—is very commonplace indeed. It is the major disorder associated with the orgasm phase of the sex response cycle and the most frequent sexual complaint cited by women in general. Masters and Johnson called this condition "orgasmic dysfunction," but the formal terminology now in use is "inhibited female orgasm." Once again, an important clinical distinction between primary and secondary forms of this disorder exists.

The woman who, like Angie Carrano, has *never* experienced orgasm under any circumstances at all is said to be suffering from "primary orgasmic dysfunction" (recently renamed "primary anorgasmia"). This female disorder is, according to Masters and Johnson, even bleaker than is primary impotence in the male, for the man with erectile difficulties has usually masturbated or perhaps achieved release by means of stimulation offered by the partner. Similarly, the retarded ejaculator can usually reach orgasm *elsewhere* than inside the partner, i.e., by himself, on his own terms, when he is feeling in control and safe.

But the primarily anorgasmic woman—although she may become aroused, experience vaginal lubrication and show other signs of sexual excitement—never reaches climax, alone or with a partner, anytime, anyplace, anywhere. Hers is a history of total inorgasmic responsivity, and it is estimated that some 8 to 10 percent of American females fall into this particular category.

Situational Orgasmic Dysfunction

Millions more are in the "secondary anorgasmia" category, to which Masters and Johnson gave the name "situational orgasmic dysfunction." This designation is, they suggested, applicable to the woman who "has experienced at least one instance of orgasmic expression," whether by means of sexual intercourse, masturbation or some other form of stimulation. She might be someone who *had been* able to attain climax at an earlier phase of her life, but is no longer capable of doing so. Or she could be orgasmic only under certain conditions—for example, when stimulating herself, but not during intercourse with a partner. She could by able to reach a climax only after extended sessions of clitoral or oral stimulation or achieve orgasmic release only while away on vacations but never while at home. Situational orgasmic dysfunction comes in a myriad of possible shapes, sizes and possibilities—all accompanied by some degree of disappointment and frustration.

The Watched Pot That Doesn't Boil

At the root of this problem, in the female, is that same involuntary inhibition of the natural orgasmic reflex which prevents the male retarded ejaculator from "letting go." She, like her masculine counterpart, cannot stop her obsessive self-observation; she is a spectator rather than an involved participant in the sexual experience. Instead of losing herself in her excited, erotic sensations and feelings, she watches fearfully and waits apprehensively for some signal of the hoped-for climactic event. It is the proverbial watched pot that fails to come to a boil.

Physical Considerations

Where female orgasmic problems are concerned, more than psychological factors alone may be involved. In some cases, the difficulty has to do with a lack of adequate stimulation; the woman's sexual tensions fail to rise above her orgasmic threshold, and so the reflex is either never or very rarely triggered. From the purely physical point of view, it must be remembered that the female's most highly sensitive and pleasurably receptive sexual organ is not the vagina but the clitoris. This organ is stimulated only indirectly during intercourse, mainly by traction of the thrusting penis as it moves against the clitoral prepuce, or hood.

The clitoris is also affected by the tugging on the inner lips of the vagina (to which it is attached, at the top) which occurs during coitus—but for some females this somewhat indirect form of clitoral stimulation doesn't prove sufficiently exciting. They simply do not respond with enough arousal, energy and steam to fuel a blast-off into the orgasmic stratosphere.

A *majority*, not a minority, of females actually cannot reach climax by means of penile thrusting alone. As Shere Hite indicates (in *The Hite Report*), only 30 percent of the 3,019 females she queried stated that they reached climax regularly without additional clitoral stimulation. "In other words," writes Hite, "the majority of women do not experience orgasm regularly as a result of intercourse."

Her figures are consistent with those of Dr. Seymour Fisher who, in *The Female Orgasm*, reports that only 20 percent of the 300 women whom he interviewed never required a final push to orgasm by means of manual stimulation. The need for clitoral stroking—in addition to the vaginal stimulation provided by the male's organ—is clearly more the rule than the exception. It is the *norm* among orgasmic females.

The Bridge Maneuver

Some couples engage in intercourse with the man stimulating the woman's clitoris simultaneously. Others do the same, with the exception that it is the female who stimulates herself. In still other instances, the male reaches climax and then brings his female partner to orgasm afterward. Finally, there is what sex therapists call the "bridge maneuver." What this involves is the man's providing clitoral stimulation until the woman reaches very high levels of excitement and then—when orgasm is near—entering and sensuously rotating his penis within her so as to bring her all the way to climax.

This tactic serves to "bridge" the distance from clitoral to coital responsiveness and provides a fine solution to what is often a fundamentally anatomical and mechanical difficulty—i.e., the vagina is not so exquisitely receptive an organ as is the clitoris, so intercourse without additional stimulation simply doesn't produce an adequate supply of pleasurable sensation. More erotic fireworks, provided by clitoral touching and stroking, are necessary if the female's sky is to be lit by her orgasm.

When the Problem Is Psychogenic

When the obstructions to orgasm are, on the other hand, primarily psychological, the "pleasuring" exercises developed by Masters and Johnson (which I will describe) can be extraordinarily helpful. These exercises are useful for teaching the anxious, overcontrolled person—who is trying to *make her orgasm happen*—how to relax and just enjoy being sexual without struggling to force something to occur. Before discussing these erotic tasks, however, I want to mention the other major female dysfunction—"vaginismus"—which is not associated with any particular phase of the sex response cycle and for which no male equivalent exists.

Vaginismus

Vaginismus is an unconscious, extremely strong contraction of the muscles surrounding the vaginal entrance—a spasm so powerful that penile penetration becomes extremely painful, difficult or downright impossible to achieve. For some peculiar reason, this problem seldom afflicts poor and uneducated women; it is a sexual malady which exists almost exclusively among women in the upper socioeconomic and educational strata.

Sexual Exercises: Sensate Focus or Pleasuring

In their brilliant treatise *Human Sexual Inadequacy* (1970) William Masters and Virginia Johnson scuttled the widespread clinical notion that sexual dysfunctions could not be dealt with successfully until the unconscious conflicts which had engendered them had been thoroughly explored and resolved.

On the contrary, Masters and Johnson demonstrated, behavioral approaches could be useful in many instances in which lengthy and expensive analytic treatment was proving to be completely fruitless and ineffective.

It was, moreover, *not* universally true that all sexual disorders involved infantile anxieties and the internal defenses that had been erected to deal with them. A great many sexual symptoms grow, the researchers explained, out of current, fairly mundane kinds of difficulties—anxieties about performance, attempts to obtain conscious control over aspects of sexual response that are not under voluntary control, "spectatoring," inability to relax, lack of sexual knowledge, ignorance of valuable techniques, and so forth. These are *not* deep and complex problems, but often rather superficial ones—easy to comprehend and not all resistant to short-term treatment. Masters and Johnson reported that they were treating a variety of sexual dysfunctions very effectively on a brief (two-week) basis, using certain behavioral methods which they had developed—erotic "homework exercises," so to speak.

The sexual tasks that they devised for dealing with the various forms of dysfunction cannot all be described here (suggestions for further reading can be found in the selected bibliography). All of these exercises do, however, remain central to the practice of sex therapy today.

Modern sex therapy tends to be an amalgam of sensual tasks and psychotherapy. That is, erotic homework assignments are given to the couple, and close attention is paid to any psychological roadblocks that may develop along the way. A wife may become frightened when her prematurely ejaculating husband becomes sexually competent, for example, because she fears that she may lose him to another woman if he is problem-free. In such a case, the erotic homework assignments would be halted temporarily while the psychological dilemmas were uncovered, worked through and resolved.

Basic Training in the Art of the Caress

The sexual exercises to which Masters and Johnson gave the name "sensate focus"—or, more simply, pleasuring—were ones they used for every couple who came to them for therapy, no matter what the nature of the complaint. Treatment *always* commenced with these particular erotic tasks; currently, some sex therapists continue this practice while others bypass sensate focus when treating specific kinds of dysfunction. The pleasuring exercises are, in any case, simple to understand and important to know about. For they are astonishingly effective in helping the overcontrolled individual learn to relax and enjoy being sexual . . . with no performance strings attached. What they involve, as the outline given below will make clear, is basic training in the art of the caress.

Exercise One: Nongenital Pleasuring

The first and most important proviso of this initial sensual training session is that *the genitals are not to be touched* throughout it. The task is devised to help the mates learn to enjoy touching, stroking, exploring, massaging and fondling all of the contours of each other's bodies. The couple is asked to find a time and place—perhaps late in the evening, when the house is quiet—which will allow them to be together without fear of interruption. They should then shower or bathe and join each other in bed, feeling attractively clean and presentable. If they are comfortable with nudity, they may be naked during this exercise; if not, they may want to start out in nightclothes or underwear.

Her Turn

One of the partners—let us say, the woman—will then lie on her stomach, while the man gently begins to stroke her body from the top of her head and moving downward. As he lightly and lazily explores the skin surfaces of her arms, back, neck, ears, buttocks (without touching any sexual organ), he is simply to "make nice" to every part of her, stroking her in the same easy way as one would stroke a purring animal. She will, in many instances, soon be purring herself. Should she, however, go on to become aroused and highly excited, her genitals are to be scrupulously avoided; sexual touching is, for the moment, out of bounds.

The male partner may want to use some light massage lotion or some baby oil to facilitate the stroking; this will smooth the passage of his hands across her skin and be helpful if his hands are those of an outdoorsman. The pressure of his touching ought, ideally, to be soft and teasing—not massage, but gentle stimulation of the skin (which, under these circumstances, becomes transformed into one vast erogenous zone). While she is being stroked, the female is enjoined to focus upon the pleasurable sensations she is experiencing and not to worry about whether her man is becoming tired or bored. He, on his part, is to concentrate upon the gratification he receives from this slow and non-goal-oriented touching (i.e., touching *not* directed toward orgasm). Both partners can relax because both will, in the words of Masters and Johnson, "give-to-get"—that is, be in both the receiving and taking positions.

After a period of time agreeable to the mates (say, fifteen minutes) the woman is instructed to turn over so that her partner can gently caress the entire front of her body—excepting, of course, the breasts and the area around the vagina. His long, slow, exploration of her body's surfaces is usually experienced as something surprising and utterly delicious. For simple touching of this kind reestablishes the intensely tactile reactions of early childhood and enhances trust at its most basic, i.e., bodily, level.

His Turn

After fifteen more minutes (or lesser or greater time segments, if these are more comfortable for the partners) the husband changes places with his wife. Now he lies on his stomach, and she reciprocates for the pleasuring she has received by softly caressing the entire back of his body. He is to tell her (as she has been asked to tell him during her turn) if anything feels especially wonderful, or tickles, or if her touch feels too soft or too heavy, or if she is moving too slowly or too quickly.

After fifteen minutes, during which he lies passively, enjoying her light-fingered exploration of his head, ears, arms, back, buttocks, inner thighs, lower legs, ankles, heels, etc., he turns over. Now she gently strokes the entire front of his body, moving from his head to his toes and from one side to another, wherever and however she pleases—avoiding only the penis and the testicles.

This total bodily caress—for the couple with or without sexual troubles—is a remarkable kind of experience. The injunction against genital touching is, in some strange way, part of what makes this exercise so erotic and exciting; nothing of a sexual nature is supposed to be *permitted* to happen. This produces the most open, childlike, trustful feelings—which have, at the same time, a decidedly aphrodisiac quality.

When the pleasuring is over, it is over; no "real sex" is allowed.

Exercise Two: Genital Pleasuring

The second phase of sensate focus, "genital pleasuring," begins at a time when the partners are well accustomed to exchanging caresses in the manner described above. Their responses to the first phase have, quite often, been nothing short of dramatic. For the man does not need to have an erect penis in order to be with his partner (since intercourse is prohibited), so he can relax and enjoy himself without having to worry about the state of erectness of his organ. . . . Erection follows, for it is the natural physiological response to erotic stimulation and will occur unless negative affects (fear, anger) interfere.

No performance, on his part, is required. Similarly, the woman, who has been unable to relax enough to experience her sexual feelings, is not worried about *having to produce* them. Frequently, however, in these supposedly asexual circumstances, she has found herself becoming unusually hot and bothered. She *can* become excited because there is no sense of being rushed or hurried. She doesn't have to respond in order to meet the needs of her partner, and this has freed her to focus on her own erotic sensations.

His Turn

Now, in the second exercise, gentle stroking of erogenous skin is added to the couple's agenda. If the genital pleasuring session begins with the male's being caressed, his partner is usually instructed to caress him in ways that will bring him to a high peak of excitation fairly quickly. She is to stroke his penis, playing with its shaft and its head, run her hand over his testes and gently touch the highly sensitive skin that lies between the anus and the scrotum. She can play with his nipples, then return to rub the head of his penis—stimulate him in any way (including orally) that she may find enjoyable.

When he becomes erect, her attention is to move to other parts of his body—his arms, legs, belly—which she will continue to stroke. During this nongenital touching, his erection may subside; that is *nothing that either partner is to worry about*. Eventually, when she pleases, she can return to the penis, caressing it with her fingers and her lips until it rises again. He, while being stimulated, is to relax, lie back, enjoy the cascade of pleasurable sensations—surrender himself completely to enjoyment of the exquisite, almost unbearably sensual feelings that she is evoking.

During this experience, it generally becomes evident that erections come and erections go, and when they do the latter, there is no cause for alarm. The loss of an erection does not mean (as the Franklins initially interpreted it to mean) that *all* is lost—i.e., that the sexual encounter is over and has been an unmitigated failure. For, during the course of genital pleasuring of the male, it becomes evident that further stimulation can frequently restore the erection, and if it doesn't, there are other enjoyable and pleasureful ways for a man and woman to enjoy being together.

The pressure is, in any case, off both partners, for during genital pleasuring intercourse is proscribed, and attaining orgasm is *not* a part of the task. The lesson being learned has to do with the joy and true eroticism non-goal-oriented sex.

Her Turn

Once again, after the man's turn at being pleasured is over, the pair change places; it is now *her turn* to be stroked and caressed. In this instance, however, he will probably not be told to try to bring her to a high state of excitement quickly in the way that she was instructed to do for him. His approach to genital touching will be more indirect, slower and more teasing.

The pleasuring of the woman begins with a gentle caressing and fondling of her entire body. The male's touch is to be light, soft, unhurried, so that his partner feels safe, tenderly admired and cared for. After a while, he commences, very slowly, to touch her breasts, play with them, kiss them. He can kiss her neck, the palms of her hands, her lips, and then return to kiss her breasts again. Then slowly, lingeringly, brushing the surface of her belly with his fingertips, he might reach down beyond it to stroke the skin around the highly sensitive clitoral area.

After a time of gentle touching, he may return to kiss her breasts and lips once again. Now, slowly and teasingly, he moves his hand across her body and to the genital region once again, touching the lips of the vagina, opening them gently, and then moving his hand off to explore her inner thighs. After a while, he will come back again, now stroking the clitoris somewhat more directly yet in the same fleeting, teasing style.

THE ART OF LONG, UNHURRIED LOVE

The male should, during the pleasuring of his mate, be sensitive to what he does that feels good and pleasing to her and what forms of stimulation might actually be turning her off. Some women particularly enjoy, it should be mentioned, the "backward-protected" position described by Masters and Johnson; it is especially designed for touching and stroking of the female. What it involves is the man sitting propped against the pillows at the head of the bed, with his legs open, and his partner lying in his arms between them. Her back leans against his chest; he can thus move his arms around in front of her body to stroke her breasts and her genitals while holding her in this position of comfort and security.

Sensate focus exercises often have astonishing effects, not only on a couple's sexual life but on many other aspects of their marriage. Writes psychiatrist Carol Nadelson: "Most couples report that this time together is remarkably revealing and gratifying. They may never have engaged in activity of this kind, and they usually report being surprised and delighted by the improvement in communication and the reinforcement of positive feelings toward each other."

Pleasuring is something that every couple—with or without a sexual problem—ought to know about, for these exercises are wonderful training in the art of long, unhurried love.

TREATING OTHER DYSFUNCTIONS:
RETARDED EJACULATION

The erotic tasks described above are crucial in the treatment of general unresponsiveness and anorgasmia, in the female, and of erectile difficulties, in the male, but they are not the therapy of choice for the retarded ejaculator. *His* anxieties are frequently of a phobic nature and therefore most amenable to the classic method of dealing with phobias—i.e., by means of behavior modification techniques. Little by little, in small and careful steps, the individual's frightened, panicky vaginal aversion is slowly desensitized.

Men who suffer from retarded ejaculation (the dysfunction is relatively rare, affecting some 5 percent of males) are often somewhat obsessive, overcontrolled people. They tend to be, like Bob Carrano, individuals who have a psychological investment in remaining unaware of certain inner states and affects, such as feelings of hostility and dependence. Thus, letting go of control is, for them, a somewhat frightening idea. What could emerge from the subterranean depths of the inner being is unfathomable and unimaginable.

In the dark of the vagina, the penis is both vulnerable to the partner and a hard, penetrating instrument experienced as potentially destructive to her with whom so much unconscious anger is associated. The individual who cannot come (occasionally or invariably) while his penis is inside his mate is frequently someone who is both afraid and angry yet out of touch with how angry and vulnerable he feels. Deconditioning of the irrational and phobic fears relating to the partner, or women, or the vagina—or some combination of the above—is the therapeutic approach which generally proves most helpful.

But the partner's assistance will be required—in this and every other form of brief sexual therapy that exists. For while the elementary curative devices used by sex therapists can be extraordinarily helpful (and often within a short period of time), they cannot work their magic when high tension and acrimony permeate the marital atmosphere. Without the willing collaboration of both members of the pair, improvements may either fail to occur or, if they do, be undercut by the partner immediately.

THE PROBLEM AND THE PARTNER

It is Masters and Johnson's credo that where sexual difficulties exist in a marriage, no such creature as an "uninvolved partner" is imaginable.

Just as the mate must be—simply by virtue of *being* the sexual partner—a part of the problem, so must he or she be an integral part of the process of resolving it. In the treatment of male premature ejaculation, for example, total cure is often attainable within a brief period of time—so long as the female partner is motivated and willing to cooperate.

PREMATURE EJACULATION: CONTROLLING THE ORGASMIC REFLEX

If the partner is willing to help, the problem of orgasmic prematurity can usually be very readily dealt with. The wife may, however, in this kind of circumstance, be a very angry person—someone who feels sexually "used" by her husband. He, predictably, comes to orgasm before she has had a chance to gain any satisfaction herself. He may, on his own part, feel sure that there is nothing he can do about it. He is often certain that he has no control over his ejaculation—when it comes, it comes, and he has no way of containing it whatsoever.

This is untrue. Unlike the erectile and the lubricatory reflexes, the orgasmic reflex *can* be brought under the control of the conscious will. It is indeed possible to hold back the ejaculate, voluntarily, just as urine and feces are retained (within bounds) until the individual's preferred moment of choice. The following procedure, developed by urologist James Semans (in 1956), is an effective technique for training the male who is unable to select the moment of his orgasm voluntarily to train himself to do so with great ease and security.

Masters and Johnson, using a minor variant of this procedure, met with a remarkably high rate of success with their patients, some of whom had suffered from the problem of premature ejaculation for periods extending back many years.

The Method

The couple may or may not begin with an initial period of pleasuring. Some sex therapists suggest commencing with sensate focus exercises because they help the partners to relax and experience the delicious drift into increasing levels of arousal without any need for "performance." For the woman, who may never have had the opportunity to reach high, plateau levels of excitement (because, as the train of *her* desire pulls out of the station, *he* is alighting from his, the journey having been completed), the sexual tasks may come as a revelation of her own hitherto unknown eroticism.

Each mate inevitably will, during that period of time devoted to these lessons in caressing, begin to understand a good deal about what is sexually pleasing—what is enjoyable and exciting to the self and what is enjoyable and exciting to the other. Much practice, in terms of the giving and receiving of delightfully pleasurable stimulation, inevitably takes place—and in a nondemanding, nonthreatening environment, for *touching* and not orgasm is the goal of these carefully structured experiences. Pleasuring is, however, not integral to the Semans method, and many sex therapists go directly to instruction in that technique, bypassing sensate focus entirely.

The procedure per se begins with the couple's exchanging embraces until the husband becomes erect. His wife, at that juncture, starts to stimulate his penis, while he lies back doing nothing but concentrating his attention upon the sensations that he is experiencing. The lesson of this task is that of getting him well acquainted with what it *feels like* when his orgasm begins to draw near. As his excitement increases and he perceives that he is about to come (or, more precisely, that the subphase of emission, or ejaculatory inevitability, is impending), the male partner tells his mate to stop stimulating him immediately. Then they wait, for about two minutes, during which his erection is likely to subside.

After that, she begins to stroke his penis again, and the entire process is repeated. The female masturbates her partner, gently and then more urgently, until he feels himself near to orgasm again. As he did the last time, he is to focus his attention upon his own sensations—the feelings associated with climbing upward, almost to the top of a very high diving board from which he will, inevitably, be forced to leap outward into climax.

He is to come very close to the top, but then stop short of getting there—by signaling his partner to stop stimulating him. His erection will probably go down, as it did before; whether it does or doesn't, however, the feelings of ejaculatory urgency will diminish. They will do so for the meanwhile, at least until his mate begins (after another two minutes) to caress and stroke his organ once again. Then the process of starting-and-stopping stimulation is repeated for a third round of the same.

Finally, on the fourth repeat, the male is not only permitted to approach orgasm but to go ahead and *have* it (extravaginally, during this first session). His ejaculation will have occurred, for the first time in his experience, at his own behest at the time that he has *chosen to have it happen*. He is, as he cannot fail to apprehend, in voluntary control of his orgasmic reflex—which can be held back or released, depending on the decision he makes.

He will usually find this entire "lesson" glorious, and his partner may enjoy it enormously as well, in ways that she finds completely surprising. (If she finds it difficult to carry out, initially, her reward will surely come to her later on.) After two sessions of this sort—in which the husband is brought to the edge of orgasm three times and finally goes on to reach climax on the fourth occasion—the "stop-start" exercises are repeated, with a lubricant such as KY jelly or Nivea oil added. The female uses this during stimulation of her mate, for it is excitingly evocative of the lubricated vaginal interior.

Taking Conscious Control

Eventually, after about four or five successful stimulation-and-stopping exercises, the pair is ready to try the process out while they engage in intercourse. The wife assumes the female-superior position, on top of her mate, while he holds her by the hips or "love handles" and guides her slowly up and down the shaft of his organ. When he begins, in time, to experience the sensations premonitory to orgasm, he is (as he did in the earlier stop-start exercises) to stop the music entirely. He must cease moving her up and down, and stop all thrusting, until the need to ejaculate subsides.

Then, after that brief time-out, the entire sequence is repeated. As was true in the noncoital exercises, three close approaches to climax—which stop short of getting there—take place before orgasmic release is allowed to occur on the fourth time around. What becomes clear is that the male *can* put his ejaculation off for as long as he likes, whenever he likes. He knows what it feels like to get near to the moment of ejaculatory inevitability and how to stop it from happening—by *stopping*—if it is happening too soon for himself or for his partner.

The couple is advised to keep in practice training, by going through a stop-start sequence at least once a week, until they are able to make use of the technique automatically during their customary lovemaking. Eventually, of course, they will want to use the method in positions other than the female-superior, and all that they need to know, by way of advice, is that most men have more difficulty controlling their ejaculation in the male-superior (man on top) position than they do in any other position whatsoever.

In time, however, this information should become irrelevant. As he becomes secure in his use of this techinique, the male partner will find himself progressively more capable of enjoying longer, more satisfying intercourse, in any position he likes, and without fear of ejaculating a moment sooner than he wants to. He will not (or at least very rarely) be overwhelmed by his orgasm; instead, he will be in conscious charge of it.

WHEN EROTIC INTEREST HAS VANISHED

A common clinical reality, not yet considered in this discussion, is that of the couple who comes into therapy because erotic interest seems to have disappeared. The spouses may, in this instance, be sexually functional and adequate—able to produce erection and lubrication, during arousal, and to attain orgasmic satisfaction—but one or the other partner is, for some mysterious reason, unmotivated and disinclined in that direction. He or she has no wish, no desire to be sexual; the drive is simply not there.

Rarely, when the pair seeks sexual therapy, is this loss of sexual appetite a mutual one. If it were, the couple would probably not require treatment; if neither individual wanted to be physically involved, there clearly would be no problem between them! (As a matter of fact, among those satisfied mates in the Pittsburgh study—people who were happy with their choice of partner and who felt that their marriages were working very well—there were two couples who indicated that their relationships were completely and totally asexual.) Usually, one partner's lack of interest in sex has become too difficult for the other one to tolerate.

"Desire" is now considered to be a separate phase of the sex response cycle—one which, obviously, precedes arousal and orgasm. The major dysfunction associated with the desire phase is absence of erotic interest—that is, neither thinking, caring, fantasizing, nor having the remotest concern about anything to do with sex or things sexual at all. "Inhibited sexual desire" is the scientific term used to designate this total or almost total sexual turnoff.

The couple's sexual abstinence or avoidance may, in some instances, be due to some underlying physical cause—in the male, androgen levels appear to be critical. As Dr. Raul Schiavi notes, hypogonadal men, i.e., those with abnormally low male hormone levels, respond to replacement therapy with a "significant increase in sexual thoughts and a reestablishment of sexual desire within two weeks." Hypogonadism is, however, a relatively uncommon condition.

More frequently encountered, clinically, are certain illnesses which have the potential to impair sexual drive in both women and men. These include thyroid problems (both overactive and underactive thyroids), pituitary tumors, and diabetes—a disease which can profoundly affect both the desire and arousal phases of the sex response cycle.

The syndrome of depression is another cause of decreased or absent interest in sex; it is, according to Helen Singer Kaplan, "the most common cause of global loss of sexual desire in young persons." Changes in libido often precede the more obvious mood changes associated with depression, as she observes, and are a common sign of a masked form of the illness.

Antihypertensive drugs (such as reserpine, methyldopa, clonidine, spironolactone, the beta-adrenergic blockers) can impair sexual drive in both sexes as well as interfere with erection in the male. This is important information to have, because an estimated 44 million Americans suffer from high blood pressure, and beta blockers are the second most frequently prescribed of all medications. (Diuretics, also used to treat hypertension, currently occupy first place.)

Sexual desire can be affected, as well, by certain psychoactive drugs—including some of the major tranquilizers, minor tranquilizers (in high doses) and the important MAO inhibitors, used in the treatment of depression—and by certain antihistamines, too (prescribed medications, not those sold over the counter). Alcohol, barbiturates and marijuana can also have deleterious effects upon sexual drive; but heroin and morphine are, among all drugs of abuse or potential abuse, those which most consistently lead to libidinal disaster. They interfere with the nervous circuitry which must be activated in order for a person to feel "turned on" and sexually motivated.

Ruling out the possibility of such organically based problems is, obviously, of critical importance. It is nevertheless true, and must be emphasized, that complaints of drastically decreased or lost desire *are most frequently psychological in origin*. These disturbances tend to be far less treatable by means of short-term, active sex therapy methods than are the maladies of the arousal and orgasm phases. Disorders of desire require longer, more extensive treatment and have a less favorable prognosis. Where erotic indifference is concerned, the problems tend to be deeper and more firmly embedded in the partners' personalities; often, they are woven into the texture of an extremely problematic and disturbed relationship. In such cases, it is one or both members of the couple—and the marriage they share—which must be treated before any of the specifically *sexual* symptoms can be addressed.

PART V

THE CHILD-LAUNCHING YEARS:

Time of Transformation

PART V

THE

16

The Second Separation

In the middle of the journey of their lives, the majority of couples must confront a dismaying variety of demands and dilemmas.

This phase of marriage is, in the view of most experts, one of the most stressful of the marital cycle. For during this time the partners must deal not only with the aging, ailing, dying of their own parents, but with the sexual and aggressive challenges coming to them from their adolescent children.

A father, disappointed by the failure of his own career aspirations, may realize that he will be outstripped by the son who has just been admitted to a far more prestigious university than he himself had attended. Or another middle-aged man, successful in having reached his goals, may feel a sense of emptiness—a sense that the struggle and the sacrifice were, somehow, not really worth it. He may be disturbed, even feel his own sense of self and integrity assaulted by the adolescent who starts acting out that disappointment for him—the son who suddenly finds competitive strivings meaningless and who appears to be opting out of the career struggle entirely.

A mother may, at this time of her life, walk down the street with her adolescent daughter and find that the male passersby are glancing appraisingly at the younger woman and ignoring her own existence completely. She may envy her ripening offspring's ability to enter a business marketplace with many more opportunities open to women and feel deprived, superannuated herself.

There is, for the middle-aged man and the middle-aged woman, a dawning, discomfiting realization that time is finite—that time is running out. What has not been accomplished, and what has not been experienced, may very well not ever be.

In the meridian of our existence, most of us experience a freshly painful confrontation with the fact of our own mortality. Living, as we have always known, is a process, one with a beginning, a middle and an ending. And in the middle, in new and disturbing ways, the time when we shall "be no more" is glimpsed; it is really *there*, ahead of us, on the road we must unavoidably travel. We halt in our tracks, shaken by the increasingly acute realization of what we knew to be true yet had not actually quite comprehended: that we will, one day, be absent from the human world. And the world, made real and palpable to us by means of our conscious perceptions of it, will continue along its ways without us—even though our own consciousness has disappeared.

The integration of this difficult knowledge, which must now be accepted at a level of being to which it had never been admitted earlier, is usually occurring in tandem with *external* shifts—profound changes in a number of our closest, most fundamental attachments. If we have been successful, as parents, then our children are becoming capable of surviving without us. What will they be to us—and what will we be to them— when we are no longer so vitally necessary? We peer backward and forward simultaneously, taking stock of what has been and assessing what may lie before us.

Were the turnings in the roadway that were chosen earlier, we wonder, the choices that were the right ones? Our own parents, who once appeared so fixed against the horizon of the future, no longer seem to intervene between ourselves and eternity; they are often dependent or infirm, or they have gone out of view entirely. It is *we* who now stand at the edge of eternity for the generation that is to follow us, and it is a strange and scary place to be.

It is no wonder, given the kaleidoscopic shifts and changes taking place—changes in relation to the last generation and changes in relation to the upcoming one (as well as in the image of the self and of the options that the future has to offer)—that marriages *do* change during this middle era of existence. How could they not? The partners in the relationship are undergoing a complex process of summing up their individual lives and shared past and are imagining themselves forward with a newly diminished sense of how much time lies before them. They are, moreover, aware that they are approching a phase of their lives when they will be a couple—just two people alone together again.

Inevitably, images of their own parents, alone after childrearing, begin rising to the surface. Fears and fantasies abound; the dusty trunks of old issues, packed away for many years but never successfully dealt with, suddenly begin to be reopened. This period is frequently made problematical, for the middle-aged partners, by the reawakening of old conflicts about leaving home.

For as their maturing children begin engaging in the long process of detaching, the parents' unresolved feelings about their own adolescent separations may suddenly erupt—and clamor for resolution once again. This, it seemed to me, was what was happening in the lives of Kathleen and Philip Gardiner, who were in their mid-forties at the time of our interviews. The Gardiners were, in the wrong season of their lives—for they should have confronted these tasks during their own adolescences— struggling with the problems of defining themselves as differentiated, independent adults and of leaving their original families behind them.

A MARITAL CRISIS

It was not until the outset of my second meeting with the Gardiners that I was able to ask Philip my typical opening question: "What first attracted you to Kathleen, would you say?" Our first interview had been taken up with a discussion of all that was happening in the Gardiners' marriage at the present moment. "What," I encouraged him, "were the particular qualities, in her, that seemed special to you, at the time that the two of you were getting to know each other?"

Philip looked at me, half-smiling, as if at the almost embarassing irrelevance of what I had asked.

For Philip had, shortly after the Thanksgiving holiday, moved out of the bedroom that he and his wife had shared for the past twenty-three years. He had retreated to the third floor where, for several months, he'd lived in a formerly unused guest room next to the bedroom occupied by sixteen-year-old Matthew. At last, when the situation became completely intolerable to her, Kathleen had demanded that her husband either return to the marriage or get out of the house entirely. To her astonishment and horror, it had been the latter path that he had chosen. Philip had moved out.

Now he shrugged. "Oh, there were lots of qualities," he murmured vaguely, "the circumstances in which we met . . . her tremendous sense of purpose . . . her sense of—of vulnerability, too." Philip grew silent, began looking around the living room, as if it were a place completely novel and strange to him. He was, at present, living in a small condominium not far from their rambling Tudor home in Boston's affluent Belmont area.

I waited, watching a lazy, halfhearted snowfall swirling downward outside a row of three frontward-facing windows. Even though it was just past three-thirty in the afternoon, Kathleen had turned on several of the lamps; an early January dusk was falling. It was cozy in here. The furniture, much of it covered in the same dark navy blue and red floral pattern, sagged comfortably as if inviting one to fill in the indentations that other visitors' bodies had created. "What *were* the circumstances of your first meeting?" I asked Philip finally, with a broad wave of my hand that included both of them.

Quickly, almost reflexively, they looked at each other and then laughed aloud. "Oh, we were young and alive, and at the beach," he replied, a note of gaiety in his voice. "I was a bachelor, without anyone in my life; she was not yet out of the doldrums about a relationship that had recently terminated. She was feeling pretty isolated, and I was a happy-go-lucky guy . . . just looking for a good time, essentially."

I glanced at his wife. Kathleen Gardiner, at forty-four, looked younger than her years. She was curvaceous to the point of plumpness, but wore a gray suit and a creamy, very plain angora sweater beneath it; the effect was crisply businesslike yet sexy. Her hair was dark brown, bobbed in loose waves that framed her face; she had fair skin and startlingly large, intense Irish blue eyes. Her bow-shaped lips were, at this moment, slightly pursed; she had, it seemed to me, been annoyed by something Philip had said. But she stared down at her hands, folded in her lap, as though determined to keep her own counsel.

"A happy-go-lucky guy," I repeated his phrase, thoughtfully, "and yet you liked *her* sense of purpose?" He gave me an odd look, yet made no reply to the question.

"And her vulnerability, too," I went on. "Wasn't that the other quality that you mentioned?"

"Well, those were two things—" he acknowledged.

"What were the other attractive things about Kathleen?" I asked.

He had found her to be someone who was "mentally challenging," he said. "She was, too, very responsive to my particular brand of humor— we seemed to have a good time together—and she began to come out of herself and to develop a similar kind of humor of her own. Which I," he added, "very much enjoyed." He sat alone, in the center of the sofa, absently smoothing out the neat creases of his elegantly cut wool trousers.

His wife, in the rocker, was staring at him through wide and anxious eyes. "Of those four qualities you mentioned," I went on calmly, although aware of her mounting tension, "that is, Kathleen's sense of purpose, her vulnerability, her humor, and her intellect, how many have remained attractive, and how many have become problematic, over the years of the marriage?" I smiled. "We're leaving aside, of course, the entire subject of being alive, young and at the beach. . . ."

She laughed shrilly as if I'd said something much funnier than I actually had; Philip merely smiled perfunctorily. "Well, although she's still vulnerable in certain ways, she has really gotten a lot stronger," he answered. "Which I think is good," he hastened to add. "So her sense of purpose is still there, and I admire that greatly. Her intellect is, too. But the humor—I think that as our marriage got harder and harder, a lot of the fun and enjoyment went out of it. There was no *playfulness*. Oh, we may have laughed every once in a while and shared a joke, but we were screaming at each other a lot of the time. And the whole idea of being alike, of sharing the same humor—it just wasn't there anymore." His tone of voice was elegiac.

Kathleen shifted in her seat, leaned forward as if to say something, but then sat back without having uttered a word. The rocker rolled gently, then stopped. "I think," Philip resumed, after a moment, "that I've always been pleased with her getting stronger and interested in the success that she was having; she's moved up very far very fast, in terms of her position, and in some ways she's doing better than *I* am!" He laughed as if at a ludicrous notion.

"And I feel pride, derivative pride, in her accomplishments," he continued. "I feel good about her, and what she is doing, and her independence . . . her *capacities*. I can't remember a time when I thought it robbed me of anything or took away something that was mine." He sounded as if he believed that *I* required reassurance on this particular topic.

Kathleen Gardiner had left college in her senior year in order to support her new husband through his final year of graduate school (he had a Ph.D. in political science). Some years later—in her early thirties—she had completed her undergraduate education and then gone on to earn a master's degree in public health administration. Since that time she had worked, at successively more impressive posts, within the state's mental health bureaucracy.

Philip, at age forty-three (he was a year younger than his spouse), was currently in the throes of establishing a new business of his own—as a pollster and political consultant. He had been, until his late thirties, a professor of government but one with a more than casual interest in state and national politics. Five years earlier he had decided to leave his tenured teaching job in order to run for a congressional nomination; the loss he'd suffered had, however, been dismaying and woundingly decisive. In the course of our previous interview, both the Gardiners had stated their belief that the marriage—already in some difficulties—had begun seriously to unravel at that point in time.

But Philip had also suggested, during that conversation, that his current need for distance and space in the relationship had to do with his experience of his wife as somewhat repressive, overly determined and powerful. "You said, last time," I reminded him, "that you felt you could not 'grow' in this marriage because Kathleen was too strong and stood in your way. And yet now I hear you saying that you rejoice in her strength and take pleausre in her growing *stronger*. . . ." I shook my head as if to ask if I was misunderstanding him or if, on the contrary, he himself was attempting to maintain two very contrary positions simultaneously.

"It's true," he admitted at once. "I *don't* have the opportunity to assert myself in certain areas; I tend to let her do the asserting instead." He directed a brief glance in Kathleen's direction, the wary look of someone expecting attack from that quarter. But she let his comment pass without challenge.

"And what would those areas be?" I asked.

He ran a hand over the top of his wavy brown hair, combed in such a way as to conceal a slightly receding hairline, then absently checked the knot of his tie. "It might be basic family decision making . . . about, oh, anything from something insignificant to—" He shrugged, as if unable to bring a particular example to mind. "It's pervasive," Philip finally declared. "It includes everything from 'What's the correct way to make a chicken with wine sauce?' to 'Whose house do we go to tonight?' As far as Kathleen's concerned, there's a right answer to these questions—there's a place to go to and a place *not* to go to, and she knows which is which. She just has a very strong feeling—which I can't really criticize her for— on almost every subject you can name!" He looked over at his wife, threw up his hands in a sudden gesture of parodied devotion and bowed his head as if mocking her oracular, goddesslike stance. Then he laughed, and she giggled, too.

But she uttered no objection, made no countercase of her own. It was as if she were afraid of making any move that would upset the applecart of his presence at this interview. He was, at the very least, at home— however briefly—and willing to talk about what was going on between them.

Kathleen considered this "progress," for Philip had refused to countenance the notion of seeing a marital therapist. What he needed, he maintained, was a period of time away from the marriage so that he could think out some crucial matters for himself. His wife had, therefore, only the haziest notions of what his recent defection from the relationship was all about.

It was obvious, however, that she saw his willingness to participate in these interviews as the most hopeful of signs—evidence that the bond they shared was, in his mind, something still alive, worthy of being talked about, and therefore viable. I myself was not sure that she was right in making such an assumption. What *was* clear to me, however, was that a mutinous uprising had occurred and that the power in this relationship had passed into his hands and out of hers.

For if, as Philip maintained, his wife had once held all of the aces in the marriage, then his move to the third floor had effectively trumped every one of them. What he had done, merely seen in terms of a spatial metaphor, was move *above her*. He had become, in very real and palpable terms, the one who was on top. Then, in response to her demand bid for him to come back to the marriage or leave the house completely, he had decided to lay his cards down, bowing out of this round of the game entirely.

Each of these withdrawing moves had enhanced his ascendancy in the relationship. *He* was now the partner in control of the emotional system that they shared, but *the system itself was not at all different*. For the relational world of the Gardiners had always contained a superpowerful person and one who was relatively weak—i.e., with little or no voice in the important matters of choice and decision making. The way in which the interpersonal system operated, *as an entity*, had therefore not altered or changed in the slightest. The spouses had simply switched roles, reversing their polarized positions.

Now it was Kathleen, the "purposeful," strong, decisive partner, who was so impotized and frightened that she could not oppose her mate in the slightest—even to explain or defend herself. Philip's present power in the relationship, which was total, derived from his wife's state of uncertainty and fear. But was he in the process of consolidating his winnings, or was he planning to leave the game on a permanent basis?

"Kathleen *knows* what she wants to do, and she knows the right and the wrong way to do it." His tone was tinged with complaint, as if he still considered himself to be the partner in the one-down position. "It's a whole sense that I don't have. . . . I mean I don't have a *strong feeling* about most things; for me it's just 'Oh, is that the way it's done? All right, I'll do it that way'—the way the other person wants it—and what I do is to just become totally accommodating." He believed, he added, that the certainties his wife had brought to the relationship had prevented him from ever developing into a person with internal standards of his own.

From the floor beneath us, an energetic rumbling could be heard. The oil heater was switching into high activity as the last rays of the sunlight faded and the outside temperature descended. I felt chilly, at that moment, and the chill resided partly within me. The threatened end of something can feel like the threatened ending of the universe, and I was finding Kathleen's terror contagious.

Philip continued speaking, his voice subdued and reflective. "Very early in the marriage, I found that I'd begun to abdicate in areas of my own personal growth because it was just *easier* on everyone if I didn't have strong opinions of my own."

He shrugged briefly, as if to characterize physically the fact that he had become resigned. "It was difficult to sustain an effort of that kind—*insisting on a position*, I mean. It was, at least, in a situation in which I was being criticized, either openly or unspokenly, for taking a stand that was not in agreement with *hers* . . . and so I just tended to hang back. But I've come to the realization, at this point in my life, that what was put aside somewhere way back there was the entire capacity to make any kind of decision about things that *I* might want. Which might be important to *me*, just for *myself*."

He had preserved intimacy and closeness in the relationship by sacrificing his autonomy entirely—or at least so he perceived it. "And that," Philip spoke as if to himself rather than to me or to his wife, "is what I gave *no importance* to earlier! For me it was just a matter of figuring out what it was that other people wanted of me—and doing whatever it was— which required not having much, if *any*, of my own agenda! And this," he added, "had repercussions in terms of what was put aside, in my political, business, and in my personal life as well."

I glanced at Kathleen; there were streaky patches of mottled red on her cheeks. She sat upright, rapt in what he was saying, her posture utterly rigid. "I—our relationship—began to feel empty," continued Philip. "I was empty . . . and I began to rebel."

"To rebel," I repeated the phrase aloud, for his use of it struck me as odd. Philip had "rebelled" because he "had to grow" and could not do so until he left his home and family and worked out reasonably firm internal standards of his own devising. Much of what he was saying, in terms of the words and imagery that he used—and the issues he seemed to be struggling with—had a markedly adolescent flavor. He sounded less like a man in the middle years of his life than he did like a young person engaged in the painful developmental tasks associated with growing up, separating from the original family, and developing an independent personal identity.

"So then," I observed, "the 'sense of purpose' that you first defined as one of Kathleen's attractive qualities actually did become a problematic issue between you?"

"Yes." The admission seemed to surprise him even as he made it. "Yes, it is a problematic area, I would say." He hesitated. "Not because it's *wrong* that she be sure of herself, but because it gets in my way. I mean it's not something that I would, in an intellectual way, ask her to change—"

"But in the interaction between you," I nodded, "her own sense of purpose—"

"Yes," he interrupted, "it gets in the way of my developing one of my own."

A SECOND ATTEMPT AT LEAVING HOME

What Philip Gardiner seemed to be reiterating, in one form or another, was that leaving home (this relationship) was a prerequisite for his growing up into a mature, autonomous adult with a "self" of his own. It was as if the developmental tasks of adolescence and young adulthood were suddenly being addressed in this, the middle epoch of his life. Propelled by powerful inner imperatives, he seemed to be circling back in time, to reconfront certain concerns that had been avoided but never surmounted earlier.

The adolescent phase of the human life cycle is characterized by a progressive and stressful detaching of the intense bond between the offspring and his parents. During this period the powerful love ties that bound the rookie human being to his base camp—the family of origin—are being slowly and painfully transformed. The developing young person is struggling to withdraw his or her own differentiated self from these old involvements and to establish new and meaningful attachments in the world of his peers.

> During this time [write Lily Pincus and Dr. Christopher Dare] the individual has to give up childhood closeness and reliance upon parents, if he is to become really adult. At the same time, in order to preserve a sense of continuity and to feel properly rooted in his life, he must retain a loyalty to his family of origin. Giving up so much of the family-linked

basis of the whole past life of the child is bound to be accompanied by a sense of loss and uncertainty, which in some ways can be seen as a mourning process. The search for a way of life that preserves a loyalty to the past—especially the past intense closeness to and dependence upon the parents while also developing an individuality that suits his psychological needs—will cause the adolescent uncertainty and discomfort too.

For some individuals the "discomfort," pain, grief-related anger, and confusion are difficult or impossible to bear. The normal developmental sequence, which demands a loosening of the primary love ties (these powerful bonds are, at least in their original intensity, *programmed* for eventual dissolution), is propelling the young person *away* from his orienting attachments and into a world that is unknown. This necessary separation from his earlier emotional moorings can bring with it feelings of terrible inner emptiness, of being adrift in an uncaring universe, terribly and frighteningly alone.

Growing up and growing away can be experienced as a kind of desertion or abandonment—even though it is the developing individual *himself* who, in response to normal growth urges, feels impelled to do the emotional detaching. In some instances, because he perceives himself as lacking in the emotional supplies necessary for journeying off on his own, the adolescent cannot endure going through this lonely and frightening (but eventually liberating) process. He cannot transform the original relationships with the parents, renounce their protection and leave the world of childhood; he feels too unready inside.

Instead, therefore, of confronting this complex and disorienting developmental challenge, he may seek to circumvent the separation process. He will, in such an instance, usually attempt to do this in one of two very different-seeming fashions. The adolescent can either fail to leave the nutrient environment which enclosed and supported him during the years of his growth and *never depart* (in the emotional or perhaps literal sense) or he may burst out of the family's emotional enclosure negatively and angrily, *cutting off* connections and behaving as if they were nonexistent or meaningless.

The results, in both circumstances, will be remarkably similar. For neither of these opposite-seeming strategies—that is, not leaving at all or severing affectional relationships entirely—will permit the normal working-through and resolution of the young person's attachments to his first, most passionately loved caretakers. A sense of fusion, of being stuck in the intense emotionality of the "world that was" lingers. . . . For what the unseparated person cannot recognize is that detaching, psychologically, from the parents involves *transforming* the relationship but not losing them entirely.

It involves forgiving them for what they did not give and giving up the idea that what was not gotten will ever be received from them—that impossible dream of being perfectly nurtured as a child which cannot be fulfilled as an adult. To the extent, however, that the individual fails to make the internal separation, he will valiantly go on trying to remake the past in the present. The fusion with the original objects of his love will become manifest, in many forms and disguises, throughout the succeeding years of the person's adult, "separate" existence.

A new intimate bond may be forged, despite the fact that the internal tasks of adolescence and young adulthood have been partly or perhaps completely avoided. To the extent that space has not been made available for the mate, however, he or she will be perceived—and responded to— as the parental stand-in. Hers or his will be a substitute role in the family drama which is being eternally re-created and replayed.

Detaching from the first, most primitive bonds is the basic precondition of developing healthy new attachments—and of working on individuation, or becoming "I, myself," the person that one *is*.

Philip Gardiner had always, as he described himself, felt devoid of strongly held views and convictions—a lack, increasingly painful, of individual personhood and identity. What Kathleen had provided in the relationship, he now believed, was the filling of the vacuum within him, of "those empty areas, in me, which I now find I *have* to move into. . . . To start developing, myself."

Hitherto his wife's "sense of purpose" had sustained him and allowed him to avoid making choices and decisions (and, by the way, having to take responsibility for their eventual outcomes!). But now he needed— and was experiencing the need with urgency—to develop insides of his own. The trajectory of his flight from the household had, moreover, included a long sojourn on the third floor as a quasi "peer" of his adolescent son.

It was as if he were attempting a second separation, in the middle of his life, because his first efforts to separate—during his own adolescence— had not been sufficiently successful. But was he, I wondered, struggling to free himself from the intimate tentacles that bound him to his original family—or to the one that he and Kathleen had created?

"HE DIDN'T LET GO"

I turned now to Kathleen.

What, I asked Kathleen, had been the basis of her initial attraction to Philip?

She had been watchfully silent through most of this meeting, as she had through much of our earlier interview. This powerful, decisive, competent woman seemed cowed and thoroughly uncertain. I had the feeling that she was sorting through every utterance that her husband made, looking for a clue—any suggestion at all—for a way to draw him back into the relationship.

She was also beginning to deal with the possibility that that might not happen.

Now she laughed lightly, met his gaze, her eyelids fluttering seductively. "I can tick them off quite easily," she answered me, but continued looking at him. "His wonderful smile; that was the first thing. His sense of humor. And there was something that I found in him, very quickly— I don't want to define it as intellectual capacity—but what it was was an enormously impressive ability to synthesize information. He can fine-tune what he hears and boil it down to its essential meaning better than anybody I have ever met." She drew in a breath, then exhaled it as a sigh. "His capacity to listen," she allowed, turning to meet my eyes directly. "The fact that he was *there* for me, always, and that he didn't let go."

Kathleen was silent for a few moments, then added ruefully, "There were times—times when the relationship regressed—when I found that quality very *annoying*." She laughed again, shook her head. "But ultimately, it became an attractive quality. His being reliable, being *there* for me, I mean."

What, then, had been its "annoying" aspect? I asked her. She shrugged her shoulders, cocked her head to one side and stared dreamily at nothing in particular. It was as if she were looking beyond me and into a past they had shared. "I wasn't sure, after we'd gone out for a period of time, that I *wanted* the relationship anymore," she said finally, as if making an embarrassing admission. "We'd dated each other, on and off, for almost four years—most of it while we were in college—and I very much wanted to experiment, to go out with other men. Which I did do. I got into other relationships, but . . . Philip was always there."

He was, she explained, not necessarily pressing her unduly. Every week or two, however, she'd receive a witty card or letter from him, letting her know that he was still there for her and that he was still a terrific person. "I used to say to him that I didn't want to marry him then, when I was in my early twenties, but later, when I was twenty-eight or so and I'd been around a bit more. But he was smart enough to call me on that one. He said, 'Marry me now, or we won't get married' and I—because of the qualities that I liked in him—said, 'Okay, I will marry you now.'"

She had assumed, in the recounting, the air of a maiden being courted and exuded that aura of exalted power and excitement. "So you liked," I asked, "his steadiness and his ability to listen?" She nodded, a happily reminiscent half smile on her features. "But you were the experimentalist in the relationship—the autonomy seeker, the one who wanted to develop her own separate self—while Philip was the one who was keeping the whole enterprise together?"

"Yes." Her response was abrupt, and Kathleen looked over at her husband swiftly. But he was staring at the Empire clock on the mantel-piece, which read 4:00 p.m., as if expecting it to chime. It didn't. "It needs fixing again," he remarked.

She shook her head, raised both hands as if in mock acknowledgment of her defeat. "It's unpredictable . . . and it was going so well there for a while." They smiled ruefully at each other, as if struck by the oddness of the moment. Then their smiles faded, and each of them looked off in a different direction.

I waited for a moment, then resumed my questioning of Kathleen. "In terms of his capacity for listening and being there for you, how much of that remains in the relationship now?" Her bitter laugh was not par-ticularly surprising. "He's *not* trying to keep the relationship together! So that's gone. . . . The other qualities that I mentioned, though," she temporized, "are probably ones that are still pretty much there."

"Including the ability to listen?" I kept my gaze fixed upon hers.

"I think he's listening *now*," she responded, in the placating tone of voice of someone who is angry yet wants to see a quarrel settled. "There was a time, though—a long period—when that wasn't happening. When I tried both verbally and in nonverbal ways to get him to listen . . . but it didn't happen. And I kept getting more and more hysterical all of the time."

"And so Philip got more and more—?" I leaned toward Kathleen, and she completed my sentence with the appropriate word. "He got more and more *distant*," she replied.

At an earlier phase of their polarized relationship, he had been the intimate chaser and she had been the one who was pressing for space in which to develop her independent personhood. But now the interaction had flip-flopped, and the race was headed off in the opposite direction—with Philip as the partner who was threatening to distance himself out of the emotional system entirely.

The Distancer and the Pursuer

"To understand the concept of distancers and pursuers, one must approach it with some warnings," writes Dr. Thomas D. Fogarty, M.D. "No one is a pure breed and the terms are used to describe the general trend of the person. . . . Over time it becomes clear that inside of every distancer is a pursuer, and inside every pursuer is a distancer. . . . The distant husband tends to move toward his wife, and pursue her as she pulls away. The pursuing wife finds that she "has no feelings" for her husband as he moves in. These different characteristics of self emerge as the context changes." In other words, depending on the circumstances, the distancer will pursue (in order not to be abandoned, totally) and the pursuer will distance (in order not to be exposed to an intimacy which might feel potentially engulfing and overwhelming).

When, I posed the question to the Gardiners, had this reversal of their roles in the relationship begun taking place? Had it been shortly after they'd married or at some later point, or had it been more recent . . . could they say? Did they remember, or was it unclear?

It had begun occurring, Philip thought, around the time that he had gotten his tenure and begun moving into various decision-making positions within the university's administration. "I think things changed—and the problems began to manifest themselves—when I got into something that I really enjoyed doing, something that really *absorbed* me professionally," he said, speaking slowly and thoughtfully. "But I don't think I was aware of a lot that was happening inside me until *after* my political campaign . . . which was a real watershed event. A watershed event, because I had to live with myself and take responsibility for what happened—or *didn't* happen, in my case. And for leaving a job which was secure and going off on the Quest . . . my losing bid for the congressional nomination, that is." He shrugged, looked pained momentarily.

At that point, he explained, a good deal of anger—"anger about my marital relationship"—had risen to the surface of his consciousness. It was, Philip now acknowledged, "probably anger at myself, that I was projecting onto Kathleen. But she was, at the same time, getting increasingly assertive and hostile." The "pleaser" was angry not only at himself but at the mate whom he could not possibly please. Having failed in her eyes, he was enraged at her, and the process of withdrawal and distancing began.

She became the intimate chaser, wielding her fistful of complaints—and these were by no means completely unrealistic. For Philip had, during this stressful period of their lives, not only suffered that political defeat; he had also, having left his former position, been out of a job for a while. Things had never quite been the same since that time.

THE EMPTYING NEST

Philip and Kathleen Gardiner were, at the time of our interviews, in their mid-forties and the parents of three children who were all in the so-called "launching stage" of the family life cycle. Matthew, at age sixteen, was the eldest and should have been first in line for takeoff.

But the Gardiners' son did not seem to be acquiring the necessary velocity to fly. Matt seemed stuck, simply immobilized on the runway. During this past year, his formerly impressive academic performance had headed into a sudden downward spiral. His schoolwork had begun to seem irrelevant and meaningless to him, as had his longtime membership on his high school's hockey team—a valued commitment which he'd precipitously abandoned. He and his father, during the period of months when they'd shared the third-floor quarters, had gotten along reasonably well, but Matthew's underlying distress was being acted out in ways that were destructive to himself.

He had gone on strike, decided that getting educated was not something he wanted to bother about; his studies no longer mattered at all. Matthew appeared to lack any notion of what the next step might be when it came to moving on, leaving the household and getting started in the direction of his own independent adulthood. The idea that he would attend a university, once taken for granted in this well-educated, upper-middle-class family, was now becoming a rapidly receding option. His overall behavior was, according to his mother, "thoroughly aimless." He was doing an alarming amount of drinking and dope smoking.

The company that her son kept, in Kathleen Gardiner's opinion, was another of his major problems; his friends, who were engaged in similar activities, were "kids who would go nowhere in their lives," in her opinion. Matt's entire way of being, so profoundly altered in the space of a year, angered and frightened her, but there was nothing she seemed able to do about it. Her eldest child was, at present, completely unreachable and uncontrollable.

Her husband appeared to be far less frightened and affected than she was; Philip seemed, at most, mildly disapproving of his adolescent son's behavior. The boy's opting out of the educational process seemed, for some reason, to be far less agitating to him—either because Philip himself was feeling friendly to rebellion or because he believed that Matthew was simply passing through a phase and would regroup and organize his life eventually.

Amy, the Gardiners' second child, was fifteen, and in a state of bubbling, eruptive turmoil. She was enraged at her father for leaving the family and furious at her mother for being the woman who had been unable to keep him there. She quarreled with Kathleen over any trivial pretext that presented itself and preserved a stony, frigid silence whenever Philip was present. Barbara, eighteen months younger (going on fourteen), was the family "angel"—her mother's confidante and caretaker during this period of crisis.

Both daughters had, to date, continued to function very ably as students and had maintained their places in their social worlds (at school and at the Congregational church to which the Gardiners belonged). But if their older brother proved unable to leave, in a nonpathological fashion, then an eventual pileup at the end of the family runway was very likely to occur.

At best, the normally difficult and painful adolescent separation process would be, for every member of this offspring generation, even more complicated and difficult to negotiate than it typically is. For as these developing persons struggled to accumulate the necessary energy and confidence to get themselves away from home base and aloft, the launching pad was literally deteriorating beneath them. Leaving home is hard enough without having home leave *you* simultaneously.

Philip Gardiner, by dropping out of the family at this critical stage of his childrens' lives, had inevitably interfered with those developmental processes which would result in their separating and eventually leaving him behind. But in his case, it occurred to me, one way of taking control of the approaching series of leave-takings might have been to take preemptive action—avoid the pain of the young generation's separation by separating from *them* beforehand.

If, in his own family of origin, separation had been a difficult and problematic issue, then Philip would have experienced it as even *more painful* than it ordinarily is when his own children began taking steps in this direction. For it is a human truth that the young person who has never gotten free of his own earliest love attachments becomes the middle-aged individual who finds it excruciatingly hard to let go and release his own children into their separate, independent lives. Not having made it away himself, in the internal sense, he experiences *their* leave-taking as a process that is almost intolerable.

It was not, I believed, coincidental that at a time when his teenaged offspring were preparing to take off, Philip Gardiner had suddenly reacted by demanding that he be first in line to leave home.

THE COMPLEMENTARY "MIDDLESCENT" CRISIS

The crisis of the adolescent years revolves around the nascent adult's struggle to liberate "I, myself" from the familial soil in which that self has been embedded; the "middlescent" crisis is a complementary one. Where the offspring must get free, the middle-aged parent must let go, relinquish primary claims upon his child's affections and surrender him to the world of his peers and his own generation. This process, no matter how healthily it proceeds, is attended by pain—the pain associated with changes and losses—which may be denied and dissociated, but is experienced keenly by both the leaver and the person or persons left behind.

Separation is a human problem which, in truth, none of us resolves so totally and definitively that no emotional strings are left hanging out. Throughout the course of our lives we must, periodically, readdress concerns relating to separateness and aloneness; they are linked to our movement through time. For each generation, the process of leaving home, selecting a mate, beginning a family, dealing with the aging and dying of grandparents and parents and, eventually, with the departure of grown children are the *expectable* transitions from one pattern of living and view of the self to another that may be radically different.

There are, as well, the less predictable losses and changes; desertion, divorce, the illness or death of a child or the untimely loss of a spouse. We deal with these successive demands and potentially overwhelming challenges with varying degrees of competence, depending upon how well we have dealt with the problems of separation and loss at earlier way stations in our lives.

The person in his middle years who, for example, was relatively successful at differentiating his own separate self from the "self that was" in the family of origin will be far more able to facilitate *his* offspring's launching into the wider world outside the household. That parent will experience some natural grief relating to his child's departure, and perhaps the resurgence of some unfinished emotional business dating back to his own leaving-home process. But he or she will nevertheless be able to accept the younger person's efforts to move outward from the family with less reactive anxiety, jealousy and despair.

This is not to say that any parent, however successfully his own adolescent transition was forded, emerges from his offspring's leave-taking years bearing no emotional scratches or scars. The adolescent detaching process is an extremely lengthy one, stretching from the first faint prepubescent stirrings of the ten- or eleven-year-old child to the ultimate departure of the adult in his late teens or early twenties. This long, difficult period strains the adaptational resources of everyone concerned, and the pressures generated can and often do reverberate into seemingly unconnected areas of the older generation's lives.

OEDIPAL TRIANGLES

As Drs. Gertrude and Rubin Blanck observe, the "potentiality for disequilibrium" in a couple's marriage inevitably increases when their child reaches puberty and enters adolescence. For each parent is, in his or her own way, affected by the metamorphosis of the cute little dependent into a challenging, demanding, sexually differentiated human being.

This stranger in the house, who used to be the youngster, is now developing breasts and curves or sprouting hair upon his face and broader muscles. His behavior is changing as well. "The reawakening of the child's sexual instincts," write Blanck and Blanck, "his struggle to cope with these, his increasing desire for and inexperience with independence, and particularly his noisy projection of these internal struggles upon the parents can constitute a strain which even the most patient parents find difficult. To this must be added the adolescent's reawakened Oedipal conflict, which usually takes its toll on each parent in different ways, aggression turning more markedly toward the parent of the same sex."

The Oedipal conflict referred to above is the erotic triangle that develops among the offspring, the opposite-sex parent and the parent of the same sex (who becomes seen as the child's competitor). King Oedipus was, of course, that royal personage who, in the Greek drama, slew his own father "mistakenly" and then, all unawares, took his own mother to the marital bed. The urge to dispose of one parent and possess the other as one's own mate develops in the earliest years, according to Freudian theory, and reaches its crescendo somewhere around the age of four or five.

During this period, the unconscious guilt associated with such lustful and aggressive feelings—and the fears that one will be punished horribly for having them—reach fever pitch. The infantile crisis that results (which Freud termed the "Oedipus complex") is resolved only when the effort to win the opposite-sex parent for one's very own love partner is sorrowfully and regretfully abandoned.

This internal renunciation is followed by intensive identification with the parent of the same sex—the one who, from the child's point of view, is "most like me" after all. The emotional truce that has been made will persist throughout the years of latency, and harmony will reign for a blessed while. Eventually, however, with the advent of puberty and of the biological changes that accompany it, those suppressed yearnings, terrifying wishes and unspeakable longings will reappear upon the household scene with a vengeance. Inchoate and disturbing, these feelings reach their greatest intensity during the adolescent period.

THE NORMAL TUG OF ATTRACTION

They become what family therapists Pincus and Dare have called "secrets in the family"—those universal fantasies which cannot be communicated in reality or, for that matter, tolerated as part of conscious thought. Denied and dissociated, these pinings for the unhaveable parent are banished from awareness—but they are *there*. And how could they not be? Parents normally and naturally, as Pincus and Dare observe, engage in what are really intense, powerful love relationships with their young and eager offspring. "For this reason," write the clinicians, "the incestuous dangers of the situation are necessarily never far below the surface.

"The child who is in absolutely no danger of its parent of the opposite sex having incestuous feelings toward him is," they point out, "more likely to become a somewhat rejected, unsure person lacking in the hope of becoming lovable and desirable, rather than (becoming) secure and confident."

The normal tug of attraction between the offspring and the opposite-sex parent is—while clearly *not* to be acted on—a natural and inevitable aspect of the development process. But, during the adolescent epoch, this process doesn't feel natural at all. The members of the household are often prey to a variety of disquieting, confusing, guilty, angry, and otherwise disturbing feelings. The eternal triangle is beginning to heat up, to become red-hot and difficult to handle.

Before long, the threesome—offspring, same-sex parent and opposite-sex parent—finds itself locked in emotional struggles which all participants are at a loss to explain. They may be involved in loud and noisy battles or in unspoken and unarticulated suffering, but the distress will in any case be very real.

This period of life marks a turning point in the lives of the parents as well as of the adolescent child, for the middle-aged person is usually struggling to deal with painful difficulties of his own. "[T]he awareness that oneself and one's spouse are no longer young and beautiful can lead to yet another development in the life cycle," state Drs. Rubin and Gertrude Blanck.

A confrontation with the aging process may occur, observe the Blancks, which can "lead to upheaval, quarreling, and the well-known last marital fling in the desperate attempt to stave off the acceptance of middle age. Sometimes, the adolescence of the child may stir up resurgence of the parent's adolescent narcissistic fantasies. . . ." The older individual may then fling himself into a new relationship as a solution to the problems of getting older and of the various disappointments that his life thus far has brought him.

THE UNHAVEABLE WOMAN

It was obvious that the question of whether or not there was another woman in the Gardiners' martial picture was one that had to be posed, and I had asked that question on the occasion of our initial interview. There was no third party, Philip responded with alacrity—at least not in terms of his being engaged in an affair.

But there *was* someone, he acknowledged, about whom he thought a great deal, with whom he had a "fantasy relationship" (although no relationship in reality).

This revelation came as no surprise to Kathleen, who said, tight-lipped, that she had been aware of the attraction from the outset. She herself was a friend of this person, whose name was Elinor; Kathleen continued to like her, to admire her style and competence. Her friend and her husband were *not* lovers; of this Kathleen felt reasonably certain. Philip echoed her by stating emphatically that Elinor was not a main actor—or, for that matter, even a factor—in what was happening in the marriage at this time.

For Elinor was married and had two young sons, about whom she cared a great deal. And while she, on her own part, was attracted to Philip—and willing to admit that this was so—she was not willing to risk endangering her own marriage or to chance compromising her family's peace and contentment.

She was thus the out-of-reach woman, the one he could not truly possess (because she belonged to another man); she was the one toward whom his thoughts, his hopes, his fantasies of perfect love and happiness could incline yearningly. The relationship with Elinor—the desired but not fully available female—was in a way an updated version of Philip's early relationship with Kathleen. *Kathleen* had been, at the time when they'd first gotten to know each other, grieving over a love affair with someone else which had recently ended. Then, when she had recovered her spirits, Kathleen had begun going out with other men; she hadn't wanted to limit herself to the relationship with Philip. She was, moreover, an "older woman" (a year older than he), and she was also more sexually experienced than he was.

Kathleen had been, in her time, the unhaveable woman—yet Philip had persisted in his courtship until he had won her for his own. Now, two and a half decades later, she herself had become the maternal stand-in, the woman from whom he needed to separate in order to realize his own self and personal identity.

THE ORIGINAL BLUEPRINT

In his own family, Philip Gardiner had been the child in the middle; he had a sister who was six years younger than he and a brother who was two years his senior. David, his older brother, had been named after their paternal grandfather; Philip had been named after their father and considered himself very much *like* him.

"Is your older brother married?" I asked, for I'd begun to make a sketch of Philip's family genogram. He nodded yes.

I asked for the name of his sister-in-law, jotted it down, and then asked whether or not the pair had any children. "They have five—" he had begun to say, when Kathleen interrupted. "Four," she stated decisively.

Philip turned to his wife. "Four?" he inquired uncertainly.

"Her three and his one," his wife replied.

He turned back to me. "One child is the product of their union, and three were hers from a former marriage, but have now been adopted by my brother." She was, he added, David's first and only wife.

How long had they been married? I inquired, and Kathleen, after a long pause, responded, "Sixteen years."

"Yesss—sixteen years—" Philip, for no apparent reason, heaved a sigh. "That's right." He himself had, as I noted, taken a bride who was slightly older than he was, someone who "had a sense of purpose" and knew her own mind. His brother, David, had wed a woman who was even more knowledgeable and experienced, having been married, and a mother, beforehand.

Philip's younger sister, Gwen, was divorced. She had two children and had adopted an orphaned relative as well. "And how long did Gwen's marriage last?" I asked, to which question Kathleen replied promptly, "Fourteen years."

We all laughed. "I wasn't sure you would have the answer," she apologized to her husband. "No, that's all right; it would have taken me a little time to figure it out, but it's perfectly all right for you to say," he assured her.

But there was a blandness in his voice which suggested that he had gone underground emotionally. Was it because he wanted less assistance and more opportunity to work the answers out for himself? I wondered.

"Are you close to them—either one of them—or to both of them?" I asked. He was, Philip answered, getting closer to his sister, but that was a very recent phenomenon. "Until the last two years, I wouldn't say that I had been close to *either*. . . ." He shrugged.

What, I asked him, are you finding that you have in common with your sister now? He paused a moment, then said, "I think we are both identifying some things about our family that have influenced our lives, and we're thinking about them pretty hard. And we're beginning to recognize the same things—things about the household that were either unspoken or unrecognized—and the kinds of reactions we've had to them."

"Is one of the things you have in common," I asked, "the fact that she's had serious problems in her marriage and that you are having them now?"

Philip shook his head in the negative. "Maybe, I don't know. It's not something I would identify—her having been through it already—but I wouldn't deny it, either. But what we talk about, for the most part, is my mother and father's relationship—the kind of person my father was." He inhaled, then added in a deeper, somber tone, "My father died in February. That brought us together, my sister and me, for some conversations, reflections. . . . We talked, as we hadn't ever done earlier."

Kathleen was, I noticed, looking at her husband almost irately, as if envious of the closeness with his sibling that he was describing. How old, I asked Philip, had his father been at the time of his dying?

"He was seventy-one—or about to be seventy-one. Actually, he was seventy years old."

"He was almost seventy-two," his wife observed.

I waited several moments, then said, "So this past year has been a tremendously upset one for you?" Philip was, I realized, dealing not only with the emancipation of his maturing children, but with the death—which is the ultimate separation—of his male parent. "It has not been an easy year," he acknowledged quietly.

"I have also been involved in getting a new business going," he remarked, moving away, in a self-protectively reflexive fashion, from the topic at hand. "I had to start earning a serious living again. I had no visible means of support after I was no longer running for the nomination. I'd been working for the university, in an excellent situation, but now I had to strike out and get a whole new operation going."

"No *invisible* means of support, either!" Kathleen's sally, and the laugh that accompanied it, had a tart edginess.

"Neither invisible nor visible; that's right," Philip allowed, his voice neutral.

The Gardiners had one child (Matthew) enrolled in a private high school and college tuitions for all three children looming before them. How, I inquired, were they managing financially?

"Borrowing, borrowing, borrowing," Philip replied. But his fledgling new firm, he assured me at once, was doing surprisingly well. He had, nevertheless, come to realize that those weaknesses in himself that he was beginning to identify were not confined to his relationship with Kathleen alone. The urge to be overly accommodating and pleasing had an insidious impact on the way he functioned in his professional life as well.

"I get no real reward," he explained, "out of doing something well just for the *feeling* of doing it well. I find it all too easy to try to satisfy the other person without any reflection about whether what is happening makes any sense to me or even whether it is a *good* or *a bad* way of approaching the problem. And that," he added, "goes back to the problem of not having any internal set of standards for myself, so that whatever is enough to make someone happy is sufficient."

I asked him why, in his opinion, those missing internal guideposts had failed to develop within him. Philip responded, with a sudden, genial grin, "I've never *needed* them, I guess. Everything went along quite nicely anyway." Then he laughed ruefully, shook his head. "No, things didn't really go along nicely, but they did *keep going*. . . ." He shifted his body, on the sofa, so that he was facing Kathleen, and they exchanged a wry, complicit smile. Whatever else was lacking in their relationship, there was obviously still understanding and affection between them—*a bond*.

"Those internal standards," I murmured, tentatively, "usually are developed as part of the leaving-home process—"

"Well, I never really did leave home," he cut in, immediately.

I smiled, chanced saying, "Yes, you seem to be dealing with some adolescent issues at this very moment—" He interrupted again. "I never really did leave home at all," he repeated.

"But the process is now getting under way, at age forty-three," I observed, "and in the wrong season of life, so to speak?" What had commenced as a comment ended up in the form of a question. "I think so, yes," Philip replied, then added fervently, "And I'm hoping it is not too late."

"And this process that is happening," I went on, "is happening in tandem with that of Matthew? And of the other kids, as well?" Philip stared at me, nodded agreement. But then he said, with some anger in his voice, "*Not*, though, in a way that makes it easy for us to communicate about it! What I've put off, Matt is putting off too! I think he is probably way behind, doing worse than even *I* was, at his age, in terms of growing up and developing responsibilities and the whole sense of—" He stopped. Kathleen leaned forward, as if about to say something, but her husband held up a hand to prevent her. She remained frozen where she was momentarily, her mouth open, but then leaned back helplessly against the cushion of the rocker.

The inability to separate—truly to grow up and leave home in the internal, psychological sense—was a burden that, dragged across the generations, was becoming heavier and heavier. It was already beginning to weigh the next generation down.

THE GOOD, HAPPY CHILD

In contrast with his own growing up and development, which Philip considered to have been "just arrested" but outwardly nontraumatic, his older brother's adolescence had been stormy and difficult. "David was, I think, beginning to develop his own ideas," he said, "but the process was a great agony to him. And he was in great conflict with my mother, all the time, about them. So the upshot was, he didn't perform well . . . he went off to Princeton, but then couldn't hack it. He felt . . . mixed up, unable to figure out whether the other guys were friends to him or not. He had to leave school and come home."

David had worked as a mechanic for a while, eventually gone back to a less prestigious college, ended up as a career officer in the armed services. "To this day," commented Philip, "my brother has to arrange his life so that he's in a highly structured situation. One where there are things to do today and he does them." He had done well in his career life and was now a high-ranking officer. But during the adolescent years, when the rules were not so clearly spelled out, David had been the bad, troubled child in the Gardiner family.

Philip, in contrast, had been the good, happy one.

What role, I inquired, had been taken by his much younger (there was a six-year age gap between them) sister, Gwen? "Gwen never really had an opportunity to develop one—at least not in adolescence—at least not so far as I knew." He glanced at his wife, as if hoping that she had some better information to offer; she shook her head, indicating that she didn't. "My sister was engaged at sixteen and married by the time she was seventeen years old."

"To an enormously wealthy man," put in Kathleen. "It was *her* way of getting out of the household. But she still resents their letting her do it. *Abrogating* their responsibilities. Because the decision was, ultimately, left up to the headmaster of the fancy private school she was attending. And he said yes, because after all, the man *was* fabulously rich. But she herself was a child."

Gwen had been married in her senior year of high school and gone on to attend Wellesley College. "Was her husband much older than she was?" I asked the couple, and Philip answered that he had been. "There was a thirteen-year age difference. He was a veteran and actually a friend of my father's. He would come to stay with us at our summer place, and that's when he became interested in my sister. But he was very *correct*. Nothing underhanded happened. One day he just asked my father if it would be all right if he asked Gwen out to dinner—"

"Let's see, he would have been around thirty-one at the time?" interrupted Kathleen, obviously taken up by the story.

"He was thirty," her husband responded.

For a moment no one said anything further. "Going back to David," I essayed, "when he had trouble with your mother, he must have gotten into trouble with your father as well?"

"Not really. Well, he—my dad and I were the mediators," he explained. "My mother was a lot more hysterical than Kathleen."

Kathleen inhaled sharply. "It is all right for *me* to refer to myself as 'hysterical'!" she said angrily. "It is *not* all right for you to do so!" There were large apple-shaped spots of red on her cheeks.

"I wasn't referring to you as hysterical." He leaned backward as if a gust of wind had hit him. "I was referring to my mother as hysterical, and what I was pointing out"—he was addressing me now—"was that they were having some of the same conflicts that Kathleen and I have, except that *she* manifested hysteria in reaction to what was going on and my father would try to calm that situation." Philip was backing down as swiftly as he possibly could.

An Either/Or World

"So your dad, too, was the mediator and pleaser?" I asked.

"I think that's true. Do you think that's true?" He turned to appeal to Kathleen.

"Yes," she replied succinctly.

He and his father, he went on to explain, tended to be the conciliators, while his brother and mother had been the family battlers. "My brother can't stand my mother, but he's *like* her. He will fight first and later on try to figure out what it was all about. Actually, being in the service has modified his behavior in that regard. Allowed him to develop control—because it's necessary—whereas my mother gets continually unleashed."

Had she continued to do so in the years since his father had died? I inquired. Philip shot me a quizzical look. "Actually, no; she has a sense of freedom about her these days," he replied.

So his mother was, I observed with a smile, less hysterical without the mediator's services? "Yes." He laughed, and I asked Philip how he could explain that. "Oh, I think it got written into their script," he shrugged lightly. "A husband and a wife give each other things to do: If you know there's a mediator, you know you can be more hysterical. People, I think, fall into natural patterns of relationships that seem to balance for a period of time—even if they are," he added, "rough on everyone emotionally."

When such "natural patterns" exist, I reflected, the "mediator's" own anxious, hysterical feelings can be expressed by the "hysterical" mate, even if those inner feelings have, at a conscious level, been thoroughly dissociated and disclaimed by him.

"How long," I asked, "were your parents married before your father died?"

It had been forty-six years, Philip replied.

"Tell me a little about their relationship," I began to say, but he waved a hand as if waving me backward. "I can't tell you anything about it," he stated decisively.

"Not, for example, whether they seemed happy, close, quarrelsome—there's nothing fairly general that you can say?" I tried to meet his eyes, but he looked away. He crossed one leg over the other, then uncrossed them and crossed them in the other direction. "I always felt that my father was suffocated," he said, finally, in a low voice.

It was a concern that he had expressed on his own behalf, a little earlier in this conversation. "Is that a worry of yours, too?" I inquired quietly.

"I don't want to be like him! I don't want to give up my growth, put off my growth, make do with where I am, and die like *he* did—or not live to my own fulfillment!" he burst out. His father, Philip seemed to be saying, had been imprisoned in an airless relationship throughout his lifetime. He, in his fear of being *like* him, was trying to reverse the situation. He was moving out of his family in order to be superliberated, wholly autonomous, to "grow" psychologically and to be free.

But the position he was moving toward was merely his father's one, turned completely inside out. Instead of remaining in the relationship—which he perceived as threatening to suffocate him—he could do the opposite, abandon the marriage. Philip inhabited an emotional system in which only these two polarized options existed. But the notion that he and Kathleen could work together to *change* the system—that there were options for being in a relationship *other* than being unable to breathe or being alone—seemed to be one that was completely foreign to him. In their system, both members operated on the assumption that you can either be close and dependent *or* disconnected and independent, but you cannot be a mixture of both. Theirs was, in other words, an either/or world. So the choices, as Philip saw them, were either suffocation or flight.

REENACTMENT

To what degree, I wondered, might an abortive mourning process—mourning for his father—be fueling Philip Gardiner's urgent need to get away from the relationship and to escape into a rosy future, dimly distinguishable, of freedom, growth, and fulfillment? "How did your father die?" I asked him.

"Heart disease. Natural causes, but after a long time. He was disabled for many years," he replied.

Then he looked at me, expectantly, as if awaiting prompting. I suggested that he simply tell me a little more about it. "My father wasn't ever *mentally* disabled," Philip hastened to reassure me, although the thought had not entered my mind. "I mean he was always alert and active and thinking. But he just never had any capacity to be *free* to do what he might want to do!" There was grief in his voice. Was he, ten months after his parent's death, behaving as his father's delegate? Was he shedding the emotional commitments in his own life and demanding liberty *on behalf of dad*, who had never been able to do it for himself?

Philip, it occurred to me, might be attempting to live out not only his own aborted adolescence but that of his father as well. "So he—your dad—never had that capacity within himself? To be free, I mean?" I asked.

He shook his head in such a way as to indicate that I was missing the point entirely. "Well, you know, at the time that he graduated from Harvard, which was in 1935, it was still the middle of the Depression. His own father had died, in 1928, when my father was just sixteen."

A startled expression must have crossed my features, for Philip stopped his recitation, waited for me to say something. I had realized, at that moment, that Philip's abrupt departure from the family had occurred when his son Matthew had reached the exact same age. It was as if an anniversary had been indelibly engraved upon the family calendar, and Philip himself were unconsciously committed to observing it.

After a few moments' pause, he continued. "He wanted desperately to become a journalist, but had to go to work as an office boy. The job—which was the only one he could find—was in a company owned by his college roommate's family. And two years later, he married my mother." He raised his arms upward, just above each of his shoulders, then slapped his trousered knees briskly as if to say that his father's fate had been sealed. He was trapped in his life, a prison constructed partly of the economic circumstances of the time and partly of the emotional commitments he had undertaken.

"He worked for that same company for twenty years, and at the end of the twentieth he said, 'That's enough,' and he quit," recounted Philip. "The next couple of years were spent in trying to get another job and in dealing with sickness. He had a mild cancer, but the treatments for it were painful. Then, after finding something else at last, he had his heart attack. So he never really . . ." He swallowed hard, unable to finish the sentence. "Well," he recommenced, "by the time his family was grown up, he was disabled. And very dependent on my mother, who did become significantly less hysterical around that time."

He gave me an odd look. "I think that's the first time I've ever said that or thought it: that her hysteria lessened after my father became so dependent. Also, she started working . . ."

Kathleen, leaning forward eagerly, added, "This all happened at the time when the children moved out of the house. Because, although there is a disparity in ages, they all left home—"

"Within three months of each other." Philip, nodding at her, was transmitting the information to me. "Yes, within three months of each other," she took up the recitation. "And within a year, Philip—his father, I mean, of course—had had his first major heart attack. So it was, I think, incredibly wrenching to have the nest emptied instantaneously like that— one son going off into the air force, another getting married and starting graduate school and Gwen marrying before she was even out of high school. And then this massive heart illness began."

"But then she calmed down," I observed, a quizzical expression on my face. I looked from one to the other of them. "He gave her another job to take care of," suggested Philip, a facetious smile on his features. "A very nice thing for him to do for her," I agreed. "Very self-sacrificing," I added, keeping my own tone light and humorous.

"And I suppose that ended it," commented Kathleen, her words accompanied by a short, harsh laugh. "He, Philip's dad, was never going to grow up and strike out on his own."

"And she *played* that role," her husband's voice throbbed with resentment. "She played it beautifully, but that's what it was. A *role*. And that's what happened: He got sick, and she got to take care of him." His expression turned stony, and he said nothing further.

I asked him, for purposes of clarification, to review his father's employment career for me once again. "He went to work, just out of Harvard, in a family-owned company that belonged to a classmate—the *family* of his classmate—and he worked for that company and essentially was an office boy."

"In the beginning," amended his wife swiftly.

"And he developed into a salesman," continued Philip, "and then became a sales manager and then rose to become the sales manager for the entire company—which was the top level he could get to in that company, because he wasn't a member of the family. I mean, there was no other growth possible for him. And he made a decision at that time, which was after he had been there for about twenty years, that he didn't want to stay there and be in that position for the rest of his life." The anxious way in which he told the story made me glance up, and I saw fear in his eyes. He looked pale. Did he believe that his father had fallen ill and become disabled because he'd been so stuck, so stymied in his life?

How old, I asked, had his dad been when he'd decided to leave his job and been out of work and then developed the disease? "He was about the same age as I am now," Philip answered, and then smiled, as if in sudden recognition. So did Kathleen.

"It's—" he began to say, then halted. "Eerie" was the word that came to my own mind; Philip was resurrecting the charged issues of the past in an hypnotic, almost trancelike fashion. His wife, her gaze fixed upon him, wore an intent, half-supplicating expression, as if she were pleading with him to awaken. "—more than coincidental," he acknowledged, at last. "Oh, God," she seconded his statement.

"Yes." Philip, checking his dates, was not talking to either one of us but to himself. "That's right. It would have been 1954, and so he would have been forty-two, and I'm just about to turn forty-three." He looked pale, sweaty and uncomfortable; Kathleen's eyes, I realized, were filling with tears.

"It's—strange," I said, in a quiet voice, and he nodded abstractedly, observed: "Almost like a pattern, repeating itself." He spoke in a flat tone, as if slightly dazed, while his wife went to get some Kleenex out of the bathroom. So much that was happening in the present generation represented not "new growth" but a repetition of what had happened earlier. Caught, unwittingly, in the skeins of the past, Philip was re-creating in the present the only intimate world he had ever known, and his fidelity to the original pattern was striking. If he was not loyal as a husband and father, he was certainly loyal as a son.

17
A Game
for Two Players

What must be held firmly in mind—for it is of vital significance—is that when partners collude to re-create charged aspects of the past, it is never a one-way process; it is not, in other words, something that one member of the couple *does to* the other one. On the contrary, *two motivated players must be involved*; otherwise the collusive game will never get going.

It might be tempting, for instance, to see Kathleen Gardiner as someone who had been conscripted into playing out her husband's family scenario—to view her as the *victim* of Philip's earlier history. But she would not have been collaborating with his need to remain emotionally fused to his original family—by taking on the part of the controlling, assertive, "suffocating" female—if he had not been doing something very similar on *her* behalf. Philip embodied, for Kathleen, the passively accommodating, reliable (until recently) male parent from whom she had precipitously separated, but never succeeded in leaving behind.

The Gardiners were resurrecting, in their marriage, aspects of earlier relational conflicts which neither one of them has been able to resolve, individually. These conflicts, *which were inside each spouse's own psyche*, had been thrust into the middle of their relationship, eventually becoming the bitterly unresolvable conflict *between them*. This had happened, moreover, in the most natural and inevitable-seeming way, for the problems that each of them had brought into the marriage, from their original families, fit together in a smoothly complementary, interlocking fashion.

Kathleen and Philip, like so many other intimate partners, were "made for each other" in that sense.

A FAMILY LOSS

Alike though the Gardiners might be, in terms of their unconscious agendas, the two members of the couple came from very different kinds of ethnic, social and economic backgrounds. Philip Gardiner derived from Boston Brahmin stock; his family had arrived in colonial America in the middle of the seventeenth century. Kathleen Curran was of mixed Irish and French-Canadian ancestry; her parents were the first "American" generation.

Philip's family belonged to the Congregational Church; Kathleen's family was Catholic (but only, as she put it, "nominally observant"). Philip's father was an executive, who had attained a relatively high managerial post over the course of his career; Kathleen's father had been a blue-collar worker, a fireman in the mixed Irish and French-Canadian enclave of Holyoke, Massachusetts, in which she and her younger sisters had been reared.

Kathleen was, I learned, the eldest of three daughters; she was the firstborn child in the Curran family. Eldest children tend, as all studies of birth order and later personality characteristics consistently find, to be leaders—people who assume control and move into positions of authority readily—*unless*, as expert Walter Toman has noted, the firstborn happens to be a girl, followed by a boy, in a family that values male children much more highly. In such a circumstance, the firstborn daughter may be treated differently and develop the personality traits usually associated with secondborn siblings instead.

Her parents, according to Kathleen Gardiner, had wanted a male child very badly. They had succeeded in having a son, when she herself was a girl of thirteen, but the infant had lived only briefly—a couple of days. Her baby brother's birth, and his death, had been "catastrophic" for everyone in the entire Curran family.

Even now, thirty-one years later, and in the midst of a crisis in her own household, Kathleen was visibly moved and upset while talking about what had happened then. "It was"—she hesitated, swallowed—"*traumatic*, in fact. My mother, you see, suffered from a lot of health problems; she'd had juvenile rheumatoid arthritis, from the age of fifteen, and she was a hemophiliac carrier also. So there were a great many difficulties just in carrying the baby, and then, when it came time for him to be born, she had a placenta previa. I remember—" Kathleen winced, halted, then took in a deep breath of air, as if needing to fortify herself before continuing.

Long before the birth itself, she resumed, her mother had become unable to get up and down the staircase. "We had taken the dining room and turned it into a bedroom, and I remember getting up to go to school one morning and looking in the room and there was—aargh!—blood *everyplace*! She was hemorrhaging, and very *badly*." Kathleen's blue eyes were wide with shock, her skin dead white, as if every blood vessel in her face had suddenly emptied.

She shuddered, added that the ambulance had come very shortly thereafter. "I was just thirteen, and *very* impressionable. My parents must have wanted that baby very much," she added, immediately, an aggrieved note entering her voice. "It—he—was the only male child they had, and I think having a male child was important to them. I don't think they would have made that effort, given my mother's health problems, unless they had been hoping against hope. And there was a *lot* of sorrow on their part, when he died." Her face was twisted with remembered grief at this moment. "My mother almost died at that time as well."

The whole family had been plunged into mourning for the lost infant. There had even been a funeral with a tiny casket. "I didn't attend," said Kathleen, her voice low with pain, "and my father had to go through all of that alone." But she'd had, in the wake of that family bereavement, to take over the daily running of the household.

For her mother, when she came home from the hospital, was convalescing but still far from well. Her health, compromised from the outset by the arthritic disease from which she suffered, had, in fact, received a blow from which she never fully recovered. The costs (mental as well as physical) of carrying and losing that baby had been enormous. So Kathleen, the eldest daughter in the household, had become the "acting mother" of the Curran family. And she'd retained that role until she went away to college and eventually married.

I noted, in pausing to survey the Gardiners' genogram, which I was constructing as we spoke—that one of those strange correspondences had emerged on the "His" and the "Hers" sides of the page. Both of the Gardiners had had a same-sex parent (Kathleen's mother, Philip's father) who'd developed a serious illness and at roughly the same point in their *own* lives—that is, when Kathleen and Philip had each been turning thirteen.

ONE TOUGH LADY

Kathleen's parents were no longer alive. Her mother had died some thirteen years earlier, at the age of forty-nine. She had been, according to her daughter, an extremely *strong* individual. "V*ery* strong," reiterated Kathleen, "and—I thought—very pretty. She was extraordinarily devoted to my father and to her children. She was also *one tough lady*." Her brief description had begun and ended with energetic assertions of her mother's strength and her toughness.

Did Kathleen mean, I wondered, to use the word "tough" in a positive or negative sense? The question, when I put it to her, brought a somewhat impish, defiant smile to her face. "During my adolescence, I meant it very negatively indeed! I thought my mother was *haaard*," she stretched the vowel out, making the word long but also deep with the tenor sound of her own profound, remembered feeling.

"But there are lots of definitions of 'tough,' " she qualified that statement immediately. "And in a way, because my mother was so extraordinarily ill and I never—except on rare occasions—heard her do much complaining about it, I *admired* that toughness, considered it a *positive* quality. But if the word is used in the sense of 'hard,' I would say that she had very high standards which she imposed on us and that there was no discussion about it: moral standards; social standards; standards about our appearance."

Kathleen's father had died—of cancer—just three years ago. He had been an extremely different sort of a person from her mother, the polar opposite of his strong, demanding wife. When I asked Kathleen to describe him a bit more, the sides of her lips turned upward in a small, almost reflexive smile. Her tone of voice, as she replied, became animated, even gay. "Warm and gentle, with a twinkle in his eye," she answered happily.

But then she added, less enthusiastically, "I think now it would have to be added that he had a tendency to be passive. . . . My mother used to get angry at him because he wouldn't stick up for himself." She laughed, suddenly, at a remembrance. "A great bone of contention in the family was the fact that as a very young man, he took the exam for fire chief and scored higher than anyone else. But he wasn't *named* chief, and my mother was just *furious* about it." She laughed again, shook her head.

Her dad was someone who, as her mother saw it, always hung back too much and did not assert himself sufficiently. But her parents' marriage had still, as Kathleen perceived it, been an extremely happy one. "I think there's no question—and my sisters would agree—that they were very much in love with each other." She spoke in a subdued, almost awed tone of voice.

"Which is not to say"—Kathleen held up a hand as if to halt any hasty conclusions on my part—"that the marriage always flowed along smoothly. But I can remember only one big quarrel—which *scared me*, as those things always do scare kids—and for the rest, a sense that they were enormously supportive of each other." Her voice remained low, hushed-sounding, romantic.

But then a bitter expression crossed her face, and she stated tersely, "My mother, as we got to be adolescents, made it clear to me *explicitly* where her devotion and care were going. . . . Once—and I will never forget it—she said to me, 'Make no mistake about it, Kathleen, given a choice between you girls and your father, I will always choose *him!*' "

The conversation had moved, with striking rapidity, from a dreamy, if slightly envious, description of her parents' relationship to an angry denunciation of her mother's forthright exclusion of her and her sisters from that bond. This certainly had an Oedipal flavor, and I could not help thinking of Kathleen as her female parent's thirteen-year-old "replacement"—which was what she had perforce become after her infant brother's death and her mother's subsequent serious illness.

At a time when a developing young woman is normally experiencing an upsurge of anxiety-laden, competitive feelings, Kathleen had been promoted to the role of her male parent's partner in running the household, thereby becoming a pseudomother of the younger children and her father's companion in the tasks of life. It was a lot of power for an adolescent girl to handle, a partial realization of the maturing female's Wish and her Fear.

The Wish is to supplant the mother in the father's affections, and the Fear is that of losing the mother's love, upon which she is still profoundly dependent. Had Kathleen's mother been telling her, in that interchange, that there were still private places in the marriage which no child would ever be able to penetrate—that the door of the parental inner sanctum, no matter how she knocked, would never really be opened to her?

"Whatever brought up the idea of her having to choose between her children and her husband?" I inquired. Kathleen shook her head, told me that she could not remember a word of the discourse that had preceded her mother's making that statement. "All that I can recall is that I was driving in the car, afterwards, and I said to myself, 'Oh well, Kathleen, that's certainly been laid out for you, clearly enough!' " She emitted a short, harsh laugh. "And it was, I realized, a conversation that I would never, ever forget."

She shrugged, as if to dismiss a matter that could be neither comprehended nor resolved. "My mother and I did not get along—not from the time I reached adolescence until after I was married."

"And then, after you were married, you *did* get along?" I asked. Kathleen, with a wry look, shook her head in the negative. "It was a distant relationship. Before she died, which was when we were just having *our* family, I did have a chance to retrieve some of the affection . . . but what I didn't have was the chance to say to her, 'Gee, Mom, I'm sorry I was such a bitch.' "

In which ways, I wondered, had her "bitchery" manifested itself?

A Precedent in History

Although both her mother and father had lived very close to their original homes—in Holyoke, within a three-mile radius of both sets of grandparents—there had been no real emotional connection between them and their families. Kathleen's grandparents had never been able to forgive her parents for eloping, which they had done when her mother was in her senior year of high school.

"My parents," Kathleen said, "weren't able to have a very wide circle of friends, given my mother's illness. They really had nobody except us—the kids."

What surprised me, I told her, was that—once the marriage was an established reality and given that her mother had become so ill—the quarrel with the maternal grandparents had not eventually been settled. "Your mother's folks never really came around, never helped her?" I inquired of Kathleen. "Can you, now, understand why that was so?"

Her jaw jutted forward angrily. "My mother's father was a very *weak* man," she responded contemptuously. "He was dominated by his wife— a successful businesswoman—who couldn't be bothered to take care of a sick daughter. I mean if she had helped my mother," her voice was heavy with irony, "she wouldn't have been able to keep up with her business or with her very active social life!"

I looked down at the partially constructed Curran family genogram. In Kathleen's extended system, the strong female/passive male dyad seemed to keep popping up again and again. It was here, on her mother's side, at least. What about her father's mother? I asked. That grandmother had, I'd already learned, been thoroughly enraged by her son's elopement. But what I didn't know was what her relationship with her own husband had been like.

My asking that question brought a grin to Philip's face. "She didn't quite *have* a husband of her own anymore! Because—you don't know this yet—but Kathleen's paternal grandfather lived in the basement of their house."

"He—what?" I gazed at him in astonishment, then turned to ask Kathleen, "What's *that* about?"

She and Philip had both started laughing; she waved a hand as if to wave off a story that was too nonsensical to be worth repeating. But Philip explained. "He—her dad's father—lived in a cellar apartment. He didn't live upstairs in the house with Kathleen's grandmother."

"That . . . grandfather lived . . . in the cellar!" Her statement, made between bursts of laughter, was no more than a repetition and confirmation of what he had said, but it sparked a fresh outburst of laughter from all of us. "Next to the furnace, yes," put in Philip, "and he kept it nice and shiny! Sometimes," he added wryly, "he was even invited *upstairs*—"

"—When she *wanted* something!" interrupted his wife, in a tone of growing hilarity. "When she *wanted* something, she would open the door and call down, 'Robert! ROBERT PATRICK!' " Her grandmother's voice, as Kathleen rendered it, had the deep, commanding tone of a bassoon. Both the Gardiners began laughing so hard that neither could say anything further. "This is a *peculiar* family," acknowledged Kathleen at last, wiping tears from the corners of her eyes with her finger. She was, it seemed to me, overjoyed at seeing Philip so amused, so happy, so *involved*.

"Yes." I nodded, smiled at her. The wave of laughter, which had overwhelmed us all for a few moments, was a tide that was rapidly receding. Our expressions grew more serious even before I spoke again, and when I spoke, I did so hesitantly.

"I am—very *struck* by one thing." My voice was bemused. "Which is that Robert Patrick went down to live in the basement while Philip went up to live in the attic." They stared at me as if they believed that I had suddenly gone mad.

Then Kathleen shook her head, began laughing again, as if a new joke had fortuitously presented itself. "It was in *her* family that this happened." Philip, laughing too, nevertheless sounded disturbed. "And my move upstairs was *my own idea*. While in your grandfather's case," he turned to demand of his wife, "it was the *woman's* decision, wasn't it?"

"Well, who knows? I don't know," she answered uncertainly.

"But *she* sent Robert Patrick to Coventry, didn't she?" he asked her, almost pleadingly. "All I know is that he was in Coventry as long as I knew him"—she shrugged—"and much, much nicer than *she* was." In both their worlds, I thought, the men tended to be "nice" and the women "powerful" (other synonyms for which were "tough," "tyrannical," "hysterical"). Neither of them really knew, however, whether her paternal grandfather had been banished to the basement or had chosen to leave his wife for a more peaceful existence belowstairs.

He, as Philip had done initially, might have separated from his mate without leaving the house. But the fact that neither of the Gardiners could even entertain the idea of a connection between a past family circumstance and a present-day occurrence was not surprising at all. Many clinicians have commented upon the extraordinary *resistance* of most people to the very notion that they are profoundly interconnected with other members of the near—and also the extended—family system.

The underlying reason for this intense resistance is probably the strong desire, active in most of us, to hold high the flag of our own individuality and uniqueness. The wish to do so is so powerful that we fail, very often, to recognize that the way in which we may be attempting to solve a problem is precisely the way we in which we saw that problem being tackled earlier.

All that I said to the Gardiners at that moment was, however, "Not that many people separate and then continue living in the same house. It has happened in your family a couple of times now."

Then I shrugged my shoulders lightly. Philip's move to the third floor had, in one sense, been a typical teenage maneuver—a way of getting space and making distance without leaving the family context entirely. But in another sense he was testing out an adaptation that he had seen put into service before. It was the weaker male's mode of retreating from a more dominant female—which is to say, by separating and yet remaining within the emotional system simultaneously.

THE DEPARTURE

That particular interchange, which occurred during the third in our series of interviews, left Kathleen with a frown upon her mobile, intelligent features. She remained silent, for a short while, then shook her head as if she'd entertained—and then rejected—an alien, insupportable (and uncomfortable) idea. "I hear what you are saying," she murmured, at last, "but it doesn't resonate. . . ." She tapped the side of her head, at the temple, as if to say, "It just doesn't resonate inside *here*."

The suggestion that she and Philip might have been re-creating (or even influenced by) a family pattern was, she protested, overly simplistic, a proposition that she could not accept. A major reason why the entire notion seemed farfetched and irrelevant, she went on to explain, was that she herself had broken away from her own family in ways that were very decisive and significant. "I have not been emotionally dependent on my parents since my early twenties," said Kathleen in a voice that was firm and clear of uncertainty. She believed, she declared, that she herself had been far more successful about making the separation from her folks than either of her younger sisters had been.

Her youngest sister, Nora, had, for example, wed a man who was sixteen years her senior—"a multimarried person," commented Kathleen, her lips pursing in a disapproval that was not verbally expressed. "I think that, to this day, Nora has unresolved feelings about both my mother and my father that she is totally unable to articulate. Whenever she was in trouble, she would always call for *Daddy*." There was scorn but also envy in this oldest sister's voice.

Here, I recognized, was another similarity on the Gardiner and Curran sides of the family map: Both Philip and Kathleen had had a younger female sibling who'd married a man who was a good deal older than she was. It was a minor matter, to be noted only in passing, but it seemed to suggest that these two brides had wed mates who, by virtue of their age seniority, would have tended to function in a fatherly as well as in a husbandly capacity.

"And Anne, who's next to me in line, never speaks of Daddy as if to say it's a relationship we share! No, she's always said '*my* father' this, and '*my* father that' . . . '*my* father' everything!" Kathleen paused, took a deep breath, then added less passionately, "That's been a big problem in Annie's *own* marriage, one that they've just started coming to grips with after twenty years—and a whole lot of trouble—as I've recently learned." Her voice held a certain sympathy for her younger sister, but also the implication that Anne's greedy territoriality about their father's love had brought a just punishment down upon her.

She was silent for a few moments, then commenced again. "I myself have been—and my sisters would, I think, bear me out on this—*much* more successful in coming to terms with my parents. While for them, my father is—to this day, and even though he's been dead for almost three years, now —very *much* a focus. He is definitely *not* a focus in my own life." Kathleen could, she added, put a fairly precise date upon the time when he had ceased to *be* one.

"He is still, I think," intervened Philip mildly, at that moment, "an important figure for all of his children. It's probably less intense, in your case," he added immediately, "than it is for Nora and Annie. But he does represent a certain standard to you."

I looked at her, met her eyes directly, asked, "What kind of standard does your father represent?"

For a moment she gazed back, not replying, as a slowly traveling blush spread itself across her features. "Goodness, with a small *g*, in a nice, warm way," she answered in a tone of pleasure and contentment. Then, appealing to her husband, she asked, "Do you—would you add anything to that?"

"I think, devotion," he answered quietly. It occurred to me, even as he said this, that Philip's own most important and attractive quality had been, for Kathleen, his willingness to *be there* for her. Whenever she had broken up with some other man, he had been accounted for and present— *reliable*, as her father had been reliable for her mother during the long years of illness and isolation from their unforgiving, uncaring families.

To the extent that Kathleen Curran had, as a growing young female child, identified with a sick and needy mother—as well as with the "tough lady" she viewed that parent as having been—it was not difficult to understand why it was so important to her to find a mate who would always *be there* to care for her—someone who would not abandon ship if and when the weather of living got rough. But Philip, selected for his reliability, was proving to be anything *but*.

"Why is it, do you think," I asked her now, "that your sisters have had more trouble in separating from your parents—and particularly your father—than you have had yourself?"

She could not, she responded, supply any answer to that question. But she could, repeated Kathleen, pinpoint the precise date, and the particular incident, around which that separation had occurred. "I was away at college and had come home for a vacation," she recounted. "My mother was in the middle of a really bad *bad* spell, and my father had been trying to get someone to live in and to help out."

That had not, given the family's financial state, been an easy task to accomplish. "Because we didn't have enormous amounts of money, he had been unable to find anyone. So one afternoon, when I was in the kitchen ironing stuff and preparing to go back to school, he asked me if I couldn't please stay at home at the end of that term and take care of my mother for a year. And I said, 'No! I won't do it!' " The expression upon her face was indignant.

"I have my own life to live," she was speaking angrily, not to me but to her father, "and she is *your* wife, and *you* are responsible!" Her sister Anne was, she paused to explain, already married by then, but Kathleen had warned her father against drafting the youngest sibling, Nora, into the job. "If you are going to ask her to do that," she was addressing her parent again, "then *I* will come home instead." The light in her narrowed eyes was fierce, unrelenting. "But you have no right to ask *her*, either— and I am telling you now, 'Don't do it'."

Her father had, I was not surprised to learn, withdrawn the request and eventually found a woman to come in to help care for his wife and assist with the running of the household. But that event had, as Kathleen perceived it, represented a last-ditch effort, on her father's part, to prevent her from leaving home. "On *his* part," she made the distinction grimly, "but not mine; for me, it *was* the departure."

The Invisible Fabric of Loyalty

For her, this act of defiance had meant the crossing of a personal Rubicon. She had left, in the wake of this assertion of her own independence from her parents, and in substantial and important ways, she had never returned. The old relationship with her mother—the affection they had shared before Kathleen's adolescence—had certainly never been restored. But what could have been the daughter's *feelings* about leaving home in this fashion?

She, who had been her mother's caretaker for so many years and who had been so responsible for her mother—could not have separated in so abrupt and definitive a manner without any feelings of self-reproach and self-directed condemnation. There was no way, it seemed to me, that Kathleen could have deserted her mother without feeling profoundly *guilty* about it. She had, in the ledger of family love, assumed an emotional debit of almost incalculable enormity.

As psychiatrist Ivan Boszormanyi-Nagy has observed,

> Loyalty commitments are like invisible but strong fibers which hold together complex pieces of relationship "behavior" in families. . . . To understand the functions of a group of people, nothing is more crucial than to know who are bound together in loyalty and what loyalty means for them. Each person maintains a bookkeeping of his perception of the balances of past, present and future give-and-take. What has been "invested" into the system through availability and what has been withdrawn in the form of support received or one's exploitative use of the others remains written into the invisible accounts of obligations.

What is woven into our very beings is a sense of existential indebtedness for what has been given to us which, suggests Dr. Boszormanyi-Nagy, constitutes "the invisible fabric of loyalty" that weaves the histories of generations of family members together.

Kathleen must in her heart of hearts—because of her own unconscious guilt and sense of having violated what the philosopher Martin Buber has called the "justice of the human world"—have suspected and feared that one day there would be a high penalty to be paid. Having failed to honor the debt of love and loyalty *justly owing* to her parents, she must, at some level, have expected that her punishment would come.

And I wondered, Did it feel "right," in some profoundly moral sense, that she who had been the abandoner was now being abandoned herself? I thought, too, of the parting words she had flung at her father: "She is *your* wife, and *you* are responsible!" Kathleen could, of course, have added to that, "She is my mother as well," but this aspect of biology and reality had been ignored or forgotten. Her intense anger, on that occasion, seemed to suggest that angry, competitive, Oedipal issues were very much alive, that the Oedipal triangle was still lit and incandescent. For the implication of that statement was that he—like her mother—had made a choice between his children and his spouse. Now, she was telling him, he was stuck with the person he had chosen.

TAKING OFF

It sounded, in a way, as if what Kathleen had actually been furious about was the close relationship between her parents—a relationship from which she was eternally barred. Instead, however, of dealing with this painful developmental dilemma (then or ever), her means of coping had been to take flight. And because she'd had to pack her emotional supplies so hurriedly, significant aspects of her own inner being were discarded and left behind.

What had been packed and brought along (because, among other things, they made leaving possible) were those strong, tough parts of her mother that Kathleen herself disapproved of and disliked. But what had been jettisoned, in the drama of the leave-taking, was any sense of her own daughterly identification with a mother who was fragile, ill and weak. Those aspects of her parent, too scary for Kathleen to incorporate as aspects of her own internal self, had been thrust out of her conscious awareness and totally denied.

The mother in Kathleen's mind was strong, one hell of a tough lady— as was Kathleen herself. That mother was powerful and demanding, someone toward whom her eldest daughter, locked in Oedipal rivalry, experienced feelings of angry competitiveness and jealousy. Had this not been the case, Kathleen might actually have been able to contemplate considering her father's request as one which certainly reflected real needs and wasn't necessarily a clear bid to keep her enslaved at home forever.

She might, in fact, have remained and cared for her mother for a period of time (having negotiated the outside limits of that period) without necessarily compromising her own separateness and integrity. But her sense of the situation had been that she had to run quickly—to escape the emotional fusion which threatened, like some cloying jungle plant of love, to wrap its petals around her and entrap her in the world of her childhood.

To be a person, felt Kathleen, she must go as quickly and decisively as possible. She had to sever the emotional connection, for the competition with her mother was a battle she was never going to win. So she had left—and viewed the finality of her separation as a healthy, psychological achievement.

The Underlying Pull Toward Fusion

But this was precisely what it was *not*. For if the Scylla of the delicate adolescent departing process is being emotionally bound and unable to leave home at all, then the Charybdis is going off in the way she had done—in anger with so many relational issues unresolved. As family theorist Dr. Murray Bowen has observed, we usually pay a heavy toll when we abruptly break off our early relationships in this fashion.

While all people, notes Dr. Bowen, have some unresolved emotional attachment to their parents, "the more intense the cutoff with the past, the more likely is the individual to have an exaggerated version of his parental family problem in his own marriage, and the more likely his own children to do a more intense cutoff with him in the next generation."

The person who runs away from his family of origin, asserts Bowen, "is as emotionally dependent as the one who never leaves home." What healthy separation involves is not necessarily geography, but the *transformation* of the original love attachments into something less highly charged, less self-defining, less urgent. Being truly separate from one's parents means having attained the ability to be *different* from them and not experiencing that differentness as a loss or a betrayal of what has been. An individual may be a separate and differentiated being yet live very near to his original family; he may, on the other hand, live a continent away and—in the internal, psychological sense—never have parted from them at all.

To the extent that Kathleen had walked out on her past, leaving so many vital matters unsettled, she had increased the likelihood that she would reenact—within her marriage and with her own children—those charged issues which had never been confronted or resolved. Had she, in other words, been able to separate more adequately from her mother, she would not have had to *become* her—the tough lady married to the nice, passive man.

As clinician Paulina McCullough writes, "In many instances, individuals [who have cut themselves off] fail to see the connection between unfinished business with the family of origin and current life crises. . . . [These] individuals deal with emotional fusion, i.e., inability to develop a strong sense of identity, by artificially separating from the family. But the underlying pull toward fusion is still there."

Kathleen's way of dealing with the passions of the Family Romance had been that of leaving hastily and slamming the door behind her. But what was present, if unaccounted for, were the remorseful feelings inside her and the yearning for the good things of the past—the deep affection for her mother, for example—which she had had to leave out of the emotional suitcase that she had carried forward with her on her life's journey.

No Longer a Woman

It was during a conversation about the Catholic faith of her childhood that the topic of Kathleen's hysterectomy emerged; the linking word between the two subjects was "blood." Protestantism was, Kathleen had been saying, a colder, less mysterious, even "bloodless" kind of religion when compared with Catholicism—the religion which she'd left behind, when she'd married Philip and toward which her thoughts now yearningly inclined.

The mention of "blood," for some reason, brought the scene she'd described earlier—her mother, hemorrhaging after that disastrous delivery—to my mind. I said so to Kathleen, and for reasons equally mysterious to me, I asked her if the word "blood" brought any associations from *her own life* to her.

For a few minutes Kathleen did not respond; she simply sat there, staring, looking either frightened or embarrassed—I wasn't sure which. At last, in a low voice, she acknowledged that the word *did* evoke a particular train of thought: It reminded her of the hysterectomy which she'd had, about four or five years earlier, which had been preceded by episodes of copious bleeding.

"I wasn't having ordinary menstrual periods before the operation," she explained, "but a huge, torrential blood flow—almost like hemorrhaging—that just couldn't be stopped." Surgery had been advised, and she had been sensible about following that advice, but to her own surprise her reaction to the procedure had been overwhelming—traumatic. "It was a huge, huge issue for me," she shrugged briefly, swallowed, "and I hadn't anticipated that it would be. Because I had had my children, and . . ." Her words trailed off; she shook her head, shrugged once again.

"And were you able to connect, emotionally, with Philip," I asked her, in a low, careful tone, "about the ways you were feeling at that time?" He stirred in his seat at that moment, shifted his position, then leaned toward her as if to be the first to hear her reply.

She shook her head in the negative. "I was feeling very . . . ah . . . defeminized, desexualized—as if I were no longer a *woman* somehow. And I don't think that he understood what I was going through or what it meant to me, at all . . ." She hesitated, as if embarrassed, then admitted with a shamefaced smile, "For two years after that if I so much as picked up a newborn baby my eyes would get all filled up." She shrugged, a shrug meant to indicate that she was now perfectly able to be objective and rational about the hysterectomy, even somewhat bemused by the degree of despair and suffering that the loss of her uterus had caused her.

ATTEMPTED SOLUTIONS

Kathleen had, it occurred to me, suffered what she had experienced as a horrible assault upon her femininity during roughly that same period of their lives when Philip had been struggling, and failing, in his efforts to secure the congressional nomination. She had felt profoundly dewomanized at a time when Philip, too, was suffering a decisive setback—in terms of recognizing that the dream for which he had put his entire career at risk would probably never be realized.

He had been, moreover, not only the loser in an election; he had, in the wake of that political bid, been completely out of work for a while. At a time when she saw herself failing as a female, he must have seen himself failing as a male, and neither one of them, it seemed, had been able to give or receive comfort or nurturance from the other. Instead, each partner's efforts to deal with his or her own individual difficulties had become the difficulties in the marriage itself.

For as Kathleen pursued her husband for reassurances (of his affection for her and of her attractiveness and femininity), he was retreating to seek some space of his own, some personal territory over which he could take command and for which he could assume responsibility. Feeling disabled, after his defeat, he perceived closeness to her as potentially overwhelming to him in the same ways that it had been overwhelming for his father.

She, in turn, had responded by intensifying her efforts to draw nearer, and he had reacted by running even faster and farther away. A clinical observation, oft repeated in the marital and family therapy literature, is that the attempted "solutions" to problems frequently become the problems themselves.

AN INTERNAL SCRIPT OF HER OWN?

Kathleen had, in the wake of that hysterectomy, felt "unwomanned" and experienced herself as utterly defeminized. Her own mother, many years earlier, had nearly bled to death and been ill for a long time after having tried to give birth to that forbidden, much desired male child.

Perhaps her mother had even (it was not at all unlikely) had a hysterectomy at that time herself. In any event, she had—when it came to the crucial matter of fertility—been clearly disqualified, dropped out of the race entirely. And her daughter had, at that point, stepped in to take her parent's place. Kathleen was not only responsible for the daily running of the household; she was, at age thirteen, just entering the garden of fecundity as her mother was being ushered out the exit.

What had the relationship *between her parents* been like, I wondered, at that terrible period of their lives? Had her father, in his own disappointment, subtly devalued her mother for having failed to produce the wanted son? Had he, because of his lonesomeness and wish for a healthy partner, become seductive in his behavior toward his daughters? Or had there been an outside relationship, one of those family secrets that everyone *knows* unconsciously yet no one really knows about, that he had become involved in as a way of finding a separate solace of his own?

I thought of the "torrents of blood"—the mother's blood and that of the daughter as well. Kathleen had, after her own hysterectomy, been *with her mother* in fantasy. She had, that is, been with those helpless, sick and vulnerable aspects of her mother which had hitherto been so vehemently denied. It was, it seemed to me, not unlikely that at that juncture all of the painful, suppressed feelings of guilt—about having deserted her mother at the dawn of her own adult life—had emerged. For the first time it occurred to me that she herself, in the trancelike way in which such family scenarios are restaged, might have been behaving in ways that would get a familiar dramatic action into motion.

To be in the same situation as her mother's—that of the abandoned person—was a way of paying off that internalized emotional debt and of being *as one* with her lost mother as well. Was it possible that Kathleen, perhaps by behaving superjealously, had been subtly encouraging Philip to act out his part in an internal script of her own? She had begun to accuse him, in the wake of that hysterectomy, of not loving her or caring about her. But had "Don't love me!" been her actual, unspoken command?

A DAUGHTER'S RATIONALIZATION

Glancing down at the Currans' side of the genogram, I noted that her father (John) had survived her mother (Marguerite) for a period of more than a decade. Had he ever remarried? I asked Kathleen, and she blinked several times, then replied shortly, "Yes. He married three months after my mother died."

My eyebrows shot up; three months were, it seemed to me, an extremely short time for mourning a long and devoted relationship—especially considering that her father would have had to spend some time courting his new wife in advance of his having married her! How, I inquired carefully, had she and her sisters felt about their father having remarried that rapidly?

"I can't really speak for my sisters," Kathleen answered. "I can only speak for myself. And I thought—I felt—that in many ways it was both a compliment to my mother and a measure of his loneliness; he could not live alone." Her voice was tender and soft.

It was a daughter's rationalization. For, stuck as she was in her original family, she would always see her father as the quintessentially good, "nice" parent and her mother as the bad one, the one who was strong, demanding and tyrannical. The polarized system that had been established in Kathleen's marriage was the one that existed in her mind. In a healthier system, she could have perceived the good and the bad in *both* her parents—and the good and the bad in herself and in her spouse.

THE FAMILIAR INTERNAL BLUEPRINT

Kathleen's fantasy was that she would, like her mother, become incapacitated and disqualified as an attractive, sexual female. Philip's fantasy was that if he stayed in the marriage, he would, like his father, develop heart disease and be disabled until the end of his days. They were working in a tradition that was familiar to both of them, one involving the dominant (bad) female and the submissive (good) male.

The notion that a woman might be strong *and* good or that a man might be passive *and* bad was one that had apparently not occurred to either one of them; it simply did not correspond to the internal blueprint with which the pair of them were familiar. In an intimate system such as the one the Gardiners had created, the way it *is* tends to be remarkably similar to the way it always *has been*.

Their marriage was, in some important sense, a mutually defensive arrangement; they interacted in ways that protected each of them from ever having to deal with difficulties stemming from within. Kathleen and Philip were colluding to see, in each other, disavowed and projected aspects of their own inner realities. What each perceived, *in the intimate other*, were parts of the self from which he or she was completely dissociated. What was being played out, in the relational system they shared, were the unresolved conflicts that neither one had been able to deal with separately.

Both of them were, in some important sense, *shielding* each other from ever having to fully confront the painful inner dilemmas with which both of them were struggling. Each partner embodied and contained, *for the mate*, repudiated and disclaimed aspects of that mate's internal being. It was by means of this mutual trade-off of disowned feelings and qualities that both were desperately attempting to master—by reenactment and repetition of problematic issues—the individual dilemmas that they had brought forward into the relationship from their own experiences in their families of origin.

THE PACT

The result was, however, that the emotional sewage which neither spouse could process was being dumped into the relationship they shared. Philip's own conflict, which actually existed *within him*, had to do with the archaic figures of an overwhelmed man and a powerful woman who had to be placated. One-half of this conflict had been acknowledged as his own—that of the good but disqualified male—but the other half was being enacted by Kathleen. She filled the role, *for him*, of the emotionally dominating caretaker who was in control, made the decisions, and filled the emptiness inside him.

He perceived her as demanding and purposeful while experiencing himself as overwhelmed by her strength and sense of certainty. What he did not seem to recognize was their mutual complicity and, above all, *his own need to have her behave in that way*. One partner cannot possibly assume the major portion of the relationship's power, burdens and responsibilities unless the other partner has *allowed* (or even urged) that situation to develop.

What Philip *could* readily recognize in his wife were the qualities of strength, assertiveness, and anger which he could not connect to as existing within his own self. These less "pleasing," less accommodating components of his internal world were split off, repressed, projected onto Kathleen, who—in accepting his projection—became ever stronger, more competent and more responsible.

Overburdened, she had become more critical and demanding as well. She could still, nevertheless, be depended upon to express enough assertiveness and anger for the pair of them, and Philip could condemn, in her, qualities that did not exist (to his knowledge) in himself. So long as she carried the aggression for the two of them, he was at liberty to be the kind, good, mediating nice guy that his father had been—and thus continue working on the still-unsettled original conflict.

That conflict was not, of course, something that he himself perceived as an ongoing struggle inside his own head—a struggle involving the passive, weaker man and the stronger, more emotional and active woman—but as a simmering battle between himself and Kathleen. Their collusive arrangement thus protected him against ever having to take conscious ownership of those parts of himself which actually might have been assertive or even frankly aggressive—might have been, that is, if it were ever possible for so nice and accommodating a man to feel deep feelings of rage.

Had he been able to experience his anger Philip would, I suspected, have gotten in touch with suppressed and painful material against which the emotional fusion with Kathleen defended him. He would, had he been able to accept his hostile feelings as something within himself and belonging to him, have gotten beyond his more readily accessible criticisms of his mother and begun to deal with how furious at his father he actually did feel.

Angry at his father for failing in his own career aspirations, for being ill and inadequate, for not taking leadership—for not showing his son how to grow up to be a man. The young Philip Gardiner had, in a very real sense, been abandoned, left to blunder his way toward masculine adulthood as well as he could, while his working model for manhood withdrew into the devitalized world of his illness and allowed himself to be "suffocated" to death.

An Ongoing Cycle of Behavior

If there was any anger in the world it was not, however, in Philip but in Kathleen. In the relationship with her he could carry on his father's struggle and try—and try again and again—to rewrite the story of his parent's life. If he could triumph where his dad had not, he would have rewritten history and made his father into the kind of parent that he had always wanted him to become. By struggling to restage the family script in the present, he was attempting to magically alter the script of the past.

In reality, of course, the only thing that can be changed in the present is the present itself. But so long as Kathleen continued to assume the role of the assertive, demanding partner, he could see himself as her polar opposite: a completely nonangry and nonaggressive person, as his good father had been. With her assistance, he could perceive his inner conflict as something that was external to himself (creating, by the way, the illusion that he could escape it by escaping *her*).

Kathleen, in turn, by becoming the marine sergeant of the household, protected her husband from any conscious awareness of his rageful emotions and permitted his internalized conflict to be acted out between them. She dominated him in the fashion that he required; it was easy, moreover, for her to become superresponsible and competent enough for the pair of them.

She had, after all, been a "parentified" child. If it was necessary to sacrifice her own human needs, weaknesses and vulnerabilities in order to be in this relationship, this was something that Kathleen was experienced at doing. Her life had taught her all that she needed to know about how to give up her childish dependencies and her natural wishes for nurturance and support.

There existed, within her, no internal prohibitions against such things as self-assertion, taking responsibility, experiencing and expressing negative emotions. She could (unlike her partner) readily tolerate her competence as a legitimate aspect of her inner reality and her outward behavior. But what Kathleen could not acknowledge, as aspects of her internal universe, were feelings of helplessness, inadequacy, uncertainty.

Although such feelings were inside her—and inescapable—they had been suppressed as completely as possible, hustled out of consciousness's sight. To make contact with her vulnerability would have been, for her, almost inexpressibly threatening and painful, for it would have exposed her to those parts of herself which were identified with a mother who had been helpless, ill and defective (not "one tough lady" in the slightest).

To be soft or weak in any way, like the sick woman who had needed her, was intolerable. Clearly, integrating these more fragile, ill aspects of her mother into her own emerging feminine identity had been too terrifying a task for the growing daughter to contemplate—so these weaker, more vulnerable components of the maternal model had been thoroughly denied and disclaimed. Neediness, frailty, dependency, and the like were parts of Kathleen's internal world which she could not recognize as *being* there.

She could not see them in herself, but she could very readily see them as they became manifest in Philip. Kathleen had, in adapting to the circumstances of her life and developing her feminine identity, integrated only those qualities of her mother's which were commanding, tough and in charge. Her intimate partner could, however, express all of the denied feelings of powerlessness, uncertainty and ineffectiveness for the relationship system as a whole.

Just as he allowed her to handle, for him, his assertiveness and his anger, she allowed him to handle, for her, the feelings of inadequacy and vulnerability which she could not consciously connect to and acknowledge. As part of their marital quid pro quo, he carried the emotional system's weakness, incompetence, irresponsibility—and its goodness and lightheartedness as well. She carried its strength, its sternness, its responsibilities, its burdens—and also its sense of limits and the ways in which those limits needed to be met.

She bemoaned, in him, the inadequacies and lack of certitude that were so thoroughly absent in herself, while he objected to her bossiness and invasiveness. Who could say, though, whether Philip Gardiner behaved irresponsibly in order to make his wife take over more of the burdens or whether Kathleen Gardiner took control and made the decisions because he was so unsure and tended to handle things so halfheartedly or badly?

The pair of them were in an ongoing cycle of behavior, in which she did what she did because he did what he did, because she did what she did, and so on ad infinitum. In a way, once such a system is in motion, what got it started doesn't matter so much as does the manner in which the partners interact in order to perpetuate it and ensure that system's survival. In intimate systems such as that of the Gardiners, one very basic rule is that each member of the couple must *forgo being different* in any way from the other person's projections. To change, grow or mature—given that each mate is responsible for containing and expressing denied feelings and attributes of the spouse—is to shirk one's job and to threaten the very basis of the relationship itself.

THE COLLUSIVE BOND

Changing is, indeed, a form of betrayal. It asserts one partner's essential *differentness* from the vision in the other partner's head. This is why, in collusive marital systems, one spouse's effort to change will generally be blocked by the other or met with a rapid compensatory move directed toward restoring the system's customary equilibrium and balance.

Had Kathleen, for instance, begun acting much less assertively and responsibly, Philip would have responded to her changed behavior in a semiautomatic fashion. He would have acted more uncertain and inadequate than ever in order to force her back into the "powerful" position that he needed to have her occupy. (He was, by the way, very powerful indeed when it came to *keeping* her there!)

And similarly, should he have begun to behave more forcefully and decisively, his wife would have tried to trip him in a minute—to gainsay him by knowing better, getting stronger and more commanding than ever. Just as he needed to see his assertiveness and anger expressed by her, so she needed to make contact with her vulnerability and uncertainty secondhand, as she recognized them in the behavior of her husband.

Collusive relationships are, write Ellen Berman, M.D., Harold Lief, M.D., and Ann Marie Williams, Ph.D., "generally tightly bonded, even if highly unpleasant, each one needing the other to carry the disavowed elements of the personality. The pain is caused by the conscious perception of the partner as oppositional, ungiving, 'impossible,' in spite of the unconscious collusion."

Marriages, suggest these authors, are indeed different from other relationships; a person's behavior can be far more irrational within the marital system than it ever is outside it. The concept of collusion goes a long way, they assert, toward explaining why this is the case: "[O]nly in the marriage does the person choose one polarized half of the conflict to act out while projecting the other half. It is important to recognize that most people do not project the same internal conflict on everyone, but only on the person with whom one allows oneself to be intimate." The closer we get to another being, the more of our craziness—by which is meant our unresolved internal conflict—is liable to surface in the relationship that develops.

THE COLLUSIVE WAY OF LOVING

We humans all do, when it comes to the question of loving, come face-to-face with certain fundamental questions: What should *happen* in relationships, and what are they all about? What, for instance, is my obligation to my partner? Is it my responsibility to do everything I can (at a conscious and unconscious level) to save him from his painful, irreconcilable inner conflicts, even if he brought those conflicts into the relationship and they have little or nothing to do with me?

It is here that, broadly speaking, two very dissimilar options for being in a marriage present themselves. They are radically *different* ways of being in an intimate attachment, not only in the manner in which they are lived out but in their implications for the future growth and development of each member of the pair.

As a partner in the first, less healthy and less flexible kind of system, I would indeed feel obligated—as part of my understanding of what love is and as a way of earning the love of my spouse—to protect him from the pain of his unresolved dilemma by carrying one side of his inner conflict for him. If, for instance, he could not experience and take ownership of his angry feelings, I might make myself responsible for expressing enough anger for the pair of us. This would happen, it must be added, in a quid pro quo fashion, for collusion *always involves an exchange, a two-way arrangement*.

While each of us, by scratching each other's back in this manner, might seemed to have solved our individual problems, the costs of our "solution" would be enormous. For by entering into this unconscious deal, we would have decreed that (a) our original dilemmas had to be reenacted in the marriage and (b) they could never be resolved. How *could* our individual conflicts be settled in the relationship, given that they had not originated there?

Caught, however, in the ongoing effort to change the past in the present, I could eternally strive—and never recognize that I was striving for the impossible. That, no matter how doggedly I might struggle, I could never make my father and/or my mother into the people I wish they'd been by attempting to change the personality or behavior of my spouse.

ANOTHER WAY OF LOVING

A very different and much healthier style of loving is predicated on the assumption that loving does not require me to carry one side of my partner's unresolvable dilemmas, but to respect his right to handle his dilemmas in his own way, as best he can. I can empathize with him, sympathize with him, support him in his efforts to deal with his problems and difficulties. But loving *precludes* my trying to take over any part of his inner pain and assuming that he cannot handle it by himself.

In this kind of emotional system, each of us is left free to struggle with his or her own individual, difficult, seemingly irreconcilable internal dilemmas, but to do so in relationship to a mate who honors the legitimacy of the pain and who does not confound the partner's problems with his own. It is out of this mutual acceptance of each person's right to deal with *what is genuinely his or her own* that resolution of their separate conflicts may eventually come—but not at the cost of the relationship.

I may, for example, sympathize with my spouse's difficulties in acknowledging his feelings of anger, but I need not help him out by being angry *for* him. And he, in turn, will not be tempted to flee the marriage because he is so dismayed and offended by the rage which he perceives as mine, and *in me*, but which I am compelled to express for the pair of us.

No one of us, to be sure, grows up in that perfect environment in which we have learned to love in the healthiest, most satisfying fashion. We all have, at some point along life's way, been confronted with very different notions of what being in a "truly loving" relationshp is all about. Many of us have, in the context of our early experiences, come to believe that we must take on the internal suffering of our intimates. Philip Gardiner was a man who understood what loving meant in this way.

Instead, therefore, of permitting his wife to struggle with the apparently unresolvable dilemma of how a person can be strong and weak at the same time, he had taken on the weakness *for her*. And Kathleen, instead of allowing her husband to struggle with the issue of how you can be a nice guy and enraged at the same time, had agreed to carry the disavowed part of his conflict *for him*. They were loving in the only way they knew how to love; this, for them, was what being in an intimate relationship was all about.

But the other possibility—the second way of loving—was one that neither one of them had been lucky enough to have lived in, tasted, felt, seen, or ever even become aware of. It was a different way of being in a relationship, entirely, one in which "loving" meant recognizing the separateness of the partner and his right to carry the pain and conflict which belonged to him and for which he alone was responsible.

WAITING

Philip, as the weeks passed, seemed disinclined to give up on the relationship but equally uncertain about returning. Kathleen felt, she told me ruefully, as if she were "twisting slowly, slowly in the wind," waiting for her fate to be decided. She was, nevertheless, discovering herself to be a far less "unidimensional" person than she had ever realized earlier. "Philip was the nurturer in our family, the loving one, while I was in the role of the disciplinarian. But what I can see now is that—even though I'm still the disciplinarian—my children love me. I guess I didn't see, when Philip was living here with us, that they really *did* love me. . . ." What she was discovering, she added, was that it was possible to be nurturant and close to her children while taking charge and setting rules simultaneously.

Before the separation, explained Kathleen (during an interview at which just the two of us were present), she had been concerned about whether or not she was, overall, a good person. "I have," she said, "grown up mostly thinking I'm a bad person, because the character attributes ascribed to me by my family—and by Philip—have always seemed to have negative connotations."

What, exactly, *were* those character attributes? I asked her.

"My mother." She squinted thoughtfully, as if gazing into the past. "You're 'the just one,' she used to say. That's a *hard* word."

"Just?" I smiled. "Why is that a hard word?" She didn't smile back, but burst out with "Because justice is blind, stern, not *joyful!* It has," she added confusedly, "none of the quality of mercy that I would like . . ." Her sentence drifted off, ended there.

"Did your mother feel that you were passing judgment on her?" I asked Kathleen finally.

"Oh, I'm sure she *did*, when she said that." She sighed, shrugged. "But my mother thought, or at least she always said, 'You're the just one.' Because if ever there was a quarrel between my father and my sisters or between my sisters, she knew she would get an evenhanded presentation of the situation by asking *me* about it."

I looked at her questioningly, shook my head. "It sounds as if she had a very *high* regard and respect for you. I don't hear this as a negative characterization. . . ."

"That may be. I think that's true. But," she spoke so quietly that it was almost hard to hear her, "there's no *softness* there." Was Kathleen saying, I wondered, that it was a word that had no femininity associated with it? Aloud, I asked, "Do you mean that too much power was laid upon your doorstep?"

"Yes," she nodded, "power, assertiveness—"

"Control," I added, nodding my own head in agreement.

"Control, aggression," she continued, "all *hard* . . . Philip used to say, 'I love you because you are so strong,' " she reported, with a note of bitterness in her voice. "All nonfeminine virtues anyway. I have never had a feminine virtue attributed to me—except lately. Lately, I've come in for—" She stopped, laughed a pleased little laugh. "I've had compliments," she said suddenly. "I feel—you know—*pretty* for the first time in my life, the first time I can ever remember."

A Beachhead of Autonomy

Philip, when I spoke with him alone, was ambivalently unwilling to return to his wife and family and still very intensely involved with them. "There was an extremely long period during which I became slowly aware of what was happening—that led up to what I would call the 'suffocation,' " he told me. "And I believe that both of us would have to know ourselves much, *much* better before we could avoid falling into our old, old patterns of being together again. I'm not comfortable, at this point, about that. I can't say that I could stop myself from going down that slippery slide and becoming—" He stopped, but I knew that the word he meant to say was "overwhelmed."

A moment later, he said it himself. "When I think about going back, I am afraid. I get afraid of being overwhelmed, and so I say to myself, '*Don't.*' All that I know is that I feel, at this moment, better about myself. I don't feel better about the relationship, and there's a lot regarding the children that I feel rotten and dirty about. But when I think about going back into the marriage—which I *do think about* . . . a lot—I get scared.

"I felt, for a long time, before moving out," he went on, "as if I weren't a—a valid person, and that's not something I ever want to feel again. It may be what my father wanted, but I don't want to be *him*." I nodded, told him that I knew that that was the battle he was fighting. But he was, I added, not necessarily fighting it in the best way—by jumping out of the relationship entirely rather than attempting to negotiate his way out of the position in which he found himself now.

He feared he could not hold his own in a negotiation. "If I start to give in and get close to Kathleen, then my desire to stay close will grow, and I will give up things to *get* closer and to *be* closer, and the same things will start happening again." His worry was that if he started getting intimate with his wife once again, his small beachhead of autonomy would be eroded immediately. If he could not return to the marriage, though, neither could Philip leave it entirely.

CHANGING PARTNERS

That the Gardiners were deeply involved with one another was not a question in my mind. During the course of the interviews, there was so much laughter, so much concern, so much intense caring as each listened to the life tale being told by the other. There was something extremely *juicy* about them! Kathleen described, at one point, a hike they had taken in the company of another couple. She and Philip had gotten to feeling intensely romantic and had managed to lose their friends for a while, sneak off behind some bushes and make passionate love to one another.

Was it really going to end after so much shared time and history together?

I myself didn't think so. And as our series of conversations drew to a close, I was not completely surprised to hear Philip's announcement that he was ready to undertake marital treatment after all. He was, it seemed to me, highly invested in the relationship, but afraid that if he returned too soon it would be business as usual and nothing between them would really have changed. The move toward therapy was a move in the homeward direction, and I'll admit that when I left them, it was with high hopes that they would work it out.

But in this I was mistaken. A year later, the Gardiners were separated and Philip was living with someone else. When I met with him, he seemed relaxed, more confident; his business was prospering and his personal life was going well. But he was, he told me, worried about the fact that many of the same things were happening in *this* relationship as had happened in the relationship with Kathleen. He had changed partners; but the conflict within him was unchanged, and so this dyadic dance could not be very different from the last one. A strong woman, to take charge of his life for him, was what he wanted—and what he found completely unbearable.

PART VI

THE POSTPARENTING PHASE:

Reintegration

18
Marital Fighting

The Sternbergs, in their late forties at the time of our interviews, were an attractive, youthful-looking pair. David was a tall, lanky man, with large features; he wore his dark hair combed directly back from his forehead, and there were strands of gray at his temples. Nancy, small-boned and slender, had an aquiline nose, large gray-blue eyes and a cap of curly blond ringlets. Both were Jewish, and they lived in a long, low brick-and-wood ranch-style house in the town of Westport, Connecticut.

David, a dynamic, extremely successful businessmen, owned a thriving firm which dealt in a variety of industrial commodities. It was a business that he had started on his own, with his savings and a loan from his father. Nancy was a medical researcher, who worked (part-time) at a major university-affiliated hospital; she also took an active role in the family business.

"I do the billing, the books, the accounting," she said. "And I do some of the labeling, and a great many of the errands, as well. I am actually a fifty percent owner," she added, "and my office is in the bedroom." She laughed, wagged her thumb in her husband's direction. "He gets to sleep with the secretary!"

The Sternbergs were the parents of three children: Jeffrey, twenty-five, now teaching at a prep school in Massachusetts; Carol, twenty-two, who was working at the Justice Department, in Washington, D.C.; and James, twenty, a junior at Yale University.

There was an aura of contentment, warmth, and intense mutual interest that seemed to surround Nancy and David throughout our conversations. Both of them felt, they said, as if they had succeeded in recapturing a former sense of closeness, of the goodness and worth of the partner and of the relationship, that had been nowhere in sight during that phase of family life when they were parenting their three very young children.

"I knew I loved him," explained Nancy, "and yet I had kids who needed me—*our* kids—and he was being mean to them, *crazily* mean, especially to our oldest son, Jeff. Once, when Jeff was five or six, he was sitting on David's lap and he kicked his daddy's shin by mistake. David got furious, threw Jeff down on the floor and started whacking him. It was—I don't know—it was all totally *irrational*. I really hoped that God would strike my husband dead at that time." But that had been, she added quickly, the "low point of our marriage." She felt as if they were different people, in a different relationship, now.

"I don't know how I could have been that stupid." David's voice was subdued, and he avoided meeting my gaze. "It was plain *stupidity* on my part," he repeated, with pain and regret in his expression. Even now, he said, he could not fully comprehend why he had responded to his eldest son in the antagonistic ways that he had. "Maybe it was because I thought Jeff was brighter than I am—he's enormously intelligent, and that was clear from the outset. Maybe he was more beautiful, with his blond curls? I don't know; I try, but I still can't explain it myself."

But what he did know, David admitted, was that he had wanted his wife's attention, and her love, and had had a sense that their child was taking these things from him. "I didn't realize, at the time that her love for him and her love for me were different—as different as apples and cheesecake." He smiled, looked shamefaced, cleared his throat and repeated that it was hard for him to believe he had ever behaved so jealously and demandingly.

But he had been, then, a man on the run—a man caught in a frantic, deadly competition with his own father. "I was a Jewish boy, well educated and from a wealthy family, and I was going to work hard, have a big home, have it all—I was going to be a millionaire."

"And most important of all," put in his wife, "he was going to show his father just how *successful* a guy he could be!"

"Yes," admitted David, "if my father were here"—he gestured with his hand, held horizontally in front of him just above eye level—"then I was going to be up *here*." His hand shot up a couple of feet. "I was going to be *more* than he was! If he had one, I was going to have two; if he had two, then I would have four; I was going to have the whole thing." He shrugged dismissively, but there was an angry energy in his voice.

Nancy had certainly heard it. "David was," she explained, "a totally driven person at that time. I couldn't understand why he was doing all of these things so frantically. He wasn't going after anything that I wanted; I'm not a materialistic person. I don't care about clothes, clubs, that kind of thing. But there he was, working three jobs, and really mean—*mean*, sometimes, to be around. Nasty to the kids and not someone it was easy to live with."

"I didn't think of myself as mean," interposed David at once. "I perceived myself entirely differently—as a good person, very harassed, yet doing his best for his family's welfare." He shook his head again. He had not realized, he added, how unhappy he really *was* at that time and how incompatible were his beliefs about himself—that he was a just and fair individual, who was struggling to create a good life for his wife and his children—with the ways in which he was actually behaving.

What had slowed David Sternberg down, and forced him to the sidelines, was an early heart attack. Not until then, he acknowledged, had he stopped to confront himself and think about the things he was doing. "I began, when I was lying there recuperating, to see myself as someone completely different from the person I'd imagined I was. And when I looked in that mirror and really saw who was there, I said to myself, 'Holy crow, you're not the person I thought you were!' There was somebody else standing there! And he wasn't such a good person after all. . . . I was making everyone around me completely miserable."

He paused momentarily, then leaned toward me as if to make certain that I would hear every word that he said. "I understood, for the first time, that I wasn't getting the value out of life that I believed would be there when I was younger—when I was twenty-two or twenty-three and fell in love with Nancy, whom I still love very much now. That I was doing things, in my relationships with her and with the kids, that I could see were not good—senseless, in fact, not for me." He had realized, added David, that he was making some big mistakes, but he had not, at that juncture of his life, had the faintest notion about how he might work on correcting them.

"WHY ARE WE FIGHTING?"

It was not until the time of their eldest son Jeffrey's departure for college—some seven years before our interviews and a full decade after David's heart attack—that a major crisis in the Sternbergs' relationship had erupted. Jeff had, for many years, been the couple's "problem child," but now, without *his* difficulties to focus upon, they'd come face-to-face with some of their own. "The two of us began having tremendous quarrels around the time of Jeff's going away," Nancy said. "David got so hypersensitive and irritable. It was just about impossible for me to disagree with him about *anything*—no matter how trivial—without sending him into a towering rage."

I turned to her husband, began asking him the obvious questions: Did this behavior resemble behavior that he had seen in his own original family? Had one or both parents, for instance, been in a state of simmering anger a lot of the time? He was nodding his agreement even as I asked the questions, an ironic expression playing around the sides of his lips.

His father, who had died recently, had been an extremely tense and combative man, according to David. His own behavior, he went on to say, "bore some similarities" to that of his parent. But, he added, he could not compare his relationship with his own wife to the one that his parents had shared; there were some important differences. His father had been much more explosive than he was, and his mother had never fought back. Nancy *did*.

"Right," she put in immediately, "I did, and it was just *awful*. But we weren't really able to get anywhere in terms of sorting things out. The two of us were not, at that time, capable of confronting each other—of putting our issues on the table, knowing what they *were*, trying to negotiate them, work them out. . . . We'd been deflecting them, for so long, into the fights about Jeffrey. We'd been *using* Jeff, and he was playing right into it. He was, as I now know, trying to protect us by keeping the heat off the problems *we* were having and on him and his problems instead."

The three of them had been locked in an emotional triangle, but then one arm of that triangle had gone away to college. The system, in the absence of the parents' major means of dealing with their own anxieties, had gone out of kilter and become thoroughly disequilibrated. For if the pair of them were not fighting about Jeffrey's problems, they were at liberty to fight about the problems *between them*. The tensions in the household had, according to Nancy, escalated to a height they had never reached before.

"We were left, the two of us, and the younger children were still at home then, too. Carol was in tenth grade, James only in eighth, and suddenly—what happened?" She put the question to me rhetorically. "We were picking on *them*," she said, supplying the correct answer herself. "I saw it happening, and it was so *clear*: that we were using the other kids, whom we had never used in this way before!" Nancy looked aghast.

She resumed, after a moment's pause. "Our daughter was a high school sophomore at that time, and there was always an—oh, an electric inter-action between herself and her father. Carol is independent and bright and has a mind of her own, and she *knows* what she's about. . . . She's just a very dynamic young woman, and I think David has a problem with women like that. He's attracted to them, and he'd never like a woman who was a simp or clingy, but he still gets aggravated—and I don't know, the pair of us started picking on her. And we started picking on *James!*" She hit the side of her temple, with her hand, as if to underscore the fact that what they'd begun doing was the impossible and incredible.

"*James*, who is the most lovable, adorable kid you would ever want to meet! He's a wonderful person, and there's hardly anything about him to pick on!" Then she shrugged, amended that statement. "Well, he has a messy room, and wasn't doing all of his homework—"

"But," agreed David, "nobody was noticing it until *then*. Now, all of a sudden, here were the other kids getting caught in the system—triangulated in. And Nancy—she realized that something weird was happening, and she told me that she thought we had to go and see someone, get some help with our problems. . . ." His voice trailed off, but he added, almost as an afterthought, "I was very reluctant; I didn't like the idea."

He stopped speaking, fixed his gaze upon his wife who, after a few moments, took up the tale. The situation had, said Nancy, deteriorated to a point at which she'd felt it necessary to go to David with a choice: He could either come with her to see a therapist or she was going to leave him. "I said," her voice trembled slightly as she spoke, " 'I *know* that our life can be better! I love you. You love me. We have a whole wonderful background of living together all these years, and a solid foundation, in terms of the commitment we've made to each other. But we *fight* all the time.' "

Their life together, in the wake of Jeff's leaving for college, had become completely untenable. The entire atmosphere was suffused with a poisonous anxiety, which the smallest match of some apparently innocuous comment could cause to explode at any moment. "Some small incident would happen," recounted Nancy, her eyes wide with fear at the recollection, "and it would turn into an incident that was big enough and important enough to destroy an entire weekend."

They cared about each other, but could not stop the fighting, nor could they begin to comprehend what the quarreling was actually about.

FUNCTIONAL AND DYSFUNCTIONAL QUARRELS

According to psychiatrist Larry B. Feldman, M.D., *the central psychodynamic issue that underlies destructive marital conflict is the wounded or impaired self-esteem of both members of the couple.* "[N]arcissistic vulnerability is," writes Dr. Feldman, "at the core of all or most conflictual marriages [and] the degree of each spouse's vulnerability is approximately the same, even though the surface manifestations may be quite different."

Thus, while one partner may *appear to be* far healthier and more competent than the other, differences at the superficial level conceal deeper, underlying similarities. Both are struggling, suggests Feldman, to maintain a sense of self-esteem which is, at best, precarious.

What are the distinctions between arguments that are "functional" and those which are "dysfunctional" in nature? In a "functional" marital quarrel (or any quarrel!), the basic issues being disagreed about can be identified in fairly specific ways. They are not lost to sight, impossible to recognize, because they have become diluted and distorted in a host of vague and global overgeneralizations. In other words, the difference is between the clear communication of a particular problem—for example, "I want you to be responsible for taking out the garbage"—and a broad, diffuse accusation, such as "You never help me; you think only about yourself!"

Statements which begin with "You never" or "You always" are usually ones that generate far more heat than they do illumination. The actual difficulties cannot be clarified when they are being buried under a slag heap of wide-ranging, irrelevant denunications.

Good, productive quarrels contain a minimum of this kind of windy grandstanding—or at least the great declamations are limited to the time when the fight is just breaking out.

In a constructive fight, each opponent listens *actively* to the other person's point of view. He doesn't, that is, merely sit there waiting for the partner to finish what she is saying so that his own complaint can be lodged. For when that happens, as Dr. Feldman notes, the pair are involved in "cross-complaining"—each spouse is talking *at* the other yet completely unable to take in what the other is saying.

Clearly, if neither person is able to receive the partner's messages, the chances of identifying the difficulties—let alone negotiating change—become hazy and unlikely indeed. Expressing one's own feelings, but being incapable of listening, is a dysfunctional way of being in a fight. So, *by definition*, is getting into any quarrel which involves physical violence of any sort—whether it be slapping, kicking, throwing things, breaking a chair, smashing a window, or indeed merely *threatening* to hit the partner.

Behavior of this kind is fundamentally unhealthy and counterproductive, as is fighting that involves verbal abuse along the lines of namecalling and character assassination ("You slimy drunk!"; "You ass kisser!"; "You're an even bigger bitch than your mother!"; and the like).

Intimate partners who revile each other in these ways and/or mistreat each other physically may fight on and on until they fall over, exhausted—but when they do, the difficulties are not much closer to being resolved. The atmosphere, in the wake of the storm, is as thick and heavy as it was during the period when the tensions between the couple were building to a climax.

The squall (or hurricane) is over, but the marital weather is the same—not surprisingly. For positive changes cannot be negotiated when neither partner has been capable of stating his own position clearly or, for that matter, discovering what the other person's position might be—that is, talking and listening effectively.

Sometimes, it should be mentioned, a modified version of task one (see Chapter Eleven, "Tasks") can be immensely useful in helping to turn a destructive conflict into one that is productive and leads to positive change. In this version of the exercise, adapted for the purpose at hand, a quarrel that appears to be going nowhere is interrupted with a cease-fire in place, and the partners take on the roles of talker and listener in the manner described in Chapter Eleven. The first speaker takes fifteen minutes to explain his subjective experience and understanding of what is happening while the spouse hears his or her case *without interrupting*; then, as in the original task, the speaker and the listener switch places.

Most quarrels, however fierce and bitter, will have real difficulty surviving this kind of treatment intact. For what is being promoted is healthy dialogue—the clarification of the basic disagreements by two separate people who, being different, naturally see the matter in different ways.

FIGHTING THE GOOD FIGHT

The good fight is one which ends with enhanced understanding, mutually negotiated compromise and realistic movement in the direction of the difficulty's resolution. The bad, dysfunctional fight is one in which the couple engages, in an ongoing fashion, without ever resolving anything. This kind of conflict can, like the most brutal kind of indoor sport, result in psychological or even physical injuries, but the game never reaches its ending. For each partner feels narcissistically wounded by the other's cruel, rejecting behavior.

There is, clearly, no human being whose self-esteem is unass completely immune to environmental blows and insults of an are all narcissistically vulnerable to some lesser or greater Dr. Feldman observes (in the paper cited earlier), self-exist at varying degrees of severity. At the most disturbed end of the continuum is the person who reacts to any sign of disapproval or rejection (whether real or imagined) with a dizzying drop in his own sense of self-worth. Such an individual may, in the absence of ongoing positive feedback from the partner, literally lose his sense of being a whole person and feel as if he is coming apart at the seams.

At the opposite end of the continuum, on the other hand, are those individuals who react to criticism and other negative stimuli with only minor diminutions in their own good feelings about themselves. A great many people are, however, somewhere in the middle of this spectrum—not pathologically disturbed or suffering from a serious narcissistic disorder, but burdened by a sense of self-esteem that is to some degree compromised and uncertain.

Such individuals are prone to be dependent upon the intimate partner for help in maintaining their own internal equilibrium. For it is their fundamental neediness, writes Feldman, "which promotes the creation of conscious and unconscious narcissistic expectations"—expectations that the spouse will be totally and consistently attentive and/or admiring. It is positive feedback from the partner which, like an ongoing transfusion, keeps good feelings about the self in the ascendent and contains the antibodies that keep *bad* feelings about the self under control.

In relationships of this kind, the members of the couple tend to become attached to each other in a predominantly attention-seeking *or* admiration-seeking style; thus, while *both have narcissistic issues*, each is attempting to deal with them in a somewhat different manner.

In the first instance, the attention seeker requires—from the partner—the heedful concern and unflagging attentiveness of a loving, strong and understanding parent. And on occasions when (as is inevitable) this constant attention is *not* forthcoming, the vulnerable person feels empty and abandoned. His or her self-esteem plummets; he experiences himself as someone bad and guilty, who is being punished. In short, unless he is being attended to by the intimate other, he finds it impossible to like himself.

The individual who, on the other hand, takes an admiration-seeking stance in the relationship, needs unending applause for his or her abilities and accomplishments. Unless a steady airflow of admiration from the partner is forthcoming, this person's inflated sense of self stands in imminent danger of deflating, collapsing into nothing at all. In the absence (however temporary) of the mate's ongoing positive reinforcement and praise, feelings of tension, guilt and self-rejection emerge. The partner's steady reassurance is necessary in order to combat the narcissistically injured person's inner sense of self-criticism and failure.

Most frequently, but certainly not invariably, it is the female spouse who—as a way of dealing with her own low self-esteem—becomes attached to an idealized, strong, "parentified" partner, whose unflagging attention is necessary if she is to continue feeling good about herself. And generally, but again not invariably, it is the male who attaches himself to someone younger, someone who will look up to him and admire his accomplishments. *His* low self-esteem is covered over by his grandiosity.

Both are, however, struggling with the same underlying problem: Good feelings about the self are in short supply within, and the failure of narcissistic supplies from outside perennially threatens. Because, observes Dr. Feldman, each person is so heavily focused upon the maintenance of his or her uncertain self-esteem, "there is little or no perception of the other as a truly separate person with independent needs and emotions."

What is missing from the relationship is empathy—the capacity to identify with the thoughts and emotions of the other. The admiration seeker, focused upon his own feelings of inadequacy, is unaware of his partner's pressing need to be heard, understood and validated. She needs his attention in much the same way that a diabetic needs insulin: to maintain her normal functioning and emotional equilibrium. But, because her tactics for coping with low self-esteem are so different from his own, he cannot begin to comprehend them.

Nor can her mate, who needs *admiration* rather than caring attentiveness, perceive that when he turns away from her she experiences his behavior as consciously hostile, mean and rejecting. She not infrequently, responds by attacking him—for she is thoroughly unaware of *his* own basic and very dissimilar requirements. What he wants is to be respected, honored and complimented for his achievements and his capabilities; he has no wish to be truly listened to, heard and understood. He would, on the contrary, prefer not to disclose who he really is and usually does his best to avoid it.

What he needs from her, in order for him to maintain a basic sense of self-worth, is a steady inflow of admiration, gratification and reassuring praise. He experiences her condemnation and anger, therefore, as a thoroughly alarming interruption of his desperately necessary supply of self-esteem and good feeling. "Each spouse," writes clinician Feldman, "behaves in ways that the other experiences as highly threatening. . . . The spouse who expects admiration is frequently inattentive or neglectful. The spouse who expects attention is frequently critical or condemning.

These behaviors strike to the core of each spouse's narcissistic vulnerability. . . ." Each, then, responds with anxiety and rage—a sense of having been willfully and perhaps even maliciously betrayed.

THE ODD THINGS OTHER COUPLES FIGHT ABOUT

There is nothing so peculiar as the sorts of things that other married people fight about! For the Sternbergs, a repetitious quarrel, which could grow so wild that it kept them up throughout the night, had to do with the state of cleanliness of the bathroom, particularly with the way the toilet bowl looked.

When I asked them to give me an example of a typical argument, Nancy rolled her eyes and said, "We just *had* one the other night. They're always about the same thing. David says the housework isn't done, the toilets need cleaning. And I'm busy, doing the filing and looking up the accounts receivable—so the kitchen table's all covered with papers. And then he, at the end of the day, says, 'I see you haven't gotten to the bathrooms.' " She was mimicking his tone, speaking in a clipped, stentorian tone of voice.

"It was eight o'clock at night by then!" her husband interrupted Nancy to protest.

"And I said," she continued recounting to me, " 'What does it look like I've been doing all day?' . . . It was so obvious that I'd been *occupied*!" She paused momentarily, then added, "I feel, when he sets out these jobs for me to do—and I decide I've got *other* things to do—that it becomes a kind of power struggle, a battle going on between us."

I nodded, asked them both whether his request that she clean the bathrooms was something that the two of them perceived as a red flag meaning "Let's have a fight"? Nancy nodded. "Yes, you know what the buttons are and you try to push them. And it's up to the other person to respond to it or not. . . ." She shrugged her shoulders lightly.

"I think that what Nancy said before is true," commented David reflectively, "about its being a fight for power between us. I feel that she is, by not cleaning up—which would take a matter of ten minutes—telling me, 'I don't have to do it if I don't want to.' "

"Right," she responded promptly. "You can't tell me what to do!" Her voice, though not loud, had an angry edge to it.

"I agree," David said to her immediately, then turned to me. "I believed I had asked her. She believed that I had ordered her to do it! And I wasn't ordering her; I was requesting. I perceived myself as being very nice and requesting something. She hears these things—and it's usually something to do with cleaning—as an order, a demand." He had begun by sounding measured and reasonable, but now he sounded irate.

Nancy shook her head, disagreeing. "In the morning he said, 'Today I think it would be appropriate for you to vacuum and do the bathrooms—' "

"That's the way you *heard* it," he intervened.

"That's the way you *said* it," she retorted swiftly. "In the morning, he said, 'Today I think it would be appropriate for you to vacuum and do the bathrooms,' " recounted Nancy, sounding outraged, "and that's all I have to hear. What am I, the paid slave? It's 'appropriate,' " she added sarcastically, "to do what *I* think I should be doing!"

I nodded my agreement, asked with a smile, "So, throughout the day, while you were filing and looking up accounts, you knew damn well that you were going to do what *you* wanted to do, and that—"

"Yes," interrupted David, "that there would be a reaction!"

"Yes," I kept my eyes fixed upon Nancy, "and you were pissed." She laughed, agreed that if she had been planning to do the bathrooms anyway, she probably would have changed her mind. She turned, looked at her husband, who said to her, "I'm glad you admitted you wouldn't have done them, because we both know that that's true."

"So this argument typically starts," I asked, "with you, David, waving the red flag that signals 'Let's have a fight'?" He laughed shortly, shrugged, said that when lots of things were bothering him, and he felt very pressured, he needed to let off steam. "That's when I push the button," he admitted. "And right now, because of pressures from my family, having to do with my father's estate and the kind of will that he left, there's a lot of tension—"

"I feel as if I'm being made into the scapegoat," interjected Nancy, at that moment. David stopped, looked at her thoughtfully, then acknowledged that there was some validity to her statement. He'd had the feeling, on the day of that quarrel, that he was in need of an enemy somehow. "I needed somebody to be mad at me," he said slowly, looking confused, as if he himself did not understand what he meant by what he had said.

He had perhaps, it occurred to me, needed *someone else* to be mad at him, lest his own negative feelings about himself—which were being stirred up by the difficulties about his father's estate—should become intolerable or even overwhelming. Getting Nancy mad at him was a way of thrusting his own self-critical thoughts and emotions out of his inner world and experiencing them as coming *at him* from outside.

DEFENDING AGAINST THE BAD FEELINGS

In the Sternbergs' marriage, it was David who, in nonconformance with the more stereotypic male behavior, tended to be the emotionally overexpressive, demanding, attention-seeking partner. While he was, in the business arena, an energetic, extremely successful entrepreneur, he was his wife's emotional dependent. Nancy, far more objective and reserved a person than her husband, was predictably capable, competent and reasonable. She had handled everything that it was necessary for her to handle in the wake of David's heart attack and of a serious postcoronary depression, which had lasted almost a year.

Her stance, in the relationship, was that of the admiration seeker. She could do it all—run the business and the family and hold down her research job—so long as a steady stream of recognition of her abilities and importance was forthcoming. "I am," she said at one point, "a caretaker, as were my mother and grandmother before me. I come from a line of self-sacrificing women." She had, in fact, fallen in love with her husband in the context of an incident (at a summer camp, where both were counselors) which had involved his becoming very upset and distressed and her "wanting to make him feel better and being able to do it."

He, on the other hand, had been attracted "not only by her beauty, which was and is obvious," but by her ability to set limits on his overexpansive, overenthusiastic nature. He had, too, been impressed by her seriousness and caringness. "She seemed," he said, "to put *my* needs before her own." This kind of attention, which he craved, was something that had never come to him before.

His relationship with his own mother had, according to David, been an extremely remote one. Not only had his parents' marriage been unhappy and conflictual, but his mother had been overinvolved with an older sister who was homely, troubled and unpopular. He himself had been considered the easygoing, self-sufficient, well-adapted child in the family—the one who was well able to take care of himself and required very little in the way of parental concern, worry or attention.

Narcissistic vulnerability, as Dr. Feldman notes in his remarkable article, stems from the relative weakness of good parental objects—internalized positive images of the loved caretaker as accepting, approving, and admiring. The internalized *negative* images are potentially much stronger. The bad—rejecting, disapproving, depreciating—parental objects lurk in the shadows just outside the citadel of consciousness and threaten to leap into the light of awareness at any moment. Without a steady flow of positive gratification from the partner, the defenses against these bad internal images are weakened.

There is, for this reason, little ability to tolerate frustration—any stoppage of the flow of acceptance and/or admiration is met by narcissistic anxiety and rage. The anxiety is generated, explains the clinician, by "a fear of repressed negative self-images. The . . . vulnerable individual is constantly threatened by unconscious images of himself or herself as inferior, unworthy, unlovable, repulsive, etc. Narcissistic modes of relating . . . are created in part as a way of coping or defending against these shame-producing self-images."

Most of us are, of course, preoccupied to some extent with preventing certain negative feelings about ourselves from entering into awareness. There are, in all of us, certain unpleasant self-images that we struggle to keep at bay, out of our own sight. In marriages where both spouses' self-esteem is very fragile, however, the partner is expected to help out with this ongoing effort. He or she is supposed to provide enough narcissistic gratification to keep the wolves—the bad feelings about the self—away from the doorstep of consciousness.

When this defensive stratagem fails, as it must, over time, a second line of defense—that of projective identification—is mobilized against the bad, unacceptable feelings. This occurs in the following kind of sequence: The partner who, for example, was expected to provide constant and unflagging attention (Nancy Sternberg was supposed to drop whatever she was doing and clean the bathrooms or even to put the children's needs aside when David needed nurturance) says or does something that threatens the other person's security. She fails, in a word, to supply the needed attentiveness. As a result, the bad internal images—"I'm no good," "I don't matter," "I'm abandoned"—begin ascending to conscious awareness.

These feelings, needless to say, make the attention-seeking partner feel anxious and uncomfortable. And he, in attempting to deal with his discomfort, executes an unconscious but quite automatic cognitive maneuver. Instead of perceiving the negative, potentially annihilating thoughts and feelings as coming from within, he begins experiencing them as coming *to* him *from* her. It is *she* who thinks that he is of no importance and doesn't matter; it is *she* who does not value him! She is all-bad, and he is her all-good innocent victim.

Not only does he experience her as indifferent, uncaring, hostile and depreciatory, but he *behaves* in ways that will turn these perceptions into a self-fulfilling prophecy. He "pushes a button"—as David Sternberg had when he had suggested that Nancy clean the toilets—which will turn the intimate partner into the harsh denunciator and cold, ungiving enemy that she is supposed to be. Suddenly, she is no longer the idealized all-good, all-accepting, all-attentive parent; she is the bad, rejecting, hateful one instead.

And he, just as suddenly, is no longer her starry-eyed, emotionally dependent admirer. She cannot continue experiencing herself as the competent, adequate, needed and adulated caretaker. She is, on the contrary, incapable of setting limits on this irrational, explosive juvenile, who is in the midst of a behavioral tantrum. He, who was relied upon to respect and applaud her, has rendered her foolish and helpless; he is terrible, impossible to deal with.

It is as if each partner's internalized bad parental object has, like an interior jack-in-the-box, leaped up from beneath its lid and out of its repressive container. This intolerable part of the self, usually kept well out of sight, must be ejected from the inner world—and is therefore projected onto the intimate other, whose escalating anger and bitter accusations come to personify what was intolerable within. Both are, in some real sense, getting their inner nightmares out—and, in the process, creating a nightmare in the relationship.

THE BEST OF QUARRELS

Since the fight about the bathrooms was a repeating one, I asked David Sternberg whether it was also a familiar one. "Did it happen, I mean, in the family that you lived in when you were growing up? Was it a fight you were ever in before you got married?"

He shook his head, in the negative, immediately. "No, this isn't carried over from—" He stopped, gave me an odd look, then said, "Well, maybe it is. My mother was very, very finicky about the ways things were kept. If you did not keep the bathroom orderly—more than any other part of the house—it made her—" He laughed, said that that was the *only* thing that he could remember her getting angry about. "If you didn't take care of the ring on the tub or wipe down the shower stall—"

"She is what you'd call 'crazy clean,' " put in Nancy.

"And in our house, the bathroom was a fetish—a key focal point." He laughed again. "I never even thought of that, but come to think of it, that was the key room that had to be kept clean. And if you didn't treat the bathroom right, that was the only time my mother, who was very passive-aggressive, would become outwardly aggressive."

He, who had experienced himself as having a lot of trouble capturing his mother's attention, had learned that he could do so by leaving the bathroom in a deplorable state. A good way of getting another person focused upon you is, of course, to engage that person in a fight—even *if* the attention that one receives is negative! Negative attention is, not infrequently, considered to be better than no attention at all.

A number of years earlier, continued David, it would have been completely impossible for him to acknowledge the part that he had played in starting the quarrel or to have empathized with Nancy's point of view in any way whatsoever. "I don't think that before we had our year of therapy, we could have avoided getting into something wild—something that went on all evening and maybe through the night. I know that I'*d* have gone into the bathroom and started yelling that the place was like Yankee Stadium—that there were towels strewn all over the place, and the toilets needed cleaning!" He laughed, turned to Nancy, who laughed too, but nevertheless looked a little bit frightened.

Then, he went on, he'd have gone storming over to the utilities closet and snatched the bowl cleaner out. Nancy would, he said, have come racing after him, crying, "I'll do it—let *me*!" but he would have refused her offer in an angry, offended fashion. "I'd have insisted that it was too late, that she ought to have done it when I *asked* her," he went on, "and she would have answered by saying she wasn't a maid—that if it bothered me, I could go clean it myself!" He grinned, looked over at Nancy, who was nodding her head up and down.

This entire scene, earlier in their marriage, would have culminated in his taking the cleaning fluids and the towels from the bathrooms and throwing them all down on the living-room rug in front of her. "I'd have been yelling my head off," recounted David, "saying things like 'Here, you can take this damn stuff, and do what you want with it, but now I can at least sit on the toilets!" The fight would escalate upward, from that point, until both of them were furious, unreachable, completely unable to halt the horrible thing that was happening. Nancy kept nodding, as if to say, "He's right; that was the typical pattern."

But it had been different this time, observed her husband, for they no longer fought in the ways that they had fought before. The quarrel had gotten under way and gone on for a while, but then he'd said to himself, "Hey, you're being crazy. Why should we be fighting about toilet bowls anyway?" He had, after cleaning up one bathroom, simply left the cleaning fluids in the hallway.

Nancy, before going to bed, had gone over the other bathrooms. Why, I asked her, had she done that? "Oh, probably to appease him," she replied, with a toss of her blond head and a shrug. She had, she added, been really angry while she did the work, but had felt, nevertheless, that she had a choice. "My choice was not to get into it. I didn't feel like getting into a big hassle and not sleeping—it wasn't worth it. So, when I saw him put the cleaning fluid down—and that he wasn't bugging me— I got up and did it myself."

I turned to David. "And did you then feel appeased, or were you still furious?" He had felt appeased, he said, sounding satisfied. "And you both felt the fight was over?" I asked, looking at him and then at her. It had been partially resolved, that evening, and then totally resolved in the morning, replied Nancy, and her husband murmured his agreement.

What had made this recent conflict—so unpleasantly familiar to both the Sternbergs—amenable to resolution without its ever getting out of control and seriously vindictive and destructive? The partners were, it seemed to me, now able to accept responsibility for the part that *each of them played* in getting the battle into motion. David was, evidently, able to make conscious contact with the fact that he'd been feeling tense *before* the entire sequence had begun. He knew that he had, for that reason, "pushed the argument button" in the first place. Nancy was aware, as she could acknowledge, of the fact that her procrastination had been a passive-aggressive way of saying no and that she should have stated (and explained) her refusal in a far more direct, clear and open manner.

This had enabled them, instead of battling each other until both had dropped, to eventually get the *real issues*—David's problems with his father's will and the bitter family feelings that it was beginning to generate—out onto the table for discussion. And Nancy's attentions became, at that point, helpful, solicitous and comforting rather than hurtful and rejecting. They even had, as she informed me with a laugh, managed to get the dirty-bathrooms dilemma worked out by deciding that since David was the one who was really disturbed by them, he should take charge of keeping them clean. He could either hire someone or do them himself, but—it was their mutual decision—she was to stay out of the matter entirely.

The best of quarrels are, I reflected, those that end with a negotiated compromise for change in a positive direction.

19

The Five Ways
in Which Couples Relate

Many spouses consider themselves far more mature than their partners, but in fact, when it comes to selecting mates, we tend to choose people who are at the same level of maturity, of emotional development, as our own.

When a couple enters marriage, as theorist Murray Bowen, M.D., observes, the degree of self-definition of each member of the pair is generally remarkably similar. "People pick spouses who [are at] the same levels of differentiation," notes Dr. Bowen. And the lower the level of separateness and individuation of each of the mates, the more intense and uncomfortable is the emotional fusion that develops.

"One spouse [may become] the dominant decision maker for the common self, while the other adapts to the situation," writes psychiatrist, Bowen. "This is one of the best examples in the borrowing and trading of self in a close relationship. One may assume the dominant role and force the other to be adaptive, or one may assume the adaptive role and force the other to be dominant." Whichever way it happens, though, this transfer of autonomy could not occur without the agreement (usually unconscious) of both parties to the bargain. Partners who were more highly separated and individuated would not get into a relationship that involved either giving up parts of the self or taking over unwanted aspects of the intimate other's inner being.

The less differentiated person who is, for example, unable to "own" and consciously experience his anger might be expected to use his internal radar to seek out the intimate partner who would take over this denied aspect of his internal world and experience and express the anger *for* him. He would, however, need to find a person at his own developmental level to do it. A potential mate who was individuated and separate enough to be capable of distinguishing her own inner self from that of her partner would never accept his projected angry feelings. She would neither take them in nor perceive them as her own, nor act them out for him—because relating, on that level, was something totally alien to her.

Her higher level of self-differentiation would, in this instance, prevent the relationship from ever getting off the ground. For he—if the intimate other balked at accepting and expressing his aggression for him—would be stuck with the thoughts and feelings that he was struggling so desperately to disavow. And she—unless she happened to be someone who was similarly burdened by unwanted parts of her inner self—would resist entering into an attachment which seemed to require her being used in this fashion.

But if, on the other hand, both individuals were dealing with aspects of the same developmental dilemma, they would be able to work out an unconscious bargain. She could accept, as hers, his repudiated and disavowed hostile feelings in exchange for his taking on those parts of her internal world which she devalued and could not consciously own as anything existing inside her.

Say, for instance, that she happened to be someone who viewed herself as eminently sane and reasonable, but that she contained—as the result of an identification with a highly disturbed, irrational parent—a well-controlled and well-disguised inner core of craziness of which she was consciously unaware. Her mate might then—in exchange for her experiencing and acting out his anger for him—take over and express *on her behalf* those parts of her inner being that were terrified, weird and illogical. He could do this by behaving impulsively, in a lunatic fashion, whenever she let him know (by means of covert and overt cues) that she needed to have him do this for her. "More differentiated spouses," writes Dr. Bowen, "have lesser degrees of [emotional] fusion, and fewer of the complications" that result from it.

Often, one member of a couple seems to be far more normal, well balanced, and mentally healthier than his or her spouse. The sober, steady, competent mate of an unstable, explosive alcoholic; the even-tempered, relatively cheerful partner of a complaining depressive; the person who moves about town, easily, yet is married to someone who is mildly phobic and afraid to go out of the house unaccompanied—all are examples of what might appear to be varying levels of maturation of the mates.

But appearances and reality may differ. For while all of the above are, indeed, examples of differing degrees of overt pathology, one spouse's sound and robust functioning may be highly dependent on the other spouse's taking over his disowned craziness. The depressed wife of the superefficient administrator may be carrying his repudiated feelings of inadequacy, vulnerability, need, unresolved mourning; that is why one partner's improvement so frequently leads to the development of symptoms in the other and possibly to the breakdown of the entire relationship.

It may appear, to those outside the marriage, as if the level of differentiation of the two partners were so strangely disparate that their having gotten together at all is almost unimaginable! But in terms of each individual's growth and maturation, *like marries like*—and if they are in a match of their own choosing (not one arranged by parents or an outsider), the spouses' basic levels of emotional development will be, for all intents and purposes, identical.

DIFFERENTIATION OF SELF: WHAT IS IT?

What, more precisely, does the word "differentiation" actually refer to? The term is one which is not easy to define. Clinician Mark Karpel, M.S., offers as lucid an exposition of the basic concept as I have yet encountered. Individuation is, he suggests, that process "by which a person becomes increasingly differentiated from a past or present relational context." Writes Karpel:

> This process encompasses a multitude of intrapsychic and interpersonal changes that share a common direction. In different relational contexts, the specific changes may vary greatly. They may involve an infant's gradual realization that the source of his gratifications is an object, a body, which is separate from his own and which becomes for him "mother"; an adolescent's determination to violate an unwritten family rule that mother chooses all of the children's clothing; a husband's struggle to see himself as capable of surviving without the painful relationship that exists between his wife and himself; a mother's recognition that her child is, in fact, *not* as anxious, dependent, shy or whatever as she has felt herself to be.
>
> Individuation, involves the subtle but crucial phenomenological shifts by which a person comes to see him/herself as separate and distinct within the relationship in which s/he has been embedded. *It is the increasing definition of an "I" within a "We"* [my italics].

The degree to which the "I" of each partner remains embedded in the "We" of his or her family of origin—in thrall to *their* emotional program—will have everything to do with how flexible, comfortable and gratifying a marriage the pair will be able to work out.

THE FIVE WAYS INTIMATE PARTNERS RELATE

By way of illustrating this last statement, let me talk about how *different* a marital relationship will be, depending on how successfully each partner has differentiated his or her own separate, distinct self from the family context in which that self developed. The framework that I shall use in the following discussion is the ingenious and wonderfully illuminating one devised by marital and family therapist Stuart Johnson, M.S.W., for use in the teaching of clinical trainees.

There are, in Johnson's schema, five possible ways in which intimate partners will be able to relate to each other—all highly dependent upon the degree of separation and individuation that the members of the couple have achieved.

Level Five: Paradox

At the very lowest level of differentiation on this developmental ladder, level five, are those mates who exist in a world that Johnson calls "paradox." In this world, the two major human needs—to be a separate self and to be emotionally connected to other human beings—cannot possibly be met. For being close to a partner and *not* being close to a partner are prospects that are equally terrifying.

For someone as poorly differentiated as are those at this level, to be intimate with another person is to negate one's individual separateness entirely. Getting closer to the partner is, in the internal world, experienced as being absorbed by the individual, swallowed up, so that one's own distinct self disappears into the relationship. Intimacy is a merging and fusion of the self and other—which involves the threat of losing one's own separate personality. Every step nearer is, therefore, accompanied by terrible anxiety, for it feels like a step closer to self-annihilation.

The very natural reaction to this threat is to move away—to run for the hills, psychologically speaking. Since closeness is a negation of separateness, getting as distant from the mate as quickly as one can becomes the order of the day. This withdrawal from intimacy is automatic, but in its wake, a new difficulty inevitably develops—for being alone and autonomous does not provide the solution, either. To be alone is, on the contrary, experienced as a terrible emptiness—an abandonment, a sense of awful nothingness, of nonbeing.

Autonomy is experienced as not mattering to anyone, as the absence of a necessary confirmation and validation of one's existence itself. *Paradoxically, the move toward separateness has produced the same results as did the move toward greater closeness: the threat of self-annihilation.* As a result, the impetus to move *toward* the partner returns, and the cycle repeats itself.

People at this lowest rung on the differentiation scale are involved in a yo-yo style of relating. Moving nearer to the mate is dangerous; one will disappear into the relationship. Moving farther away is equally so; one will dissolve in the echoing spaces of an indifferent universe. Every effort to solve the problem contains its own contradiction. Both the need to be a separate self and the need to be emotionally connected to another human being are experienced as desperately and hopelessly ungratifiable.

Intimacy, in this individual's world, is the very negation of autonomy; autonomy is the negation of closeness. This is an unresolvable dilemma—and many of the people in this level five category are schizophrenics or suffer from severe borderline disorders. Their close relationships tend to be difficult, transient and unstable. How could they not be, since being close and being separate *feel* equally dangerous?

Level Four: Projective Identification

The next step upward on the differentiation scale is called "projective identification"—that relational world in which so many married partners become mired for long periods of time or for their entire lives together. There is, it must be said immediately, a huge and marked contrast between couples at this level and those at the one below it. For at level five, the twin problems of how to meet one's needs for separateness and one's needs for emotional connectedness are equally unresolvable and insolvable. At level four, the dilemma has been partially—but by no means fully and healthily—worked out.

People who are at this stage of differentiation are capable of taking conscious ownership of *one-half* of the closeness/separateness polarity. They can be intimate *or* be autonomous, but they experience intimacy and autonomy as mutually exclusive. There is, in their interpersonal system, a clear-cut choice to be made: You can assert and express your need for warmth, openness and nearness to the partner *or* your need for distance and personal space in which to develop your own separate self, but you cannot do both simultaneously. While level four mates are *both* struggling with an inner conflict—about being close and achieving a separate, individual identity—they deal with it by dividing it up between them. Each splits off, represses and projects onto the partner whichever side of the internal dispute he or she has disowned and repudiated.

At level five *neither* set of needs—to maintain one's own distinct identity, to be emotionally attached—could be met and satisfied. At level four, the partners can and do consciously assert and express either one of them—and then retain contact with the repressed part of the controversy via the thoughts, feelings and behavior of the mate. Thus, the person who is fully aware of her autonomy needs, but has devalued and rejected her intimacy needs, finds someone in a complementary position. She falls in love with someone who, for reasons of his own, can be intimate but has difficulties recognizing and legitimizing his own need to be separate, self-sufficient person.

Suppose that she happens to be someone who was raised in a traditional, somewhat sexist family and that she has become strongly affected by the feminist movement during her late adolescence and early adulthood. She is, at the time of meeting the man who is to become her partner, in rebellion against what she considers to be the woman trap, i.e., becoming the intimacy carrier in the family. She has seen, by observing the experiences of her mother and the other females in the family, how thankless and unvalued a position this can be; she is aware, moreover, of the new possibilities opening up for women like herself.

Such an intellectual position would be fine, if she did not—as an individual at this emotional level would tend to do—deal with the softer, more pliant, adaptive and closeness-seeking aspects of her inner self by splitting them off and repressing them decisively. The result of this unconscious maneuver would be her losing touch with her own intimate needs so completely that she would experience herelf as totally without them—a being sufficient, emotionally speaking, unto herself.

The partner she chose, or was chosen by, would have to be someone who was in a complementary position. He might be an individual who, like his mate, was reared in a fairly traditional setting—one in which the man earned the living and maintained a superior position and the woman took charge of the household and occupied a secondary place—but someone who had gotten insufficient nurturance along the way. Perhaps he was made to feel guilty about his needs, or perhaps his mother, in order to retain her own area of command, tried to keep him infantilized and dependent as long as was possible. He, for whatever historical reasons, experiences himself as needy, and he wants a self-sufficient woman to take care of him.

Therefore, he applauds her superautonomous stance, finds it enormously attractive. The male partner, in the emotional system that this pair has created, would be the closeness seeker, while his wife expressed the autonomy needs for the pair of them. She would assume *his need* to be a separate person and assert it for him, along with her own. He would carry *her need* for warmth and relationship, along with his own, well within his conscious awareness—because staying close to the mate is his area of specialty. And inevitably a pursuer-distancer relationship would develop, with each spouse in a polarized position.

Frustration and confusion are foredoomed because the rules of the system decree that neither can get what he or she seems to desire so ardently . . . and in a way both members of the pair seem to know it. In truth, the intimacy seeker has promised to chase but never to overtake the partner, just as the autonomy seeker has promised to run but never to get too distant from her breathless, dissatisfied pursuer.

Suppose, in this situation, that the wife were offered a job that required her spending long periods of time away from her spouse. She would tend, in the course of the decision-making process, to recognize her autonomous needs primarily and perhaps exclusively, while her husband could only see and assert another side of the conflict: the competing needs for togetherness and emotional closeness. As a result, they would polarize around the issue and come out of their corners swinging—instead of recognizing that *both* of them want to be intimate and *both* of them want space in which to develop their own self-interests and separate talents.

The dilemma that each person has—an internal conflict about how to satisfy his or her valid needs for separateness and for connectedness—will then be fought out as a problem between them, with each partner in an opposing corner of the conjugal ring. And, so long as he continues to demand more intimacy, she will fail to recognize the fact that there is a similar call coming from within her own being. Her partner will, in turn, never become aware—not so long as she keeps battling blindly for her independence and autonomy—that he, too, might enjoy a little more distance and room to call his own in the relationship they share. Instead, each will go on trying to batter the other into accepting his or her own grossly oversimplified position.

What is fought out between the mates, at level four, is the problem that neither one of them has been able to address internally—the problem of how to be a distinct and separate individual while remaining emotionally attached to another human being. The core issue for these couples is each mate's inability to contain, internally, both sides of the autonomy/intimacy polarity. But the polarizations of the pair's ambivalence are by no means limited to dilemmas having to do with personal space and the need for closeness to the partner. While this is, indeed, the core issue, the spouses can and do square off about any human relationship issue that can be imagined: competence/incompetence, logic/emotionality, strength/weakness, martyr/tyrant, caretaker/wounded bird, angry/never angry, irascible/even-tempered, devil/angel, and so forth. If the issue can be placed on a continuum, the spouses will be at either end of it.

What one partner is, the other partner *is not*, or so it seems, at the surface of the relationship. Underneath, however, self and other are inextricably and confusingly intertwined. For it is impossible, when spouses use projection as a major means of relating to each other, for one mate really to know whether the anger is in himself or whether it is in the intimate other.

In these marriages, the partners' underground wiring is crossed. A depressed wife may be hauling her husband's unacknowledged vulnerability and sorrow for him while he is assuming her disowned healthiness—disowned because, in an earlier context, she learned that she was not lovable unless she was weak, needy and dependent. Level four relationships are always characterized by such unconscious quid pro quos.

Neither mate, at this level of separation and individuation, has come into the marriage feeling like a discrete, autonomous creature—someone who can stand on his or her own feet and function yet connect emotionally to another human being who is similarly separate, different and autonomous. The overriding problem, for both of the spouses, is that of recognizing just where one person ends and the other person begins. But so long as the projections continue to be exchanged, that problem remains unresolvable.

Level Three: Conscious Splitting

This level may best be thought of as a bridge or way station between the two very different interpersonal worlds which exist above and below it. Partners at this level, when swept up in a marital battle, are likely to behave and even *feel like* level four couples, but eventually, when they calm down, they can acknowledge the existence of their own internal ambivalences.

The key difference, at level three, is that even though the spouses *are* projecting unwanted thoughts and feelings onto one another, there is not so much unconscious process involved. Each is able, when the smoke clears, to take ownership of that dark, "split-off" side of the internal battle—the conflictual needs to be close and to be a separate individual—which has been banished from awareness and is being connected to only in the thoughts, feelings and behavior of the intimate other.

Partners at this level may, and do, process unwanted mental materials through each other—in other words, engage in level four behavior—but they are able to achieve some insight about what they are doing. A husband and wife whom I interviewed had, for example, a story to tell which I think is illustrative of the level three couple's tendencies to (1) identify, projectively, with the intimate partner and (2) eventually be able to comprehend, consciously, what one has done and the way in which it has happened.

The pair, who were in the postparental phase of their lives—they were in their early fifties at the time of our talks—had gone to Italy for what was to be a working vacation for him, and for her a purely relaxing and pleasureful interlude. But once in Rome, the husband had become more and more involved with his Italian colleagues; he was the owner of a successful family corporation and was thinking of forming an Italian subsidiary.

His wife was left fuming and miserable, in their hotel or out sightseeing, and lunching, and sometimes even eating dinner by herself. The tensions between them rose as she continued to demand more of his time and attention and he maintained that she had to be more tolerant of his need to devote himself and his energies to the important decision that was at hand. The trip, which was disastrous, culminated in one of those marital quarrels that neither partner finds it bearable to think about afterward.

What, exactly, had happened? To begin at the beginning of this sequence, the husband had asked his wife to accompany him—an intimate request on his part. Traveling together to a foreign country is, however, an intensely closeness-fostering experience and a couple often gets into much more emotional contact in these circumstances than they do during their round of daily activities at home. He had, apparently, responded to what he perceived as intensified demands for intimacy by withdrawing, running away. Something about the situation had scared him, and his reaction had been to assert autonomy for the pair of them.

Later on, he could acknowledge this and was able to say, "Sure, I knew that I wanted to spend more time together, but she started haranguing me about my other arrangements almost from the time we got there! So while I did, initially, want to be with her, she didn't give me much space in which to feel that!

"My feeling was," he continued, "that I was being *dogged*, that she was chasing after me so hard that I'd better never stop running, or there wouldn't be a minute that belonged to me!" His own needs and wishes for closeness had, in their interaction, been thoroughly disowned—but he could, upon reflection, recognize that such needs really did exist inside him and had indeed been responsible for the original invitation. A level four individual could not have made conscious contact with these repressed, denied aspects of the self at all.

The wife, it should be noted immediately, had accompanied her spouse on this vacation in a less than totally willing frame of mind. She herself was a clinical psychologist, with a demanding practice. Their trip to Rome had required her taking two weeks from a busy schedule—and then sitting there tapping her heels in a European hotel lobby, when she would have been far more contented to have remained at home. She could, however, admit that she had been unusually demanding and irritable because she disliked traveling and hadn't really wanted to go along with him in the first place.

Why, then, had she gone? Her answer, given with a shrug and a wry toss of her head, was that she had decided to do so because *he* was so keen on it! It had been, given his enthusiasm, impossible for her to refuse him. So, even before embarking upon the journey, she was championing the togetherness and intimacy in the relationship while her autonomous needs and wishes were being discounted. Little wonder that she had been so provoked by his withdrawal; she had sacrificed her own separate self-wishes and self-needs on the altar of their mutual closeness! They had polarized, in the course of their Italian sojourn, around the question of who wanted intimacy and who wanted to withdraw.

But each was, in retrospect, capable of becoming aware of the "split-off" side of her or his internal conflict—her suppressed desire to be separate and his suppressed wish to be close. Couples at level four cannot do this. They cannot recognize that there is any inner battle going on, for the autonomy carrier perceives himself as uniquely without feelings and the intimacy carrier perceives herself as wanting only warmth and togetherness. At *level three, what is introduced is an increasing awareness of complexity—of a dilemma within the self as well as a dilemma involving the intimate partner.*

Level three is not really an experiential world unto itself, as are the others I have described, but a mezzanine of sorts between the levels below and above it. One could, in fact, think of level three as a large waiting room, with various couples milling around in it and with moving stairways bringing other couples down from level two and still others up from level four.

Those arriving from below would be partners whose relationships are improving—because both are in the process of taking conscious ownership of those devalued aspects of the self which have been being projected onto the mate. These are couples who are moving upward, on our metaphorical scale, as their capacity for being intimate *and* autonomous (not one or the other) increases, and they become capable of negotiating their desires for closeness and for separateness with less invasion of each other's personal boundaries.

Those couples coming down from above would, on the other hand, be level two people whose relationships—owing to great stress or to difficulties arising around a life cycle shift—are deteriorating and becoming far less functional. Such a pair may, if their problems remain unresolved, continue their regressive journey downward; the relationship may even break apart. Or the partners may, after a period of time at this level, spontaneously move onto the Up escalator and return to that far healthier transactional world with which they are already familiar.

Level Two: Tolerating Ambivalence

This level is called "ambivalence," for ambivalence is what each partner is now able to contain and to tolerate. The spouses can, at this higher level of separation and individuation, take conscious ownership of *both* sides of the inner conflict—of the competing needs, within each one of them, to be close to the partner and to be a separate, distinct person. They do not have to dichotomize and oversimplify the internal situation, so that one always presses for more autonomy and the other for more intimacy, as do couples at lower levels of self-differentiation.

The level two individual experiences the inner tug-of-war between his self-needs and closeness-needs as a struggle which is taking place *within*. He is, however, able to endure the tensions generated by this struggle without thrusting them outside himself—transforming them into a struggle between himself and his mate. He can accept responsibility for his psychological innards, because he perceives himself to be self-sufficient inside—a separate and independent creature who can stand on his own two feet and function. He feels, in a word, complete—which, in human terms, means being able not only to take care of himself but to bond intimately with another human being.

Couples at this level of development can recognize, with relative ease, where each one of them ends and where the other person begins. The husband who is angry can, for example, accept conscious ownership of that feeling—*know* that the anger is within himself and not in his intimate partner. The wife who feels uncertain about whether she wants to spend her Sunday afternoon painting or go out walking in the woods with her spouse is able *to experience* these competing wishes as a conflict that is inside her. People who inhabit a level two world can take responsibility for their ambivalent needs, thoughts, feelings and desires.

They are capable, for this reason, of accepting responsibility for both sides of the internalized dilemma—their need to be intimate and yet to be different, distinct individuals. The mates' capacity for tolerating ambivalence, at higher levels of self-differentiation, makes it possible for them to engage in a far richer, more complex process of intimate negotiation.

These couples tend, in dealing with the ongoing business of the relationship, to work matters out in what might be thought of as a two-step process. First, each of the partners recognizes and honestly addresses his or her own inner ambivalence—the competing needs to be intimate and to be separate which are experienced as warring forces within each person's being. Secondly, each brings an up-to-the-minute report on his or her own conflict into their mutual discussion.

The wife who is engaged in choosing between remaining in her studio and painting (an autonomous activity) or going walking with her spouse (an intimate activity) must concern herself with her own ambivalent urges as well as with any potential conflict with her mate. If she should experience her needs for closeness as existing only in *him* (as a level four or level three individual would do), she might agree to go out walking yet end up feeling exploited and annoyed—because her "owned" need was to spend that time painting, alone, in her studio. But at level two, both members of the pair would be far more likely to consult all of the cards in their inner decks and play out a transactional game which was much more mutually gratifying.

Partners at lower levels of differentiation tend to omit the crucial first step of this process; they fail to address the internalized conflict. Instead of taking ownership of the ambivalence within, they "split off" and repress one-half of it, then project that disowned aspect of the self onto the intimate other. One young couple whom I interviewed were, to cite an instance of this sort, engaged in an ongoing quarrel about what he saw as *her* refusal to entertain his friends in their apartment.

The husband, a shy and somewhat retiring assistant professor of English, thought it important that they invite a new and illustrious colleague to their place and have a small dinner party in his honor. But, as became clear in the course of our conversation, he was annoyed with his wife because he was certain that she did not want to and was, in fact, refusing to do it.

His strong feelings about this matter, while not in the forefront of his consciousness for much of the time, emerged whenever they got into a disagreement of any kind, on any subject whatsoever—and then he let her know that he was completely furious about her behavior. His wife maintained, however, that whenever she asked him to set a date for the dinner, he put her off; the present moment was, for one reason or another, always an inconvenient one.

She had, as she admitted readily in the course of the discussion, not insisted upon his settling upon a date for entertaining a guest whom she barely knew and whom she had not been particularly impressed by. She was, she added, an uncertain cook and hostess and had welcomed putting off the occasion for as long as possible. So their negotiation about the matter had gotten nowhere; they'd made no decision to have or not to have the dinner and were in a state of paralysis about it. This had left the husband feeling angry at his wife—especially because he had never dealt with his own ambivalence about the matter in the first place.

He himself did have, as he was eventually able to acknowledge, somewhat negative feelings about this particular individual. He actually did not like his new colleague very much, but still felt that, for political reasons, he did have to be invited to their home for dinner. Nevertheless, instead of taking inner responsibility for his own conflicted thoughts and emotions, he had dealt with them by insisting (and believing) that it was his wife who was the reluctant one. That important first step of the negotiation—recognizing his own inner dilemma—had not been taken before he'd opened the discussion with his partner, and the conflict had spilled into their relationship.

Partners who are more highly individuated do not get into these kinds of difficulties very frequently, for the boundary between the self and the other tends to be far clearer, more distinct and more definite. The above transaction, carried on by a level two couple, would have proceeded in a very different fashion. The husband, for example, having recognized the struggle going on within him, might have said to his wife, "I'm feeling frustrated about this, and I myself don't like Professor X, but I think I've got to have him to the house. I know this is an imposition, for you, because you don't like entertaining that much, but I guess, given the circumstances, that I need to ask you to help me."

His forthright statement of his own conflicted feelings would have given *her* the option to share her own ambivalent feelings with him—the first important move in their effort to work out a jointly acceptable resolution. Her response, in a healthier emotional climate, might have been to say something like "You're right, I don't really want to do it, but I will do it if you feel it's important to you."

Or she might have helped him explore the entire question of whether or not he himself actually wanted the dinner. Was it really necessary for him to get caught up in departmental politics, and was courting this particular fellow important to him and to his career? She could, in other words, acknowledge her own inner pros and cons—including her fears about her possible inadequacies as a hostess—while supporting him in working out a decision with which both of them could be comfortable.

The final phase of this more functional kind of marital transaction would be a working out of the logistics: Would the dinner be on a weekend or a weeknight? And what other guests could be included who, if added to the group, might make the evening more enjoyable for both of them?

The husband had, in the original situation, asserted an autonomous need—to bring in an associate from his separate world, the work environment which existed outside the marriage. The wife, rebuffing his need by means of her foot-dragging reluctance, was asserting the intimacy in the relationship—indicating that it was the world *inside* the marriage which really counted most. These partners, being less well differentiated than a level two pair, experienced themselves as having to be autonomous *or* to be close; they inhabited an either/or planet.

More highly self-delineated individuals are able to assert *both* needs and take conscious ownership of their existence inside themselves. Being close and being separate persons are, in a level two world, not perceived as being wants and needs that are by definition mutually exclusive. The inner experience, at this level, is that autonomy and intimacy exist on a spatial continuum—a sliding ruler, of sorts. Moving nearer to the partner on that ruler—by making love, listening to her talk about her problems, going out to dinner together—means losing some degree of separateness, for one could have read a book, or done some work of one's own, or spent some time with a friend or a colleague.

Every inch closer to the mate, at level two, involves a sacrifice of that inch of the self's autonomy. But there is not, as there is at levels three and four, the same stark sense that one must choose between having the full twelve inches of autonomy or no inches whatsoever or, alternatively, twelve inches of intimacy or no intimacy at all.

Both partners can, in a level two system, acknowledge their ambivalent needs for nearness to the mate and individual separateness as conflicting forces that exist inside each person's own head. There is, in these spouses' relational world, a greater appreciation of complexity; they do not, as do less well-differentiated pairs, lock into rigidified, oversimplified, inflexible, polarized stances in the relationship.

Both members of the couple can, at this higher and more functional developmental level, have angry and peaceful feelings, be competent and incompetent; both can assert their weaknesses and their strengths. They can be bad and be good, sad and cheerful, the babied one and the one who is being cared for. They can—and this constitutes the very heart of the matter—tolerate their needs for intimacy and for autonomy simultaneously.

Level One: Integrated

Level one on the scale—"integrated"—is relational heaven itself. It is, suggests therapist Johnson, less an interpersonal reality than it is an ideal. Couples who exist at this Olympian level no longer conceive of their needs for independence and their needs for togetherness as conflicting forces within each partner's head or as a conflict between them. *Instead, autonomy and intimacy are experienced as integrated aspects of each partner's personhood and of the relationship that the two of them share.*

This peak of healthy functioning can be conceived of as the level five experience turned outside out. For at that lowest level of individuation being close and being a separate person were experienced as equally dangerous; they amounted to the same thing. At level one, the two needs have collapsed in upon themselves in a similar fashion, but now the inner experience is that being close and being separate are both equally safe and gratifying. Both are acceptable, all of the time, and there is no conflict between them that requires resolution.

What has to be negotiated by the partners, in this interpersonal world, is the *activity* to be engaged in—not the internalized conflict about whether to assert one's intimate needs or one's self-needs at any given point in time. Thus, if one member of a couple wanted to finish watching a television program and the other one wanted to go to bed and make love, the matter could be worked out fairly easily.

For the mate watching TV would not tend to feel that the other person was crowding him, trying to take away his autonomy (his choice about the way in which he wants to spend his time). He might indicate to his wife that he wanted to complete the autonomous piece of behavior in which he was engaged but couldn't do that and make love to her at the same time. . . . So could she delay? Or could she wait until he is feeling a bit more interested himself? A couple at this level will easily work out some kind of mutually acceptable quid pro quo because the fact that one feels differently from the other—and *is* a fundamentally different person— is not experienced as a threat or a betrayal.

Couples in an integrated relationship of this kind perceive autonomy and intimacy as states of being—not, as in level two, spatial positions on a closeness-distance ruler. At level two, being close or being separate was fundamentally tied to *what the partners happened to be doing.* If they were making love, each had sacrificed a certain degree of his or her own separateness and autonomy. If each was involved in independent activities—if she was at the library and he was at the zoo with their son—some metaphorical inches, on the sliding autonomy/intimacy ruler, had of necessity been surrendered.

At level one, however, intimacy and autonomy are perceived as integrated states of being—the way the members of the couple *are* rather than what activities they happen to be engaged in at the moment. During lovemaking, for example, a partner may be doing something highly intimate, but his essential separateness is not being obliterated or denied. The feeling, at this highest level of self-differentiation, is that while he cannot exercise his autonomy, at that particular moment, being close to the partner will not bring his separateness into question. On the contrary, he experiences himself as more fully able to be himself—*who he really is*—in the presence of the intimate other. Being close to the partner supports being a distinct, separate person.

And being separate supports a sense of closeness, because to the degree that my spouse lets me know that he recognizes and feels comfortable with my essential differentness, I can feel safe about letting my hair down and being who I really am, with him. And even though I may be visiting a dear family member in Texas, while he remains at home in Connecticut, I carry my feelings of closeness to him within me. Intimacy is an internalized state of being; I can feel near to him no matter where I am and whatever I happen to be doing at that moment. So his championing and protection of my autonomous needs (such as making that visit) enhance my ability to be close to him.

At this integrated level of relationship, partners can live comfortably with their differences, even with differences about certain deeply held beliefs and values. One highly functional couple whom I interviewed were, for instance, in their late twenties. The husband owned an automobile radio sales and repair shop, and the wife worked in the mayor's office of a small Connecticut city. They had one small daughter and an important religious difference: She was a devout and believing Catholic, and he was a lapsed Catholic who was not interested in religion at all.

She regretted, she said, that he could not share a belief that was so important to her, but the agreement, worked out between them, was that he would support her churchgoing activities and not undermine him with their child. He, in turn, would never be asked to do anything that would make him feel compromised or ridiculous—nor would she cast him in a bad or wrong light in the eyes of the upcoming generation (she was pregnant, and their second baby was due very shortly).

The negotiation of this important difference supported each person's otherness and separateness in a way that both of them could live with relatively easily. Most important, in order to work out the arrangement, each had had not only to understand *that the partner was a different person* but also to recognize the particular ways in which his or her differentness manifested itself. Each had had to ask the other, in the course of their ongoing dealings with their religious problem, "How are you different from me? How do you feel about this particular question that is now going to arise?" Recognition of the partner's otherness is, in this situation, another way of getting to know who he or she *is*. Separateness feeds closeness, and closeness feeds the capacity for being the different person that one is.

At higher levels of separation and individuation, observes clinician Mark Karpel, a couple's intimate relationship takes the form of a *dialogue* between separate beings rather than the form of fusion and interpersonal merger that it does in the less differentiated levels below. He writes:

> Dialogue represents the mature stage of human development in which the poles of "I" and "We" are integrated in such a way that they nourish and foster one another.
>
> Individuation (the differentiated "I"), and dialogue (the differentiated "We") are complementary parts of the overall process of both partners' simultaneous self-delineation in relationship. . . . [D]ialogue represents the mode of relationship that maximally fosters continuing individuation of both partners. Unlike fusion, where difference is avoided, in dialogue it is sought and affirmed. Partners aim toward an ideal of responding to the other as a whole and truly *other* person and not merely as a part of their own experience.

Autonomy and intimacy are, in these circumstances, mutually self-supporting and self-enhancing states of being.

20

"We Have
a Good Time"

David Sternberg's father had, according to his son, "made a considerable amount of money" in the wholesale dairy products business. Money had, added David, always been an issue in the household in which he had grown up; money had been a stand-in for control, dominance, power and, most insidiously of all, for love. "His father was an illiterate immigrant," observed Nancy in an objective tone of voice, "the most self-involved person I have ever known. All he ever thought about was himself and money. Money as a means of controlling the people around him." Control, she observed flatly, had been the top priority on her father-in-law's agenda.

I looked at David, my eyebrows raised, as if inviting objections on his part. But he merely nodded, said, "I knew I was a prisoner of my dad and of his money craziness. When we bought our first house, for instance, he gave us part of the down payment—five thousand dollars—and then insisted that he owned one of the rooms. It belonged to him! So if he was visiting and wanted to lie down, one of us might say, 'Why don't you take a rest in Jeff's room?' (The house we were in, at that time, wasn't this one; it was tiny, just a cottage.) 'What do you mean, *Jeff's* room?' he'd demand. 'This is *my* room, I paid for it, and I'm just letting Jeff use it!' "

"And that was the signal," put in his wife, "for the pair of them to go for each other's throats. I never knew why David let himself get suckered into it. . . . If his dad wanted to act like a jackass, I didn't know why *he* had to join him!" Typically, she recounted, two days before his parents were due to arrive for a visit, the fighting between David and her would begin. "We'd fight about our son Jeff or about the cleaning; David would go looking through the closets and drawers, saying things like 'Where did this moth come from?' " She laughed, shook her head as if at the absurdity of his search for her housewifely crimes.

The only things that tended to defuse the tension of these visits would be sickness or a failure of some kind. "If David happened to be having some pain, after the heart attack," explained Nancy, "or if he were having a business setback, it would be easier." "What my father loved most," acknowledged her spouse wryly, "was to hear that I wasn't making money, wasn't a success. If he heard I wasn't succeeding, then he wouldn't attack me."

"Then, you see," Nancy hastened to underscore her earlier statement, "his dad would feel he was more in control. Money, sickness, whatever—control was where it was *at* for him."

There was a short silence, after which her husband said, his tone mournful, "Still, he was a remarkable man, my father! The way anything and everything interested him—the interest he took and the knowledge he had about the news, politics, everything going on around him! He cared about, believed in, the importance of the workingman and in work benefits and in paying decent wages—which he did, in his own business, when not too many other business people were doing it!" David's voice was gathering enthusiasm even as he spoke.

"He gave a great deal of money away to charities, Jewish and otherwise as well," he continued. "And the man came to this country without a cent in his pocket—an orphan, in his late teens—who could barely read! His mother—my grandmother, who of course, I never knew—had died giving birth to him, and my grandfather barely took care of him and of his older brother. Then he, too, died when my dad was not yet twelve years old."

David's father had been on his own very early in life. The stories of his difficult boyhood had come to his son via his uncle; his dad had never wanted to discuss his childhood and its privations. "But that the man could arrive in this country," continued David admiringly, "and work himself up into the position of being able to start his own company—and understand the stock market and make *money* on it! And know the name of every senator—who he was, along with the whole history of his voting record—and know whether or not he supported the interests of the common man! My father was deeply concerned about social justice, and he was, in that way, a compassionate man. But he was not," the admission that ended this paean of praise came out with the expiration of a sigh, "compassionate on a one-to-one basis."

The tone of the Sternberg household had been argumentative and demanding, with each person pulling his or her own oar against the emotional currents of the other members of the family. "No one ever had any real concern for *you*," recounted David, "though everyone came in complaining, looking for support." This was what had made Nancy's family seem so enormously attractive to him. "They could sit together without sniping or fighting. There was real interest in hearing what the other person had to say."

THE DEVIL AND THE ANGEL

His wife's background had, indeed, been very different from David's own. Nancy Fein's father had been an executive vice-president of a major New York advertising concern, and she had grown up in affluent Greenwich, not very far from where she lived now. The Feins had not, at least by suburban Westchester standards, been extremely well-to-do. "My folks had to borrow money from my grandmother and Dad's brother in order to buy our house. They were short, a lot of the time, but I never learned about it until later. That didn't affect me, when I was young; there was nothing that I didn't have, nothing that I wanted and felt was lacking."

Nancy's mother, before her marriage, had been an artist—very talented, according to her daughter. She had sacrificed her own career in order to marry and to raise her family. Then, when her children were grown and she might have returned to explore her artistic interests, she had become ill with the cancer which claimed her life at the age of fifty-one.

Nancy's father, who had remarried within the year after her mother's death, had himself died of a heart attack several years later. There was no member of her nuclear family left but her brother—six years older than she was—with whom she had very little contact. He was a highly successful Hollywood screenwriter who, she said, "inhabited a different planet" from the one that she and David lived upon.

She missed having close relatives sorely and wished her parents were there to see their grandchildren turning into adults. Her mother, relatively young at the time of her death, had been someone who loved people, loved life, opened herself out to everyone. "My dad, too, was lots of fun— a witty, urbane man, very likable." She smiled. "His friends used to call him 'Come-to-Me-Frankie', because every other conversation ended with an invitation to come by that evening, for a drink, a game of cards, a talk."

But her dad had been extremely possessive in his relationship with her mother, and, for that reason, he had deeply resented her older brother's birth. "He did *not* want a child, at the time that Roger was born. He was a night reporter then, on a Long Island newspaper, and he—from what I can gather—disliked my brother from the very beginning." She paused momentarily, then remarked that matters had been very different in her own case. "I, by the time I came along, was *wanted*—and I was a girl— so I had a different father than Roger did."

The family environment in which she had been reared had been calm, caring, affectionate and very civilized—with the exception of the quarreling between her father and her brother, which became more fequent during Roger's adolescence and which could get fierce. "I, whenever the fights broke out, tried to disappear. I would hide in my room. Once, though, my brother ran in and hid in my closet, and my father came after him with a tennis racket." She shuddered, as if to indicate how terrifying an experience that had been.

And what position, I inquired, had her mother taken when these two rivals had been battling for her attention? Nancy, looking thoughtful, hesitated before answering. "She was the person in the middle," she replied. "Often, she allied herself with my brother, tried to explain my father's behavior to him." Her mother had, while attempting to assist her son, always tried to do so without alienating her husband.

"And who," I inquired, "was *your* best ally in the family?"

"I didn't need an ally," she responded promptly, "because there was no enemy. But the worse Roger was, the better I tried to be . . . predictably." She grinned. There had been a devil and an angel in her original household—a not uncommon family phenomenon. And the more her brother had played out the designated script of the bad child, the more she herself had been motivated (or condemned) to occupy the role of the good one.

That place in the emotional system, while to all outward appearances the more attractive one, is as unrealistic and demanding a slot as is that of the family outlaw. What it requires is that the person who occupies it be angelic on an around-the-clock basis—the all-good, unambivalent counterpart to her all-bad, unambivalently demonic opposite.

Things had not been, I suspected, perfectly easy for Nancy in her family of origin, either, but they had been difficult in a less obvious fashion for her than they had for her brother. For while the angel of the household can be (or *must* be) positive, competent and accommodating, she is being called upon to negate her feelings of unhappiness, rebelliousness, sadness, distress—to deny and disavow such feelings in her inner experience and in her outward behavior.

"She was scared," commented David thoughtfully, in what seemed to me a wonderful act of mind reading, "of her parents' turning on her, someday, and treating her the way they treated Roger." He glanced at his wife. "You know you've *said* that to me," he asserted, as if expecting some objection on her part. But Nancy merely shrugged, nodded her agreement.

If she had been the perfect paragon of a daughter, it was nothing less than the situation had demanded of her.

Unresolved Mourning

Nancy's mother, whose name was Helen, had been an extraordinary person, according to both her daughter and her son-in-law. "She was— I feel like a traitor even saying it—more like a real mother to me than my *own* mother ever was," said David, lovingly and enthusiastically.

"I'm a person who—I tend to get very excitable, upset about things, and Nancy's mother would sit me down in this special way that she had. And she'd say, 'Son, I want to talk over these problems with you, from start to finish, no matter how long it takes us doing it. Let's put our heads together and understand what's happening.' And we would . . . talk not only about me, and what was on my mind, but her and her life—*everything*. There was nothing that I couldn't talk about *to* her!" His eyes, I realized with a start, had grown moist with tears as he spoke. "She was someone—" he started to add and then stopped, as if continuing would be too difficult.

Nancy, seated next to him on the sofa, remained dry-eyed, but she placed a hand upon her spouse's shoulder, squeezed it lightly. Helen Fein's painful descent into death—the cancer had been a breast tumor which was not discovered until after it had metastasized into other areas of the body and was beyond control—had, I learned, taken place during the same year that David's heart attack had occurred. He had, in fact, been stricken a mere six weeks after his mother-in-law's death.

This was a time of his life when he'd been, as both members of the couple agreed, behaving like a whirling dervish: getting his own business started and holding down two other part-time jobs simultaneously. There had been, as David now realized, a frantic quality to his behavior, a sense that it was now or never when it came to beating his father out—or at least demonstrating that he was as good a man as his parent.

In point of fact, disturbing events were occurring on his own side of the family as well as on his wife's. For during this selfsame period, his father had become involved in a flagrant affair. "My dad never *had* had any time for my mother," stated David with a brief shrug. "He was an ebullient guy, a big partygoer; she was a homebody, someone who wallowed in her migraines and insomnia."

They were a mismatch, according to their son, and his mother had always regretted having rejected another suitor and chosen his father instead. But her husband had (she later maintained) come into her life and courted her with all the irresistible force of a tornado. It was she who had, nevertheless—according to the story circulated throughout the family by David's father—ultimately rejected her spouse. She had decided, in her early sixties, that it was time to write finis to the sexual aspects of their relationship.

His father's response had been a humiliating demonstration, paraded before everyone, that if *she* were done with sex he could avail himself of a partner who wasn't. The woman he had taken up with was actually married to his own wife's brother, and the scandal that ensued upon this "romance" had been enormous.

David himself, during this period, was drifting into an outside relationship of his own. He had met a young woman, the daughter of a client, with whom he'd begun having a series of long, intimate luncheon dates. "She was a very lovely, very compassionate person," he said, "and I was desperately in need of someone to *talk to*—a sounding board, a listener— even though I did feel guilty about it and did feel that I was doing what I believed to be wrong."

His own wife, bent upon what was happening to her mother, seemed frozen and unavailable. For Nancy, instead of beginning the process of advance mourning for the terrible loss that was to occur, was being her usual positive, helpful and competent self—as good a child as she ever had been. It was as if, having been bred to disavow that which was painful, sad and distressing, she could not take in, experience and integrate the grievous event that was actually then taking place. The sorrow of this time was something that her entire life had left her unprepared for dealing with. The painful feelings were inside her, but she, being who she was, could do no other than resist them and deny their very existence.

It was two weeks before David's heart attack—and a month after his mother-in-law's death—that the flirtation in which he was engaged reached its moment of decision. The romantic lunches with his client's daughter had been taking place in New London, Connecticut, where his business brought him on a weekly basis. That evening, he was staying over—and his young friend came to his motel. "I don't know how true it's going to sound," he told me, looking embarrassed, "but she came there and invited herself in. I guess, for me, there was kind of an ambivalent feeling. I was thirty-five, almost thirty-six, and I really thought she was very attractive. She was, at the time, around twenty-three years old."

He was blushing; his cheeks had turned a deep rosy color. I glanced at Nancy, who did not look particularly uncomfortable. "She had also brought some alcohol, and we had a drink or two, and before I knew it, we were getting undressed," he continued. "And we ended up in bed. Suddenly, I realized I couldn't do anything—because if I did it, I couldn't say to myself that this is *not* what I want from my wife! I couldn't demand, of Nancy, that type of loyalty and commitment and discipline. It wasn't that I didn't want to make love then—I definitely *did* want to—but I knew that I could never be able to tell her, 'Don't do it,' or claim that *I* never had." He shrugged, lifted his shoulders, as if to indicate the total impasse at which he had arrived.

"He cannot lie," put in Nancy, as if by way of explanation. "The man cannot; it's just constitutionally impossible. He can *try*, but he simply can't go on with it. . . ." Her voice, and her entire expression, bespoke her pleasure in this fact and her approval.

"Naturally," he resumed, "the young lady thought I was wacko, impotent, or both. All I said was 'I can't do it, I just can't,' and she asked me, 'What are you telling me? Am I not pretty enough?' And she had on, I remember, these small panties—I felt as if I were being torn in half. It was the animal instinct and the intellectual instinct, the two things pulling against each other. There was also—for me, the deciding factor—morality. If I did this, it would be a complete breakdown of what I believed was the way a man and woman lived together . . . a total breakdown of loyalty and trust."

His relationship with this young woman had ended with this incident; David had, however, continued experiencing a great deal of turmoil about it. Their flirtation, though physically unconsummated, had been a long secret he had been keeping from his wife. And even though it had ended, he went on feeling guilty and upset about it.

Then he had had his heart attack. Nancy's focus of concern—the recent loss of her beloved parent—had of necessity to shift radically and immediately to the family emergency at hand. All else had been put aside, as she ran her household, cared for the children, took over a major portion of David's business activities and worked to preserve his health and well-being. Her performance, during this time, had been exemplary. But what she had found it impossible to do, throughout this entire period, was to mourn—to process the awful feelings of grief and desolation and to integrate her mother's death into the fibers of her own understanding and being.

"I'm not the kind of person who gets depressed," she acknowledged evenly, in the course of our conversations. "I get upset but never depressed. And one of the things that we learned in therapy is that David carries my depression for me. He deals with these problems for me, because it's so hard for *me* to deal with them. . . . When he lay down, in the period after his heart attack—which was the period after my mother's death— he was really lying down for *both* of us. And I was feeding into that, making him stay there much longer—because he was carrying for me what I couldn't carry for myself."

She fell silent, and for a space of time no one said a word. "Nancy," commenced her husband, at last, "has—in the same way that I'm overly expressive and even hypochondriacal at times—a tendency to suppress everything, never admit that anything might be troubling, or a problem, or something that was disturbing her. That's her family: 'Don't complain.' Her mother was dying and in terrible pain, and you never heard a word about it. . . ."

David, with his ready emotionality, had been recruited to do the complaining (and, to some large degree, the feeling of the pain) for his wife. For to be lovable, in Nancy's deepest understanding, was to be a happy, healthy, adequate and always superpositive individual. She, the perennially good child of her parents, had never learned to recognize or accept responsibility for those aspects of her internal being that were negative, distressed, or even frankly despairing. Challenged, during the terrible months of her mother's final illness, she had been totally incapable of experiencing and expressing the grief that lay like a solid stone deep inside her.

Her husband, stressed by *her* stress and by his own pain about Nancy's mother's death, was burdened by the requirement that he feel and express her sorrow as well as his own. Because of his overinvolved relationship with an angry and competitive father, he was, moreover, struggling with a great many self-critical, self-condemnatory feelings and thoughts. For the message being beamed to him from his parent was that any act of healthy independence or success was to be viewed as a personal affront. To win his dad's love, he would have to remain under his control—which meant, at that point in David's own adult life, being either ill or a failure.

As his father's son he had, on the other hand, needed to identify with, and wanted to emulate, a man whom he very much admired—a person who cared about his fellow human beings, who had succeeded against incredible odds, and who had demonstrated so much ingenuity and bravery. To *be a man* meant doing deeds that were similar to his parent's.

David had, however, internalized the terrible stream of reproach attendant upon any act of independence or healthy aggression that he undertook. He could not succeed as a competent, successful male without evoking, within himself, his father's savage anger and criticism. Being lovable, as he had learned to understand it, meant being needy, dependent and controlled by the other person in the relationship. To be strong and healthy was associated with guilt and terrible reproaches of the self.

Inevitably, then, his own urges toward mastery and success elicited the angry, critical voice inside him. David's way of dealing with his own ambivalent, unmanageable feelings—and achieving some semblance of a resolution of his inner conflict—had been, routinely, to see the anger as existing in Nancy. He would provoke her, when he needed an enemy, to turn upon him the rage of a furious parent. He put his anger into her—in the same way that he had put his sense of health and adequacy into his intimate partner's safekeeping.

Nancy's role, in the projective identification world they had formerly inhabited, was to represent the well-being and competency in the relationship; David's was to carry the distress, illness, the messy, sloppy emotionality. Disentangling their exchanged projections, in the course of therapy, had involved *her* learning to take conscious ownership of the hurting that went on inside her and *his* becoming able to experience himself as a competent male without undue self-reproach or self-hatred.

The Sternbergs had, in other words, moved up from level four and were now living (for much, though not all of the time) in the very different land of level two. This movement up the ladder had been accomplished by means of psychotherapy combined with the remarkably effective behavioral homework assignments described earlier (see Chapter Eleven, "Tasks").

ASCENDING THE SCALE

A couple's move upward, on the metaphoric scale described earlier, can be caused by any of a variety of differing reasons. It may happen, as was true in the Sternbergs' case, as a result of therapeutic attention to the relationship. Or it may occur because *one* partner is ready (either as the result of individual therapy or because of some gut impulse toward growth) to have it better and is able to convince the other partner to follow him or her on what feels like a perilous journey.

A shift upward may, on the other hand, be due to changing circumstances in the partners' lives—a good phase during which both feel so confident that a spurt of self-generated growth very naturally takes place. Or it may come about as a consequence of the pair's agreeing to go through a carefully calibrated set of behavioral tasks (such as those described in Chapter Eleven) which are designed to *produce* changes in their customary way of transacting the emotional business between them.

Intimate partners must, in any case, be relatively healthy and functional to allow changes in their marriage to occur because *what most of us need, and need in the most profound way, is predictability in our relationships.* We need to know what the other person is likely to do next, even if what he or she does is highly pathological and makes us feel miserable much of the time. This is the reason why changing anything at all can feel so terrifying. The consequences of interacting differently are unfathomable.

For Nancy Sternberg, the consequences of being different had proved to be surprisingly delightful. "I think we would not be married now," she had told me straightforwardly, on the telephone, before our first meeting, "if we hadn't gotten a lot of matters between us straightened out." Not only had they been able to deal with a lot of the bad stuff between them, she'd added, but they had liberated a lot of the good stuff—the loving feelings—that had been buried underneath so much suspicion and mistrust.

The changes in the marriage, as the Sternbergs described them, were pervasive. "Take money," said Nancy. "The fact that we handle it in the ways we do now is nothing short of a miracle, considering David's background. Considering that, in his family, money was love, and love was money. One of the major pieces of work that David did in our therapy—to my mind—was to learn to dissociate the two things."

I knew, I commented, turning to her husband, that money had been a hot issue between him and his father. But how, I asked, had it become an issue between him and his wife? "In what specific ways," I further clarified the question, "did the problem actually manifest itself?"

David looked at me wryly, cocked his head to one side. "I was using money in the same ways," he replied. "Just as I wanted my father to give me money—which is to say, love—I was beginning to do the same kinds of things around here: accumulate it, *have* it, but not use it. And naturally, my children would see this: that my money was my love, which I doled out to them. I would be very tight, when it came to giving them their allowances and make the same kinds of overtures that my dad did: 'Look, I'm giving you two dollars for your allowance. You're very lucky; you're getting more than other people get and doing absolutely nothing for it. But I'm giving it to you because I love you.' "

"Or," she took up the tale, "the kids would do some kind of work that their father had promised to pay them for. And then one of them would come and say, 'Okay, Dad, I did it,' and he would answer, 'Oh, well, I'm glad that job is done.' And this would force the kid into the unpleasant position of having to say, 'But you promised you would pay for it.' David then would answer by saying, 'Do you think *my* customers pay me right away? That I can just walk in and get the money the minute that the job is done?' And he would play games of that sort."

I glanced at David, who nodded, as if to corroborate the testimony his wife was offering. "Then," she resumed, "the kid would ask him four days later, for the third time, and he'd reply, 'You're asking me for that money again! Why don't you stop pestering me about it?' It was *awful*," she stated, a note of anger resounding in her voice.

"Everything in my life had always revolved around money. Everything was converted into—" began David, but Nancy interrupted him in mid-sentence. "This went on between the two of us as well. David would say to me, 'Here is your money for the week.' He had his little stockpile, and whenever he needed something, he went into that and took it. But when I needed it, there was a set amount, and I wasn't allowed to go over it! Heaven forbid that I got left with a car with no gas in it! I had to take it out of the food money and then be forced to say, 'David, I need more cash.' " She drew herself up, and mimicked the stern reply that the question would elicit: "How *come* you need more money, and what in the world did you spend it on?"

"That went on," put in David uncomfortably, "for the first ten years of our marriage."

"It was just a very paternalistic way to behave," Nancy swept on. "And it made me very, very angry, because on a practical level I am just as thrifty a person as he is. I don't spend money on things I don't need, or don't want—I've never done that. Even as a child, I was a saver."

"But it was a real guilt and power thing for me," admitted her spouse. "Exactly," she said, with a brief nod of her head. "It was, I mean, *love* and power," he amended, "because at that point, following in my dad's footsteps, the two things were mixed up in my head. I thought I had a very human, kind approach, that I was developing a sense of values for my wife, my children. . . . I was teaching them." He smiled a rueful smile. "I didn't realize what strings I was pulling."

"And here am I, a grown woman—an adult—with children, running a household, knowing perfectly well what things cost and having someone try to teach me something that it was not his business to teach me! Because I already knew anyway . . . and this whole situation fomented a great deal of resentment. So one of the arrangements we made, when we became able to negotiate with each other so much more effectively—which we did, during therapy—was to have a place for funds to be kept, into which either one of us could go for cash, when we needed it."

Once David was able to separate "love" and "money" in the relationship with his wife, he'd found the same dilemmas in his relationships with his children readily and easily solvable as well. Money was now, as both members of the couple agreed, a nonissue in the family and between them.

So was sex, which had also been a problematical issue at times.

"If," explained Nancy, "I didn't feel like having sex on a particular night, David would take it so badly—as if I were rejecting him as a human being. And so, many times, I felt that I couldn't say no, because he would overreact."

Had this issue, I inquired, resolved itself in therapy as well? "Yes," she answered promptly, "because it wasn't a function of sex per se, but of where we were over this power thing. I felt, for many years, that David had—"

"I can see," he interrupted, with anger in his voice, "how, when we get into this kind of discussion and regress to what was happening then, I get certain feelings back again."

"This is making him annoyed," commented his wife, looking at her spouse with questioning eyes. "Yes," he said.

There was a silence. "Well . . . ?" Nancy asked him finally. "No, go on," he told her, with a wave forward of his hand. She was flustered. "I forgot what I was saying. . . . Oh . . . I always felt that there was, in David, a certain resentment of women with strength, yet strong women are the very ones to whom he is attracted. And I think, at that time, that both things—money, sex . . . probably the children, too—really had to do with how strong and powerful he himself happened to be feeling."

"Is what you're saying," I asked her straightforwardly, "that he was very much in need of control?"

She blinked several times, but replied with equal forthrightness, "Control . . . yes, that's the word. He had to make sure he had the upper hand. Can you *imagine*," she added, "the kind of distance the pair of us had to come, to get to where we are now?"

"It wasn't control," objected David, at that moment, "so much as it was rejection. I felt—well, I was always a very sexual kind of person. That's an enjoyable part of my life and I always was, and hope will be, fairly demanding in that area. So my feeling was that if the other person was making excuses it was in some way a reflection on myself. Either I was being rejected because I wasn't a good lover or I wasn't doing the things that satisfied her, but whatever! In some way, the causes lay in me, not in her."

He paused, then continued reflectively. "There was also the feeling—and this gets into the whole female dominance issue—that this was the way that a woman could really anger a man, flaunt her power. I guess I saw that in my own home, with my mother, because sex was—it was almost nonexistent. I have the feeling that, when I was a kid, there was a big sexual war going on in my household . . . the war that ended with my father carrying on with an aunt of mine.

"So." He shrugged as if to say the connection he was making was obvious. "If Nancy wanted to read or to knit and it was nine o'clock and I wanted to shut the lights off and make love, I would be livid. I felt this was her way of getting back at me for the other controlling cards that I held—such as the money, for example. She had the sex control, because she knew I wouldn't go outside the marriage. In fact, in the encounter that I almost had—with that young woman in New London—the big thing for me was probably that I was getting involved with somebody who wanted it as against someone whom I had to *ask*. . . ."

"That was your perception," said Nancy tartly.

"That was my perception," he agreed. "And not until we got into treatment did I realize that a lot of the problem was due to misreading—not understanding the basic fact that we are different people, and if she doesn't feel like having sex at certain times, hey, that's okay, too! She can say to me, 'Maybe not that way,' or 'I'm really not in the mood for it,' or, 'I'm not in the mood but I can see you're really up for it, so let's go.' And I can honestly say I really don't care; she can decide."

His wife looked at him, laughed, then turned and said to me, "He can usually change my mind very rapidly." I noticed, at that moment, that her hand rested in between his two hands, though I hadn't noticed it getting there.

It seemed an opportune time to ask them a question that I asked of every couple at some point or other during our interviews: "If you were thinking about sex, and wondering about some particular aspect of it—some question such as 'How often do other couples have intercourse?' or, 'How many women have multiple orgasms?' or whatever—what thing would come to your mind?"

They glanced at each other, in puzzlement, then smiled, turned and stared at me blankly for a brief time. It was Nancy who elected to respond to me first. "I don't think it would be any question about the mechanics. I think I have a fairly large store of physical knowledge. But what I might wonder is . . . I was a virgin, when I got married, and never fooled around. . . . Is this it? One partner in my whole life? What would it be like to have a little affair on the side? How exciting would it be?"

I laughed, said to David, "How exciting was it—almost?"

"My mother always said almost doesn't count!" countered Nancy, laughing too. "He *couldn't*."

"But if he had?" I asked her, and she shook her head immediately. "That would not be the deciding factor. If my need to experience it were, in the first place, strong enough to take the risk of forming an emotional attachment to someone else—when I already have one that makes me very happy—I'd have to weigh into it the whole question of whether I'd want to do something that might upset the balance, might lead to more unhappiness than happiness eventually. So my desire to actually go out and satisfy this curiosity is really insufficient to me. I'm not curious enough to jeopardize what I have now."

She paused, then added, after several moments of reflection, "In the second place, what—when you think about it—could possibly happen? How many things can you do? Sex is a finite type of thing. I feel that it probably would be a disappointment to me, given the fact that we have a very exciting and full sex life, right now. . . . I don't know what more it can bring. Except," she grinned, "to say, 'Okay, I've had more than one partner, so I can die now, knowing that!' "

Nancy, having considered the question, had clearly reached her own conclusion. She realized, she added, that some couples did get into open marriage sorts of arrangements, ones in which they agreed to have other sexual partners but remain faithful to the emotional attachment that the two of them shared. "I don't know how well it really works for them," her voice was dubious, "but for us it would not work, given the kind of people that we are. We are both very conservative, very traditional—"

"It's hypocrisy!" snorted David, at that moment.

"It would be hypocritical for you," she returned, equably, "but it could possibly work for *them*. I don't think it could possibly work for me—for us—for we're both loyal types—"

"I would like to hear the way in which they discuss the affectional bond with which they honor each other!" he said, shaking his head as if to dismiss the entire idea. "And the sexual bond, which they go out and experience with other people! I honestly don't know what they perceive the sexual act as being. Is it just like playing baseball or basketball—you come home, towel off, say that was a good game, and that's the end of it? I don't know; if that's the way they see it, maybe there's no hypocrisy involved. But I find it hard to believe it can be done. To me, what they are doing is rationalizing away the emotional tie that exists between them."

"And if there is no emotional tie, then it *is* all an athletic exercise," agreed Nancy. I observed, dryly, that sometimes married people went outside the relationship and found outside partners—and discussed them with each other—because there was not that much for them to talk about, otherwise.

"For me," David responded passionately, "it is so difficult to understand that this would be a subject that a couple would be able to converse about! And *not* be able to converse and understand each other about their other, deeper emotions—about what life is, and what death is, and what family is, and what money is, and what education is, and racism is. . . . For Nancy and myself, this is our *bond*, a bond of how it is that we really think and what we feel! And what we want our children to follow us in and to feel as well. To have the only area we could discuss be the sexual area—it's beyond my comprehension, it's so *thin*! But I see it," he acknowledged, "it's very prevalent, in what I read, what I see on television."

"The amount of sex that is involved—" he added, but never went on, never completed the sentence. "I know," he declared, "that what I consider to be the basic joys of life—relating to people, relating totally—" He stopped again, then commenced anew. "As for the sexual part, my fantasy is different from her fantasies." They looked at each other and smiled.

"How are they different?" I inquired.

"Mine are all mechanical—doing different things. But again"—he held up a hand as if to prevent me from drawing false inferences—"the risk factor is very, very high."

"The risk factor?"

"Yes, because his thing is—he would be looking for two women at the same time," explained his wife comfortably and knowledgeably. "At *least* two." David laughed.

"And in my case," she pointed out, "I would be only looking for one guy."

What he wondered about—and this, he told me, would be his own question about sex—was whether males fantasized much more than females did. "For me, each time I drive around, the fantasies are a little bit different. And I think that what Mr. Carter said about lust in his heart is true for a lot of guys. I truly believe the man was being very honest and honorable; there is lust in a lot of men. I will catch sight of a young girl, and I will wonder what sex would be like with her. How different would it be? And since I'm an older man, what kind of an experience would it be for *her*? I wouldn't dwell on it—I might be driving past some college campus—but it passes by; it is not a reality. There's no chance of its being a reality; it's only something that is a . . . a curiousness."

Both their responses to my question had, I remarked, been very similar. The only thing that each of them wondered about was what sex would be like with another partner.

"Yes," said Nancy thoughtfully, "I don't know what else there is to wonder about. I mean, if you want to know how many times other people have intercourse, the Kinsey reports will tell you. . . ." Her voice had drifted off, and a dreamy expression was settling in upon her features. "We went to Washington, a couple of weeks ago," she went on, in an apparent change of subject. "We took James with us and visited Carol, who's working for the Justice Department right now. And we stayed at the Marriott, which overlooks all of downtown D.C."

I nodded, waited for her to continue. "The last time we'd been there, we'd had a really crummy room. We didn't like it; it was on a slab, in the back, almost like a motel room in a unit behind the hotel building itself. So I said to the guy at the front desk, 'Please don't give us one of those back rooms; I want to be in the main part of the hotel.' And he said, 'Oh, did you have a bad experience last time? Then this time we'll make it up to you.' And he gave us the Marriott suite—at the same price— which is two monster rooms on the top floor. It has," she said happily, "a panoramic view of Georgetown and Washington."

"And a bar, three televisions." David sighed.

"A bar, three televisions," she repeated.

"A telephone in the bathroom," he added, sounding delighted.

"It was really unbelievable," Nancy agreed. "And we had a bed, as big as this room." She swung her arm around, to include the entire expanse of the den in which we were seated—an area of some twelve by sixteen feet. "And we opened up the drapes, so that we could see all of downtown Washington. And that," she concluded meaningfully, "is how we spent our entire evening . . . in bed."

"I thought you were going to get even more graphic," said David, teasing. She shook her head no.

"She's not mentioning that we were directly by the George Washington Monument," David said.

"Right, the big phallic symbol." Nancy laughed. "And there we were, all lined up in front of it! But we are, right now, freer, more loose; there's no tension in us about these matters. Neither one of us is tied up in knots about anything so far as sex is concerned. We enjoy ourselves." She hesitated, met my gaze directly, a pleased look upon her features. "I took my satin nightgown to Washington," she told me. "Because at home I wear flannel pajamas." David put his arm around the back of her shoulders.

"We have a good time," she said.

Works Cited

INTRODUCTION

Elisabeth A. Carter, M.S.W., "The Challenge of the Middle Years." Keynote address presented at the New York Chapter of the American Association for Marital and Family Therapy, Jamaica, West Indies, 1985.

Stanley Kunitz, "Route Six," in: *The Poems of Stanley Kunitz 1928–1978* (Boston: Atlantic-Little, Brown, 1979).

Monica McGoldrick; John K. Pearce; and Joseph Giordano, *Ethnicity and Family Therapy* (New York/London: The Guilford Press, 1982).

Carol Nadelson; Derek Polonsky; and Mary Alice Mathews, "Marriage as a Developmental Process," in *Marriage and Divorce: A Contemporary Perspective*, eds. Carol C. Nadelson and Derek C. Polonsky (New York/London: The Guilford Press, 1984).

Anthony P. Thompson, "Extramarital Sex: A Review of the Research Literature," *The Journal of Sex Research*, vol. 19, art. 1 (February 1983).

Abigail Trafford, *Crazy Time: Surviving Divorce* (New York: Harper & Row: 1982).

Mark Zborowski, *People in Pain* (San Francisco: Jossey-Bass, 1969).

CHAPTER ONE. THE ATTRACTION

Peter Berger and Hansfried Kellner, "Marriage and the Construction of Reality: An Exercise in the Microsociology of Knowledge," *Diogenes*, vol. 46 (Summer 1964).

Henry V. Dicks, *Marital Tensions: Clinical Studies Towards a Psychological Theory of Interaction* (New York: Basic Books, 1967).

Lily Pincus and Christopher Dare, *Secrets in the Family* (New York: Pantheon Books, 1978).

CHAPTER TWO. WHERE THE PAST AND THE PRESENT CONVERGE: GENOGRAMS

Patricia H. Meyer, "Between Families: The Unattached Young Adult," in *The Family Life Cycle: A Framework for Family Therapy*, eds. Elizabeth A. Carter and Monica McGoldrick (New York: Gardner Press, Inc., 1980).
Pincus and Dare, op. cit.

CHAPTER THREE. AUTONOMY AND INTIMACY

Walter Toman, *Family Constellation: Its Effect on Personality and Social Behavior* (New York: Springer, 1961).

CHAPTER FOUR. LOVE ITSELF

John Bowlby, *Attachment and Loss*, vol. 1, *Attachment* (London: Hogarth Press, 1969).
Henry V. Dicks, "Object Relations Theory and Marital Studies," *British Journal of Medical Psychology*, vol. 36 (1963).
Selma Fraiberg, "How a Baby Learns to Love," *Redbook* (May 1971).
Colin Murray Parkes, "Psycho-Social Transitions: A Field for Study," *Social Science and Medicine*, vol. 5, (1971).
Theodore Lidz, *The Person: His and Her Development Throughout the Life Cycle*, rev. ed. (New York: Basic Books, Inc., 1976).
Michael R. Liebowitz, *The Chemistry of Love* (Boston: Little, Brown and Co., 1983).
Pincus and Dare, op. cit.
Sydney Smith, "The Golden Fantasy: A Regressive Reaction to Separation Anxiety," *International Journal of Psychoanalysis*, vol. 58 (1977).
René A. Spitz, "Hospitalism: An Inquiry into the Genesis of Psychiatric Conditions in Early Childhood," in *Psychoanalytic Study of the Child*, vol. 1: eds., Anna Freud, Hans Hartmann, and Ernst Kris (New York: International Universities Press, 1945).

CHAPTER FIVE. HAPPILY EVER AFTER

Christopher Lasch, *Haven in a Heartless World: The Besieged Family* (New York: Basic Books, 1977).

CHAPTER SIX. MARRIAGES AS SYSTEMS

Murray Bowen, *Family Therapy and Clinical Practice* (New York/London: Jason Aronson, Inc., 1978).

Sigmund Freud, *Introductory Lectures on Psycho-Analysis*, tr. James Strachey (New York: W. W. Norton, 1977).

Froma Walsh, "Family Therapy: A Systemic Orientation to Treatment," in *Handbook of Clinical Social Work*, eds. Aaron Rosenblatt and Diana Waldfogel (San Francisco: Jossey-Bass, 1983).

CHAPTER SEVEN. AN INTIMATE SYSTEM: THE CARETAKER AND THE WOUNDED BIRD

Lucille K. Forer, *Birth Order and Life Roles* (Springfield, Ill.: Charles C. Thomas, 1969).

Jay Haley, "Toward a Theory of Pathological Systems," in *The Interactional View*, eds. Paul Watzlawick and John H. Weakland (New York: W. W. Norton, 1977).

Salvador Minuchin, *Families and Family Therapy* (Cambridge, Mass.: Harvard University Press, 1974).

Clifford Sager, *Marriage Contracts and Couple Therapy: Hidden Forces in Intimate Relationships* (New York: Brunner/Mazel, Inc., 1976).

Walter Toman, op. cit.

CHAPTER EIGHT. MARITAL INFIDELITY

Janice L. Francis, "Toward the Management of Heterosexual Jealousy," *Journal of Marriage and Family Counseling*, vol. 3 (1977).

Bernard L. Greene, Ronald R. Lee, and Noel Lustig, "Conscious and Unconscious Factors in Marital Infidelity," *Medical Aspects of Human Sexuality* (September 1974).

Frederick G. Humphrey, "Treating Extramarital Sexual Relationships in Sex and Couples Therapy," in *Couples Therapy for Sexual Problems*, eds. Gerald Weeks and Larry Hof (New York: Brunner/Mazel, Inc., 1986).

A. C. Kinsey, W. B. Pomeroy, and C. E. Martin, *Sexual Behavior in the Human Male* (Philadelphia: W. B. Saunders, 1948).

A. C. Kinsey, W. B. Pomeroy, and P. H. Gebhard, *Sexual Behavior in the Human Female* (Philadelphia: W. B. Saunders, 1953).

Gilbert D. Nass, Roger W. Libby, and Mary Pat Fisher, *Sexual Choices* (Belmont, Calif.: Wadsworth, 1981).

Betsy Stone, personal communication.

Thompson, op. cit.

———. "Extramarital Sexual Crisis: Common Themes and Therapy Implications," *Journal of Marriage Therapy*, vol. 10, no. 4 (Winter 1984).

Robert N. Whitehurst, "Extramarital Sex: Alienation or Extension of Normal Behavior?," in *Extramarital Relations*, ed. G. Neubeck (Englewood Cliffs, N.J.: Prentice-Hall, 1969).

CHAPTER NINE. EMOTIONAL TRIANGLES

Bowen, op. cit.

Carter, and McGoldrick, op. cit.

Lynn Hoffman, *Foundations of Family Therapy: A Conceptual Framework for Systems Change* (New York: Basic Books, Inc., 1981).

Stuart Johnson, personal communication.

Kitty La Perriere, "On Children, Adults and Families: The Critical Transition from Couple to Parents," in *Family Therapy: Combining Psychodynamic and Family Systems Approaches*, eds. John K. Pearce and Leonard J. Friedman (New York: Grune & Stratton, Inc., 1980).

Monica McGoldrick, "The Joining of Families Through Marriage: The New Couple," in *The Family Life Cycle*, loc. cit.

Stanley Willis, Commentary on a paper delivered by Greene, Lee, and Lustig, op. cit.

CHAPTER TEN. WHAT MARITAL PROBLEMS ARE MADE OF: COUPLES IN COLLUSION

David A. Berkowitz, "An Overview of the Psychodynamics of Couples: Bridging Concepts," in *Marriage and Divorce: A Contemporary Perspective*, loc. cit.

Ellen Berman, Harold Lief, and Ann Marie Williams, "A Model of Marital Interaction," in *The Handbook of Marriage and Marital Therapy*, ed. G. Pirooz Sholevar (Jamaica, N.Y.: Spectrum Medical and Scientific Books, 1981).

W. Ronald D. Fairbairn, *An Object Relations Theory of the Personality* (New York: Basic Books, Inc., 1952).

Larry B. Feldman, "Dysfunctional Marital Conflict: An Integrative Interpersonal-Intrapsychic Model," *Journal of Marriage and Family Therapy*, vol. 8, no. 4, October 1982.

Freud, op. cit.

――――. *A General Introduction to Psychoanalysis* (New York: Boni & Liveright, New York, 1916–17).

――――. "Some Psychological Consequence of the Anatomical Distinction Between the Sexes," in *The Standard Edition of the Complete Psychological Works of Sigmund Freud*, ed. James Strachey, vol. 19 (London: Hogarth Press, 1961).

――――. "Female Sexuality," in *The Standard Edition of the Complete Psychological Works of Sigmund Freud*, vol. 21 (London: Hogarth Press, 1961).

Melanie Klein, "Notes on Some Schizoid Mechanisms," in *International Journal of Psychoanalysis*, vol. 27 (1946).

――――. "On Identification," in *New Directions in Psychoanalysis*, eds. Melanie Klein, Paula Heimann, and R. E. Money-Kyrle (New York: Basic Books, Inc., 1956).

Pincus, and Dare, op. cit.

A. G. Thompson, "Introduction" to *Marriage: Studies in Emotional Conflict and Growth*," ed. Lily Pincus (London: Institute of Marital Studies, The Tavistock Institute of Human Relations, 1960).

John Zinner and Roger Shapiro, "Projective Identification as a Mode of Perception and Behaviour in Families of Adolescents," *International Journal of Psychoanalysis*, 53. 523–530 (1972).

CHAPTER ELEVEN. TASKS

Stuart Johnson: Personal interview.

CHAPTER TWELVE. A CLASSIC SYSTEM: THE SILENT HUSBAND AND THE HYSTERICAL WIFE

American Psychiatric Association, *Diagnostic and Statistical Manual of Mental Disorders*, 3d ed. (Washington, D.C.: American Psychiatric Association, 1980).

Anthony Storr, *The Art of Psychotherapy* (New York: Methuen, Inc., 1980).

Jurg Willi, "The Hysterical Marriage," in *Contemporary Marriage: Structure*,

Dynamics and Therapy, eds. Henry Grunebaum and Jacob Christ (Boston: Little, Brown and Co., 1976).

CHAPTER THIRTEEN. SEXUAL SYMPTOMS: PSYCHOLOGY, BIOLOGY, OR BOTH?

Carol Botwin, *Is There Sex After Marriage?* (Boston: Little, Brown and Co., 1985).

Sigmund Freud, "Some Character Types Met with in Psychoanalytic Work," in *Standard Edition*, vol. 14 (London: Hogarth Press, 1961).

William H. Masters and Virginia E. Johnson, *Human Sexual Inadequacy* (Boston: Little, Brown and Co., 1970).

Richard F. Spark, R. A. White, and P. B. Connolly, "Impotence Is Not Always Psychogenic: Newer Insights into Hypothalamic-Pituitary-Gonadal Dysfunction," *JAMA*, vol. 243 (1980).

CHAPTER FOURTEEN. WHAT, PRECISELY, HAPPENS DURING SEX?

William H. Masters and Virginia E. Johnson, *Human Sexual Response* (Boston: Little, Brown and Co., 1966).

CHAPTER FIFTEEN. SEXUAL CURES

Seymour Fisher, *The Female Orgasm: Psychology, Physiology, Fantasy* (New York: Basic Books, Inc., 1973).

Ellen Frank, Carol Anderson, and Debra Rubenstein, "Frequency of Sexual Dysfunction in 'Normal' Couples," *New England Journal of Medicine* (1978).

Sigmund Freud, "Three Essays on the Theory of Sexuality" (1905), in *The Standard Edition of the Complete Psychological Works of Sigmund Freud*, Vol. 8 (London: Hogarth Press, 1953).

Shere Hite, *The Hite Report*. (New York: Dell, 1981).

Helen Singer Kaplan, *Disorders of Sexual Desire and Other New Concepts and Techniques in Sex Therapy* (New York: Simon and Schuster, 1979).

————. *The New Sex Therapy: Active Treatment of Sexual Dysfunctions* (New York: Brunner/Mazel, 1974, 1981).

Carol C. Nadelson, "Problems in Sexual Functioning," in *Treatment Interventions in Human Sexuality*, eds. Carol C. Nadelson and David B. Marcotte (New York: Plenum, 1983).

Raul C. Schiavi, "Evaluation of Impaired Sexual Desire: Biological Aspects," in

Comprehensive Evaluation of Disorders of Sexual Desire, Helen Singer Kaplan, ed. (Washington, D.C.: American Psychiatric Press, 1984).

James H. Semans, "Premature Ejaculation: A New Approach," *Southern Medical Journal*, vol. 49 (1956).

CHAPTER SIXTEEN. THE SECOND SEPARATION

Rubin Blanck and Gertrude Blanck, *Marriage and Personal Development* (New York: Columbia University Press, 1968).

Thomas D. Fogarty, "The Distancer and the Pursuer," *The Family*, vol. 7, no. 1 (1979).

Sigmund Freud, "From the History of an Infantile Neurosis," in *The Standard Edition*, vol. 18 (London: Hogarth Press, 1955).

Pincus and Dare, op. cit.

CHAPTER SEVENTEEN. A GAME FOR TWO PLAYERS

Berman, Lief, and Williams, op. cit.

Ivan Boszormenyi-Nagy and Geraldine M. Spark, *Invisible Loyalties*. (Hagerstown, Md./Evanston/San Francisco/London: Harper & Row, 1973).

Bowen, op. cit.

Martin Buber, "Guilt and Guilt Feelings," *Psychiatry*, vol. 20 (1957).

Paulina McCullough, "Launching Children and Moving On," in *The Family Life Cycle. A Framework for Family Therapy*, loc. cit.

Toman, op. cit.

CHAPTER EIGHTEEN. MARITAL FIGHTING

Feldman, op. cit.

CHAPTER NINETEEN. THE FIVE WAYS IN WHICH COUPLES RELATE

Bowen, op. cit.

Stuart Johnson: Personal interview.

Mark Karpel, "Individuation: From Fusion to Dialogue," *Family Process*, vol. 15 (1976).

Selected Bibliography

American Psychiatric Association. *Diagnostic and Statistical Manual of Mental Disorders, Third Edition.* Prepared by the Task Force on Nomenclature and Statistics. Washington, D.C.: American Psychiatric Association, 1980.

Ananth, J. "Hysterectomy and Depression." *Obst. & Gynec.*, 52:724-730, No. 6, 1978.

Appleton, William S. *Fathers and Daughters.* Garden City, New York: Doubleday, 1981.

Bach, George R., and Peter Wyden. *The Intimate Enemy.* New York: Avon, 1981.

Bannister, Kathleen, and Lily Pincus. *Shared Phantasy in Marital Problems: Therapy in a Four-Person Relationship.* East Greenwich, London, England: Institute of Marital Studies, the Tavistock Institute of Human Relations, 1965.

Beavers, W. Robert. *Successful Marriage: A Family Systems Approach to Couples Therapy.* New York: W. W. Norton, 1985.

Benedek, Therese. "Parenthood as a developmental phase: A contribution to the libido theory." *J. Am. Psychoanalytic Assoc.*, 7:389-416, 1959.

Berger, Peter, and Hansfried Kellner. "Marriage and the Construction of Reality: An Exercise in the Microsociology of Knowledge." *Diogenes*, 46:1-24, Summer 1964.

Berkowitz, David A. "An Overview of the Psychodynamics of Couples: Bridging Concepts," in *Marriage and Divorce: A Contemporary Perspective*, eds. Carol C. Nadelson and Derek C. Polonsky. New York: Guilford Press, 1984.

Berman, Ellen M., and Harold I. Lief. "Marital therapy from a psychiatric perspective: An overview." *Am. J. Psych.*, 132:583-592, June 1975.

———, et al. "A Model of Marital Interaction," in *The Handbook of Marriage and Marital Therapy*, ed. G. Pirooz Sholevar. Jamaica, N.Y.: Spectrum Medical and Scientific Books, 1981.

Bjorksten, Oliver, J.W. *New Clinical Concepts in Marital Therapy.* Washington, D.C.: American Psychiatric Press, Inc., 1985.

Blanck, Rubin, and Gertrude Blanck. *Marriage and Personal Development*. New York: Columbia University Press, 1968.

Boszormenyi-Nagy, Ivan. "From family therapy to a psychology of relationships: Fictions of the individual and fictions of the family." *Comp. Psych.*, 7:408-423, October 1966.

———, and Geraldine M. Spark. *Invisible Loyalties*. New York: Harper & Row, 1973.

Botwin, Carol. *Is There Sex After Marriage?* Boston: Little, Brown, 1985.

Bowen, Murray. *Family Therapy and Clinical Practice*. New York/London: Jason Aronson, Inc., 1978.

Bowlby, John. *Attachment and Loss: Vol. 1. Attachment*. London: Hogarth Press, 1969.

Bradt, Jack Oldham, and Carolyn Johnson Moynihan, eds. *Systems Therapy* (published by the authors). Washington, D.C.: Groome Child Guidance Center, 1971.

Buber, Martin. "Guilt and Guilt Feelings." *Psychiatry*, 20:114-129, 1957.

Carter, Elizabeth A., and Monica McGoldrick. *The Family Life Cycle: A Framework for Family Therapy*. New York: Gardner Press, Inc., 1980.

Center for Family Learning. *The Best of the Family*. New Rochelle, N.Y.: The Center for Family Learning, 1979.

Cherlin, Andrew J. *Marriage, Divorce, Remarriage*. Cambridge, Mass.: Harvard University Press, 1981.

Cohler, Bertram J., and Henry U. Grunebaum. *Mothers, Grandmothers, and Daughters*. New York: John Wiley & Sons, 1981.

Dicks, Henry V. "Object relations theory and marital studies." *Brit. J. Med. Psychol.*, 36:125-129, 1963.

———. "Concepts of Marital Diagnosis and Therapy as Developed at the Tavistock Family Psychiatric Units, London, England," in *Marriage Counselling in Medical Practice*, eds. E. Nash, L. Jessner, and D. Base. Chapel Hill, N.C.: University of North Carolina Press, 1964.

———. *Marital Tensions: Clinical Studies Towards a Psychological Theory of Interaction*. New York: Basic Books, 1967.

Erikson, Erik H. *Identity and the Life Cycle*. New York: W. W. Norton, 1980.

Fairbairn, W. Ronald D. *Psychoanalytic Studies of the Personality*. London: Tavistock Publications, Ltd., 1952.

———. *An Object Relations Theory of the Personality*. New York: Basic Books, 1952.

Feldman, Larry B. "Dysfunctional marital conflict: An integrative interpersonal-intrapsychic model." *J. Marr. Fam. Ther.*, 8: 17-428, No. 4.

Ferber, Andrew, et al. *The Book of Family Therapy*. Boston: Houghton Miflin, 1973.

Fisher, Seymour. *The Female Orgasm: Psychology, Physiology, Fantasy*. New York: Basic Books, 1973.

Flag, Michael F., et al. "Impotence in medical clinic outpatients." *JAMA*, 249:1736-1742, 1983.

Fogarty, Thomas F. "Family Structure in Terms of Triangles," in *Systems Therapy*, eds. Jack Oldham Bradt and Carolyn Johnson Moynihan. Published by the authors, Washington, D.C., 1971.

———. "The distancer and the pursuer," in *The Family*, Vol. 7:11–16, No. 1, 1979.

Foley, Vincent D. *An Introduction to Family Therapy*. New York: Grune & Stratton, 1974.

Forer, Lucille K. *Birth Order and Life Roles*. Springfield, Il.: Charles C. Thomas, 1969.

Fraiberg, Selma. "How a baby learns to love." *Redbook magazine*, 76:164-171, May 1971.

Framo, James L. *Explorations in Marital and Family Therapy*. New York: Springer Publishing Co., 1982.

Francis, Janice L. "Toward the management of heterosexual jealousy." *J. Marr. Fam. Couns.*, 3:61–69, 1977.

Frank, Ellen, et al. "Frequency of sexual dysfunction in 'normal' couples." *N. Engl. J. Med.*, 299:199–215, 1978.

———, and Carol Anderson. "The sexual stages of marriage." *Family Circle*, 64:146-149, February 19, 1980.

Freud, Sigmund. *A General Introduction to Psychoanalysis*. New York: Boni & Liveright, 1916–1917.

———. "From the History of an Infantile Neurosis," in *The Standard Edition of the Complete Psychological Works of Sigmund Freud*, Vol. 18, ed. James Strachey. London: Hogarth Press, 1955.

———. "Some Character Types Met with in Psychoanalytic Work," in *Standard Edition*, Vol. 14. London: Hogarth Press, 1961.

———. "Some Psychological Consequences of the Anatomical Distinction Between the Sexes," in *The Standard Edition of the Complete Psychological Works of Sigmund Freud*, Vol. 19. London: Hogarth Press, 1961.

———. "Female Sexuality," in *The Standard Edition of the Complete Psychological Works of Sigmund Freud*, Vol. 21, London: Hogarth Press, 1961.

———. *Introductory Lectures on Psycho-Analysis*, tr. James Strachey. New York: W. W. Norton, 1977.

Greene, Bernard L., ed. *The Psychotherapies of Marital Disharmony*. New York: The Free Press, 1965.

———, et al. "Conscious and Unconscious Factors in Marital Infidelity." *Med. Aspects Hum. Sexuality*, 8:87-105, September 1974.

Greenspan, Stanley I., and Fortune V. Mananino. "A model for brief intervention with couples based on projective identification." *Am. J. Psych.*, 131:1103-1106, October 1974.

Group for the Advancement of Psychiatry: Committee on the Family. *The Field of Family Therapy*. New York; Brunner/Mazel, 1970.

Grunebaum, Henry, and Jacob Christ, eds. *Contemporary Marriage: Structure, Dynamics, and Therapy*. Boston: Little, Brown, 1976.

Guerin, Philip J., ed. *Family Therapy: Theory and Practice*. New York: Gardner Press, Inc., 1976.

Guntrip, Harry. *Psychoanalytic Theory, Therapy and the Self*. New York: Basic Books, 1971, 1973.

Gurman, A.S., and D.P. Kniskern. *Handbook of Family Therapy*. New York: Brunner/Mazel, 1981.

Haley, Jay. "Marriage therapy." *Arch. Gen. Psych.*, 8:213-234, March 1963.

————, ed. *Changing Families: A Family Therapy Reader*. New York/London: Grune & Stratton, 1971.

————. *Uncommon Therapy: The Psychiatric Techniques of Milton H. Erickson, M.D.* New York: W. W. Norton, 1973.

————. "Toward a Theory of Pathological Systems," in *The Interactional View*, eds. Paul Watzlowick and John H. Weakland. New York: W. W. Norton, 1977.

————. *Problem Solving Therapy: New Strategies for Effective Family Therapy*. San Francisco: Jossey-Bass, 1978.

Hite, Shere. *The Hite Report*. New York: Dell, 1981.

Hoffman, Lynn. *Foundations of Family Therapy: A Conceptual Framework for Systems Change*. New York: Basic Books, 1981.

Hofling, Charles K., and Jerry M. Lewis, eds. *The Family: Evaluation and Treatment*. New York: Brunner/Mazel, 1980.

Humphrey, Frederick G. "Extramarital affairs: clinical approaches in marital therapy." *Psych. Clinics. of North America*, 5:581-593, December 1982.

————. "Treating Extramarital Sexual Relationships in Sex and Couples Therapy," in *Couples Therapy for Sexual Problems*, eds. Gerald Weeks and Larry Hof. New York: Brunner/Mazel, 1986.

Institute of Marital Studies, the Tavistock Institute of Human Relations. *The Marital Relationship as a Focus for Casework*. East Greenwich, London, England: Victoria Hall, 1975.

Jackson, Don D. "The Individual and the Larger Contexts," in *General Systems Theory and Psychiatry*, eds. W. Gray et al. Seaside, Cal., Intersystems Publishers, 1982.

————. "Family Rules: Marital Quid Pro Quo." *Arch. Gen. Psych.*, 12:589-594, June 1965.

Jacobson, Gary, and Robert G. Ryder. "Parental loss and some characteristics of the early marriage relationship." *Amer. J. Orthopsychiat.*, 39:779-787, No. 5, October 1969.

Johnson, Stuart. Personal communication.

Kantor, David, and William Lehr. *Inside the Family: Toward a Theory of Family Process*. New York: Harper & Row, 1976.

Kaplan, Helen Singer. *The New Sex Therapy: Active Treatment of Sexual Dysfunctions*. New York: Brunner/Mazel, 1974, 1981.

————. *The Illustrated Manual of Sex Therapy*. New York: Quadrangle/The New York Times Book Co., 1975.

————. *The Evaluation of Sexual Disorders: Psychological and Medical Aspects.* New York: Brunner/Mazel, 1983.

Karpel, Mark. "Individuation: From fusion to dialogue." *Family Process,* 15:65–82, 1976.

Katchadourian, Herant A., and Donald T. Lunde. *Fundamentals of Human Sexuality,* 2nd Ed. New York: Holt, Rinehart and Winston, 1975.

Kernberg, O. "Barriers to falling in love and remaining in love." *J. Am. Psychoanal. Assoc.,* 22:486-511, 1974.

Kinsey, A.C., et al. *Sexual Behavior in the Human Male.* Philadelphia: W. B. Saunders, 1948.

————, et al. *Sexual Behavior in the Human Female.* Philadelphia: W. B. Saunders, 1953.

Klein, Melanie. "Notes on Some Schizoid Mechanisms." *Internatl. J. Psychoanal.* 27:99-110, 1946.

————. "On Identification," in *New Directions in Psychoanalysis,* eds. Melanie Klein, Paula Heimann, and R. E. Money-Kyrle. New York: Basic Books, 1956.

Kohl, Richard N. "Pathological reactions of marital partners to improvements of patients." *Amer. J. Psych.,* 118:1036-1041, No. 11, May 1962.

Kohut, H. "The psychoanalytic treatment of narcissistic personality disorders." *Psychoanalytic Study of the Child,* 23:86-113, 1968.

————. "Thoughts on narcissism and narcissistic rage." *Psychoanalytic Study of the Child,* 27:360-400, 1972.

Kopp, Sheldon B. *If You Meet the Buddha on the Road, Kill Him: The Pilgrimage of Psychotherapy Patients.* New York: Bantam Books, 1976.

Laing, R.D. "Family and Individual Structure," in *The Predicament of the Family: A Psycho-Analytical Symposium,* ed. Peter Lomas. London: Hogarth Press, 1967.

La Perriere, Kitty. "On Children, Adults and Families: The Critical Transition from Couple to Parents," in *Family Therapy: Combining Psychodynamic and Family Systems Approaches,* eds. John K. Pearce and Leonard J. Friedman. New York: Grune & Stratton, 1980.

Lederer, William J., and Don D. Jackson. *The Mirages of Marriage.* New York: W. W. Norton, 1968.

Levinson, Daniel J. *The Seasons of a Man's Life.* New York: Alfred A. Knopf, 1978.

Lidz, Theodore. *The Person: His and Her Development Throughout the Life Cycle,* Revised Edition. New York: Basic Books, 1976.

Liebowitz, Michael R. *The Chemistry of Love.* Boston: Little, Brown, 1983.

Lowenthal, Marjorie Fiske, et al. *Four Stages of Life.* San Francisco: Jossey-Bass, 1975.

McCullough, Paulina. "Launching Children and Moving On," in *The Family Life Cycle: A Framework for Family Therapy,* eds. Elizabeth A. Carter and Monica McGoldrick. New York: Gardner Press, Inc., 1980.

McGoldrick, Monica. "The Joining of Families Through Marriage: The New Couple," in *The Family Life Cycle: A Framework for Family Therapy,* eds. Elizabeth A. Carter and Monica McGoldrick. New York: Gardner Press, Inc., 1980.

————, and Randy Gerson. *Genograms in Family Assessment*. New York: W. W. Norton, 1985.

————, et al. *Ethnicity and Family Therapy*. New York: Guilford Press, 1982.

Mahler, Margaret, et al. *The Psychological Birth of the Human Infant*. New York: Basic Books, 1975.

Main, T.F. "Mutual projection in a marriage." *Compreh. Psych.*, 7:432-449, No. 5, October 1966.

Marshall, John R., and John Neill. "The removal of a psychosomatic symptom: Effects on the marriage." *Family Process*, 16:273-280, 1977.

Masters, William H., and Virginia E. Johnson. *Human Sexual Inadequacy*. Boston: Little, Brown, 1970.

————. *Human Sexual Response*. Boston: Little, Brown, 1966.

Mathews, Mary Alice, et al. "Process of Disillusionment and Adjustment in Marriage," in *Marriage and Divorce: A Contemporary Perspective*, eds. Carol Nadelson and Derek Polonsky. New York: Guilford Press, 1984.

Meyer, Patricia H. "Between Families: The Unattached Young Adult," in *The Family Life Cycle: A Framework for Family Therapy*, eds. Elizabeth A. Carter and Monica McGoldrick. New York: Gardner Press, Inc., 1980.

Minuchin, Salvador. *Families and Family Therapy*. Cambridge, Mass.: Harvard University Press, 1974.

————, et al. *Psychosomatic Families: Anorexia nervosa in Context*. Cambridge, Mass.: Harvard University Press, 1978.

————, and H. Charles Fishman. *Family Therapy Techniques*. Cambridge, Mass.: Harvard University Press, 1981.

Mittelmann, Bela. "The Concurrent Analysis of Marital Couples," in *Psychoanalytic Quarterly*, 17:182-197, 1948.

Nadelson, Carol C. "Problems in Sexual Functioning," in *Treatment Interventions in Human Sexuality*, eds. Carol C. Nadelson and David B. Marcotte. New York: Plenum, 1983.

————, et al., "Conjoint marital psychotherapy: Treatment techniques." *Dis. Nerv. Syst.*, 37:898-903, November 1977.

————, et al., "Marital stress and symptom formation in mid-life," *Psychiatric Opinion*, 15:29-32, September 1978.

————, et al. "Marriage as a Developmental Process," in *Marriage and Divorce: A Contemporary Perspective*, eds. Carol C. Nadelson and Derek C. Polonsky. New York: Guilford Press, 1984.

Nash, Ethel M., et al., *Marriage Counseling in Medical Practice*. Chapel Hill, N.C.: University of North Carolina Press, 1964.

Nass, G.D., R.W. Libby, and M. Fisher. *Sexual Choices*. Belmont, Ca.: Wadsworth, 1981.

Offit, Avodah K. *The Sexual Self*. New York: Congdon & Weed, 1983.

Palazzoli, Mara Selvini, et al. *Paradox and Counterparadox*. New York: Jason Aronson, Inc., 1981.

Paolino, Thomas J., Jr., and Barbara S. McCrady, eds. *Marriage & Marital Therapy*. New York: Brunner/Mazel, 1978.

Parkes, Colin Murray. "Psycho-social transitions: A field for study." *Soc. Sci. & Med.*, 5:101–115. Printed in Great Britain: Pergamon Press, 1971.

Pearce, John K., and Leonard J. Friedman, eds. *Family Therapy: Combining Psychodynamic and Family Systems Approaches*. New York: Grune & Stratton, 1980.

Person, Ethel Spector. "Women working: fears of failure, deviance and success." *J. Am. Acad. Psychoanal.*, 10:67-84, No. 1, 1982.

Pincus, Lily. *Death in the Family: The Importance of Mourning*. New York: Pantheon Books, 1974.

———, ed. *Marriage: Studies in Emotional Conflict and Growth*. London: Institute of Marital Studies, the Tavistock Institute of Human Relations, 1976.

———, and Christopher Dare. *Secrets in the Family*. New York: Pantheon Books, 1978.

Rubinstein, David, and Joan F. Timmins. "Depressive dyadic and triadic relationships." *J. Marriage. & Fam. Counsel*, 4:13-23, No. 1, January 1978.

Safilios-Rothschild, Constantina. *Love, Sex and Sex Roles*. Englewood Cliffs, N.J.: Prentice-Hall, 1977.

Sager, Clifford. *Marriage Contracts and Couple Therapy: Hidden Forces in Intimate Relationships*. New York: Brunner/Mazel, 1976.

———, et al. "The marriage contract." *Family Process*, 10:311-326, No. 3, September 1971.

Sarrel, Lorna, J., and Philip M. Sarrel. *Sexual Turning Points: The Seven Stages of Adult Sexuality*. New York: Macmillan, 1984.

Satir, Virginia. "Family Communication and Conjoint Family Therapy," in *Conjoint Family Therapy*, ed. Virginia Satir. Palo Alto, Ca.: Science and Behavior Books, 1967.

Scherz, Frances H. "The crisis of adolescence in family life." *Social Casework*, 209-215, April 1967.

Schiavi, Raul C. "Evaluation of Impaired Sexual Desire: Biological Aspects," in *Comprehensive Evaluation of Disorders of Sexual Desire*, ed. Helen Singer Kaplan. Washington, D.C.: American Psychiatric Press, 1984.

Semans, James H. "Premature ejaculation: a new approach." *Southern Med. J.*, 49:353-357, 1956.

Sholevar, G. Pirooz. *The Handbook of Marriage and Marital Therapy*. New York: SP Medical Publications, 1981.

Slipp, Samuel. *Object Relations: A Dynamic Bridge Between Individual and Family Treatment*. New York: Jason Aronson, Inc., 1984.

Smelser, Neil J., and Erik, H. Erikson, eds. *Themes of Work and Love in Adulthood*. Cambridge, Mass.: Harvard University Press, 1980.

Smith, Sydney. "The golden fantasy: A regressive reaction to separation anxiety." *Int. J. Psychoanal.*, 58:311-324, 1977.

Spark, Richard F., et al. "Impotence is not always psychogenic: Newer insights into hypothalamic-pituitary-gonadal dysfunction." *JAMA*, 243:750-755, No. 8, 1980.

Spitz, René A. "Hospitalism: An inquiry into the genesis of psychiatric conditions in early childhood," in *Psychoanalytic Study of the Child, Vol. 1*: 53-74, eds. Anna Freud, Hans Hartmann, and Ernst Kris. New York: International Universities Press, 1945.

Stewart, Ralph H., et al. "An object-relations approach to psychotherapy with marital couples, families, and children." *Family Process*, 14:161-178, No. 2, June 1975.

Stierlin, Helm. *Psychoanalysis & Family Therapy*. New York: Jason Aronson, Inc., 1977.

———. "The dynamics of owning and disowning: Psychoanalytic and family perspectives." *Family Process*. 15:277-288, 1976.

———. *Separating Parents and Adolescents: Individuation in the Family*. New York: Jason Aronson, Inc., 1981.

———. "Family Therapy—A Science or an Art?" *Family Process*, 22:413-423, December 1983.

Stone, Betsy. Personal communication.

Storr, Anthony. *The Art of Psychotherapy*. New York: Methuen, Inc., 1980.

Tavris, Carol, and Susan Sadd. *The Redbook Report on Female Sexuality*. New York: Delacorte Press, 1975, 1977.

Thompson, A.G. "Introduction" to *Marriage: Studies in Emotional Conflict and Growth*, ed. Lily Pincus. London: Institute of Marital Studies, the Tavistock Institute of Human Relations, 1960.

Thompson, Anthony P. "Extramarital Sex: A review of the research literature." *The Journal of Sex Research*, 19:1-22, February 1983.

———. "Extramarital sexual crisis: common themes and therapy implications." *J. Marr. Ther.*, 10:239-254, Winter 1984.

Toman, Walter. *Family Constellation: Its Effect on Personality and Social Behavior*. New York: Springer, 1961.

Trafford, Abigail. *Crazy Time: Surviving Divorce*. New York: Harper & Row, 1982.

Vogel, E., and N. Bell. "The Emotionally Disturbed Child as the Family Scapegoat," in *A Modern Introduction to the Family*, eds. E. Vogel, and N. Bell. New York: Free Press, 1960.

Walsh, Froma. "Family Therapy: A Systemic Orientation to Treatment," in *Handbook of Clinical Social Work*, eds. Aaron Rosenblatt and Diana Waldfogel. San Francisco: Jossey-Bass, 1983.

Watzlawick, Paul, et al. *Pragmatics of Human Communication*. New York: W. W. Norton, 1967.

Weiss, Robert S. *Marital Separation*. New York: Basic Books, 1975.

Wexler, Joan and John Steidl. "Marriage and the Capacity to Be Alone." *Psychiatry*, 41:72-82, No. 1, February 1978.

Whitehurst, Robert N. "Extramarital Sex: Alienation or Extension of Normal Behavior?," in *Extramarital Relations*, ed. G. Neubeck. Englewood Cliffs, N.J.: Prentice-Hall, 1969.

Willi, Jurg. "The Hysterical Marriage," in *Contemporary Marriage: Structure, Dynamics and Therapy*, eds. Henry Grunebaum and Jacob Christ. Boston: Little, Brown, 1976.

————. *Couples in Collusion: The Unconscious Dimension in Partner Relationships*. Claremont, Ca.: Hunter House, Inc., 1982.

Willis, Stanley. Commentary on a paper delivered by Bernard L. Greene, Ronald R. Lee, and Noel Lustig. *Med. Aspects Hum. Sexuality*, 8:105-111, September 1974.

Winnicott, D.W. *The Maturational Processes and the Facilitating Environment*. New York: International Universities Press, 1965.

Zinner, John, and Roger Shapiro. "Projective Identification as a Mode of Perception and Behaviour in Families of Adolescents." *Int. J. Psychoanal.*, 53:523-530, 1972.

Index

abortion, 137
"additional requests" task, 200–201
adolescence:
  "aborted," 310
  guilt felt in, 323–24
  identity problems in, 18, 325–26
  independence sought in, 323–24
  as "launching stage," 297–99
  Oedipal conflict in, 300–301
  rebellion in, 122, 123, 124, 290,
    316
  separation process in, 18–19, 122,
    290–93, 298–300, 305, 320–23
  sexuality in, 17, 64, 109, 300–301
  unresolved conflicts of, 283, 290–
    91
adoption, 118–20, 134, 136, 158,
  167, 168
adrenaline, 263
affairs, extramarital, 127–40
  as adaptive maneuvers, 132, 146
  alienation as cause of, 132
  anger about, 107–8, 129
  attitudes toward, 127, 128–29
  autonomy vs. intimacy in, 131–32,
    133

as betrayals, 136, 158–59
blame for, 131–32, 136, 137, 138,
  139–40
as catastrophic events, 128
causes of, 130–31, 139, 159
clues left in, 134–36, 153, 154,
  155–56, 165, 167, 169, 178
continuance of, 137–38
curiosity about, 389–91
deception in, 56–58, 90–91, 96,
  138, 140, 153–54, 157, 165, 169
divorce and, 138, 153
as "emotional distance regulators,"
  131–32, 139, 147
as EMS (extramarital sex), 127–28,
  130, 131, 132, 133, 139, 151–53
extramarital partner in, 138–39,
  146–47, 151, 160–63
fantasy in, 161, 162, 164, 302–3
fault shared in, 131–32
of females and of males, 127–28,
  129, 133–36
as forms of communication, 131,
  147, 157
frequency of, 20, 127–28
friendship and, 153, 161, 169

affairs, extramarital (*continued*)
  guilt feelings from, 128–29, 130, 135, 136, 137, 138, 139, 156, 168
  inner reality of, 129
  internal conflict caused by, 128
  jealousy in, 129
  as last marital flings, 302
  in marital cycle, 15
  marriage threatened by, 20–21, 137–38, 143, 147, 165–66
  morality of, 127, 128, 129
  power struggles in, 130, 133, 143, 152–53, 170
  as psychological strain, 128–30
  as rebellions, 159
  as repetitions of family relationships, 133–36, 141–42, 151, 167–68
  revelation of, 6, 130, 137, 152, 154
  revenge in, 137
  secrecy and, 132, 147
  self-esteem in, 130, 133, 134, 139, 152–53, 159–60
  stability and, 145, 146–47
  stress caused by, 129
  as subject of quarrels, 130, 137, 166–67
  tension relieved by, 146–47, 152
  therapy "tasks" for, 107–8
  time frame for, 20
  as triangles, 56–57, 129–30, 141–56
alcohol, 280
alcoholism, 46, 51, 52–53, 68, 81, 104, 110, 182, 360
alienation, 132
ambivalence, 186–87, 193, 365, 366, 369–72, 384
American, The (James), 28
androgen levels, 279

anger:
  from extramarital affairs, 107–8, 129
  in families, 52
  in projective identification, 62, 178, 179, 182–83, 199, 216, 220–21, 224, 225, 226, 296–97, 330–32, 334, 335, 336, 359–60, 366, 369, 371, 384
  as relational problem, 23, 178–79
  sexual problems and, 243, 244, 245, 247–50, 251
anorexia, 144
anorgasmic females, 231–32, 261, 266–68
anxiety:
  in children, 317
  in intimate relationships, 90, 142–43, 145, 158, 185, 355
  sexual problems and, 245–50, 262–63, 275
arthritis, 314, 315
Art of Psychotherapy, The (Storr), 222
"assumptive world," 72
asthma, 68
Attachment (Bowlby), 77
autonomic nervous system, 263
autonomy/intimacy:
  in extramarital affairs, 131–32, 133
  in marriages, 16, 20–24, 31–32, 33, 44, 54, 59–71, 192–93, 194, 198–99, 223, 336, 351, 359, 362–75
  in projective identification, 189–204, 226–27

"backward-protected" position, 274
barbiturates, 280
Bateson, Gregory, 106
Berger, Peter, 35
Berkowitz, David, 182, 187–88

Berman, Ellen, 179, 334
beta-adrenergic blockers, 234, 280
birth order, 65–66, 116–17, 314, 315
Birth Order and Life Roles (Forer), 117
Blanck, Rubin and Gertrude, 302
bolus, 258
Boszormanyi-Nagy, Ivan, 323
Botwin, Carol, 234
Bowen, Murray, 108, 142, 325, 359, 360
Bowen Family Systems, 108
Bowlby, John, 77
Brett, Laura and Tom:
  autonomy vs. intimacy as problem of, 59–71, 84–86, 90, 94, 96–98
  deception as problem of, 43–45, 57–58, 65, 85–86, 94, 96, 98–100
  as "dreamer" and "observer," 64–71, 80–81
  emotional problems of, 87–100
  ex-girlfriend as problem for, 28, 32–39, 54–56, 57–58, 71, 85–86, 89–94, 107–8
  family backgrounds of, 7–8, 40–58, 80–84, 85–86, 90, 92–93, 98–100
  genogram of, 7–8, 39, 40–58, 80–84, 90
  initial attraction of, 27–28, 43, 68
  jealousy as problem of, 89–90, 93–94, 97
  marital tasks of, 14
  occupations of, 28
  past as threat to, 81–83, 85–86, 88–89, 99
  projective identification as problem of, 63
  relationship of, 59–60, 92–98
  in therapy, 14, 28, 89, 107–8
Buber, Martin, 323

Cancer Ward, The (Solzhenitsyn), 28
Carrano, Angie and Bob:
  autonomy vs. intimacy as problem of, 210–14, 221
  children of, 15, 205, 216
  family backgrounds of, 207, 227–28
  genogram of, 212
  as "hysterical wife" and "silent husband," 205–28
  initial attraction of, 205–8, 209, 211–12, 217, 221
  occupations of, 12, 16, 206
  power struggle as problem of, 210
  previous relationships of, 206–8, 209
  projective identification as problem of, 205
  relational problems of, 15–16, 214–15
  separation of, 212, 213, 214, 215–16
  sexual problems of, 16, 209–10, 215–16, 231–33, 234, 266, 275
Carter, Elizabeth, 19, 158
Carter, Jimmy, 390
Chemistry of Love, The (Liebowitz), 77–78
children:
  "abandoned," 328–29, 331
  abused, 216, 219
  adopted, 118–20, 134, 136, 158, 167, 168
  as "angels" vs. "devils," 378–80, 383
  anxiety in, 317
  birth order of, 65–66, 116–17, 314, 315

children (*continued*)
  as caretakers, 65–66, 115, 224, 315, 322–23
  developing autonomy of, 144
  discipline of, 13
  divorce and, 5–6, 227–28
  eldest, 66, 314, 315
  fathers and, 157–58
  illegitimate, 48
  latency period of, 301
  male, 315
  middle, 116–17, 121, 303
  "misbehavior" of, 144–45
  mourning process of, 227–28, 329
  neglect of, 222
  "only," 66
  "parentified," 224, 227–28, 332
  parents and, 114–15, 142, 143–45, 146, 159, 175, 317, 346–47
  personality development of, 66
  "problem," 345–46
  sexuality of, 174, 301
  "special," 53
  youngest, 66
clitoral prepuce, 268
clitoris, 254–55, 261, 267, 268–69, 274
clonidine, 280
coition, artificial, 252
condoms, 232
contraception, 127
"control sharing" task, 201–4
corpora cavernosa, 253, 258
corpus spongiosum, 253, 258
couples, married:
  asexual, 279
  as bonded pairs, 87, 96, 175, 334
  buzzwords used by, 30, 242
  as "caretaker" and "wounded bird," 15, 121–26, 134, 136–37, 159–60, 163, 168, 169, 239, 250

collusion of, 34, 41, 169, 173–88, 190, 192, 193, 205, 226, 313, 330–35
compatibility of, 22, 30, 163, 164, 313
as "distancer" and "pursuer," 192–93, 194, 199, 296–97, 364–65
"distress barometer" of, 145
as "dreamer" and "observer," 64–71, 80–81
former relationships of, 27, 28, 32–39
friends of, 8, 30
as "hysterical wife" and "silent husband," 205–28
identical and opposite traits of, 27, 30, 59–60
as individuals, 110, 112
initial attraction of, 27–39, 185, 187
in-laws of, 8, 146
interviews of, 3, 9–11, 48, 237
meta-communication between, 43, 44, 68
"middlescent" crisis of, 297–300
as newlyweds, 8, 15
as "passive male" and "strong female," 296–97, 318–20, 329–33, 336, 337, 338, 339
psychological legacies of, 41, 53
as "social mammals," 41
therapy "homework" for, 34, 36–38, 107–8, 189–204, 349, 385
see also individual couples

Dare, Christopher, 38, 45–46, 47, 50, 51, 79, 186, 291–92, 301
Dartmouth Medical School, 10
daughters:
  emerging sexuality of, 17, 64, 109

fathers and, 46–47, 50–51, 68–69, 119, 179, 317, 324
mothers and, 9, 52–55, 113–16, 150–51, 315–18, 324, 325–26, 332–33
depersonalization, 122
depression:
in projective identification, 62–63, 182–83, 185, 206–7, 214
as relational problem, 23, 53, 68, 81, 104, 109, 129, 144, 360–61, 366, 383
diabetes mellitus, 234, 280
Dicks, H. V., 35, 79–80
diuretics, 235–37, 280
divorce:
aftermath of, 23–24
children and, 5–6, 227–28
extramarital affairs and, 138, 153
frequency of, 14, 88
interpreters of, 7
drug abuse, 121–22, 123, 125, 126

ejaculation:
control of, 258, 263, 265, 276–79
drugs and, 266
premature, 17, 231, 260, 264–65, 276–79
retarded, 232, 265–66, 267, 275
eloping, 48–49, 318
emotional fusion, 59–60, 360, 362
emotions:
"demilitarized zones" for, 233–34
dissociated, 62, 124, 178–79, 182–83, 185, 192, 193, 222–23, 224, 225, 226, 227, 332–33, 361, 368–69, 379, 381
expression of, 11–12, 47–48, 84–86, 178–79
hiding of, 33, 44
overload of, 37–38

regulation of, 131–32, 139, 147
sharing of, 31–32, 38
empathy, 27, 149–50, 223, 351
erection, male:
aging and, 240–44, 246, 247, 273
drugs and, 234, 235–36
frequency of, 238, 260
length of, 256
physiology of, 253–54
as sexual response, 248, 272
variations in, 263
estrogen levels, 246

Fairbairn, Ronald D., 175
families:
academic, 205
affectivity in, 52
anger handled in, 52
authority in, 114
birth order in, 65–66, 116–17, 314, 315
conflictual issues in, 80
decision making in, 210–11, 288, 296, 365
devotion in, 322
dilemmas in, 45, 47–48, 49, 365
disapproval in, 48–49
as "drama," 41, 293, 332
dysfunctional, 107–8
as emotional systems, 8, 11–12, 17–18, 40–41, 45, 47–48, 64, 107–8, 144
environment created by, 106, 146, 376–77, 379
expectations of, 17, 40, 109
expressions of feelings in, 11–12
extended, 8, 9, 320
extramarital affairs and relationships in, 133–36, 141–42, 151, 167–68
familiarity based on, 38, 50–53, 68, 79, 88–89

families (*continued*)
  health problems in, 314–15, 326–27, 328, 329
  humiliation in, 67
  illegitimacy in, 48
  incestuous feelings in, 300–301
  individuals in, 103–5, 106, 109, 320, 323–25
  intact, 6
  "investment" in, 323
  Irish, 11–12
  Italian, 11
  Jewish, 12
  labels and roles in, 64–65
  large, 68
  life cycle of, 17, 184
  loyalty in, 323–24
  modern theories of, 106, 107, 108, 117, 174–81
  nonexpressive, 182
  original, 7, 14, 18, 20, 40–41, 52, 53, 65, 80, 109, 158, 227, 325, 326, 346
  "outsider status" in, 67–68, 70
  as "patient," 107–8
  power struggles in, 66, 114–16
  projection process of, 142
  quarrels in, 81–84, 316–17
  relational issues in, 323–26
  repetition of patterns in, 7–8, 9, 13, 18, 20, 40–41, 46–49, 50–54, 88–89, 93, 227–28, 303–12, 313, 318–20, 328–29, 332, 335, 346
  role-playing in, 106–7, 110
  rules of behavior in, 11–12, 17–18, 40, 110
  "sacrificial member" of, 106–7
  secrets of, 48, 301, 328
  self-definition in, 110
  self-destructive behavior in, 144–45
  separation from, 290–93, 298–300

  sexist, 364
  sibling rivalry in, 321
  as social systems, 45, 49, 105
  "spokesman" for, 109
  stability of, 107
  subculture of, 35, 40, 53
  subliminal alarms in, 17
  suppression of past in, 64
  symbols of, 5–6
  symptoms of disturbance in, 109, 144–45
  therapy for, 10, 103–10
  as transactional network, 109
  transformation of relationships in, 292–93, 325–26
  transgenerational stresses in, 158–59
  triangles in, 8–9, 70–71, 81, 84, 98, 114–16, 119, 141–42, 146, 150–51
  see also individual members
Family Constellation (Toman), 65–66, 117
Family Institute of Westchester, 10, 40
Family Life Cycle, The (Carter and McGoldrick), 52
fantasy:
  in extramarital affairs, 161, 162, 164, 302–3
  in intimate relationships, 14, 15, 21–22, 38, 53, 176–78, 301, 329–30, 390–91
  projective identification and, 187
fathers:
  children and, 157–58
  daughters and, 46–47, 50–51, 68–69, 119, 179, 317, 324
  as examples of failure, 46–47, 50–51
  "inner," 176
  passive, 316

sons and, 344, 353, 354, 356–57, 383

Feldman, Larry B., 186, 347–48, 349, 350, 351

Female Orgasm, The (Fisher), 268

female-superior position, 278

feminist movement, 127, 364

fertility, 326–27, 328

"fight or flight" responses, 263

Fisher, M. P., 128

Fisher, Seymour, 268

Fogarty, Thomas D., 296

foreplay, 241, 242, 244, 248

Forer, Lucille, 117

Fraiberg, Selma, 73–74

Francis, J. L., 129

Franklin, Bruce and Sara:
  as "caretaker" and "wounded bird," 239, 250
  occupations of, 239, 240
  separation of, 239
  sexual problems of, 239–51
  in therapy, 239, 241, 243–44, 246, 249

Freud, Sigmund, 103, 104, 105, 174, 175, 249, 261, 301

frigidity:
  impotence as comparable to, 261–62
  as inhibited sexual desire, 215–16, 231, 237, 247

Gardiner, Kathleen and Philip:
  autonomy vs. intimacy as problem of, 288, 289–91, 293, 295, 305, 308, 309, 327–28, 334, 336, 338–39
  careers of, 287–88, 296, 327–28, 331
  children of, 18, 285, 297–99, 310

as "distancer" and "pursuer," 296–97

education of, 287

family backgrounds of, 291, 298, 303–33, 337–38

genogram of, 315, 318, 329

initial attraction of, 285–87, 291, 294–95

mid-life crisis of, 285–312

"other woman" and, 302–3

as "passive male" and "strong female," 296–97, 318–20, 329–33, 336, 337, 338, 339

as polarized relationship, 295–96, 309

power struggle of, 289–90, 334, 338

projective identification as problem of, 296–97, 330–33

separation of, 285–86, 318–20, 337, 338–39

in therapy, 288

"genital pleasuring," 272–74

genograms, 40–58
  behavioral remission shown in, 52–53
  construction of, 7–8, 40–43, 45
  definition of, 8
  emotional problems shown in, 47–48
  as "family tree," 40
  generational conflicts depicted in, 41, 45, 46–49
  insights gained from, 41–42, 67, 70–71
  past vs. present in, 40–43, 49–50
  relationships in, 40
  similarities in, 79
  symbols used in, 42, 67

Gibran, Kahlil, 70

Giordano, Joseph, 12

Greene, Bernard L., 131

G-spot, 242
guilt:
    in adolescence, 323–24
    from extramarital affairs, 128–29,
        130, 135, 136, 137, 138, 139,
        156, 168
    in projective identification, 194,
        221
    sexual problems and, 243, 244,
        245, 247–50, 251

Haley, Jay, 116
heart disease, 46, 310–12, 345, 354,
        377, 378, 380, 382
heroin, 280
Hite, Shere, 268
Hite Report, The (Hite), 268
Hoffman, Lynn, 143–44
hormones, 246, 279
housework, 148–49, 352–53, 356–58
Human Sexual Inadequacy (Masters
        and Johnson), 241, 252–53, 261,
        264, 265, 267, 269, 271, 274,
        276
Human Sexual Response (Masters and
        Johnson), 252–59
Humphrey, Frederick, 131
hypertension, 234, 235–37, 280
hypochondria, 383
hypogonadism, 279
hysterectomies, 326–27, 328, 329

imagos, 175–76
impotence, sexual, 16, 17, 231
    aging and, 240–42, 243
    drugs as cause of, 234–35
    frigidity vs., 261–62
    primary, 262
    secondary, 237, 262–63
incest, 78–79, 300–301
infants:

abandonment felt by, 18, 75–77,
        134, 136, 176–77
attachment behaviors of, 74, 76,
        174–78
attention given to, 157–58
"bad objects" of, 177–78
fear experienced by, 76, 177
foundling home, 74
human vs. primate, 76, 77–78
inborn sexual drives of, 174
internalized images of, 174, 175–76
libidinal strivings of, 175
mothers and, 72–80, 174–81, 361
needs and wishes of, 105
smiles of, 76
survival of, 177
trauma experienced by, 261
interaction models, 35
internalization, 35, 72, 174–76, 354
intimate relationships:
    admiration or attention in, 350–51,
        354, 355, 357, 367
    anxiety in, 90, 142–43, 145, 158,
        185, 355
    betrayal in, 14, 21
    breakdown of, 87, 325–26
    casual relationships vs., 90–91, 92
    challenge in, 29–31
    changes in, 17–20, 110, 145, 189–
        90, 203–4, 208, 309, 333, 334,
        385
    competency in, 148–49
    confusion in, 22, 59, 179, 365
    deception in, 31–32, 33, 43–45
    developmental tasks in, 19, 158–59
    as dialogue, 95–96, 375
    emotional fusion in, 59–60, 360,
        362
    emotionally "demilitarized zones"
        in, 233–34
    empathy in, 27, 149–50, 223, 251

exclusiveness in, 73–74

familiarity in, 38, 50–53, 68, 79, 88–89

fantasy in, 14, 15, 21–22, 38, 53, 176–78, 301, 329–30, 390–91

fear of emptiness in, 222–23

freedom desired in, 93–98

honesty in, 29, 31, 44, 45

hostile feelings in, 178–79

hypocrisy in, 389–90

illusion in, 44

incestuous fears in, 78–79, 300–301

intellectual levels of, 149, 150, 163, 364

"internal blueprint" for, 329–31

irrational behavior in, 92

jealousy in, 89–90, 93–94, 129, 245

life cycles and, 13–14

manipulation in, 45, 66, 203

maturity in, 7, 14, 41, 359

misrepresentation in, 43–45, 330–31

models for, 78–79

needs fulfilled in, 60–61, 74–80, 364

objective vs. subjective reality in, 35, 36, 75–77, 124, 176, 181, 183

obsessional behavior in, 218–19

past relationships and, 7, 27, 28, 32–39, 183–84, 188

predictability in, 385

primary, 174–80

privacy in, 94, 134, 135, 155–56, 164, 317

reflexive actions in, 34–35

rejection in, 387–88

repression in, 105

respect in, 30, 225

restaging core experiences in, 49–54

role-playing in, 35, 44, 60–61, 97–98, 295–97, 310–12, 313, 329–33

role reversals in, 97–98, 295–97

as romance, 95–96

"scary places" of, 95–96

self-annihilation in, 362–63

self-definition in, 18–22, 34, 72–76, 85, 176–79, 212–14, 289–93, 296, 299–300, 330, 350–51, 359, 360–61, 369–75

self-esteem in, 94, 95, 124, 125, 126, 130, 133, 134, 139, 152–53, 159–60, 180, 222, 239, 347–52

separation problems in, 53, 77–78, 79, 122

shadow relationships in, 54–56, 57

sincerity in, 29, 45

superior-to-inferior mode in, 225

threat of abandonment in, 75–77, 79

"toxic" issues in, 46, 53, 89, 158

"truly loving," 335–36

unconscious processes in, 23, 41, 51–52, 60, 72–73, 159–60, 360

vicious cycles in, 223

vulnerability in, 67, 198, 332–33, 334, 366

see also marriages

Is There Sex After Marriage? (Botwin), 234

James, Henry, 28

jealousy, 89–90, 93–94, 97, 129, 245

Johnson, Stuart, 145, 190, 192, 194, 196, 362, 373

Johnson, Virginia, 239, 241, 252–59, 261, 264, 265, 267, 269, 271, 274, 276

Journal of the American Medical Association, 238

Junior League, 10

Kaplan, Helen Singer, 264–65, 280

Karpel, Mark, 361, 375

Kearney, Gordon and Jo Ann:
  autonomy vs. intimacy as problem of, 150, 163–65
  as "caretaker" and "wounded bird," 15, 121–26, 134, 136–37, 159–60, 163, 168, 169
  child of, 15, 112, 137, 152, 153–55, 156, 157–58, 164, 170
  extramarital affair as problem of, 15, 121, 126, 133–40, 147–70, 178
  family backgrounds of, 112–21, 150–51, 158
  genogram of, 112, 150
  household responsibilities as shared by, 148–49
  initial attraction of, 149–50
  journals kept by, 134–36, 153
  as middle children, 116–17, 121
  occupations of, 112, 118, 148, 152
  separation of, 160, 165–66, 168–70
  siblings of, 116, 117, 118–19

Kellner, Hansfried, 35

Kinsey, A. C., 10, 127, 128, 391

Klein, Melanie, 174, 176, 177

Kunitz, Stanley, 7

labia majora, 255

labia minora, 255

La Perriere, Kitty, 157

Lasch, Christopher, 88

Laughter in the Dark (Nabokov), 28

Lee, Ronald R., 131

Libby, R. W., 128

Lidz, Theodore, 78–79

Liebowitz, Michael, 77–78

Lief, Harold, 179, 334

Locke, Elliot and Jessie:
  marital crisis of, 236, 237
  sexual problems of, 235–37
  in therapy, 236–37

love:
  in adult relationships, 72
  attachments of, 72
  as basis of survival, 74–75
  between mother and child, 72–80
  capacity for, 94, 95
  definition of, 72–73
  "falling in," 38, 68, 78–79
  as feelings of security and safety, 74–75, 77
  "magic circle" of, 74
  money as substitute for, 386–87, 388
  psychobiological preparation for, 75
  self-, 125, 126, 160

LSD, 122, 123, 126

Lustig, Noel, 131

McCullough, Paulina, 326

McGoldrick, Monica, 12, 146, 158

male-superior position, 278

MAO inhibitors, 280

marijuana, 280

marriages:
  abuse in, 216–18, 219, 232
  accommodation in, 16, 87, 289–90, 293, 305, 308
  agenda of, 14, 314
  age-related problems in, 13–14, 16, 17, 19, 231, 239–51, 273
  ambivalence in, 27, 70, 213, 369–72, 384
  assumptions about, 7, 41, 72
  author's research on, 3–24
  autonomy /intimacy in, 16, 20–24,

31–32, 33, 44, 54, 59–71, 192–
93, 194, 198–99, 223, 336, 351,
359, 362–75
behavioral language in, 64, 332–33,
335
characterization of, 36
choice of mate in, 7, 78–80
claustrophobia in, 226–27
commitment to, 16, 17, 32, 96,
157, 203–4, 227, 382
communication in, 35, 36–37, 54,
64, 152, 179, 196, 199, 214–15,
223, 236, 242, 306
complementarity in, 38, 109–10
conflict in, 27, 63, 88–89, 179,
180, 187–88, 313, 330, 332,
334, 335, 353, 363, 365, 369,
370, 371, 373, 384
"conscious splitting" level of, 366–
69
contracts in, 34, 36–37, 41, 43,
124–26, 159–60, 221, 330–31,
335
control in, 34–35, 94, 124, 170,
195–204, 212–13, 223, 224, 226,
338
cycles in, 13–17, 184, 332–33,
335, 369
dependence in, 310–12
dilemmas of, 335, 336, 368, 387
disappointment and disenchantment
phase in, 14–15, 21
as "dramatic acts," 35–36, 99
early conflicts replayed in, 38–39,
45–49
early phase of, 35
"emotional deals" in, 124–26, 335
as emotional systems, 12, 13, 35,
103–10, 145, 159, 160, 181,
184, 190, 194, 205, 228, 289,
309, 333, 365, 389–90

equilibrium maintained in, 104–5,
109–10, 125, 129, 334–35, 346,
350, 351
as equivalent to child-parent relationship, 79–80
ethnic factors in, 11–12
expectations for, 87–89, 350
extramarital affairs as threat to, 20–
21, 137–38, 143, 147, 165–66
familial patterns repeated in, 7–8,
9, 13, 18, 20, 40–41, 46–49, 50–
54, 88–89, 93, 227–28, 303–12,
313, 318–20, 328–29, 332, 335,
346
forming of, 7, 12, 32, 36
"Golden Fantasy" in, 78–80
happiness in, 12, 87–100, 260–61,
279, 316, 361, 373–75
as "haven in heartless world," 88,
128
healthy ways of relating in, 335–36
housework as issue in, 148–49,
352–53, 356–58
hysterical, 219–28, 310–11
idealization phase in, 14
innocence of, 128
"integrated" level of, 373–75
interpersonal conflicts vs. intraper-
sonal problems in, 61–62, 105,
108, 109, 110, 175, 181, 182,
189, 216, 233, 234, 235, 236,
250, 361, 373
interpreters of, 7
intimacy in, 16, 20–24
as leaving home, 150–51, 291–93
leisure time in, 8
loyalty in, 382, 389
marital models for, 78–81, 112–14,
168, 182
marital scenario in, 35–36, 60, 99,
308, 328–29

marriages (*continued*)
mid-life crisis and, 21, 47, 241, 283–312, 326
money problems in, 8, 12, 13, 116, 197, 385–87, 388
morality in, 382
mortality as issue in, 284–85
negotiation in, 368, 370–72, 387
nurturing in, 124–26
open, 96–98, 389–90
"paradox" level of, 362–63
as part of larger relationship system, 42–43, 50–53, 88
as "patients," 108
personal growth in, 288, 290–91, 305, 309, 338–39
"personal space" in, 22, 59, 60, 110, 157, 163–64, 193, 223, 226, 327, 363, 365, 367, 368
polarized, 181, 183, 186–88, 189, 193, 202, 226–27, 329, 332, 334, 363, 365, 368
power sharing in, 36–38
power struggles in, 12–13, 34–37, 130, 133, 143, 152–53, 170, 190, 201–4, 249–50
pregnancy as issue in, 87, 137, 152, 157–58, 217–18
"private places" of, 317
productivity phase of, 14, 15–16, 21, 227
"projective identification" level of, 363–66, 384
of psychiatrists, 125
quid pro quo arrangements in, 333, 335, 366
redefinition and child-launching phase of, 14, 18, 20, 21
reintegration and postparenting phase of, 14, 19, 20, 367

relational levels of, 362–75
as relationships, 7, 12–13, 14, 15, 32, 37, 49–50, 88, 110, 163, 188, 190, 203–4, 334, 359–75
religious differences in, 374–75
"repetitive sequences of partnership" in, 46
responsibility in, 136–37, 180, 183, 200, 221, 327–28, 332, 369–70
rules of behavior in, 11, 173, 189–90, 193, 202, 228
second, 55–58
secret, 48–49, 318
separateness in, 21–22, 33
stability in, 6, 16, 54, 208–9, 217, 221, 222, 295
supportive behavior in, 165–66
as therapeutic relationships, 110, 188
therapy for, 10, 13, 28, 34, 36–38, 103, 107–8, 161, 169, 182, 189–204, 349, 385
as "transactional games," 370
unconscious agreements in, 7, 14, 41, 43, 60, 159–60, 360
vows of exclusivity in, 128
"warp and woof" of, 163
"win/lose" framework of, 37, 163
see also couples, married
massagers, electric, 252
Masters, William, 239, 241, 252–59, 261, 264, 265, 267, 269, 271, 274, 276
masturbation, 232, 252, 262, 267
Mathews, Mary Alice, 14, 17
menopause, 246
menstruation, 326
methyldopa, 234, 280
Meyer, Patricia, 52

mid-life crisis, 21, 47, 241, 283–312, 326
morphine, 280
mothers:
  abandonment by, 18, 75–77, 134, 136, 176–77
  as "attachment figures," 74, 76, 174–78
  as caretakers, 74, 77–78
  daughters and, 9, 52, 55, 113–16, 150–51, 315–18, 324, 325–26, 332–33
  domineering, 114–15, 118, 120–21, 122, 134, 150–51
  infants and, 72–80, 174–81, 361
  as nurturers, 133–36, 175
  pseudo-, 317
  sons and, 70–71
  as strong individuals, 316–18, 324, 326, 332–33, 337
  substitute, 133–34
  wives as, 133–36, 158, 168
mothers-in-law, 8, 146
mourning process:
  of adults, 77, 309–12
  of children, 227–28, 329
  cultural assumptions in, 12
  of infants, 76
  for old relationships, 94
  of parents, 315, 329
  protest-despair-detachment process of, 77
  separation and, 309–12
  unresolved, 380–84
myotonia, 253, 254, 256, 257

Nabokov, Vladimir, 28
Nadelson, Carol, 14, 17, 274
Nass, G. D., 128
"never angry" person, 23, 62

"never sad" person, 62–63
nipple erection, 264
"nongenital pleasuring," 270–72

object relations theory, 174–81
"odd day, even day" task, 195, 203
Oedipus conflict, 174, 175, 300–301, 317, 324
orgasm:
  absence of, 231–32, 261, 266–68
  clitoral vs. vaginal, 261
  ejaculation phase of, 257–58
  emission phase of, 257
  of females, 231–32, 258–59, 261, 266–69
  inhibited, 266–67
  in males, 232, 257–58, 264–66
  multiple, 388
  number and quality of, 242, 258–59, 388
  "platform" phase of, 256, 257
  situational dysfunction of, 267–68
  threshold of, 268

Palazzoli, Mara Selvini, 197
Palmer, David and Virginia:
  family backgrounds of, 182
  projective identification as problem of, 182–84
"paradoxical" communication, 196
parasympathetic nervous system, 263
parents:
  adoptive vs. natural, 119–20, 134, 136
  authority of, 9, 197, 337
  as caretakers, 18, 354–55, 356
  caring for, 323–25
  children and, 114–15, 142, 143–45, 146, 159, 175, 317, 346–47
  death of, 285, 310–12, 314
  disabled, 310–12

parents (*continued*)
  as disciplinarians, 337
  emotional dependence on, 75, 320–21
  fusion with, 325–26, 331
  identification with, 301, 322, 324, 332–33, 354–55
  manipulation by, 120
  mourning process of, 315, 329
  post-childrearing period of, 18, 19
  separation of, 5–6
  standards imposed by, 316, 321–22, 337
  surrogate, 159
Parkes, C. Murray, 72
Pearce, John K., 12
penis, 243–44, 246, 255
Person, The (Lidz), 78
personality:
  authoritarian, 225
  of the child, 66
  "defeated," 222
  development of, 73, 174, 176–77, 360
  differentiation of, 290–93, 299–300
  disavowed elements of, 334
  dynamics of, 184
  fragile, 129
  histrionic, 219–28
  hysterophile, 220
  internalized negative images of, 354–55
  obsessive-compulsive, 219–28
  passive-aggressive, 356–57
  projective identification and, 185–86, 194
  unintegrated aspects of, 226
phobias, 144, 360
Pincus, Lily, 38, 45–46, 47, 50, 51, 79, 186, 291–92, 301
pituitary gland, 280

placenta previa, 314
"pleasuring" exercises, 269–74, 277
Polonsky, Derek, 14, 17
pregnancy, 87, 137, 152, 157–58, 217–18
projective identification:
  ambivalence and, 186–87, 193, 365, 366, 369–72, 384
  anger expressed in, 62, 178, 179, 182–83, 199, 216, 220–21, 224, 225, 226, 296–97, 330–32, 334, 335, 336, 359–60, 366, 369, 371, 384
  autonomy vs. intimacy in, 189–204, 226–27
  as collusion, 178–80, 181, 182–85, 192, 193
  conflict expressed in, 179, 180, 187–88, 330, 332, 336
  counteracting of, 173, 191
  as defense mechanism, 178, 186–87, 188, 199, 355
  definition of, 22–23
  depression expressed in, 62–63, 182–83, 185, 206–7, 214
  dissociated feelings in, 62, 124, 178–79, 182–83, 185, 192, 193, 222–23, 224, 225, 226, 227, 332–33, 361, 368–69, 379, 381
  examples of, 176–77, 182–84
  as exchanges, 63, 169, 173, 178, 180–81, 185–86, 188, 221–22, 227–28, 330–31, 333, 360–61
  as expression of inner reality, 124, 176, 181, 183, 185, 199–200, 203, 222–23, 225, 330, 332, 356
  as externalization, 179–80, 183
  fantasy and, 187
  as "game without end," 188, 202
  guilt expressed in, 194, 221
  in hysterical marriages, 219–28

identification in, 366
individuation vs., 362–69
insights into, 366–67, 368
introjection and, 185
as mental act, 186
pathology in, 360–61
personalities distorted in, 185–86, 194
in polarized relationships, 181, 183, 186–88, 189, 193, 202, 226–27, 329, 332, 334, 363, 365, 368
process of, 62–63, 173–74, 184, 186–87, 188
in quarrels, 181, 184, 201, 356, 365, 367
as relational level, 363–66, 384
repression in, 225, 363–64
role-playing and, 180–81, 185
self-image and, 177–179, 187, 193–94, 198, 218, 221–22
separateness vs., 192–93
"splitting off" and, 177, 185–86, 187, 193, 228, 363, 366–69, 370
symbiotic fusion in, 221–22, 226–27
therapeutic tasks for, 189–204
of transgenerational problems, 180–81, 183–84, 187–88
unconscious level of, 174, 178, 185, 186, 187, 366, 370, 372
vicarious gratification in, 178–79
vicious cycle of, 192
Prophet, The (Gibran), 70
prostate gland, 258
psychoactive drugs, 122, 123, 126, 280
psychosis, 122
psychotherapy:
behavioral tasks in, 33–34, 36–38, 107–8, 189–204, 349, 385
conceptual bridges in, 181
"cooling down system" in, 112
for extramarital affairs, 107–8
family, 10, 103–10
Freudian, 103, 104, 105, 174, 175, 249, 261, 301
"intimacy requests" in, 195–204
metacontrol in, 201–4
multigenerational approach to, 108
object relations school of, 174–81
undermining of, 105, 106–7

quarrels:
accusations in, 35, 36
causes of, 4–6, 8–9, 12–13, 31, 32–35, 343–58
cognitive maneuvers in, 355
as communication, 348–49
compromises as result of, 349, 358
cross-complaining in, 348
dysfunctional vs. functional, 347–49
escalation of, 357
extramarital affairs as subject of, 130, 137, 166–67
family, 81–84, 316–17
inner conflicts expressed by, 353
between parents and children, 114–15
physical violence in, 348, 349
as power struggles, 352–53
productive, 347–52
projective identification in, 181, 184, 201, 356, 365, 367
psychodynamic issues in, 347–48, 354–56
repetitious, 352
self-esteem and, 347–48, 349–52, 355
settlement of, 33–34
start of, 352, 353, 355–56, 358

quarrels (*continued*)
 therapy for, 33–34, 36–38, 107–8,
  189–204, 349, 385
 unresolvable, 89

Reproductive Biology Research Foundation, 253
reserpine, 234, 280
"Route Six" (Kunitz), 7

Sager, Clifford, 124
Schiavi, Raul, 279
schizophrenia, 105, 106–7, 363
Secrets in the Family (Pincus and
  Dare), 79
Semans, James, 265, 276
Semans method, 265, 276–79
"sensate focus" exercises, 269–74, 277
sex:
 abstinence from, 279
 acting-out in, 21
 bridge maneuver in, 268–69
 erotic feelings and, 232
 extramarital (EMS), 127–28, 130,
  131, 132, 133, 139, 151–53
 foreplay in, 241, 242, 244, 248
 knowledge of, 7, 16–17, 238, 239–
  51, 270, 388–91
 lust and, 390–91
 oral, 244, 267
 pain and, 246–47
 physiology of, 252–59, 261
 positions for, 242, 274, 278
 as power struggle, 387–88
 premarital, 49
 promiscuity in, 109
 responsivity in, 240
 "revolution" in, 127
 taboos of, 249
sex drive, 174, 279–80
"sex flush," 256

*Sexual Behavior in the Human Fe-
  male* (Kinsey), 127
Sexual Behavior in the Human Male
  (Kinsey), 127
sexuality:
 adolescent, 17, 64, 109, 300–301
 aging and, 16, 17, 231, 239–51,
  273
 biological factors in, 16
 as bond, 388–92
 of children, 174, 301
 as closeness, 90, 92
 domination and, 51
 psychological factors in, 16
sexual problems:
 aging and, 239–51
 anger and guilt in, 243, 244, 245,
  247–50, 251
 anxiety and, 249–50, 262–63, 275
 of arousal phase, 262–64
 behavioral techniques for, 17, 260–
  80
 biological vs. psychological causes
  of, 231–51, 260, 267, 269, 270,
  280
 cultural influences on, 260
 desexualized feelings as, 279–80,
  326–27, 328, 329, 333
 drugs as cause of, 234–35, 266, 280
 of females, 231–32, 261, 266–69
 frequency of, 8, 12, 15, 16, 197,
  260–61
 illness as cause of, 234, 260, 279–
  80
 of males, 262–63, 275–79
 misinterpretation of, 245–46
 as negative cycle, 231, 236, 237
 of orgasm stage, 231, 264–69
 psychotherapy for, 233–34, 236–38,
  239, 241, 243–44, 246, 249,
  261, 270

self-esteem and, 232, 234, 239, 240, 243, 245, 267
shared responsibility for, 275–76
types of, 16–17
sexual response cycle, 252–59
arousal phase of, 262–64
excitement phase of, 253–56, 262
laboratory studies of, 252–53
muscular contractions in, 257, 258, 269
myotonia in, 253, 254, 256, 257
orgasm stage of, 231, 257–58, 264–69
plateau stage of, 256, 262, 276
refractory period of, 258–59
resolution phase of, 258–59
"tenting" effect in, 255, 258
vasocongestion in, 253–55, 256, 257, 263
Shapiro, Roger, 178
Solzhenitsyn, Aleksandr, 28
sons:
fathers and, 344, 353, 354, 356–57, 383
mothers and, 70–71
spironolactone, 280
Spitz, René, 74
"splitting off," 177, 185–86, 187, 193, 228, 363, 366–69, 370
Sternberg, David and Nancy:
careers of, 344–45
children of, 20, 343, 344, 345–47, 376, 387, 390
close relationship of, 19, 20, 343–44
extramarital affair as problem of, 380–82
family backgrounds of, 344, 353, 354, 356–57, 376–81, 383
jealousy as problem of, 344

power struggle of, 352–53, 376–77, 386, 387–88
quarrels of, 343–58, 376–78, 385–87
sexual relationship of, 381, 387–92
in therapy, 347, 383, 384, 387
Stone, Betsy, 131–32
Storr, Anthony, 222, 224, 225
success, fear of, 249–50
suicide, 129

"talking and listening" task, 190–95, 201, 203, 349
"tenting" effect, 255, 258
Thompson, Anthony, 129, 130
thyroid glands, 279
Toman, Walter, 65–66, 117, 314
Trafford, Abigail, 23–24
tranquilizers, 280
transudate, 254
triangles:
causes of, 142–43
as cross-generational coalitions, 81, 84, 98, 114–15, 116, 119
as emotional systems, 49–50, 141, 346
"eternal," 15, 142, 146–47, 301
extramarital affairs as, 56–57, 129–30, 141–56
family, 8–9, 70–71, 81, 84, 98, 114–15, 119, 141–42, 146, 150–51
fixed, 116
in-laws and, 8, 146
intensity lowered by, 141, 143
Oedipal, 174, 175, 300–301, 317, 324
patterns in, 9, 53, 114–15
"perverse," 115–16, 141, 143
repetition of, 9, 56, 81, 84, 98

triangles (*continued*)
  as "three-legged tables," 145, 147
  transient, 145–46

Unfinished Business (Scarf), 10
urethra, 257
uterus, 254

vagina:
  expansion of, 255–56
  during intercourse, 255–56
  lubrication of, 244, 246, 248, 254,
    264
vaginismus, 269
vaginitis, 244, 246
vasectomies, 232
vasocongestion, 253–55, 256, 257,
    263
vibrators, 252
vulva, 255

Walsh, Froma, 109–10
Western Psychiatric Institute, 260
Willi, Jurg, 220
Williams, Ann Marie, 179, 334
Willis, Stanley, 159
women:
  extramarital affairs of, 127–28, 129,
    133–36
  orgasms of, 231–32, 258–59, 261,
    266–69
  sexual problems of, 231–32, 261,
    266–69
women's liberation movement, 127,
    364

Yale Psychiatric Institute, 190

Zborowski, Mark, 11
Zinner, John, 178

MAGGIE SCARF, the author of *Secrets, Lies, Betrayals; Unfinished Business;* and *Intimate Worlds,* is a Visiting Fellow at the Whitney Humanities Center, Yale University, and a Fellow of Jonathan Edwards College, Yale University. She lives in Connecticut with her husband and is the mother of three daughters.